Orison Swett Marden

Pushing to the Front; or Success under Difficulties

A Book of Inspiration and Encouragement to All who are Struggling for...

Orison Swett Marden

Pushing to the Front; or Success under Difficulties
A Book of Inspiration and Encouragement to All who are Struggling for...

ISBN/EAN: 9783337143558

Printed in Europe, USA, Canada, Australia, Japan

Cover: Foto ©ninafisch / pixelio.de

More available books at **www.hansebooks.com**

Copyright, 1901, M. P. Rice.

ABRAHAM LINCOLN

"With malice toward none, with charity for all, with firmness in the right as God gives us to see the right, let us strive on to finish the work we are in."

PUSHING TO THE FRONT

OR, SUCCESS UNDER DIFFICULTIES

A BOOK OF INSPIRATION AND ENCOURAGEMENT TO
ALL WHO ARE STRUGGLING FOR SELF-ELEVATION
ALONG THE PATHS OF KNOWLEDGE
AND OF DUTY

BY

ORISON SWETT MARDEN

*ILLUSTRATED WITH TWENTY-FOUR FINE
PORTRAITS OF EMINENT PERSONS*

> We live in a new and exceptional age. America is another name for Opportunity. Our whole history appears like a last effort of the Divine Providence in behalf of the human race.
> — EMERSON

BOSTON AND NEW YORK
HOUGHTON, MIFFLIN AND COMPANY
The Riverside Press, Cambridge
1894

PREFACE.

The author's excuse for one more postponement of the end "of making many books" can be briefly given. He early determined that if it should ever lie in his power, he would write a book to encourage, inspire, and stimulate boys and girls who long to be somebody and do something in the world, but feel that they have no chance in life. Among hundreds of American and English books for the young, claiming to give the "secret of success," he found but few which satisfy the cravings of youth, hungry for stories of successful lives, and eager for every hint and every bit of information which may help them to make their way in the world. He believed that the power of an ideal book for youth should lie in its richness of concrete examples, as the basis and inspiration of character-building; in its uplifting, energizing, suggestive force, more than in its arguments; that it should be free from materialism, on the one hand, and from cant on the other; and that it should abound in stirring examples of men and women who have brought things to pass. To the preparation of such a book he had devoted all his spare moments for ten years, when a fire destroyed all his manuscript and notes. The memory of some of the lost illustrations of difficulties overcome stimulated to another attempt; so once more the gleanings of odd bits of time for years have been arranged in the following pages.

The author's aim has been to spur the perplexed youth to act the Columbus to his own undiscovered possibilities; to urge him not to brood over the past, nor dream of the future, but to get his lesson from the hour; to encourage him to make every occasion a great occasion, for he cannot tell when fate may take his measure for a higher place; to show him that he must not wait for his opportunity, but make it; to tell the round boy how he may get out of the square hole, into which he has been wedged by circumstances or mistakes; to help him to find his right place in life; to teach the hesitating youth that in a land where shoemakers and farmers sit in Congress no limit can be placed to the career of a determined youth who has once learned the alphabet. The standard of the book is not measured in gold, but in growth; not in position, but in personal power; not in capital, but in character. It shows that a great checkbook can never make a great man; that beside the character of a Washington, the millions of a Crœsus look contemptible; that a man may be rich without money, and may succeed though he does not become President or member of Congress; that he who would grasp the key to power must be greater than his calling, and resist the vulgar prosperity that retrogrades toward barbarism; that there is something greater than wealth, grander than fame; that *character is success*, and *there is no other*.

If this volume shall open wider the door of some narrow life, and awaken powers before unknown, the author will feel repaid for his labor. No special originality is claimed for the book. It has been prepared in odd moments snatched from a busy life, and is merely a new way of telling stories and teaching lessons that have been told and taught by many others from Solomon down. In these well-worn and trite topics lie "the marrow of the wisdom of the world."

> " Though old the thought, and oft expressed,
> 'T is his at last who says it best."

If in rewriting this book from lost manuscript, the author has failed to always give due credit, he desires to hereby express the fullest obligation. He also wishes to acknowledge valuable assistance from Mr. Arthur W. Brown, of West Kingston, R. I.

43 BOWDOIN STREET, BOSTON, November 11, 1894.

CONTENTS.

CHAPTER		PAGE
I.	THE MAN AND THE OPPORTUNITY	5
	Don't wait for your opportunity; *make* it.	
II.	BOYS WITH NO CHANCE	25
	Necessity is the priceless spur.	
III.	AN IRON WILL	55
	Give a youth resolution and the alphabet, and who shall place limits to his career?	
IV.	POSSIBILITIES IN SPARE MOMENTS	63
	If a genius like Gladstone carries through life a book in his pocket, lest an unexpected spare moment slip from his grasp, what should we of common abilities not resort to, to save the precious moments from oblivion?	
V.	ROUND BOYS IN SQUARE HOLES	74
	Man is doomed to perpetual inferiority and disappointment if out of his place, and gets his living by his weakness instead of by his strength.	
VI.	WHAT CAREER?	89
	Your talent is your call. "What can you do?" is the interrogation of the century. Better adorn your own than seek another's place.	
VII.	CONCENTRATED ENERGY	106
	One unwavering aim. Don't dally with your purpose. Not many things indifferently, but one thing supremely.	
VIII.	"ON TIME," OR THE TRIUMPH OF PROMPTNESS	121
	Don't brood over the past or dream of the future; but seize the instant, and get your lesson from the hour.	
IX.	CHEERFULNESS AND LONGEVITY	133
	You must take joy with you, or you will not find it even in heaven.	
X.	A FORTUNE IN GOOD MANNERS	146
	The good-mannered can do without riches: all doors fly open to them, and they enter everywhere without money and without price.	
XI.	THE TRIUMPHS OF ENTHUSIASM	170
	"What are hardships, ridicule, persecution, toil, sickness, to a soul throbbing with an overmastering enthusiasm?"	
XII.	TACT OR COMMON SENSE	187
	Talent is no match for tact; we see its failure everywhere. In the race of life, common sense has the right of way.	

CONTENTS.

XIII. SELF-RESPECT AND SELF-CONFIDENCE 202
>We stamp our own value upon ourselves, and cannot expect to pass for more.

XIV. GREATER THAN WEALTH 210
>A man may make millions and be a failure still. He is the richest man who enriches mankind most.

XV. THE PRICE OF SUCCESS 232
>"Work or starve" is Nature's motto, — it is written on the stars and the sod alike, — starve mentally, starve morally, starve physically.

XVI. CHARACTER IS POWER 250
>Beside the character of a Washington the millions of many an American look contemptible. Character is success, and there is no other.

XVII. ENAMORED OF ACCURACY 273
>Twenty things half done do not make one thing well done. There is a great difference between going just right and a little wrong.

XVIII. LIFE IS WHAT WE MAKE IT 292
>We get out of life just what we put into it. The world has for us just what we have for it.

XIX. THE VICTORY IN DEFEAT 304
>To know how to wring victory from our defeats, and make stepping-stones of our stumbling-blocks, is the secret of success.

XX. NERVE — GRIT, GRIP, PLUCK 318
>There is something grand and inspiring in a young man who fails squarely after doing his level best, and then enters the contest a second and a third time with undaunted courage and redoubled energy.

XXI. THE REWARD OF PERSISTENCE 337
>"Mere genius darts, flutters, and tires; but perseverance wears and wins."

XXII. A LONG LIFE, AND HOW TO REACH IT 356
>The first requisite to success is to be a first-class animal. Even the greatest industry cannot amount to much, if a feeble body does not respond to the ambition.

XXIII. BE BRIEF 372
>"Brevity is the soul of wit." Boil it down.

XXIV. ASPIRATION 375
>"A man cannot aspire if he looks down." Look upward, live upward.

XXV. THE ARMY OF THE RESERVE 389
>We never can tell what is in a man until an emergency calls out his reserve, and he cannot call out an ounce more than has been stored up.

LIST OF PORTRAITS.

                                                                             PAGE

ABRAHAM LINCOLN. From an original unretouched negative, made in 1864, at the time the President commissioned Ulysses S. Grant lieutenant-general and commander of all the armies of the republic. It is said that this negative, with one of General Grant, was made in commemoration of that event.
Frontispiece.

NAPOLEON. After Painting by Charles de Chatillon	6
BENJAMIN FRANKLIN. After Painting by Désnoyers	26
BISMARCK. After the Lenbach Portrait	56
HARRIET BEECHER STOWE. After an English Engraving by R. Young, from an original portrait taken about the time that "Uncle Tom's Cabin" was published	64
JAMES WATT. After an English Engraving	74
FRANCIS PARKMAN. After Photograph	106
JOHN QUINCY ADAMS. After Painting by Healy in Corcoran Gallery, Washington, D. C.	122
OLIVER WENDELL HOLMES. After Photograph	134
MADAME DE STAËL. After Painting by Baron François Gérard	146
SIR HUMPHRY DAVY. After Painting by Sir Thomas Lawrence	170
HORACE GREELEY. After Photograph	188
GEORGE PEABODY. After Photograph	202
WILLIAM LLOYD GARRISON. After Photograph	210
PROFESSOR S. F. B. MORSE. After Photograph	232
GEORGE WASHINGTON. After the Stuart Painting in Museum Fine Arts, Boston	250
GALILEO GALILEI. After Painting by Sustermans in the Ufizzi Palace, Florence	274
HENRY WARD BEECHER. After Etching by Rajon	292
GENERAL ROBERT E. LEE. After Photograph	304
GENERAL ULYSSES S. GRANT. After Photograph	318
CHARLES ROBERT DARWIN. After an Etching by Rajon	338
WILLIAM EWART GLADSTONE. After Photograph	356
DAVID GLASGOW FARRAGUT. After Treasury Department Engraving	376
DANIEL WEBSTER. After Daguerreotype	390

Most of these portraits are from original sources, and have never been used before.

PUSHING TO THE FRONT.

CHAPTER I.

THE MAN AND THE OPPORTUNITY.

No man is born into this world whose work is not born with him. — LOWELL.

No royal permission is requisite to launch forth on the broad sea of discovery that surrounds us — most full of novelty where most explored. — EDWARD EVERETT.

Things don't turn up in this world until somebody turns them up. — GARFIELD.

We live in a new and exceptional age. America is another name for Opportunity. Our whole history appears like a last effort of the Divine Providence in behalf of the human race. — EMERSON.

Vigilance in watching opportunity; tact and daring in seizing upon opportunity; force and persistence in crowding opportunity to its utmost of possible achievement — these are the martial virtues which must command success. — AUSTIN PHELPS.

"I will find a way or make one."

There never was a day that did not bring its own opportunity for doing good, that never could have been done before, and never can be again. — W. H. BURLEIGH.

"Are you in earnest? Seize this very minute;
What you can do, or dream you can, *begin* it."

"IF we succeed, what will the world say?" asked Captain Berry in delight, when Nelson had explained his carefully formed plan before the battle of the Nile.

"There is no *if* in the case," replied Nelson. "That we shall succeed is certain. Who may live to tell the tale is a very different question." Then, as his captains rose from the council to go to their respective ships, he added: "Before this time to-morrow I shall have gained a peerage or Westminster Abbey." His quick eye and daring spirit saw an opportunity of glorious victory where others saw only probable defeat.

"Is it POSSIBLE to cross the path?" asked Napoleon of the engineers who had been sent to explore the dreaded pass of St. Bernard. "Perhaps," was the hesitating reply, "it is within the limits of *possibility*." "FORWARD, THEN," said the Little Corporal, heeding not their account of difficulties, apparently insurmountable. England and Austria laughed in scorn at the idea of transporting across the Alps, where "no wheel had ever rolled, or by any possibility could roll," an army of sixty thousand men, with ponderous artillery, and tons of cannon balls and baggage, and all the bulky munitions of war. But the besieged Massena was starving in Genoa, and the victorious Austrians thundered at the gates of Nice. Napoleon was not the man to fail his former comrades in their hour of peril.

The soldiers and all their equipments were inspected with rigid care. A worn shoe, a torn coat, or a damaged musket was at once repaired or replaced, and the columns swept forward, fired with the spirit of their chief.

"High on those craggy steeps, gleaming through the mists, the glittering bands of armed men, like phantoms, appeared. The eagle wheeled and screamed beneath their feet. The mountain goat, affrighted by the unwonted spectacle, bounded away, and paused in bold relief upon the cliff to gaze at the martial array which so suddenly had peopled the solitude. When they approached any spot of very special difficulty, the trumpets sounded the charge, which reëchoed with sublime reverberations from pinnacle to pinnacle of rock and ice. Everything was so carefully arranged, and the influence of Napoleon so boundless, that not a soldier left the ranks. Whatever obstructions were in the way were to be at all hazards surmounted, so that the long file, extending nearly twenty miles, might not be thrown into confusion." In four days the army was marching on the plains of Italy.

NAPOLEON

"There shall be no Alps."
"Impossible is a word to be found only in the dictionary of fools."

THE MAN AND THE OPPORTUNITY. 7

When this "impossible" deed was accomplished, others saw that it might have been done long before. Many a commander had possessed the necessary supplies, tools, and rugged soldiers, but lacked the grit and resolution of Bonaparte. Others excused themselves from encountering such gigantic obstacles by calling them insuperable. He did not shrink from mere difficulties, however great, but out of his very need made and mastered his opportunity.

Grant at New Orleans had just been seriously injured by a fall from his horse, when he received orders to take command at Chattanooga, so sorely beset by the Confederates that its surrender seemed only a question of a few days; for the hills around were all aglow by night with the camp-fires of the enemy, and supplies had been cut off. Though in great pain, General Grant gave directions for his removal to the new scene of action immediately.

On transports up the Mississippi, the Ohio, and one of its tributaries; on a litter borne by horses for many miles through the wilderness; and into the city at last on the shoulders of four men, he was taken to Chattanooga. Things assumed a different aspect immediately. *A Master* had arrived who was *equal to the situation*. The army felt the grip of his power. Before he could mount his horse, he ordered an advance. Soon the surrounding hills were held by Union soldiers, although the enemy contested the ground inch by inch.

Were these things the result of chance, or were they compelled by the indomitable determination of the injured General?

Did things *adjust themselves* when Horatius with two companions held ninety thousand Tuscans at bay until the bridge across the Tiber had been destroyed?—when Leonidas at Thermopylæ checked the mighty march of Xerxes?—when Themistocles, off the coast of Greece, shattered the Persian's Armada?—when Cæsar, finding his army hard pressed, seized spear and buckler, fought while he reorganized his men, and snatched victory from defeat? — when Winkelried gathered to his breast a sheaf of Austrian spears, thus opening a path through which his comrades pressed to freedom? — when Benedict Arnold, by desperate daring at Saratoga, won the battle which seemed doubtful to Horatio Gates, loitering near his distant tent? — when for years, Napoleon did not lose a single battle in which he was personally engaged? — when Wellington fought in many climes without ever being conquered? — when Ney, on a hundred fields, changed apparent disaster into brilliant triumph? — when Perry left the disabled Lawrence, rowed to the Niagara, and silenced the British guns? — when Sheridan arrived from Winchester just as the Union retreat was becoming a rout, and turned the tide by riding along the line? — when Sherman signaled his men to hold the fort, though sorely pressed; and they held it, knowing that their leader was coming?

History furnishes thousands of examples of men who have seized occasions to accomplish results deemed impossible by those less resolute. Prompt decision and whole-souled action sweep the world before them.

True, there has been but one Napoleon; but, on the other hand, the Alps that oppose the progress of the average American youth are not as high or dangerous as the summits crossed by the Corsican.

Don't wait for extraordinary opportunities. *Seize common occasions and make them great.*

On the morning of September 6, 1838, a young woman in the Longstone Lighthouse, between England and Scotland, was awakened by shrieks of agony rising above the roar of wind and wave. A storm of unwonted fury was raging, and her parents could not hear the cries; but a telescope showed nine human beings clinging to the windlass of a wrecked vessel whose bow was hanging on the rocks half a mile away. "We can do nothing," said William Darling, the light-keeper. "Ah, yes, we must go to the rescue," exclaimed his daughter, pleading tearfully with both father and mother until the former replied: "Very well, Grace, I will let you persuade me, though it is against my better judgment." Like a feather in a whirlwind the little boat was tossed on the tumultuous sea, and it seemed to Grace that she could feel her brain reel amid the maddening swirl. But borne on the blast that swept the cruel surge, the shrieks of those shipwrecked sailors seemed to change her weak sinews into cords of steel. Strength hitherto unsuspected came from somewhere, and the heroic girl pulled one oar in even time with her father. At length the nine were safely on board. "God bless you; but ye're a bonny English lass," said one poor fellow, as he looked wonderingly upon this marvelous girl, who that day had done a deed which added more to England's glory than the exploits of many of her monarchs.

A cat-boat was capsized in 1854 near Lime Rock Lighthouse, Newport, R. I., and four young men were left struggling in the cold waves of a choppy sea. Keeper Lewis was not at home, and his sick wife could do nothing; but their daughter Ida, twelve years old, rowed out in a small boat and saved the men. During the next thirty years she rescued nine others, at various times. Her work was done without assistance, and showed skill and endurance fully equal to her great courage.

"If you will let me try, I think I can make something that will do," said a boy who had been employed as a scullion at the mansion of Signor Faliero, as the story is told by George Cary Eggleston. A large company had been invited to the banquet, and just before the hour the confectioner, who had been making a large ornament for the table, sent word that he had spoiled the piece. "You!" exclaimed the head servant, in astonishment; "and who are you?" "I am Antonio

Canova, the grandson of Pisano the stone-cutter," replied the pale-faced little fellow.

"And, pray, what can you do?" asked the major-domo. "I can make you something that will do for the middle of the table, if you'll let me try." The servant was at his wit's end, so he told Antonio to go ahead and see what he could do. Calling for some butter, the scullion quickly moulded a large crouching lion, which the admiring major-domo placed upon the table.

Dinner was announced, and many of the most noted merchants, princes, and noblemen of Venice were ushered into the dining-room. Among them were skilled critics of art work. When their eyes fell upon the butter lion, they forgot the purpose for which they had come, in their wonder at such a work of genius. They looked at the lion long and carefully, and asked Signor Faliero what great sculptor had been persuaded to waste his skill upon a work in such a temporary material. Faliero could not tell; so he asked the head servant, who brought Antonio before the company.

When the distinguished guests learned that the lion had been made in a short time by a scullion, the dinner was turned into a feast in his honor. The rich host declared that he would pay the boy's expenses under the best masters, and he kept his word. But Antonio was not spoiled by his good fortune. He remained at heart the same simple, earnest, faithful boy, who had tried so hard to become a good stone-cutter in the shop of Pisano. Some may not have heard how the boy Antonio took advantage of this first great opportunity; but all know of Canova, one of the greatest sculptors of all time.

Weak men wait for opportunities, strong men make them.

"The best men," says E. H. Chapin, "are not those who have waited for chances but who have taken them; besieged the chance; conquered the chance; and made chance the servitor."

"Oh, how I wish I were rich!" exclaimed a bright,

industrious drayman in Philadelphia, who had many mouths to fill at home. "Well, why don't you get rich?" asked Stephen Girard, who had overheard the remark. "I don't know how, without money," replied the drayman. "You don't need money," replied Mr. Girard. "Well, if you will tell me how to get rich without money, I won't let the grass grow before trying it."

"A ship-load of confiscated tea is to be sold at auction to-morrow at the wharf," said the millionaire. "Go down and buy it, and then come to me." "But I have no money to buy a whole ship-load of tea with," protested the drayman. "You don't need any money, I tell you," said Girard sharply; "go down and bid on the whole cargo, and then come to me."

The next day the auctioneer said that purchasers would have the privilege of taking one case, or the whole ship-load, buying by the pound. A retail grocer started the bidding, and the drayman at once named a higher figure, to the surprise of the large crowd present. "I'll take the whole ship-load," said he coolly, when a sale was announced. The auctioneer was astonished, but when he learned that the young bidder was Mr. Girard's drayman, his manner changed, and he said it was probably all right.

The news spread that Girard was buying tea in large quantities, and the price rose several cents per pound. "Go and sell your tea," said the great merchant the next day. The young man secured quick sales by quoting a price a trifle below the market rate, and in a few hours he was worth fifty thousand dollars. The author does not endorse this method of doing business, but tells the story merely as an example of seizing an opportunity.

There may not be one chance in a million that you will ever receive aid of this kind; but opportunities are often presented which you can improve to good advantage, if you will only *act*.

"You are too young," said the advertiser for a factory manager in Manchester, England, after a single glance at an applicant. "They used to object to me on that score four or five years ago," replied Robert Owen, "but I did not expect to have it brought up now." "How often do you get drunk in the week?" "I never was drunk in my life," said Owen, blushing. "What salary do you ask?" "Three hundred (pounds) a year." "Three hundred a year! Why I have had I don't know how many after the place here this morning, and all their askings together would not come up to what you want."

"Whatever others may ask, I cannot take less. I am making three hundred a year by my own business."

The youth, who had never been in a large cotton mill, was put in charge of a factory employing five hundred operatives. By studying machines, cloth, and processes at night, he mastered every detail of the business in a short time, and was soon without a superior in his line in Manchester.

The lack of opportunity is ever the excuse of a weak, vacillating mind. Opportunities! Every life is full of them. Every lesson in school or college is an opportunity. Every examination is a chance in life. Every patient is an opportunity. Every newspaper article is an opportunity. Every client is an opportunity. Every sermon is an opportunity. Every business transaction is an opportunity, — an opportunity to be polite, — an opportunity to be manly, — an opportunity to be honest, — an opportunity to make friends. Every proof of confidence in you is a great opportunity. Every responsibility thrust upon your strength and your honor is priceless. Existence is the privilege of effort, and when that privilege is met like a man, opportunities to succeed along the line of your aptitude will come faster than you can use them. If a slave like Fred Douglass can elevate himself into an orator, editor, statesman, what ought the poorest white boy to do, who is rich in opportunities compared with Douglass, who did not even own his body?

It is the idle man, not the great worker, who is always complaining that he has no time or opportunity. Some young men will make more out of the odds and ends of opportunities, which many carelessly throw away, than others will get out of a whole lifetime. Like bees, they extract honey from every flower. Every person they meet, every circumstance of the day, must add something to their store of useful knowledge or personal power.

"There is nobody whom Fortune does not visit once in his life," says a Cardinal; "but when she finds he is not ready to receive her, she goes in at the door and out at the window."

"What is its name?" asked a visitor in a studio, when shown, among many gods, one whose face was concealed by hair, and which had wings on its feet. "Opportunity," replied the sculptor. "Why is its face hidden?" "Because men seldom know him when he comes to them." "Why has he wings on his feet?" "Because he is soon gone, and once gone, cannot be overtaken."

Life pulsates with chances. They may not be dramatic or great, but they are important to him who would get on in the world.

Cornelius Vanderbilt saw his opportunity in the steamboat, and determined to identify himself with steam navigation. To the surprise of all his friends, he abandoned his prosperous business and took command of one of the first steamboats launched, at one thousand dollars a year. Livingston and Fulton had acquired the sole right to navigate New York waters by steam, but Vanderbilt thought the law unconstitutional, and defied it until it was repealed. He soon became a steamboat owner. When the government was paying a large subsidy for carrying the European mails, he offered to carry them free and give better service. His offer was accepted, and in this way he soon built up an enormous freight and passenger traffic.

Foreseeing the great future of railroads in a country like ours, he plunged into railroad enterprises with all his might, laying the foundation for the vast Vanderbilt system of to-day.

Young Philip Armour joined the long caravan of Forty-Niners, and crossed the "Great American Desert" with all his possessions in a prairie schooner drawn by mules. Hard work and steady gains carefully saved in the mines enabled him to start, six years later, in the grain and warehouse business in Milwaukee. In nine years he made five hundred thousand dollars. But he saw his great opportunity in Grant's order, "On to Richmond." One morning in 1864, he knocked at the door of Plankinton, partner in his venture as a pork packer. "I am going to take the next train to New York," said he, "to sell pork 'short.' Grant and Sherman have the rebellion by the throat, and pork will go down to twelve dollars a barrel." This was his opportunity. He went to New York and offered pork in large quantities at forty dollars per barrel. It was eagerly taken. The shrewd Wall Street speculators laughed at the young Westerner, and told him pork would go to sixty dollars, for the war was not nearly over. Mr. Armour kept on selling. Grant continued to advance. Richmond fell, and pork fell with it to twelve dollars a barrel. Mr. Armour cleared two millions of dollars.

John D. Rockefeller saw his opportunity in petroleum. He could see a large population in this country, with very poor lights. Petroleum was plenty, but the refining process was so crude that the product was inferior, and not wholly safe. Here was his chance. Taking into partnership Samuel Andrews, the porter in a machine shop where both had worked, Mr. Rockefeller started a single barrel still in 1870, using an improved process discovered by his partner. They made a superior grade of oil and prospered rapidly. They soon admitted the third partner, Mr. Flagler, but Andrews soon became dissatisfied. "What will you take for your interest?" asked Rockefeller. Andrews wrote carelessly on a piece of paper, "One million dollars." Within twenty-four hours Mr. Rockefeller handed him the amount, saying, "Cheaper at one million than ten." In twenty years the business of the little refinery, not worth one thousand dollars for building and apparatus, had grown into the Standard Oil Trust, capitalized at ninety millions of dollars, with stock quoted at 170, giving a market value of one hundred and fifty millions.

These are illustrations of seizing opportunity for the purpose of making money. But fortunately there is a new generation of electricians, of engineers, of scholars, of artists, of authors, and of poets, who find opportunities, thick as thistles, for doing something *nobler than merely becoming rich.* Wealth is not an end to strive for, but an opportunity; not the climax of a man's career, but the beginning.

Mrs. Elizabeth Fry, a Quaker lady, saw her opportunity in the prisons of England. From three hundred to four hundred half-naked women, as late as 1813, would often be huddled in a single ward of Newgate, London, awaiting trial. They had neither beds nor bedding, but women, old and young, and little girls, slept in filth and rags on the floor. No one seemed to care for them, and the Government furnished simply food to keep them alive. She visited Newgate, calmed the howling mob, and told them she wished to establish a school for the young women and the girls, and asked them to select a schoolmistress from their own number. They were amazed, but chose a young woman who had been committed for stealing a watch. In three months these "wild beasts," as they were sometimes called, were tame, and became harmless and kind. The reform spread until the Government legalized the system, and good women throughout Great Britain became interested in the work of educating and clothing these outcasts. Fourscore years have passed, and her plan has been adopted throughout the civilized world.

A boy in England had been run over by the cars, and the bright blood spurted from a severed artery. No one seemed to know what to do until another boy, Astley Cooper, took his handkerchief and stopped the bleeding by pressure above the wound. The praise which Astley received for thus saving the boy's life encouraged him to become a surgeon, the foremost of his day.

" The time comes to the young surgeon," says Arnold, "when, after long waiting, and patient study and experiment, he is suddenly confronted with his first critical operation. The great surgeon is away. Time is pressing. Life and death hang in the balance. Is he equal to the emergency ? Can he fill the great surgeon's place, and do his work ? If he can, he is the one of all others who is wanted. *His opportunity confronts him.* He and it are face to face. Shall he confess his ignorance and inability, or step into fame and fortune ? It is for him to say."

Are you prepared for a great opportunity ?

"Hawthorne dined one day with Longfellow," said James T. Fields, "and brought a friend with him from Salem. After dinner the friend said, 'I have been trying to persuade Hawthorne to write a story based upon a legend of Acadia, and still current there, — the legend of a girl who, in the dispersion of the Acadians, was separated from her lover, and passed her life in waiting and seeking for him, and only found him dying in a hospital when both were old.' Longfellow wondered that the legend did not strike the fancy of Hawthorne, and he said to him, 'If you have really made up your mind not to use it for a story, will you let me have it for a poem?' To this Hawthorne consented, and promised, moreover, not to treat the subject in prose till Longfellow had seen what he could do with it in verse. Longfellow seized his opportunity and gave to the world 'Evangeline, or the Exile of the Acadians.'"

Of what value was the old story of Shylock and his pound of flesh (contained in a dozen lines) till Shakespeare touched it with his magic pen and transformed it into a realistic drama?

Open eyes will discover opportunities everywhere; open ears will never fail to detect the cries of those who are perishing for assistance; open hearts will never want for worthy objects upon which to bestow their gifts; open hands will never lack for noble work to do.

Everybody had noticed the overflow when a solid is immersed in a vessel filled with water, although no one had made use of his knowledge that the body displaces its exact bulk of liquid; but when Archimedes observed the fact, he perceived therein an easy method of finding the cubical contents of objects, however irregular in shape. Everybody knew how steadily a suspended weight, when moved, sways back and forth until friction and the resistance of the air bring it to rest, yet no one considered this information of the slightest practical importance; but the boy Galileo, as he watched a lamp left swinging by accident in the cathedral at Pisa, saw in the regularity of those oscillations the useful principle of the pendulum. Even the iron doors of a prison were not enough to shut him out from research, for he experimented with the straw of his cell, and learned valuable lessons about the relative strength of tubes and rods of equal diameters. For ages astronomers had been familiar with the rings of Saturn, and regarded them merely as curious exceptions to the supposed law of planetary formation; but Laplace saw that, instead of being exceptions, they are the sole remaining visible evidences of certain stages in the invariable process of star manufacture, and from their mute testimony he added a valuable chapter to the scientific history of Creation. There was not a sailor in Europe who had not wondered what might lie beyond the Western Ocean, but it remained for Columbus to steer boldly out into an unknown sea and discover a new world. Innumerable apples had fallen from trees, often hitting heedless men on the head as if to set them thinking, but not before Newton did any one realize that they fall to the earth by the same law which holds the planets in their courses, and prevents the momentum of all the atoms in the universe from hurling them wildly back to chaos. Lightning had dazzled the eyes, and thunder had jarred the ears of men since the days of Adam, in the vain attempt to call their attention to the all-pervading and tremendous energy of electricity; but the discharges of Heaven's artillery were seen and heard only by the eye and ear of terror until Franklin, by a simple experiment, proved that lightning is but one manifestation of a resistless yet controllable force, abundant as air and water.

Like many others, these men are considered great, simply because they improved opportunities common to the whole human race. Read the story of any successful man and mark its moral, told thousands of years ago by Solomon: "Seest thou a man diligent in his business? he shall stand before kings." This proverb is well illustrated by the career of the industrious Franklin, for he stood before five kings and dined with two.

He who improves an opportunity sows a seed which will yield fruit in opportunity for himself and others. Every one who has labored honestly in the past has aided to place knowledge and comfort within the reach of a constantly increasing number.

Avenues greater in number, wider in extent, easier of access than ever before existed, stand open to the sober, frugal, energetic and able mechanic, to the educated youth, to the office boy and to the clerk — avenues through which they can reap greater successes than ever before within the reach of these classes within the history of the world. A little while ago there were only three or four professions — now there are fifty. And of trades, where there was one, there are a hundred now.

"Opportunity has hair in front," says a Latin author; "behind she is bald; if you seize her by the forelock, you may hold her, but, if suffered to escape, not Jupiter himself can catch her again."

But what is the best opportunity to him who cannot or will not use it?

"It was my lot," said a shipmaster, "to fall in with the ill-fated steamer Central America. The night was closing in, the sea rolling high; but I hailed the crippled steamer and asked if they needed help. 'I am in a sinking condition,' cried Captain Herndon. 'Had you not better send your passengers on board directly?' I asked. 'Will you not lay by me until morning?' replied Captain Herndon. 'I will try,' I answered, 'but had you not better send your passengers on board *now?*' 'Lay by me till morning,' again shouted Captain Herndon.

"I tried to lay by him, but at night, such was the heavy roll of the sea, I could not keep my position, and I never saw the steamer again. In an hour and a half after the Captain said, 'Lay by me till morning,' his vessel, with its living freight, went down. The Captain and crew and most of the passengers found a grave in the deep."

Captain Herndon appreciated the value of the opportunity he had neglected when it was beyond his reach, but of what avail was the bitterness of his self-reproach when his last moments came? How many lives were sacrificed to his unintelligent hopefulness and indecision! Like him the feeble, the sluggish, and the purposeless too often see no meaning in the happiest occasions, until too late they learn the old lesson that the mill can never grind with the water which has passed.

Such people are always a little too late or a little too early in everything they attempt. "They have three hands apiece," said John B. Gough; "a right hand, a left hand, and a little behindhand." As boys, they were late at school, and unpunctual in their home duties. That is the way the habit is acquired; and now, when responsibility claims them, they think that if they had only gone yesterday they would have obtained the situation, or they can probably get one to-morrow. They remember plenty of chances to make money, or know how to make it some other time than *now;* they see how to improve themselves or help others in the future, but perceive no opportunity in the present. They are always at the pool, but somehow, when the angel troubles the water, there is no one to put them in. They cannot *seize their opportunity.*

Joe Stoker, rear brakeman on the ——— accommodation train, was exceedingly popular with all the railroad men. The passengers liked him, too, for he was eager to please and always ready to answer questions. But he did not realize the full responsibility of his position. He "took the world easy," and occasionally tippled; and if any one remonstrated, he would give one of his brightest smiles, and reply in such a good-natured way that the friend would think he had overestimated the danger: "Thank you. I'm all right. Don't you worry."

One evening there was a heavy snowstorm, and his train was delayed. Joe complained of extra duties because of the storm, and slyly sipped occasional draughts from a flat bottle. Soon he became quite jolly; but the conductor and engineer of the train were both vigilant and anxious.

Between two stations the train came to a quick halt. The engine had blown out its cylinder head, and an express was due in a few minutes upon the same track.

The conductor hurried to the rear car, and ordered Joe back with a red light. The brakeman laughed and said:

"There's no hurry. Wait till I get my overcoat."

The conductor answered gravely, "Don't stop a minute, Joe. The express is due."

"All right," said Joe, smilingly. The conductor then hurried forward to the engine.

But the brakeman did not go at once. He stopped to put on his overcoat. Then he took another sip from the flat bottle to keep the cold out. Then he slowly grasped the lantern and, whistling, moved leisurely down the track.

He had not gone ten paces before he heard the puffing of the express. Then he ran for the curve, but it was too late. In a horrible minute the engine of the express had telescoped the standing train, and the shrieks of the mangled passengers mingled with the hissing escape of steam.

Later on, when they asked for Joe, he had disappeared; but the next day he was found in a barn, delirious, swinging an empty lantern in front of an imaginary train, and crying, "Oh, that I had!"

He was taken home, and afterward to an asylum, for this is a true story, and there is no sadder sound in that sad place than the unceasing moan, "Oh, that I had!" "Oh, that I had!" of the unfortunate brakeman, whose criminal indulgence brought disaster to many lives.

"Oh, that I had!" or "Oh, that I had not!" is the silent cry of many a man who would give life itself for the opportunity to go back and retrieve some long-past error.

"There are moments," says Dean Alford, "which are worth more than years. We cannot help it. There is no proportion between spaces of time in importance nor in value. A stray, unthought-of five minutes may contain the event of a life. And this all-important moment — who can tell when it will be upon us?"

"What we call a turning-point," says Arnold, "is simply an occasion which sums up and brings to a result previous training. Accidental circumstances are nothing except to men who have been trained to take advantage of them." *An opportunity will only make you ridiculous unless you are prepared for it.*

The trouble with us is that we are ever looking for a princely chance of acquiring riches, or fame, or worth. We are dazzled by what Emerson calls the "shallow Americanism" of the day. We are expecting mastery without apprenticeship, knowledge without study, and riches by credit. Because the politician acquires power by bribing the caucus, influence by "standing in" with the saloon keeper, wealth by fraud, and immunity from conviction by packing the jury, we are cozened into looking at life through a distorted lens. These are opportunities to be shunned like the cholera. They appear to rest upon a solid foundation, but they lead to infamy, and crime, and harmfulness to mankind, and perhaps suicide.

It is a common saying that "Luck beats science every time." But this is the gambler's maxim, the fool's motto.

Young men and women, why stand ye here all the day idle? Was the land all occupied before you were born? Has the earth ceased to yield its increase? Are the seats all taken? the positions all filled? the chances all gone? Are the resources of your country fully developed? Are the secrets of nature all mastered? Is there no way in which you can utilize these passing moments to improve yourself or benefit another? Is the competition of modern existence so fierce that you must be content to simply gain an honest living? Have you received the gift of life in this progressive age, wherein all the experience of the past is garnered for your inspiration, merely that you may increase by one the sum total of purely animal existence?

The new is supplanting the old everywhere. The machinery of ten years ago must soon be sold as old iron to make room for something more efficient. The methods of our fathers are daily giving place to better systems. Those who have devoted their lives to the cause of labor and progress are constantly falling in the ranks; and, as the struggle grows more intense, men and women with even stronger arms and truer hearts are needed to take the vacant places in the Battle of Life.

Born in an age and country in which knowledge and opportunity abound as never before, how can you sit with folded hands, asking God's aid in work for which He has already given you the necessary faculties and strength? Even when the Chosen People supposed their progress checked by the Red Sea, and their leader paused for Divine help, the Lord said, "Wherefore criest thou unto me? Speak unto the children of Israel, *that they go forward.*"

With the world full of work that needs to be done; with human nature so constituted that often a pleasant word or a trifling assistance may stem the tide of disaster for some fellow-man, or clear his path to success; with our own faculties so arranged that in honest, earnest, persistent endeavor we find our highest good; and with countless noble examples to encourage us to dare and to do, each moment brings us to the threshold of some new opportunity.

Don't *wait* for your opportunity. *Make it,* — make it as the shepherd-boy Ferguson made his when he calculated the distances of the stars with a handful of glass beads on a string. Make it as George Stephenson made his when he mastered the rules of mathematics with a bit of chalk on the grimy sides of the coal wagons in the mines. Make it, as Napoleon made his in a hundred "impossible" situations. Make it, as *all leaders of men,* in war and in peace, have made their chances of success. Make it, as *every man must*, who would accomplish *anything* worth the effort. Golden opportunities are nothing to laziness, but industry makes the commonest chances golden.

> " There is a tide in the affairs of men,
>   Which, taken at the flood, leads on to fortune;
>   Omitted, all the voyage of their life
> Is bound in shallows and in miseries;
>   And we must take the current when it serves,
>   Or lose our ventures."

> " 'T is never offered twice; seize, then, the hour
> When fortune smiles, and duty points the way;
> Nor shrink aside to 'scape the spectre fear,
> Nor pause, though pleasure beckon from her bower;
> But bravely bear thee onward to the goal.'

CHAPTER II.

BOYS WITH NO CHANCE.

In the blackest soils grow the fairest flowers, and the loftiest and strongest trees spring heavenward among the rocks. — J. G. HOLLAND.

Poverty is very terrible, and sometimes kills the very soul within us, but it is the north wind that lashes men into Vikings; it is the soft, luscious south wind which lulls them to lotus dreams. — OUIDA.

> Want is a bitter and a hateful good,
> Because its virtues are not understood;
> Yet many things, impossible to thought,
> Have been by need to full perfection brought.
> The daring of the soul proceeds from thence —
> Sharpness of wit and active diligence.
> Prudence at once and fortitude it gives,
> And if in patience taken, mends our lives.
>   DRYDEN.

Poverty is the sixth sense. — GERMAN PROVERB.

It is not every calamity that is a curse, and early adversity is often a blessing. Surmounted difficulties not only teach, but hearten us in our future struggles. — SHARPE.

There can be no doubt that the captains of industry to-day, using that term in its broadest sense, are men who began life as poor boys. — SETH LOW.

> 'T is a common proof,
> That lowliness is young ambition's ladder!
>   SHAKESPEARE.

"*I* AM a child of the court," said a pretty little girl at a children's party in Denmark; "*my* father is Groom of the Chambers, which is a very high office. And those whose names end with 'sen,'" she added, "can never be anything at all. We must put our arms akimbo, and make the elbows quite pointed, so as to keep these 'sen' people at a great distance."

"But my papa can buy a hundred dollars' worth of bonbons, and give them away to children," angrily exclaimed the daughter of the rich merchant Peter*sen*. "Can your papa do that?"

"Yes," chimed in the daughter of an editor, "my papa can put your papa and everybody's papa into the newspaper. All sorts of people are afraid of him, my papa says, for he can do as he likes with the paper."

"Oh, if I could be one of them!" thought a little boy peeping through the crack of the door, by permission of the cook for whom he had been turning the spit. But no, *his* parents had not even a penny to spare, and his name ended in "sen."

Years afterwards, when the children of the party had become men and women, some of them went to see a splendid house, filled with all kinds of beautiful and valuable objects. There they met the owner, once the very boy who thought it so great a privilege to peep at them through a crack in the door as they played. He had become the great sculptor Thorwald*sen*.

This sketch is adapted from a story by a poor Danish cobbler's boy, whose name did not keep him from becoming famous, — Hans Christian Ander*sen*.

"There is no fear of my starving, father," said the deaf boy, Kitto, begging to be taken from the poorhouse and allowed to struggle for an education; "we are in the midst of plenty, and I know how to prevent hunger. The Hottentots subsist a long time on nothing but a little gum; they also, when hungry, tie a ligature around their bodies. Cannot I do so, too? The hedges furnish blackberries and nuts, and the fields, turnips; a hayrick will make an excellent bed."

This poor deaf boy with a drunken father, who was thought capable of nothing better than making shoes as a pauper, became one of the greatest biblical scholars in the world. His first book was written in the workhouse.

Creon was a Greek slave, as a writer tells the story in Kate Field's "Washington," but he was also a slave of the Genius of Art. Beauty was his god, and he worshiped it with rapt adoration. It was after the

BENJAMIN FRANKLIN

"Seest thou a man diligent in his business? He shall stand before kings."
"I have made the most out of the stuff."

repulse of the great Persian invader, and a law was in force, that under penalty of death no one should espouse art except freemen. When the law was enacted he was engaged upon a group for which he hoped some day to receive the commendation of Phidias, the greatest sculptor living, and even the praise of Pericles.

What was to be done? Into the marble block before him Creon had put his head, his heart, his soul, his life. On his knees, from day to day, he had prayed for fresh inspiration, new skill. He believed, gratefully and proudly, that Apollo, answering his prayers, had directed his hand and had breathed into the figures the life that seemed to animate them; but now, — now, all the gods seemed to have deserted him.

Cleone, the devoted sister of Creon, felt the blow as deeply as her brother. "O Aphrodite!" she prayed, "immortal Aphrodite, high enthroned child of Zeus, my queen, my goddess, my patron, at whose shrine I have daily laid my offerings, be now my friend, the friend of my brother!"

Then to her brother she said: "O Creon, go to the cellar beneath our house. It is dark, but I will furnish light and food. Continue your work; the gods will befriend us."

To the cellar Creon went, and guarded and attended by his sister, day and night, he proceeded with his glorious but dangerous task.

About this time all Greece was invited to Athens to behold an exhibit of works of art. The display took place in the Agora. Pericles presided. At his side was Aspasia. Phidias, Socrates, Sophocles, and other renowned men stood near him.

The works of the great masters were there. But one group, far more beautiful than the rest, — a group that Apollo himself must have chiseled, — challenged universal attention, exciting at the same time no little envy among rival artists.

"Who is the sculptor of this group?" None could tell. Heralds repeated the question, but there was no answer. "A mystery, then! Can it be the work of a slave?" Amid great commotion a beautiful maiden with disarranged dress, disheveled hair, a determined expression in her eyes, and with closed lips, was dragged into the Agora. "This woman," cried the officers, "this woman knows the sculptor; we are sure of this; but she will not tell his name."

Cleone was questioned, but was silent. She was informed of the penalty of her conduct, but her lips remained closed. "Then," said Pericles, "the law is imperative, and I am the minister of the law. Take the maid to the dungeon."

As he spoke, a youth with flowing hair, emaciated, but with black eyes that beamed with the flashing light of genius, rushed forward, and flinging himself before Pericles, exclaimed: "O Pericles, forgive and save the maid. She is my sister. I am the culprit. The group is the work of my hands, the hands of a slave."

The indignant crowd interrupted him and cried, "To the dungeon, to the dungeon with the slave." "As I live, no!" said Pericles rising. "Behold that group! Apollo decides by it that there is something higher in Greece than an unjust law. The highest purpose of law should be the development of the beautiful. If Athens lives in the memory and affections of men, it is her devotion to art that will immortalize her. Not to the dungeon, but to my side bring the youth."

And there, in the presence of the assembled multitude, Aspasia placed the crown of olives, which she held in her hands, on the brow of Creon; and at the same time, amid universal plaudits, she tenderly kissed Creon's affectionate and devoted sister.

The Athenians erected a statue to Æsop, who was born a slave, that men might know that the way to honor is open to all. In Greece, wealth and immortality were the sure reward of the man who could distinguish himself in art, literature, or war. No other country ever did so much to encourage and inspire struggling merit. Genius, achievement, beauty, were worshiped by the Greeks.

"I was born in poverty," said Vice-President Henry Wilson. "Want sat by my cradle. I know what it is to ask a mother for bread when she has none to give. I left my home at ten years of age, and served an apprenticeship of eleven years, receiving a month's schooling each year, and, at the end of eleven years of hard work, a yoke of oxen and six sheep, which brought me eighty-four dollars. I never spent the sum of one dollar for pleasure, counting every penny from the time I was born till I was twenty-one years of age. I know what it is to travel weary miles and ask my fellow men to give me leave to toil. . . . In the first month after I was twenty-one years of age, I went into the woods, drove a team, and cut mill-logs. I rose in the morning before daylight and worked hard till after dark, and received the magnificent sum of six dollars for the month's work! Each of these dollars looked as large to me as the moon looks to-night."

Mr. Wilson determined to never lose an opportunity for self-culture or self-advancement. Few men knew so well the value of spare moments. *He seized them as though they were gold* and would not let one pass until he had wrung from it every possibility. He managed to read a thousand good books before he was twenty-one — what a lesson for boys on a farm! When he left the farm he started on foot for Natick, Mass., over one hundred miles distant, to learn the cobbler's trade. He went through Boston that he might see Bunker Hill monument and other historical landmarks. The whole trip cost him but one dollar and six cents. In a year he was at the head of a debating club at Natick. Before eight years had passed, he made his great speech against slavery, in the Massachusetts Legislature. Twelve years later he stood shoulder to shoulder with the polished Sumner in Congress. With him, *every occasion was a great occasion.* He ground every circumstance of his life into material for success.

"Don't go about the town any longer in that outlandish rig. Let me give you an order on the store. Dress up a little, Horace." Horace Greeley looked down on his clothes as if he had never before noticed how seedy they were, and replied: "You see, Mr. Sterrett, my father is on a new place, and I want to help him all I can." He had spent but six dollars for personal expenses in seven months, and was to receive one hundred and thirty-five from Judge J. M. Sterrett of the Erie "Gazette" for substitute work. He retained but fifteen dollars and gave the rest to his father, with whom he had moved from Vermont to Western Pennsylvania, and for whom he had camped out many a night to guard the sheep from wolves. He was nearly twenty-one; and, although tall and gawky, with tow-colored hair, a pale face and whining voice, he resolved to seek his fortune in New York City. Slinging his bundle of clothes on a stick over his shoulder, he walked sixty miles through the woods to Buffalo, rode on a canal boat to Albany, descended the Hudson in a barge, and reached New York, just as the sun was rising, August 18, 1831.

He found board over a saloon at two dollars and a half a week. His journey of six hundred miles had cost him but five dollars. For days Horace wandered up and down the streets, going into scores of buildings and asking if they wanted "a hand;" but "no" was the invariable reply. His quaint appearance led many to think he was an escaped apprentice. One Sunday at his boarding-place he heard that printers were wanted at "West's Printing-office." He was at the door at five o'clock Monday morning, and asked the foreman for a job at seven. The latter had no idea that the country greenhorn could set type for the Polyglot Testament on which help was needed, but said: "Fix up a case for him and we'll see if he *can* do anything." When the proprietor came in, he objected to the new-comer and told the foreman to let him go when his first day's work was done. That night Horace showed a proof of the largest and most correct day's work that had then been done. In ten years Horace was a partner in a small printing-office. He founded the "New Yorker," the best weekly paper in the United States, but it was not profitable. When Harrison was nominated for President in eighteen hundred and forty, Greeley started "The Log-Cabin," which reached the then fabulous circulation of ninety thousand. But on this paper at a penny a copy, he made no money. His next venture was "The New York Tribune," price one cent. To start it he borrowed a thousand dollars and printed five thousand copies of the first number. It was difficult to give them all away. He began with six hundred subscribers, and increased the list to eleven thousand in six weeks. The demand for the "Tribune" grew faster than new machinery could be obtained to print it. It was a paper whose editor, whatever his mistakes, always tried to be *right*.

James Gordon Bennett had made a failure of his "New York Courier" in eighteen hundred twenty-five, of the "Globe" in eighteen hundred thirty-two, and of the "Pennsylvanian" a little later, and was only known as a clever writer for the press, who had saved a few hundred dollars by hard labor and strict economy for fourteen years. In eighteen hundred thirty-five he asked Horace Greeley to join him in starting a new daily paper, the "New York Herald." Greeley declined, but recommended two young printers, who formed a partnership with Bennett, and the "Herald" was started May 6, eighteen hundred thirty-five, with a cash capital sufficient to pay expenses for *ten days*. Bennett hired a small cellar on Wall Street, furnished it with a chair and a desk composed of a plank supported by two barrels; and there, doing all the work except the printing, began the work of making a really great daily newspaper, a thing then unknown in America, as all its predecessors were party organs. Steadily the young man struggled towards his ideal, giving the news, fresh and crisp, from an ever widening area, until his paper was famous for giving the current history of the world as fully and quickly as any competitor, and often much more thoroughly and far more promptly. Neither labor nor expense was spared in obtaining prompt and reliable information on every topic of general interest. It was an up-hill job, but its completion was finally marked by the opening at the corner of Broadway and Ann Street of the most complete newspaper establishment then known.

One of the first things that attracts the attention on entering George W. Child's private office in Philadelphia is this motto, which was the key-note of the success of a boy who started with "no chance:" "Nihil sine labore." It was his early ambition to own the "Philadelphia Ledger" and the great building in which it was published; but how could a poor boy working for $2.00 a week ever hope to own such a great paper? However, he had great determination and indomitable energy; and as soon as he had saved a few hundred dollars as a clerk in a bookstore, he began business as a publisher. He made "great hits" in some of the works he published, such as "Kane's Arctic Expedition." He had a keen sense of what would please the public, and there seemed no end to his industry.

In spite of the fact that the "Ledger" was losing money every day, his friends could not dissuade him from buying it, and in eighteen hundred sixty-four the dreams of his boyhood found fulfillment. He doubled the subscription price, lowered the advertising rates, to the astonishment of everybody, and the paper entered upon a career of remarkable prosperity, the profits sometimes amounting to over four hundred thousand dollars a year. He always refused to lower the wages of his employes even when every other establishment in Philadelphia was doing so.

At a banquet in Lyons, nearly a century and a half ago, a discussion arose in regard to the meaning of a painting representing some scene in the mythology or history of Greece. Seeing that the discussion was growing warm, the host turned to one of the waiters and asked him to explain the picture. Greatly to the surprise of the company, the servant gave a clear and concise account of the whole subject, so plain and convincing that it at once settled the dispute.

"In what school have you studied, Monsieur?" asked one of the guests, addressing the waiter with great respect. "I have studied in many schools, Monseigneur," replied the young servant: "but the school in which I studied longest and learned most is the school of adversity." Well had he profited by poverty's lessons; for, although then but a poor waiter, all Europe soon rang with the fame of the writings of the greatest genius of his age and country, Jean Jacques Rousseau.

The smooth sand beach of Lake Erie constituted the foolscap on which, for want of other material, P. R. Spencer, a barefoot boy with no chance, perfected the essential principles of the Spencerian system of penmanship, the most beautiful exposition of graphic art.

With thirteen halfpence in his pocket William Cobbett started on foot to find work in the King's Gardens at Kew. "When my little fortune had been reduced to threepence," he says, "I was trudging through Richmond in my blue smock-frock and my red garters tied under my knees, when, staring about me, my eyes fell upon a little book in a bookseller's window, on the outside of which was written, 'The Tale of a Tub. Price 3d.' The title was so odd that my curiosity was excited. I had threepence, but then I could not have any supper. In I went and got the little book, which I was so impatient to read, that I got over into a field at the upper corner of Kew Gardens, where there stood a haystack." Here he read until he fell asleep, to be awakened by the birds at dawn. He found work at Kew, and for eight years followed the plough, when he ran away to London, copied law papers for eight or nine months, and enlisted in an infantry regiment. During his first year of soldier life he subscribed to a circulating library at Chatham, read every book in it, and began to study.

"I learned grammar when I was a private soldier on the pay of sixpence a day. The edge of my berth, or that of the guard-bed, was my seat to study in; my knapsack was my bookcase; a bit of board lying on my lap was my writing-table, and the task did not demand anything like a year of my life. I had no money to purchase candles or oil; in winter it was rarely that I could get any evening light but that of the fire, and only my turn, even, of that. To buy a pen or a sheet of paper I was compelled to forego some portion of my food, though in a state of half starvation. I had no moment of time that I could call my own, and I had to read and write amidst the talking, laughing, singing, whistling, and bawling of at least half a score of the most thoughtless of men, and that, too, in the hours of their freedom from all control. Think not lightly of the *farthing* I had to give, now and then, for pen, ink, or paper. That farthing was, alas! a great sum to me. I was as tall as I am now, and I had great health and great exercise. The whole of the money not expended for us at market was *twopence a week* for each man. I remember, and well I may! that upon one occasion I had, after all absolutely necessary expenses, on a Friday, made shift to have a half-penny in reserve, which I had destined for the purchase of a red herring in the morning, but when I pulled off my clothes at night, so hungry then as to be hardly able to endure life, I found that I had lost my half-penny. I buried my head under the miserable sheet and rug, and cried like a child."

But Cobbett made even his poverty and hard circumstances serve his all-absorbing passion for knowledge and success. "If I," said he, "under such circumstances could encounter and overcome this task, is there, can there be in the whole world, a youth to find any excuse for its non-performance?"

Humphry Davy had but a slender chance to acquire great scientific knowledge, yet he had true mettle in him, and he made even old pans, kettles, and bottles contribute to his success, as he experimented and studied in the attic of the apothecary-store where he worked.

"Many a farmer's son," says Thurlow Weed, "has found the best opportunities for mental improvement in his intervals of leisure while tending 'sap-bush.' Such, at any rate, was my own experience. At night you had only to feed the kettles and keep up the fires, the sap having been gathered and the wood cut before dark. During the day we would always lay in a good stock of 'fat-pine' by the light of which, blazing bright before the sugar-house, in the posture the serpent was condemned to assume, as a penalty for tempting our first grandmother, I passed many a delightful night in reading. I remember in this way to have read a history of the French Revolution, and to have obtained from it a better and more enduring knowledge of its events and horrors and of the actors in that great national tragedy, than I have received from all subsequent reading. I remember also how happy I was in being able to borrow the books of a Mr. Keyes after a two-mile tramp through the snow, shoeless, my feet swaddled in remnants of rag carpet."

"May I have a holiday to-morrow, father?" asked Theodore Parker one August afternoon. The poor Lexington millwright looked in surprise at his youngest son, for it was a busy time, but he saw from the boy's earnest face that he had no ordinary object in view, and granted the request. Theodore rose very early the next morning, walked through the dust ten miles to Harvard College, and presented himself as a candidate for admission. He had been unable to attend school regularly since he was eight years old, but he had managed to go three months each winter, and had reviewed his lessons again and again as he followed the plough or worked at other tasks. All his odd moments had been hoarded, too, for reading useful books, which he borrowed. One book he could not borrow, but he felt that he must have it; so on summer mornings he rose long before the sun and picked bushel after bushel of berries, which he sent to Boston, and so got the money to buy that coveted Latin dictionary.

"Well done, my boy!" said the millwright, when his son came home late at night and told of his successful examination; "but, Theodore, I cannot afford to keep you there!" "True, father," said Theodore, "I am not going to stay there; I shall study at home, at odd times, and thus prepare myself for a final examination, which will give me a diploma." He did this; and, by teaching school as he grew older, got money to study for two years at Harvard, where he was graduated with honor. Years after, when, as the trusted friend and adviser of Seward, Chase, Sumner, Garrison, Horace Mann, and Wendell Phillips, his influence for good was felt in the hearts of all his countrymen, it was a pleasure for him to recall his early struggles and triumphs among the rocks and bushes of Lexington.

"The proudest moment of my life," said Elihu Burritt, "was when I had first gained the full meaning of the first fifteen lines of Homer's Iliad. I took a short triumphal walk, in favor of that exploit." His father died when he was sixteen, and Elihu was apprenticed to a blacksmith in his native village of New Britain, Conn. He had to work at the forge ten or twelve hours a day; but while blowing the bellows, he would solve mentally difficult problems in arithmetic.

In a diary kept at Worcester, whither he went some ten years later to enjoy its library privileges, are such entries as these, — "Monday, June 18, headache, 40 pages Cuvier's 'Theory of the Earth,' 64 pages French, 11 hours' forging. Tuesday, June 19, 60 lines Hebrew, 30 Danish, 10 lines Bohemian, 9 lines Polish, 15 names of stars, 10 hours' forging. Wednesday, June 20, 25 lines Hebrew, 8 lines Syriac, 11 hours' forging." He mastered 18 languages and 32 dialects. He became eminent as the "Learned Blacksmith," and for his noble work in the service of humanity. Edward Everett said of the manner in which this boy with no chance acquired great learning: "It is enough to make one who has good opportunities for education hang his head in shame."

The barefoot Christine Nilsson in remote Sweden had little chance, but she won the admiration of the world for her wondrous power of song, combined with rare womanly grace.

"Let me say in regard to your adverse worldly circumstances," says Dr. Talmage to young men, "that you are on a level now with those who are finally to succeed. Mark my words, and think of it thirty years from now. You will find that those who, thirty years from now, are the millionaires of this country, who are the orators of the country, who are the poets of the country, who are the strong merchants of the country, who are the great philanthropists of the country,— mightiest in the church and state, — are now on a level with you, not an inch above you, and in straightened circumstances now.

"No outfit, no capital to start with? Young man, go down to the library and get some books, and read of what wonderful mechanism God gave you in your hand, in your foot, in your eye, in your ear, and then ask some doctor to take you into the dissecting-room and illustrate to you what you have read about, and never again commit the blasphemy of saying you have no capital to start with. *Equipped? Why, the poorest young man is equipped as only the God of the whole universe could afford to equip him.*"

A newsboy is not a very promising candidate for success or honors in any line of life. A young man can't set out in life with much less chance than when he starts his "daily" for a living. Yet the man who more than any other is responsible for the industrial regeneration of this continent, started in life as a newsboy on the Grand Trunk Railway. Thomas Alva Edison was then about fifteen years of age. He had already begun to dabble in chemistry, and had fitted up a small itinerant laboratory. One day, as he was performing some occult experiment, the train rounded a curve, and the bottle of sulphuric acid broke. There followed a series of unearthly odors and unnatural complications. The conductor, who had suffered long and patiently, now ejected the youthful devotee, and in the process of the scientist's expulsion added a resounding box upon the ear.

Edison passed through one dramatic situation after another — always mastering it — until he has attained at an early age the scientific throne of the world. When recently asked the secret of his success, he said he had always been a total abstainer and singularly moderate in everything but work.

Daniel Manning, who was President Cleveland's first campaign manager and afterwards Secretary of the Treasury, started out as a newsboy with apparently the world against him. So did Thurlow Weed; so did

David B. Hill. New York seems to have been prolific in enterprising newsboys.

What nonsense for two uneducated and unknown youths who met in a cheap boarding-house in Boston, to array themselves against an institution whose roots were embedded in the very constitution of our country, and which was upheld by scholars, statesmen, churches, wealth, and aristocracy, without distinction of creed or politics! What chance had they against the prejudices and sentiment of a nation? But these young men were fired by a lofty purpose, and they were thoroughly in earnest. One of them, Benjamin Lundy, had already started in Ohio a paper called "The Genius of Universal Liberty," and had carried the entire edition home on his back from the printing-office, twenty miles, every month. He had walked four hundred miles on his way to Tennessee to increase his subscription list. He was no ordinary young man.

With William Lloyd Garrison, he started to prosecute his work more earnestly in Baltimore. The sight of the slave-pens along the principal streets; of vessel-loads of unfortunates torn from home and family and sent to Southern ports; the heartrending scenes at the auction blocks, made an impression on Garrison never to be forgotten; and the young man whose mother was too poor to send him to school, although she early taught him to hate oppression, resolved to devote his life to secure the freedom of these poor wretches.

In the very first issue of his paper, Garrison urged an immediate emancipation, and called down upon his head the wrath of the entire community. He was arrested and sent to jail. John G. Whittier, a noble Friend in the North, was so touched at the news that, being too poor to furnish the money himself, he wrote to Henry Clay, begging him to release Garrison by paying the fine. After forty-nine days of imprisonment he was set free. Wendell Phillips said of him, "He was imprisoned for his opinion when he was twenty-four. He had confronted a nation in the bloom of his youth."

Garrison did not propose to lose his time just because he was imprisoned. While in jail, he prepared several lectures; but what could he do with them? Churches and halls were closed to him; but he was not to be suppressed. In Boston, with no money, friends, or influence, in a little upstairs room, he started the "Liberator." Read the declaration of this poor young man with "no chance," in the very first issue: "I will be as harsh as truth, as uncompromising as justice. I am in earnest. I will not equivocate, I will not excuse; I will not retreat a single inch, and I will be heard." What audacity for a young man, with the world against him!

Hon. Robert Y. Hayne, of South Carolina, wrote to Otis, mayor of Boston, that some one had sent him a copy of the "Liberator," and asked him to ascertain the name of the publisher. Otis replied that he had found a poor young man printing "this insignificant sheet in an obscure hole, his only auxiliary a negro boy, his supporters a few persons of all colors and little influence."

But this poor young man, eating, sleeping, and printing in this "obscure hole," had set the world to thinking, and must be suppressed. The Vigilance Association of South Carolina offered a reward of fifteen hundred dollars for the arrest and prosecution of any one detected circulating the "Liberator." The governors of one or two States set a price on the editor's head. The legislature of Georgia offered a reward of five thousand dollars for his arrest and conviction.

The youth with no chance had stirred up a nation. Twelve "Fanatics" met one stormy night in the basement of the African church in Boston and organized the New England Anti-Slavery Society. The contest grew bitter. Prudence Crandall admitted a few colored girls to her school in Connecticut, patronized by wealthy people residing in Boston and New York, and hoodlums filled her well with refuse. Merchants refused to sell her anything, and a midnight mob threatened to destroy the schoolhouse and lay violent hands upon the teacher. Garrison and his coadjutors were denounced everywhere. A clergyman named Lovejoy was killed by a mob in Illinois for espousing the cause, while defending his printing-press, and in the old "Cradle of American Liberty" the wealth, power, and culture of Massachusetts arrayed itself against the "Abolitionists" so outrageously, that a mere spectator, a young lawyer of great promise, asked to be lifted upon the high platform, and replied in such a speech as was never before heard in Faneuil Hall. "When I heard the gentleman lay down principles which place the murderers of Lovejoy at Alton side by side with Otis and Hancock, with Quincy and Adams," said Wendell Phillips, pointing to their portraits on the walls, "I thought those pictured lips would have broken into voice to rebuke the recreant American. the slanderer of the dead. For the sentiments that he has uttered, on soil consecrated by the prayers of the Puritans and the blood of patriots, the earth should have yawned and swallowed him up."

The whole nation was wrought to fever heat. Charles Sumner was stricken down in the United States Senate by a blow from Preston S. Brooks, of South Carolina, for his speech against the extension of slavery in Kansas. That State came into being amid the "very tempest and whirlwind of passion," the slaveholding oligarchy "colonizing voters" with all its might, while from New England's hills emigrants poured westward by thousands, singing Whittier's lines: —

> "We cross the prairie as of old
> The Pilgrims crossed the sea,
> To make the West, as they the East,
> The homestead of the free!"

Between the Northern pioneers and Southern chivalry the struggle was long and fierce even in far California. The drama culminated in the shock of civil war. When the war was ended, and, after thirty-five years of untiring, heroic conflict, Garrison was invited as the nation's guest, by President Lincoln, to see the stars and stripes unfurled once more above Fort Sumter, an emancipated slave delivered the address of welcome, and his two daughters, no longer chattels, presented Garrison with a beautiful wreath of flowers.

About this time Richard Cobden, another powerful friend of the oppressed, died in London. John Bright afterwards unveiled a marble statue in Bradford, England, bearing in bold letters the word "Cobden," encircled by the inscription: "Free Trade, Peace and Good Will among Men."

Richard Cobden's father died leaving nine children almost penniless. The boy earned his living by watching a neighbor's sheep, but had no chance to attend school until he was ten years old. He was sent to a boarding-school, where he was abused, half starved, and allowed to write home only once in three months. At fifteen he entered his uncle's store in London as a clerk. He learned French by rising early and studying while his companions slept. He was soon sent out in a gig as a commercial traveler.

He called upon John Bright to enlist his aid in fighting the terrible "Corn-Laws" which were taking bread from the poor and giving it to the rich. He found Mr. Bright in great grief, for his wife was lying dead in the house. "There are thousands of homes in England at this moment," said he, "where wives, mothers, and children are dying of hunger. Now, when the first paroxysm of grief is passed, I would advise you to come with me, and we will never rest until the Corn-Laws are repealed." They formed the "Anti-Corn-Law League," which, aided by the Irish famine, — for it was hunger that at last ate through those stone walls of protection, — secured the repeal of the law in 1846. Mr. Bright said: "There is not in Great Britain a poor man's home that has not a bigger, better, and cheaper loaf through Richard Cobden's labors."

John Bright himself was the son of a poor working man, and in those days the doors of the higher schools were closed to such as he; but the great Quaker heart of this handsome, resolute youth was touched with pity for the millions of England's and Ireland's poor, starving under the "Corn-Laws." Cobden could no longer see the poor man's bread stopped at the Custom-House and taxed for the benefit of the landlord and farmer, and he threw his whole soul into this great reform. "This is not a party question," said he, "for men of all parties are united upon it. It is a pantry question,— a question between the working millions and the aristocracy." During the famine, which cut off two millions of Ireland's population in a year, John Bright was more powerful than all the nobility of England. The whole aristocracy trembled before his invincible logic, his mighty eloquence, and his commanding character. Except possibly Cobden, no other man did so much to give the laborer a shorter day, a cheaper loaf, an added shilling.

Over a stable in London lived a poor boy named Michael Faraday, who carried newspapers about the streets to loan to customers for a penny apiece. He was apprenticed for seven years to a bookbinder and bookseller. When binding the Encyclopædia Britannica, his eyes caught the article on electricity, and he could not rest until he had read it. He procured a glass vial, an old pan, and a few simple articles, and began to experiment. A customer became interested in the boy, and took him to hear Sir Humphry Davy lecture on chemistry. He summoned courage to write the great scientist and sent the notes he had taken of his lecture. One night, not long after, just as Michael was about to retire, Sir Humphry Davy's carriage stopped at his humble lodging, and a servant handed him a written invitation to call upon the great lecturer the next morning. Michael could scarcely trust his eyes as he read the note from the great Davy. In the morning he called as requested, and was engaged to clean instruments and take them to and from the lecture-room. He watched eagerly every movement of Davy, as he developed his safety-lamp and experimented with dangerous explosives, with a glass mask over his face. Michael studied and experimented, too, and it was not long before this poor boy with no chance was invited to lecture before the great philosophical society.

He was appointed professor at the Royal Academy at Woolwich, and became the wonder of the age in science. Tyndall said of him, "He is the greatest experimental philosopher the world has ever seen." When Sir Humphry Davy was asked what was his greatest discovery, he replied, "Michael Faraday."

"What has been done can be done again," said the boy with no chance who became Lord Beaconsfield, England's great Prime Minister. "I am not a slave, I am not a captive, and by energy I can overcome greater obstacles." Jewish blood flowed in his veins and everything seemed against him, but he remembered the example of Joseph, who became Prime Minister of Egypt four thousand years before, and that of Daniel, who was Prime Minister to the greatest despot of the world five centuries before the birth of Christ. He pushed his way up through the lower classes, up through the middle classes, up through the upper classes, until he stood a master, self-poised upon the topmost round of political and social power. Rebuffed, scorned, ridiculed, hissed down in the House of Commons, he simply said, "The time will come when you will hear me." The time did come, and the boy with no chance but a determined will, swayed the sceptre of England for a quarter of a century.

Henry Clay, the "mill-boy of the slashes," was one of seven children of a widow too poor to send him to any but a common country school, where he was drilled only in the "three R's." But he used every spare moment to study without a teacher, and in after years he was a king among self-made men. The boy who had learned to speak in a barn, with only a cow and a horse for an audience, became one of the greatest of American orators and statesmen.

See Kepler struggling with poverty and hardship, his books burned in public by order of the state, his library locked up by the Jesuits, and himself exiled by public clamor. For seventeen years he works calmly upon the demonstration of the great principles, that planets revolve in ellipses, with the sun at one focus; that a line connecting the centre of the earth with the centre of the sun passes over equal spaces in equal times, and that the squares of the times of revolution of the planets about the sun are proportional to the cubes of their mean distances from the sun. This boy with no chance became one of the world's greatest astronomers.

"When I found that I was black," said Alexander Dumas, "I resolved to live as if I were white, and so force men to look below my skin."

How slender seemed the chance of James Sharples, the celebrated blacksmith artist of England! He was very poor, but he often rose at three o'clock to copy books he could not buy. He would walk eighteen miles to Manchester and back after a hard day's work, to buy a shilling's worth of artist's materials. He would ask for the heaviest work in the blacksmith shop, because it took a longer time to heat at the forge, and he could thus have many spare minutes to study the precious book, which he propped up against the chimney. He was a great miser of spare moments and used every one as though he might never see another. He devoted his leisure hours for five years to that wonderful production, "The Forge," copies of which are to be seen in many a home.

What chance had Galileo to win renown in physics or astronomy, when his parents compelled him to go to a medical school? Yet while Venice slept, he stood in the tower of St. Mark's Cathedral and discovered the satellites of Jupiter and the phases of Venus, through a telescope made with his own hands, because he was too poor to buy one. When compelled on bended knee to publicly renounce his heretical doctrine that the earth moves around the sun, all the terrors of the Inquisition could not keep this feeble man of threescore years and ten, from muttering to himself, "Yet it does move." When thrown into prison, so great was his eagerness for scientific research that he proved by a straw in his cell that a hollow tube is relatively much stronger than a solid rod of the same size. Even when totally blind, he kept constantly at work.

Imagine the surprise of the Royal Society of England when the poor, unknown Herschel sent in the report of his discovery of the star Georgium Sidus, its orbit and rate of motion; and of the rings and satellites of Saturn. The boy with no chance, who had played the oboe for his meals, had with his own hands made the telescope through which he discovered facts unknown to the best equipped astronomers of his day. He had ground two hundred specula before he could get one perfect.

George Stephenson was one of eight children whose parents were so poor that all lived in a single room. George had to watch cows for a neighbor, but he managed to get time to make engines of clay, with hemlock sticks for pipes. At seventeen he had charge of an engine, with his father for fireman. He could neither read nor write, but the engine was his teacher, and he a faithful student. While the other hands were playing games or loafing in liquor shops during the holidays, George was taking his machine to pieces, cleaning it, studying it, and making experiments in engines. When he had become famous as a great inventor of improvements in engines, those who had loafed and played called him lucky.

The famous English artist, Martin, went to the baker's with his last shilling, to buy a loaf of bread. The baker snatched the loaf from his hands and told him the shilling was counterfeit. Martin returned to his home, and finding a dry crust in his trunk, went about his work with that determination which knows no defeat.

Without a charm of face or figure, Charlotte Cushman resolved to place herself in the front rank as an actress, even in such characters as Rosalind and Queen Katherine. The star actress was unable to perform, and Miss Cushman, her understudy, took her place. That night she held her audience with such grasp of intellect and iron will that it forgot the absence of mere dimpled feminine grace. Although poor, friendless, and unknown before, when the curtain fell upon her first performance at the London theatre, her reputation was made. In after years, when physicians told her that she had a terrible, incurable disease, she flinched not a particle, but quietly said, "I have learned to live with my trouble."

A poor colored woman in a log cabin in the South had three boys, but could afford only one pair of trousers for the three. She was so anxious to give them an education, that she sent them to school by turns. The teacher, a Northern girl, noticed that each boy came to school only one day out of three, and that all wore the same pantaloons. The poor mother educated her boys as best she could. One became a professor in a Southern college, another a physician, and the third a clergyman. What a lesson for boys who plead "no chance" as an excuse for wasted lives!

"I want a Greek Testament," said John Brown of Carpow, Scotland, to a bookseller at St. Andrew's. The dealer stared at the shepherd boy, rough and unkempt from a night walk of twenty miles to buy a book, and had begun to make sport of so strange a request from a small country lad, when a college professor entered. "Now," said the professor, after learning what John wanted, "if you will read a verse of that Testament and translate it to me, you shall have the book for nothing." The boy translated several verses with ease and marched proudly home with his prize. He had mastered both Greek and Latin while tending his flock, and laid the foundation for the ripe scholarship for which he became noted.

Sam Cunard, the whittling Scotch lad of Glasgow, wrought out many odd inventions with brain and jack-knife, but they brought neither honor nor profit until he was consulted by Burns & McIvor, who wished to increase their facilities for carrying foreign mails. The model of a steamship which Sam whittled out for them was carefully copied for the first vessel of the great Cunard Line, and became the standard type for all the magnificent ships since constructed by the firm. When Samuel Cunard was knighted, he did not forget that he owed his honors and his wealth to conscientious whittling.

The New Testament and the speller were Cornelius Vanderbilt's only books at school, but he learned to read, write, and cipher a little. He wished to buy a boat, but had no money. To discourage him from following the sea, his mother told him if he would plough, harrow, and plant with corn, before the twenty-seventh day of the month, ten acres of rough, hard, stony land, the worst on his father's farm, she would lend him the amount he wished. Before the appointed time the work was done, and well done. On his seventeenth birthday Cornelius bought the boat, but on his way home it struck a sunken wreck and sank just as he reached shallow water.

But Cornelius Vanderbilt was not the boy to give up. He at once began again. In three years he saved three thousand dollars. He often worked all night, and soon had far the largest patronage of any boatman in the harbor. During the War of 1812 he was awarded the Government contract to carry provisions to the military stations near the metropolis. He fulfilled this contract by night, that he might run his ferry boat by day between New York and Brooklyn.

The boy who gave his parents all his day earnings and half of what he got at night, was worth thirty thousand dollars at the age of thirty-five, and when he died at an advanced age, he left to his thirteen children one of the largest fortunes in America.

Lord Eldon might well have pleaded "no chance" when a boy, for he was too poor to go to school or even to buy books. But no; he had grit and determination, and was bound to make his way in the world. He rose at four o'clock in the morning and copied law books which he borrowed, the voluminous "Coke upon Littleton" among others. He was so eager to study, that sometimes he would keep it up until his brain refused to work, when he would tie a wet towel about his head, to enable him to keep awake and to study. His first year's practice brought him but nine shillings, yet he was bound not to give up. The Master of Rolls once decided a law point against him; but on his appeal, the House of Lords reversed the decision.

When Eldon was leaving the chamber, the Solicitor tapped him on the shoulder and said, "Young man, your bread and butter's cut for life." The boy with "no chance" became Lord Chancellor of England, and one of the greatest lawyers of his age.

Stephen Girard had "no chance." He left his home in France when ten years old, and came to America as a cabin boy. His great ambition was to get on and to succeed at any cost. There was no work, however hard and disagreeable, that he would not undertake. Midas like, he turned to gold everything he touched, and became one of the wealthiest merchants of Philadelphia. His abnormal love of money cannot be commended, but his thoroughness in all he did, his public spirit at times of national need, and willingness to risk his life to save strangers sick with the deadly yellow fever, are traits of character well worthy of imitation.

John Wanamaker walked four miles to Philadelphia every day, and worked in a bookstore for one dollar and twenty-five cents a week. He next worked in a clothing store at an advance of twenty-five cents a week. From this he went up and up until now he counts his wealth by millions. He was appointed Postmaster-General by President Harrison in 1888, and in that capacity showed great executive ability. Give a boy a purpose and determination, no matter how poor his chance, and you will hear from him.

The men who manipulate to-day the levers that move the world were nearly all poor boys.

Prejudice against her race and sex did not deter the colored girl, Edmonia Lewis, from struggling upward to honor and fame as a sculptor.

Fred Douglass started in life with less than nothing, for he did not own his own body, and he was pledged before his birth to pay his master's debts. To reach the starting-point of the poorest white boy, he had to climb as far as the distance which the latter must ascend if he would become President of the United States. He saw his mother but two or three times, and then in the night, when she would walk twelve miles to be with him an hour, returning in time to go into the field at dawn. He had no chance to study, for he had no teacher, and the rules of the plantation forbade slaves to learn to read and write. But somehow, unnoticed by his master, he managed to learn the alphabet from scraps of paper and patent medicine almanacs, and no limits could then be placed to his career. He put to shame thousands of white boys. He fled from slavery at twenty-one, went North and worked as a stevedore in New York and New Bedford. At Nantucket he was given an opportunity to speak in an anti-slavery meeting, and made so favorable an impression that he was made agent of the Anti-Slavery Society of Massachusetts. While traveling from place to place to lecture, he would study with all his might. He was sent to Europe to lecture, and won the friendship of several Englishmen, who gave him $750, with which he purchased his freedom. He edited a paper in Rochester, N. Y., and afterwards conducted the "New Era" in Washington. For several years he was Marshal of the District of Columbia. To-day he is the first colored man in the United States, the peer of any man in the country.

Henry Dixey, the well-known actor, began his career upon the stage as the hind legs of a cow.

P. T. Barnum rode a horse for ten cents a day. George W. Childs worked as an errand boy for four dollars a month; and from similar small beginnings have grown most of the large fortunes on record.

Gideon Lee could not even get shoes to wear in winter, when a boy, but he went to work barefoot in the snow. He made a bargain with himself to work sixteen hours a day. He fulfilled it to the letter, and when from interruption he lost time, he robbed himself of sleep to make it up. He became a wealthy merchant of New York, mayor of the city, and a member of Congress.

Andrew Johnson, apprenticed to a tailor at ten years of age by his widowed mother, was never able to attend school.

It was a boy born in a log-cabin, without schooling,

or books, or teacher, or ordinary opportunities, who won the admiration of mankind by his homely practical wisdom while President during our Civil War, and who emancipated four million slaves.

Behold this long, lank, awkward youth, felling trees on the little claim, building his homely log-cabin, without floor or windows, teaching himself arithmetic and grammar in the evening by the light of the fireplace. In his eagerness to know the contents of Blackstone's Commentaries, he walked forty-four miles to procure the precious volumes, and read one hundred pages while returning. Abraham Lincoln inherited no opportunities, and acquired nothing by luck. His good fortune consisted of untiring perseverance and a right heart.

In another log-cabin, in the backwoods of Ohio, a poor widow is holding a boy eighteen months old, and wondering if she will be able to keep the wolf from her little ones. The boy grows, and in a few years we find him chopping wood and tilling the little clearing in the forest, to help his mother. Every spare hour is spent in studying the books he has borrowed, but cannot buy. At sixteen he gladly accepts a chance to drive mules on a canal towpath. Soon he applies for a chance to sweep floors and ring the bell of an academy, to pay his way while studying there.

His first term at Geauga Seminary cost him but seventeen dollars. When he returned the next term he had but a sixpence in his pocket, and this he put into the contribution box at church the next day. He engaged board, washing, fuel, and light of a carpenter at one dollar and six cents a week, with the privilege of working nights and Saturdays all the time he could spare. He had arrived on a Saturday and planed fifty-one boards that day, for which he received one dollar and two cents. When the term closed, he had paid all expenses and had three dollars over. The following winter he taught school at twelve dollars a month and "board around." In the spring he had forty-eight dollars, and when he returned to school he boarded himself at an expense of thirty-one cents a week.

Soon we find him in Williams College, where in two years he is graduated with honors. He reaches the State Senate at twenty-six and Congress at thirty-three. Twenty-seven years from the time he applied for a chance to ring the bell at Hiram College, James A. Garfield became President of the United States. The inspiration of such an example is worth more to the young man of America than all the wealth of the Astors, the Vanderbilts, and the Goulds.

Among the world's greatest heroes and benefactors are many others whose cradles were rocked by want in lowly cottages, and who buffeted the billows of fate without dependence, save upon the mercy of God and their own energies.

"The little gray cabin appears to be the birthplace of all your great men," said an English author who had been looking over a book of biographies of eminent Americans.

With five chances on each hand and *one unwavering aim*, no boy, however poor, need despair. There is bread and success for every youth under the American flag, who has energy and ability to *seize his opportunity*. It matters not whether the boy is born in a log-cabin or in a mansion; if he is dominated by a resolute purpose, and upholds himself, neither men nor demons can keep him down.

> The rich man's son inherits lands,
>   And piles of brick and stone and gold,
> And he inherits soft white hands,
>   And tender flesh that fears the cold,
> Nor dare he wear a garment old:
>   A heritage, it seems to me,
> One scarce would wish to hold in fee.

The rich man's son inherits cares ;
　　The bank may break, the factory burn,
A breath may burst his bubble-shares ;
　　Then, soft white hands could hardly earn
A living that would serve his turn.

What doth the poor man's son inherit?
　　Stout muscles, and a sinewy heart,
A hardy frame, a hardier spirit !
　　King of two hands, he does his part
In every useful toil and art:
　　A heritage it seems to me,
A king might wish to hold in fee.

　　　　　　　　　　　　　　LOWELL.

CHAPTER III.

AN IRON WILL.

The truest wisdom is a resolute determination. — NAPOLEON I.

He wants wit, that wants resolved will. — SHAKESPEARE.

When a firm decisive spirit is recognized, it is curious to see how the space clears around a man and leaves him room and freedom. — JOHN FOSTER.

A strong, defiant purpose is many-handed, and lays hold of whatever is near that can serve it; it has a magnetic power that draws to itself whatever is kindred. — T. T. MUNGER.

People do not lack strength; they lack will. — VICTOR HUGO.

He who has resolved to conquer or die is seldom conquered; such noble despair perishes with difficulty. — CORNEILLE.

Every man stamps his own value upon himself, and we are great or little according to our own will. — SAMUEL SMILES.

The saddest failures in life are those that come from not putting forth of the power and will to succeed. — WHIPPLE.

As men in a crowd instinctively make room for one who would force his way through it, so mankind makes way for one who rushes toward an object beyond them. — DWIGHT.

In idle wishes fools supinely stay;
Be there a will, and wisdom finds a way.
CRABBE.

"I CAN'T! it is impossible!" said a lieutenant to Alexander, after failing to take a rock-crested fortress. "Begone!" thundered the great Macedonian; "there is nothing impossible to him who will try;" and at the head of a phalanx he swept the foe from the stronghold.

"You can only half will," Suwarrow would say to people who failed. He preached willing as a system. "I don't know," "I can't," and "impossible" he would not listen to. "Learn!" "Do!" "Try!" he would exclaim.

Napoleon in Egypt visited those sick with the plague,

to show that a man who is never afraid can vanquish that scourge. A will power like this is a strong tonic to the body, and it will stimulate to almost superhuman undertakings. Such a will has taken many men from apparent death-beds, and enabled them to perform wonderful deeds of valor.

Aaron Burr was dangerously sick when he joined Arnold in leading the expedition against Canada. General Wolfe, sick with fever, led his troops up the heights of Abraham, defeated Montcalm, and compelled impregnable Quebec to surrender. But five days before, he wrote home to England: "My constitution is entirely ruined, and without the consolation of having rendered any considerable service to the State, or without prospects of it."

When told by his physicians that he must die, Douglas Jerrold said, "And leave a family of helpless children? I won't die." He kept his word, and lived for years.

After a sickness in which he lay a long time at death's door, Seneca said: "The thought of my father, who could not have sustained such a blow as my death, restrained me, and I commanded myself to live."

Professor George Wilson, of Edinburgh University, was so fragile that no one thought he ever could amount to much; but he became a noted scholar in spite of discouragements which would have daunted most men of the strongest constitutions. Disaster, amputation of one foot, consumption, frightful hemorrhages, — nothing could shake his imperious will. Death itself seemed to stand aghast before that mighty resolution, hesitating to take possession of the body after all else had fled.

At fifty-five years of age, Sir Walter Scott owed more than six hundred thousand dollars. He determined that every dollar should be paid. This iron resolution gave confidence and inspiration to the other faculties

BISMARCK

"The iron will of one stout heart shall make a thousand quail."

and functions of the body and brain. Every nerve and fibre said, "*The debt must be paid;*" every drop of blood caught the inspiration and rushed to the brain to add its weight of force to the power which wielded the pen. And the debt was paid. In his diary he wrote: "I have suffered terribly and often wished that I could lie down and sleep without waking. But I will fight it out if I can." His imperious will worked on and on after it seemed that every other faculty had abandoned his mind.

"Is there one whom difficulties dishearten?" asked John Hunter. "He will do little. Is there one who will conquer? That kind of a man never fails."

"Six o'clock A. M. — I, Edward Irving, promise, by the grace of God, to have mastered all the words in alpha and beta before eight o'clock." The young man had written this on his Greek lexicon. He added later: "Eight o'clock A. M. — I, Edward Irving, by the grace of God, have done it."

"Nothing is impossible to the man who can will," said Mirabeau. "Is that necessary? then that shall be. This is the only law of success."

"We have a half belief," said Emerson, "that the person is possible who can counterpoise all other persons. We believe that there may be a man *who is a match for events,* — one who never found his match, — against whom other men being dashed are broken, — one who can give you any odds and beat you."

"There are three kinds of people in the world," says a writer in the "Eclectic Magazine," "the wills, the won'ts, and the can'ts. The first accomplish everything; the second oppose everything; the third fail in everything."

"There is so much power in faith," says Bulwer, "even when faith is applied but to things human and earthly, that let a man but be firmly persuaded that he is born to do some day, what at the moment seems impossible, and it is fifty to one but what he does it before he dies."

What can you do with a man who has an invincible purpose in him; who never knows when he is beaten; and who, when his legs are shot off, will fight on the stumps? Difficulties and opposition do not daunt him. He thrives upon persecution; it only stimulates him to more determined endeavor. Give a man the alphabet and an iron will, and who shall place bounds to his achievements? Imprison a Galileo for his discoveries in science, and he will experiment with the straw in his cell. Deprive Euler of his eyesight, and he but studies harder upon mental problems, thus developing marvelous powers of mathematical calculation. Lock up the poor Bedford tinker in jail, and he will write the finest allegory in the world, or will leave his imperishable thoughts upon the walls of his cell. Burn the body of Wycliffe and throw the ashes into the Severn; but they will be swept to the ocean, which will carry them, permeated with his principles, to all lands. *The world always listens to a man with a will in him.* You might as well snub the sun as such men as Bismarck and Grant.

The shores of fortune, as Foster says, are covered with the stranded wrecks of men of brilliant ability, but who have wanted courage, faith, and decision, and have therefore perished in sight of more resolute but less capable adventurers, who succeeded in making port. Hundreds of men go to their graves in obscurity, who have been obscure only because they lacked the pluck to make a first effort; and who, could they only have resolved to begin, would have astonished the world by their achievements and successes.

"Why not try for one of the prizes offered by the London Society of Arts?" asked Mrs. Ross of her son William, then not twelve years old. "I will try," was his reply, and his painting of the "Death of Wat

Tyler" won the first prize. In after years he became miniature painter to Queen Victoria, and was knighted.

Quentin Matsys despaired of becoming a painter, although desperately in love with his master's daughter; but when told that he could not marry her unless he produced a picture of merit, he went to work with a will which knows no defeat, and painted the "Misers," one of the masterpieces of art. It is such intensity of purpose that accomplishes the "*impossible.*"

Balzac's father tried to discourage his son from the pursuit of literature. "Do you know," said he, "that in literature a man must be either a king or a beggar?" "Very well," replied the boy, "*I will be a king.*" His parents left him to his fate in a garret. For ten years he fought terrible battles with hardship and poverty, but won a great victory at last.

Who could look into the pale, emaciated face of Rufus Choate without seeing the mighty conflict raging between the mind and the body, or realizing that death was held at bay by an unconquerable will? When a friend remonstrated with him for injuring his constitution, he replied, "Good heavens! my constitution was gone long ago, and I am living on the by-laws." A parallel example was that of William M. Evarts. It almost seemed as if his mighty will was domiciled in a skeleton, and refused to leave after all other servants had abandoned the wreck. Robert Hall made a miserable failure of his first sermon, and cried like a child in the pulpit. The second sermon was worse yet, but perseverance finally made him the great pulpit orator of England.

A young French officer used to pace his room, exclaiming, "*I will be Marshal of France and a great general.*" He became a great commander, and died a Marshal of France.

When asked why he repaired a magistrate's bench with so unusual care, a carpenter replied, "Because I wish to make it easy against the time when I come to sit on it myself." In a few years he did sit as a magistrate on that bench.

Some one told the elder Pitt that a certain project was impossible. "Impossible?" said he; "I trample upon impossibilities." His power in Parliament seemed more than mortal: his royal will overwhelmed that of the proudest peers.

One secret of England's great power over her colonies and those of other nations has been her indomitable will; her grasp is like that of Destiny. But she does not always remember that her children are of the same blood, or she would have hesitated to arouse the spirit voiced by Patrick Henry: "Is life so dear or peace so sweet as to be purchased at the price of chains and slavery? Forbid it, Almighty God! I know not what course others may take; but, as for me, give me liberty or give me death." Animated by such a spirit, the American colonies could not be conquered, as Chatham, himself a man of iron determination, clearly understood. It was the weak, vacillating, obstinate, and stupid George III. who precipitated the conflict, from which his Minister sought to dissuade him. "Four regiments," wrote the king, "will bring them [the colonies] to their senses; they will only be lions while we are lambs."

"Impossible," said Napoleon, "is a word found only in the dictionary of fools." He would have melted the rocks of St. Helena before he would have remained a prisoner there, had he not lost that imperious will before which all Europe trembled.

When General Grant took command of the Northern armies, the Confederates knew that their doom was sealed, for in that mighty will they felt the grip of Fate. "*On to Richmond!*" was his watchword. Old commanders shook their heads, but the silent man with the iron will, who never knew when he was beaten, swerved not a hair's breadth from his purpose until Lee surrendered his sword at Appomattox.

Garrison wrote in the very first issue of the "Liberator:" "I am in earnest. I will not equivocate. I will not excuse. I will not retreat a single inch; and I will be heard." Such uncompromising determination was not only the making of himself, but also of such heroes as Lincoln and Grant, and the thousands of unknown heroes dead upon the field of honor. That was a will worth having.

At the close of the Revolutionary War, that consummate debater and unequaled master of sarcasm, the younger Pitt, began his long administration as Prime Minister of England. His policy was strongly opposed to the French Revolution. But at the end of many successes Austerlitz proved his death-blow. Hearing of Napoleon's victory, he pointed to a map of Europe and said, "Roll up that chart; it will not be wanted these ten years." He then fell into a stupor, from which he awoke but once, murmuring faintly, "Alas, my country!" Napoleon's supreme will had overborne and crushed a mind and will of the very highest order; a mind sagacious enough to measure very accurately the force of events, as it was, almost to a day, ten years to Waterloo.

What a mighty will Darwin had! He was in continual ill health. He was in constant suffering. His patience was marvelous. No one but his wife knew what he endured. "For forty years," says his son, "he never knew one day of health;" yet during those forty years he unremittingly forced himself to do the work from which the mightiest minds and the strongest constitutions would have shrunk. He had a wonderful power of sticking to a subject. He used almost to apologize for his patience, saying that he could not bear to be beaten, as if it were a sign of weakness. One of his favorite sayings was: "*It's dogged that does it.*" A proof of his wonderful patience, perseverance, and carefulness is that he collected his material for his "Origin of Species" during twenty years, and for his "Descent of Man" during nearly thirty.

Tupper may be a little old-fashioned, but he has written four lines which can never die : —

"Confidence is conqueror of men; victorious both over them and in them;
The iron will of one stout heart shall make a thousand quail;
A feeble dwarf, dauntlessly resolved, will turn the tide of battle,
And rally to a nobler strife the giants that had fled."

CHAPTER IV.

POSSIBILITIES IN SPARE MOMENTS.

Dost thou love life? Then do not squander time, for that is the stuff life is made of. — FRANKLIN.

Eternity itself cannot restore the loss struck from the minute. — ANCIENT POET.

Pereunt et imputantur, — the hours perish and are laid to our charge. — INSCRIPTION ON A DIAL AT OXFORD.

I wasted time, and now doth time waste me. — SHAKESPEARE.

Every hour in a man's life has its own special work possible for it, and for no other hour within the allotted span of years, and once gone it will not return. — NOEL PATON.

A man that is young in years may be old in hours, if he have lost no time. — BACON.

Believe me when I tell you that thrift of time will repay you in after life, with a usury of profit beyond your most sanguine dreams, and that waste of it will make you dwindle alike in intellectual and moral stature, beyond your darkest reckoning. — GLADSTONE.

There is not an hour of youth but is trembling with destinies — not a moment of which, once past, the appointed work can ever be done again, or the neglected blow struck on the cold iron. — RUSKIN.

Lost! Somewhere between sunrise and sunset, two golden hours, each set with sixty diamond minutes. No reward is offered, for they are gone forever. — HORACE MANN.

Give me insight into to-day, and you may have the antique and future worlds. — EMERSON.

There is no business, no avocation whatever, which will not permit a man who has an inclination, to give a little time every day to the studies of his youth. — WYTTENBACH.

And the plea that this or that man has no time for culture will vanish as soon as we desire culture so much that we begin to examine seriously into our present use of time. — MATTHEW ARNOLD.

"WHAT is the price of that book?" at length asked a man who had been dawdling for an hour in the front store of Benjamin Franklin's newspaper establishment. "One dollar," replied the clerk. "One dollar," echoed the lounger; "can't you take less than that?" "One dollar is the price," was the answer.

The would-be purchaser looked over the books on sale awhile longer, and then inquired: "Is Mr. Franklin in?" "Yes," said the clerk, "he is very busy in the press-room." "Well, I want to see him," persisted the man. The proprietor was called, and the stranger asked: "What is the lowest, Mr. Franklin, that you can take for that book?" "One dollar and a quarter," was the prompt rejoinder. "One dollar and a quarter! Why, your clerk asked me only a dollar just now." "True," said Franklin, "and I could have better afforded to take a dollar than to leave my work."

The man seemed surprised; but, wishing to end a parley of his own seeking, he demanded: "Well, come now, tell me your lowest price for this book." "One dollar and a half," replied Franklin. "A dollar and a half! Why, you offered it yourself for a dollar and a quarter." "Yes," said Franklin coolly, "and I could better have taken that price then than a dollar and a half now."

The man silently laid the money on the counter, took his book, and left the store, having received a salutary lesson from a master in the art of transmuting time, at will, into either wealth or wisdom.

Time-wasters are everywhere.

On the floor of the gold-working room in the United States Mint at Philadelphia, there is a wooden lattice-work which is taken up when the floor is swept, and the fine particles of gold-dust, thousands of dollars yearly, are thus saved. So every successful man has a kind of network to catch "the raspings and parings of existence, those leavings of days and wee bits of hours" which most people sweep into the waste of life. He who hoards and turns to account all odd minutes, half hours, unexpected holidays, gaps "between times," and chasms of waiting for unpunctual persons, achieves results which astonish those who have not mastered this secret.

HARRIET BEECHER STOWE

"Oh, the power of ceaseless industry to perform miracles."

"All that I have accomplished, or expect, or hope to accomplish," said Elihu Burritt, "has been and will be by that plodding, patient, persevering process of accretion which builds the ant-heap — particle by particle, thought by thought, fact by fact. And if ever I was actuated by ambition, its highest and warmest aspiration reached no further than the hope to set before the young men of my country an example in employing those invaluable fragments of time called moments."

"I have been wondering how Ned contrived to monopolize all the talents of the family," said a brother, found in a brown study after listening to one of Burke's speeches in Parliament; "but then I remember, when we were at play, he was always at work."

The days come to us like friends in disguise, bringing priceless gifts from an unseen hand; but, if we do not use them, they are borne silently away, never to return. Each successive morning new gifts are brought, but if we failed to accept those that were brought yesterday and the day before, we become less and less able to turn them to account, until the ability to appreciate and utilize them is exhausted. Wisely was it said that lost wealth may be regained by industry and economy, lost knowledge by study, lost health by temperance and medicine, but lost time is gone forever.

"Oh, it's only five minutes or ten minutes till mealtime; there's no time to do anything now," is one of the commonest expressions heard in the family. But what monuments have been built up by poor boys with no chance, out of broken fragments of time which many of us throw away. The very hours you have wasted, if improved, might have insured your success.

"While the students at Andover were waiting for breakfast at the boarding-house," said a lady, "the rest of the young men would stand chaffing each other; but Joseph Cook, if there were only a half minute to spare, would turn to the big dictionary in the corner of the room, and learn the synonyms of a word, or search out its derivation." It is a cheap thing to say that Joseph Cook has evidently swallowed the dictionary, and cheap people often make the remark; but our age has not produced many nobler geniuses nor a more magnificent specimen of true self-culture.

Marion Harland has accomplished wonders, and she has been able to do this by economizing the minutes to shape her novels and newspaper articles, when her children were in bed and whenever she could get a spare minute. Though she has done so much, yet all her life has been subject to interruptions which would have discouraged most women from attempting anything outside their regular family duties. She has glorified the commonplace as few other women have done. Harriet Beecher Stowe, too, wrote her great masterpiece, "Uncle Tom's Cabin," in the midst of pressing household cares. Beecher read Froude's "England," a little each day that he had to wait for dinner. Longfellow translated the "Inferno" by snatches of ten minutes a day, while waiting for his coffee to boil, persisting for years until the work was done.

Hugh Miller, while working hard as a stone-mason, found time to read scientific books, and write the lessons learned from the blocks of stone he handled.

Madame de Genlis, when companion of the future queen of France, composed several of her charming volumes while waiting for the princess to whom she gave her daily lessons. Burns wrote many of his most beautiful poems while working on a farm. The author of "Paradise Lost" was a teacher, Secretary of the Commonwealth, Secretary of the Lord Protector, and had to write his sublime poetry whenever he could snatch a few minutes from a busy life. John Stuart Mill did much of his best work as a writer while a clerk in the East India House. Galileo was a surgeon, yet to the improvement of his spare moments the world owes some of its greatest discoveries.

POSSIBILITIES IN SPARE MOMENTS.

If a genius like Gladstone carries through life a little book in his pocket lest an unexpected spare moment slip from his grasp, what should we of common abilities not resort to, to save the precious moments from oblivion? What a rebuke is such a life to the thousands of young men and women who throw away whole months and even years of that which the " Grand Old Man " hoards up even to the smallest fragments. Many a great man has snatched his reputation from odd bits of time which others, who wonder at their failure to get on, throw away. In Dante's time nearly every literary man in Italy was a hard-working merchant, physician, statesman, judge, or soldier.

While Michael Faraday was employed binding books, he devoted all his leisure to experiments. At one time he wrote to a friend, "Time is all I require. Oh, that I could purchase at a cheap rate some of our modern gentleman's spare hours, — nay, days."

Oh, the power of ceaseless industry to perform miracles!

Alexander von Humboldt's days were so occupied with his business that he had to pursue his scientific labors in the night or early morning, while others were asleep.

Oh, what wonders have been performed in " one hour a day!"

One hour a day withdrawn from frivolous pursuits, and profitably employed, would enable any man of ordinary capacity to master a complete science. One hour a day would make an ignorant man a well-informed man in ten years. One hour a day would earn enough to pay for two daily and two weekly papers, two leading magazines, and a dozen good books. In an hour a day a boy or girl could read twenty pages thoughtfully — over seven thousand pages, or eighteen large volumes in a year. An hour a day might make all the difference between bare existence and useful, happy living. An hour a day might make — nay, has made — an unknown man a famous one, a useless man a benefactor to his race. Consider, then, the mighty possibilities of two — four — yes, six hours a day that are, on the average, thrown away by young men and women in the restless desire for fun and diversion!

Every young man should have a hobby to occupy his leisure hours, something useful to which he can turn with delight, whenever he has a little leisure time. It might be in line with his work or otherwise, only his *heart must be in it.* A stone-cutter had butterflies for a hobby; and, when he died, he had one of the best collections in the world.

If one chooses wisely, the study, research, and occupation that a hobby confers will broaden character and transform the home.

"He has nothing to prevent him but too much idleness, which I have observed," says Burke, "fills up a man's time much more completely and leaves him less his master, than any sort of employment whatsoever."

Some boys will pick up a good education in the odds and ends of time which others carelessly throw away, as one man saves a fortune by small economies which others disdain to practice. What young man is too busy to get an hour a day for self-improvement? Charles G. Frost, the celebrated shoemaker of Vermont, resolved to devote one hour a day to study. He became one of the most noted mathematicians in the United States. He also gained an enviable reputation in other departments of knowledge. John Hunter, like Napoleon, allowed himself but four hours of sleep, and it took Professor Owen ten years to arrange and classify the specimens in Comparative Anatomy, over twenty-four thousand in number, which Hunter's industry had collected. What a record for a boy who began his studies while working as a carpenter!

John Q. Adams complained bitterly when robbed of

his time by those who had no right to it. An Italian scholar put over his door the inscription: "Whoever tarries here must join in my labors." Carlyle, Tennyson, Browning, and Dickens signed a remonstrance against organ-grinders who disturbed their work. Baxter once had callers who said, "We fear we break in upon your time." "To be sure you do," said the man who hoarded his moments as a miser hoards his gold.

"My morning haunts," said Milton, "are where they should be, at home; not sleeping, or concocting the surfeits of an irregular feast, but up and stirring; in winter, often ere the sound of any bell awakens men to labor or devotion; in summer, as oft with the bird that first rouses, or not much tardier, to read good authors, or cause them to be read, till attention be weary or memory have its full freight, then with useful and generous labors preserving the body's health and hardiness."

"When one begins to turn in bed," says Wellington, "it is time to turn out."

Many of the greatest men of history earned their fame outside of their regular occupations in odd bits of time which most people squander. Spenser made his reputation in his spare time, while Secretary of the Lord Deputy of Ireland. Sir John Lubbock's fame rests on his pre-historic studies, prosecuted outside of his busy banking-hours. Southey, seldom idle for a minute, wrote a hundred volumes. Hawthorne's note-book shows that he never let a chance thought or circumstance escape him. Franklin was a tireless worker. He crowded his meals and sleep into as small compass as possible, that he might gain time for study. When a child, he became impatient of his father's long grace at table, and asked him if he could not say grace over a whole cask once for all, and save time. He wrote some of his best productions on shipboard, such as his "Improvement of Navigation" and "Smoky Chimneys."

What a lesson there is in Raphael's brief thirty-seven years to those who plead "no time" as an excuse for wasted lives!

Great men have ever been misers of moments. Cicero said: "What others give to public shows and entertainments, nay, even to mental and bodily rest, I give to the study of philosophy." A great Chancellor of France wrote a valuable work in odd moments while waiting for his meals. Lord Bacon's fame springs from the work of his leisure hours while Chancellor of England. During an interview with a great monarch, Goethe suddenly excused himself, went into an adjoining room and wrote down a thought for his "Faust," lest it should be forgotten. Sir Humphry Davy achieved eminence in spare moments in an attic of an apothecary's shop. Pope would often rise in the night to write out thoughts that would not come during the busy day. Grote wrote his matchless "History of Greece" during the hours of leisure snatched from his duties as a banker.

George Stephenson seized the moments as though they were gold. He educated himself and did much of his best work during his spare moments. He learned arithmetic during the night shifts when he was an engineer. Mozart would not allow a moment to slip by unimproved. He would sometimes write two whole nights and a day without intermission. He would not stop his work long enough to sleep. He wrote his famous "Requiem" on his death-bed.

Cæsar said: "Under my tent in the fiercest struggle of war I have always found time to think of many other things." He was once shipwrecked, and had to swim ashore; but he carried with him the manuscript of his "Commentaries," upon which he was at work when the ship went down.

Samuel Budgett seemed born to work. "Doing, doing, ever doing," says his biographer, "he seemed to abhor idleness more than Nature abhors a vacuum. An idle hour would have been a sort of purgatory." In his notes he speaks of a "joyless and an uncomfortable Sabbath; and no wonder," he adds, "for I did not rise till half past five o'clock."

Dr. Mason Good translated "Lucretius" while riding to visit his patients in London. Dr. Darwin composed most of his works by writing his thoughts on scraps of paper wherever he happened to be. Watt learned chemistry and mathematics while working at his trade of a mathematical instrument-maker. A boy in Manchester, England, learned Latin and French while running errands. Henry Kirke White learned Greek while walking to and from the lawyer's office where he was studying. Dr. Burney learned Italian and French on horseback. Matthew Hale wrote his "Contemplations" while traveling on his circuit as judge.

Jeremy Bentham thought it a calamity to lose the least bit of time, and so arranged his work that not a moment would be wasted.

The present time is the raw material out of which we make whatever we will. Do not brood over the past, or dream of the future, but seize the instant and *get your lesson from the hour*. The man is yet unborn who rightly measures and fully realizes the value of an hour. As Fénelon says, God never gives but one moment at a time, and does not give a second until he withdraws the first.

Lord Brougham could not bear to lose a moment, yet he was so systematic that he always seemed to have more leisure than many who did not accomplish a tithe of what he did. He achieved distinction in politics, law, science, and literature.

Dr. Johnson wrote "Rasselas" in the evenings of a single week, to meet the expenses of his mother's funeral.

The wise Cato said that he regretted only three

things in his life: telling his wife a secret, going once by sea when he could have gone by land, and passing one day without doing anything.

Lincoln studied law during his spare hours while surveying, and learned the common branches unaided while tending store. Mrs. Somerville learned botany and astronomy, and wrote books while her neighbors were gossiping and idling. At eighty she published "Molecular and Microscopical Science."

The worst of a lost hour is not so much in the wasted time as in the wasted power. Idleness rusts the nerves and makes the muscles creak. Work has system, laziness has none. President Quincy never went to bed until he had laid his plans for the next day.

Dalton's industry was the passion of his life. He made and recorded over two hundred thousand meteorological observations. He seldom lost a moment.

In factories for making cloth a single broken thread ruins a whole web; it is traced back to the girl who made the blunder and the loss is deducted from her wages. But who shall pay for the broken threads in life's great web? We cannot throw back and forth an empty shuttle; threads of some kind follow every movement as we weave the web of our fate. It may be a shoddy thread of wasted hours or lost opportunities that will mar the fabric and mortify the workman forever; or it may be a golden thread which will add to its beauty and lustre. We cannot stop the shuttle or pull out the unfortunate thread which stretches across the fabric, a perpetual witness of our folly.

Don't defer your good deeds until you have time to do them. Very little good was ever done during hours of leisure. It is the men and women who are crowded with work who build hospitals, churches, and orphan asylums, and do the great charities of the world.

No one is anxious about a young man while he is

busy in useful work. But where does he eat his lunch at noon? Where does he go when he leaves his boarding-house at night? What does he do after supper? Where does he spend his Sundays and holidays? The way he uses his spare moments reveals his character. The great majority of youth who go to the bad are ruined after supper. Most of those who climb upward to honor and fame devote their evenings to study or work or the society of the wise and good. For the right use of these leisure hours, what we have called the waste of life, the odd moments usually thrown away, the author would plead with every youth. Each evening is a crisis in the career of a young man. There is a deep significance in the lines of Whittier: —

> "This day we fashion Destiny, our web of Fate we spin:
> This day for all hereafter choose we holiness or sin."

Time is money. We should not be stingy or mean with it, but we should not throw away an hour any more than we would throw away a dollar-bill. Waste of time means waste of energy, waste of vitality, waste of character in dissipation. It means bad companions, bad habits. It means the waste of opportunities which will never come back. Beware how you kill time, for all your future lives in it.

> "Of memory many a poet sings; and Hope hath oft inspired the rhyme;
> But who the charm of music brings to celebrate the present time?
> Let the past guide, the future cheer, while youth and health are in their prime;
> But, oh, be still thy greatest care — that awful point — *the present time!*"

"And it is left for each," says Edward Everett, "by the cultivation of every talent, by watching with an eagle's eye for every chance of improvement, by redeeming time, defying temptation, and scorning sensual pleasure, to make himself useful, honored, and happy."

CHAPTER V.

ROUND BOYS IN SQUARE HOLES.

> To business that we love, we rise betimes,
> And go to it with delight.
> SHAKESPEARE.

The high prize of life, the crowning fortune of a man, is to be born with a bias to some pursuit, which finds him in employment and happiness. — EMERSON.

How often we find, in the history of men of genius, that they neglected the studies or the business to which they were put, and took to something more congenial to their tastes! How often we find them rebelling against the injunctions and the arrangements of parents and guardians, and making arrangements of their own! — ROBERT WATERS.

If you choose to represent the various parts in life by holes in a table of different shapes, — some circular, some triangular, some square, some oblong, — and the persons acting these parts by bits of wood of similar shapes, we shall generally find that the triangular person has got into the square hole, the oblong into the triangular; while the square person has squeezed himself into the round hole. — SYDNEY SMITH.

I cannot too often repeat that no man struggles perpetually and victoriously against his own character. — SIR H. L. BULWER.

> "What the child admired,
> The youth endeavored, and the man acquired."

There is hardly a poet, artist, philosopher, or man of science mentioned in the history of the human intellect, whose genius was not opposed by parents, guardians, or teachers. In these cases Nature seems to have triumphed by direct interposition; to have insisted on her darlings having their rights, and encouraged disobedience, secrecy, falsehood, even flight from home and occasional vagabondism, rather than the world should lose what it cost her so much pains to produce. — E. P. WHIPPLE.

> I hear a voice you cannot hear,
> Which says, I must not stay;
> I see a hand you cannot see,
> Which beckons me away.
> TICKELL.

"JAMES WATT, I never saw such an idle young fellow as you are," said his grandmother; "do take a book and

JAMES WATT

"You are trying to make that boy another you; one is enough."

employ yourself usefully. For the last half-hour you have not spoken a single word. Do you know what you have been doing all this time? Why, you have taken off and replaced, and taken off again, the teapot lid, and you have held alternately in the steam, first a saucer and then a spoon, and you have busied yourself in examining and collecting together the little drops formed by the condensation of the steam on the surface of the china and the silver. Now, are you not ashamed to waste your time in this disgraceful manner?"

The world has certainly gained much through the old lady's failure to tell James how he could employ his time to better advantage!

"But I'm good for something," pleaded a young man whom a merchant was about to discharge for his bluntness. "You are good for nothing as a salesman," said his employer. "I am sure I can be useful," said the youth. "How? Tell me how." "I don't know, sir, I don't know." "Nor do I," said the merchant, laughing at the earnestness of his clerk. "Only don't put me away, sir, don't put me away. Try me at something besides selling. I cannot sell; I know I cannot sell." "I know that, too," said the principal; "that is what is wrong." "But I can make myself useful somehow," persisted the young man; "I know I can." He was placed in the counting-house, where his aptitude for figures soon showed itself, and in a few years he became not only chief cashier in the large store, but an eminent accountant.

Thomas Edward of Aberdeen, Scotland, celebrated his acquisition of the art of walking by losing himself, so that father, and mother, and neighbors were about to give up the search in despair, when some one happened to look in the pig-pen, and there lay the scamp fast asleep by the side of some little pigs, the brood of a sow so savage that no grown person dared venture into the sty. He had formed a taste for excursions into the wide world, and almost every day he would bring home priceless treasures, such as tadpoles, beetles, frogs, crabs, mice, rats, spiders, and bugs. These pets he would liberate, and watch them run around and hide, greatly to his own delight, and the terror of everybody else. Whipping and scolding only seemed to stimulate him to greater exertions in his work of capturing living curiosities.

His mother tied him by the leg to a table; but Thomas dragged the table to the fire, burned off the rope and escaped, returning at dusk with a large collection of living creatures. She hid all his clothes, but he had a grand trip in an old petticoat, bringing back some fine specimens, and a fever which nearly killed him. As soon as he could get out again, he brought back, hid in his shirt, a nest full of wasps of the most enterprising kind. The wasps seemed on the best of terms with Thomas, but they took exceptions to every other member of the family, until peace was finally restored when his father plunged the whole nest into hot water.

Tommy had taken all the conceit out of his parents as to their ability to control him, but before giving him up altogether, they resolved to see if the schoolmaster could not reclaim him. He tried. He failed. Tommy would play truant most of the time, or turn the school into a menagerie. One morning a jackdaw poked his head out of Tommy's pocket, and began to caw during prayers, and Thomas Edward was dismissed in disgrace. He was sent to another school, until one day, a lot of horse-leeches escaped from a bottle and crawled up the legs of nearly every boy in school, drawing blood. He was again dismissed. His parents tried to reinstate him. "I would not take him back for twenty pounds," said the teacher with a shudder.

A third school was tried. A centipede was found in another boy's desk, and Thomas knew nothing about it. It was in accord with the eternal fitness of things for him to be guilty, so the teacher whipped him severely and said: "Go home and tell your father to get you on board a man-of-war, as that is the best school for irreclaimables such as you."

He was six years old and could not write his name. He refused absolutely to go to school again, and his discouraged parents consented for him to go out and earn his living. *Re*pression of every kind had been tried in vain upon his upspringing instincts and propensities for the study of animal life; restraint at last removed, what glorious *ex*pression they found! How hard he worked that he might gain leisure for study! He learned the trade of a shoemaker, and worked at the bench for life, rearing a family of eleven children and storing away a wonderful amount of knowledge of birds and beasts and insects. But, from the lack of ability to read and write, he could not classify and use what he learned. So, slowly and laboriously, he acquired these useful arts. In the hope of getting money to study to better advantage, he once sold six cart-loads of specimens, the result of nine years of labor, for only twenty pounds.

He often tried to get employment as a naturalist, and failed only because he could not read and write rapidly. If he had been encouraged as a child to catch and study his charming specimens, and to learn to read and write about them, who shall say that his unequaled love of investigation would not have led him to become more than an Agassiz or a Tenney? But he had been wedged so tightly into a square hole that he never got out!

You cannot look into a cradle and read the secret message traced by a divine hand, and wrapped up in that bit of clay, any more than you can see the North Star in the magnetic needle. God has loaded the needle of that young life so it will point to the star of its own destiny; and though you may pull it around by artificial advice and unnatural education, and compel it to point to the star which presides over poetry, art, law, medicine, or your own pet calling, until you have wasted years of a precious life, yet, when once free, the needle flies back to its own star.

"Rue it as he may, repent it as he often does," says Robert Waters, "the man of genius is drawn by an irresistible impulse to the occupation for which he was created. No matter by what difficulties surrounded, no matter how unpromising the prospect, this occupation is the only one which he will pursue with interest and pleasure. When his efforts fail to procure means of subsistence, and he finds himself poor and neglected, he may, like Burns, often look back with a sigh and think how much better off he would be had he pursued some other occupation, but he will stick to his favorite pursuit, nevertheless."

Civilization will mark its highest tide when every man has chosen his proper work. No man can be ideally successful until he has found his place. Like a locomotive he is strong on the track, but weak anywhere else. "Like a boat on a river," says Emerson, "every boy runs against obstructions on every side but one. On that side all obstruction is taken away, and he sweeps serenely over a deepening channel into an infinite sea."

Only a Dickens can write the history of "Boy Slavery," of boys whose aspirations and longings have been silenced forever by ignorant parents; of boys persecuted as lazy, stupid, or fickle, simply because they were out of their places; of square boys forced into round holes, and oppressed because they did not fit; of boys compelled to pore over dry theological books when the voice within continually cried "Law," "Medicine," "Science," "Art," or "Business;" of boys tortured because they were not enthusiastic in employments which they loathed, and against which every fibre of their being was uttering perpetual protest.

It is often a narrow selfishness in a father which

leads him to wish his son a reproduction of himself. "You are trying to make that boy another you. One is enough," said Emerson. John Jacob Astor's father wished his son to be his successor as a butcher, but the instinct of commercial enterprise was too strong in the future merchant.

Nature never duplicates men. She breaks the pattern at every birth. The magic combination is never used but once. Frederick the Great was terribly abused because he had a passion for art and music and did not care for military drill. His father hated the fine arts and imprisoned the boy. He even contemplated killing his son, but his own death placed Frederick on the throne at the age of twenty-eight. This boy, who was thought good for nothing, because he loved art and music, made Prussia one of the greatest nations of Europe.

The perusal of a book, the execution of a model, or the superintendency of a water-wheel of his own construction, whirling the glittering spray from some neighboring stream, absorbed all of Isaac Newton's thoughts when a boy, whilst the sheep were going astray and the cattle were devouring or treading down the neighbors' corn. This convinced his mother that her son was not made for a farmer, as she had hoped.

How stupid and clumsy is the blinking eagle at perch, but how keen his glance, how steady and true his curves, when turning his powerful wing against the clear blue sky!

Ignorant parents compelled the boy Arkwright to become a barber's apprentice, but Nature had locked up in his brain a cunning device destined to bless humanity, and do the drudgery of millions of England's poor; so he must needs say "hands off" even to his parents, as Christ said to his mother, "Wist ye not that I must be about my Father's business?"

The parents of Michael Angelo had declared that no

son of theirs should ever follow the discreditable profession of an artist, and even punished him for covering the walls and furniture with sketches. The fire burning in his breast was kindled by the Divine Artist, and would not let him rest until he had immortalized himself in the architecture of St. Peter's, in the marble of his Moses, and on the walls of the Sistine Chapel.

Hugh Miller's parents dedicated their son to the ministry, the Scotch poor being always anxious to have at least one son " wag his maw in the poopit." An uncle offered to pay his way in college, but a voice within spoke louder than his parents or uncle. The stone-quarry was his college, and he preferred to hammer his education from the old red sandstone.

Galileo was set apart for a physician, but when compelled to study anatomy and physiology, he would hide his Euclid and Archimedes, and stealthily work out the abstruse problems. He was but eighteen when he discovered the principle of the pendulum in the lamp left swinging in the cathedral at Pisa. He invented both the microscope and telescope, enlarging knowledge of the vast and minute alike.

Pascal's father determined that his son should teach the dead languages, but the voice of mathematics drowned every other call, haunting the boy until he laid aside his grammar for Euclid.

The father of Joshua Reynolds rebuked his son for drawing pictures, and wrote on one : " Done by Joshua out of pure idleness." Yet this " idle boy " became one of the founders of the Royal Academy.

Turner was intended for a barber in Maiden Lane, but became the greatest landscape-painter of modern times.

Claude Lorraine, the painter, was apprenticed to a pastry-cook ; Molière, the author, to an upholsterer; and Guido, the famous painter of Aurora, was sent to a music school. The Quakers called a meeting to decide what should be done with Benjamin West, as painting was not in accord with their belief. One Friend at length arose and said: "God has bestowed on this youth a genius for art; shall we question his wisdom?" The women kissed the lad, and the men, laying their hands upon his head, consecrated him to the career of an artist.

Schiller was sent to study surgery in the military school at Stuttgart, but in secret he produced his first play, "The Robbers," whose first performance he had to witness in disguise. The irksomeness of his prison-like school so galled him, and his longing for authorship so allured him, that he ventured, penniless, into the inhospitable world of letters. A kind lady aided him, and soon he produced the two splendid dramas which made him immortal.

The physician Händel wished his son to become a lawyer, and so tried to discourage his fondness for music. But the boy got an old spinet and practiced on it secretly in a hayloft. When the doctor visited a brother in the service of the Duke of Weisenfelds, he took his son with him. The boy wandered unobserved to the organ in a chapel, and soon had a private concert under full blast. The duke happened to hear the performance, and wondered who could possibly combine so much melody with so much evident unfamiliarity with the instrument. The boy was brought before him, and the duke, instead of blaming him for disturbing the organ, praised his performance, and persuaded Dr. Händel to let his son follow his bent. Nature never lets a man rest until he has found his place. She haunts him and drives him until all his faculties give their consent, and he falls into his proper niche.

Daniel Defoe had been a trader, a soldier, a merchant, a secretary, a factory manager, a commissioner's accountant, an envoy, and an author of several indifferent books, before he wrote his masterpiece, "Robinson Crusoe."

Wilson, the ornithologist, failed in five different professions before he found his place.

Erskine spent four years in the navy, and then, in the hope of more rapid promotion, joined the army. After serving more than two years, he one day attended a court, out of curiosity, in the town where his regiment was quartered. The presiding judge, an acquaintance, invited Erskine to sit near him, and said that the pleaders at the bar were among the most eminent lawyers of Great Britain. Erskine took their measure as they spoke, and believed he could excel them. He at once began the study of law, in which he soon stood alone as the greatest forensic orator of his country.

A. T. Stewart studied for the ministry, and became a teacher, before he drifted into his proper calling as a merchant, through the accident of having lent money to a friend. The latter, with failure imminent, insisted that his creditor should take the shop as the only means of securing the money.

"Jonathan," said Mr. Chace, when his son told of having nearly fitted himself for college, "thou shalt go down to the machine-shop on Monday morning." It was many years before Jonathan escaped from the shop, to work his way up to the position of a man of great influence as a United States Senator from Rhode Island.

James Smeaton's father intended his son for a lawyer, but Nature had marked her bias for engineering upon every fibre of his being too deep to be erased by his parents. He was found one day in petticoats on the top of his father's barn, fixing the model of a windmill which he had made.

It has been well said, that if God should commission two angels, one to sweep a street crossing, and the other to rule an empire, they could not be induced to exchange callings. Not less true is it that he who feels that God has given him a particular work to do can be happy only when earnestly engaged in its performance. Happy the youth who finds the place which his dreams have pictured. If he does not fill that place, he will not fill any to the satisfaction of himself or others. A parent might just as well decide that the magnetic needle will point to Venus or Jupiter without trying it, as to decide what profession his son shall adopt.

In a fable in Judges the fig-tree, among others, was invited to become king over the forest. After the olive-tree had refused to give up its fatness which "pleased God and man," to reign over the trees, the fig-tree replied, "Why should I forsake my sweetness and good fruit and go to be promoted over the trees?"

What a rebuke in this beautiful fable to the thousands of people who forsake the sweetness and richness of their own nature to do something for which they are totally unfitted!

As king over the stalwart oak and lofty pine, the fig-tree would have been a dead failure, and as much out of place as some of our politicians are in Congress; but for bearing figs the oak and pine are its inferiors. Bearing figs is the grandest thing in the world for a fig-tree. It shines in its own sphere; but, stripped of its fig-bearing power, it has no excuse for existence. Sometimes a mother, who reigns a majestic queen in her own household, forsakes her quiet sweetness of home rule for a noisy, rough, public career, for which she has not the slightest qualification.

What a ridiculous exhibition a great truck-horse would make on the race-track; yet this is no more incongruous than the popular idea that law, medicine, and theology are the only desirable professions. How ridiculous, too, for fifty-two per cent. of our American college graduates to study law! How many young men become poor clergymen by trying to imitate their fathers, who were good ones; or poor doctors and lawyers for the same reason. The country is full of men who are out of place, "disappointed, soured, ruined, out of office, out of money, out of credit, out of courage, out at elbows, out in the cold." The fact is, nearly every college graduate who succeeds in the true sense of the word, prepares himself in school, but makes himself after he is graduated. The best thing his teachers have taught him is *how* to study. The moment he is beyond the college walls he ceases to use books and helps which do not feed him, and seizes upon those that do.

We must not jump to the conclusion that because a man has not succeeded in what he has really tried to do with all his might, he cannot succeed at anything. Look at a fish floundering on the sand as though he would tear himself to pieces. But look again: a huge wave breaks higher up the beach, and covers the unfortunate creature. The moment his fins feel the water, he is himself again, and darts like a flash through the waves. His fins mean something now, while before they beat the air and earth in vain, a hindrance instead of a help.

If you fail after doing your level best, examine the work attempted, and see if it really be in the line of your bent or power of achievement. Goldsmith found himself totally unfit for the duties of a physician; but who else could have written the "Vicar of Wakefield" or the "Deserted Village"? Cowper failed as a lawyer. He was so timid that he could not plead a case, but he wrote some of our finest poems. Molière found that he was not adapted to the work of a lawyer, but he left a great name in literature. Voltaire and Petrarch abandoned the law, the former choosing philosophy, the latter, poetry. Cromwell was a farmer until forty years old.

Very few of us, before we reach our teens, show great genius or even remarkable talent for any line of work or study. The great majority of boys and girls, even when given all the latitude and longitude heart could desire, find it very difficult before their fifteenth or even before their twentieth year to decide what to do for a living. Each knocks at the portals of the mind, demanding a wonderful aptitude for some definite line of work, but it is not there. That is no reason why the duty at hand should be put off, or why the labor that naturally falls to one's lot should not be done well. Samuel Smiles was trained to a profession which was not to his taste, yet he practiced it so faithfully that it helped him to authorship, for which he was well fitted. Fidelity to the work at hand, and a genuine feeling of responsibility to our parents or our employers, ourselves, and our God, will eventually bring most of us into the right niches at the proper time.

Garfield would not have become President if he had not previously been a zealous teacher, a responsible soldier, a conscientious statesman. Neither Lincoln nor Grant started as a baby with a precocity for the White House, or an irresistible genius for ruling men. So no one should be disappointed because he was not endowed with tremendous gifts in the cradle. His business is to do the best he can, wherever his lot may be cast, and advance at every honorable opportunity in the direction towards which the inward monitor points. Let duty be the guiding-star, and success will surely be the crown, to the full measure of one's ability and industry.

Most work is uncongenial, and the great majority of men and women think they would be happier in some other place. To almost every one the day of choice comes. What career? What shall my life's work be? If instinct and heart ask for carpentry, be a carpenter; if for medicine, be a physician. With a firm choice and earnest work, a young man or woman cannot help but succeed. But if there be no instinct, or if it be weak or faint, one should choose cautiously along the line of his best adaptability and opportunity. No one need doubt that the world has use for him, but great honor and fortune are not for all. True success lies in acting well your part, and this every one can do. Better be a first-rate hod-carrier than a second-rate anything.

The world has been very kind to many who were once known as dunces or blockheads, after they have become very successful; but it was very cross to them while they were struggling through discouragement and misinterpretation. Such lives do not show, however, that a numskull is sure to climb to the top. Because the last boy in his class became the great Henry Ward Beecher, there is no reason to conclude that the last boy in the next class, or the next, must become anything great at all. There must be some life in the boy, or he will not rise under any circumstances until the day appointed for the resurrection of the dead. If he starts out in life as a failure, he will end as one, unless he gets thoroughly waked up in some way. Give every boy and girl a fair chance and reasonable encouragement, and do not condemn them because of even a large degree of downright stupidity; for many so-called good-for-nothing boys, blockheads, numskulls, dullards, or dunces, were only boys out of their places, round boys forced into square holes.

"Let us people who are so uncommonly clever and learned," says Thackeray, "have a great tenderness and pity for the folks who are not endowed with the prodigious talents which we have. I have always had a regard for dunces,—those of my own school days were among the pleasantest of the fellows, and have turned out by no means the dullest in life; whereas, many a youth who could turn off Latin hexameters by the yard, and construe Greek quite glibly, is no better than a feeble prig now, with not a pennyworth more brains than were in his head before his beard grew."

George Stephenson, at twenty years of age, could neither read nor write, yet his name is inseparably linked with the introduction and development of railways.

Wellington was considered a dunce by his mother. At Eton he was called dull, idle, slow, and was about the last boy in school of whom anything was expected. He showed no talent, and had no desire to enter the army. His industry and perseverance were his only redeeming characteristics, in the eyes of his parents and teachers. But at forty-six he had defeated the greatest general living, except himself.

Goldsmith was the laughing-stock of his schoolmasters. He was graduated "Wooden Spoon," a college name for a dunce. He tried to enter a class in surgery, but was rejected. He was driven to literature. Dr. Johnson found him very poor and about to be arrested for debt. He made Goldsmith give him the manuscript of the "Vicar of Wakefield," sold it to the publishers, and paid the debt. This manuscript made its author famous.

John Harvard was called a boy of no promise, but he founded Harvard College, and became one of the real benefactors of the race.

Robert Clive bore the name of "dunce" and "reprobate" at school, but at thirty-two, with three thousand men, he defeated fifty thousand at Plassey and laid the foundation of the British Empire in India. Sir Walter Scott was called a blockhead by his teacher. When Byron happened to get ahead of his class, the master would say: "Now, Jordie, let me see how soon you will be at the foot again." Sheridan's mother tried in vain to teach him the most elementary studies. Her death aroused his slumbering talents, as has happened in hundreds of cases, and he became one of the most brilliant men of his age. Dr. Chalmers was expelled from St. Andrews school because of his stupidity.

Dr. Isaac Barrow was such a dullard that his father said, "If it is God's will to take any of my children by death, I hope it may be Isaac." "Why do you tell that blockhead the same thing twenty times over?" asked

John Wesley's father. "Because," replied his mother, "if I had told him but nineteen times, all my labor would have been lost, while now he will understand and remember."

Young Linnæus was called by his teachers almost a blockhead. Not finding him fit for the church, his parents sent him to college to study medicine. But the silent teacher within, greater and wiser than all others, led him to the fields; and neither sickness, misfortune, nor poverty could drive him from the study of botany, the choice of his heart, and he became the greatest botanist of his age.

David Drew was one of the dullest and most listless boys in his neighborhood, yet after an accident by which he nearly lost his life, and after the death of his brother, he became so studious and industrious that he could not bear to lose a moment. He read at every meal, using all the time he could get for self-improvement. He said that Paine's "Age of Reason" made him an author, for it was by his attempt to refute its arguments that he was first known as a strong, vigorous writer.

We live in a superficial age, and we hurry along in a happy-go-lucky way, ignorant or heedless of the capacities of our minds and bodies. The precocious youth, the boy or girl of average intelligence, or the dunce, should alike study his own strength, his weakness, his likes, his dislikes, his bent. "Know thyself," was spoken of old at Delphi; and, though the oracle has long been mute, the words are of eternal significance. No better advice was ever given to man. Philosophy finds its highest province in the study of our own natures. Knowledge thus gained, and that alone, will teach the round boy to avoid the square holes as he would shun falsehood and dishonor. It has been well said that no man ever made an ill figure who understood his own talents, nor a good one who mistook them.

CHAPTER VI.

WHAT CAREER?

Brutes find out where their talents lie;
A bear will not attempt to fly,
A foundered horse will oft debate
Before he tries a five-barred gate.
A dog by instinct turns aside
Who sees the ditch too deep and wide.
But man we find the only creature
Who, led by folly, combats nature;
Who, when she loudly cries — forbear!
With obstinacy fixes there;
And where his genius least inclines,
Absurdly bends his whole designs.
SWIFT.

The crowning fortune of a man is to be born to some pursuit which finds him in employment and happiness, whether it be to make baskets, or broadswords, or canals, or statues, or songs. — EMERSON.

And he who waits to have his task marked out,
Shall die and leave his errand unfulfilled.
LOWELL.

Whatever you are by nature, keep to it; never desert your line of talent. Be what nature intended you for, and you will succeed; be anything else, and you will be ten thousand times worse than nothing. — SYDNEY SMITH.

In the measure in which thou seekest to do thy duty shalt thou know what is in thee. But what is thy duty? The demand of the hour. — GOETHE.

Do noble things, not dream them, all day long,
And so make life, death, and the vast forever, one grand, sweet song.
CHARLES KINGSLEY.

"EVERY man has got a Fort," said Artemus Ward. "It's some men's fort to do one thing, and some other men's fort to do another, while there is numeris shiftless critters goin' round loose whose fort is not to do nothin.

"Twice I've endevered to do things which they was n't my Fort. The first time was when I undertook to lick a owdashus cuss who cut a hole in my tent and krawld threw. Sez I, 'My jentle sir, go out, or I shall fall onto you putty hevy.' Sez he, 'Wade in, Old Wax Figgers,' whereupon I went for him, but he cawt me powerful on the hed and knockt me threw the tent into a cow pastur. He pursood the attack and flung me into a mud puddle. As I aroze and rung out my drencht garmints, I concluded fitin wasn't my fort. I'le now rize the curtain upon seen 2nd. It is rarely seldom that I seek consolation in the Flowin Bole. But in a certain town in Injianny in the Faul of 18—, my orgin grinder got sick with the fever and died. I never felt so ashamed in my life, and I thought I'd hist in a few swallers of suthin strengthnin. Konsequents was, I histed so much I did n't zackly know whereabouts I was. I turned my livin wild beasts of Pray loose into the streets, and split all my wax-works. I then Bet I cood play hoss. So I hitched myself to a kanawl bote, there bein two other hosses behind and anuther ahead of me. But the hosses bein onused to such a arrangemunt, begun to kick and squeal and rair up. Konsequents was, I was kicked vilently in the stummuck and back, and presently, I found myself in the kanawl with the other hosses, kikin and yellin like a tribe of Cussearoorus savajis. I was rescood, and as I was bein carried to the tavern on a hemlock bored I sed in a feeble voice, 'Boys, playin hoss is n't my Fort.'

"Moral: *Never don't do nothin which is n't your Fort, for ef you do you'll find yourself splashin round in the kanawl, figgeratively speakin.*"

The following advertisement, which appeared day after day in a Western paper, did not bring a single reply :—

"Wanted. — Situation by a Practical Printer, who is competent to take charge of any department in a printing and publishing house. Would accept a professorship in any of the academies. Has no objection to teach ornamental painting and penmanship, geometry, trigonometry, and many other sciences. Has had some experience as a lay preacher. Would have no objection to form a small class of young ladies and gentlemen to instruct them in the higher branches. To a dentist or chiropodist he would be invaluable; or he would cheerfully accept a position as bass or tenor singer in a choir."

At length there appeared this addition to the notice:—

"P. S. Will accept an offer to saw and split wood at less than the usual rates." This secured a situation at once, and the advertisement was seen no more.

Your talent is your *call*. Your legitimate destiny speaks in your character.

If you have found your place, your occupation has the consent of every faculty of your being.

If possible, choose that occupation which focuses the largest amount of your experience and tastes. You will then not only have a congenial vocation, but will utilize largely your skill and business knowledge, which is your true capital.

Follow your bent. You cannot long fight successfully against your aspirations. Parents, friends, or misfortune may stifle and suppress the longings of the heart, by compelling you to perform unwelcome tasks; but, like a volcano, the inner fire will burst the crusts which confine it and pour forth its pent-up genius in eloquence, in song, in art, or in some favorite industry. Beware of "a talent which you cannot hope to practice in perfection." Nature hates all botched and half-finished work, and will pronounce her curse upon it.

Better be the Napoleon of bootblacks, or the Alexander of chimney-sweeps, let us say with Matthew Arnold, than a shallow-brained attorney who, like necessity, knows no law.

"The ignorance of men who know not for what time and to what thing they be fit," said Roger Ascham, "causeth some to wish themselves rich for whom it were better a great deal to be poor; some to desire to be in the court, which be born and be fitter rather for the cart; some to be masters and rule others, who never yet began to rule themselves; some to teach, which rather should learn; some to be priests, which were fitter to be clerks."

Half the world seems to have found uncongenial occupation, as if the human race had been shaken up together and exchanged places in the operation. A servant girl is trying to teach, and a natural teacher is tending store. Good farmers are murdering the law, while Choates and Websters are running down farms, each tortured by the consciousness of unfulfilled destiny. Boys are pining in factories who should be wrestling with Greek and Latin, and hundreds are chafing beneath unnatural loads in college who should be on the farm or before the mast. Artists are spreading "daubs" on canvas who should be whitewashing board fences. Behind counters stand clerks who hate the yard-stick, and neglect their work to dream of other occupations. A good shoemaker writes a few verses for the village paper, his friends call him a poet, and the last, with which he is familiar, is abandoned for the pen which he uses awkwardly. Other shoemakers are cobbling in Congress, while statesmen are pounding shoe-lasts. Laymen are murdering sermons while Beechers and Whitefields are failing as merchants, and people are wondering what can be the cause of empty pews. A boy who is always making something with tools is railroaded through the university and started on the road to inferiority in one of the three honorable professions. Real surgeons are handling the meat-saw and cleaver, while butchers are amputating human limbs. How fortunate that —

> "There's a divinity that shapes our ends,
> Rough-hew them how we will."

"He that hath a trade," says Franklin, "hath an estate; and he that hath a calling hath a place of profit and honor. A ploughman on his legs is higher than a gentleman on his knees."

A man's business does more to make him than anything else. It hardens his muscles, strengthens his body, quickens his blood, sharpens his mind, corrects his judgment, wakes up his inventive genius, puts his wits to work, starts him on the race of life, arouses his ambition, makes him feel that he is a man and must fill a man's shoes, do a man's work, bear a man's part in life, and show himself a man in that part. No man feels himself a man who is not doing a man's business. A man without employment is not a man. He does not prove by his works that he is a man. A hundred and fifty pounds of bone and muscle do not make a man. A good cranium full of brains is not a man. The bone and muscle and brain must know how to do a man's work, think a man's thoughts, mark out a man's path, and bear a man's weight of character and duty before they constitute a man.

"No man is fit to win," says Bulwer, "who has not sat down alone to think; and who has not come forth with purpose in his eye, with white cheeks, set lips, and clenched palms, able to say: 'I am resolved what to do.'"

Go-at-it-iveness is the first requisite for success. Stick-to-it-iveness is the second. Under ordinary circumstances, and with practical common sense to guide him, one who has these requisites will not fail.

Don't wait for a higher position or a larger salary. Enlarge the position you already occupy; put originality of method into it. Fill it as it never was filled before. Be more prompt, more energetic, more thorough, more polite than your predecessor or fellow workmen. Study your business, devise new modes of operation, be able to give your employer points. The art lies not in giving satisfaction merely, not in simply filling your place, but in doing better than was expected, in surprising your employer; and the reward will be a better place and a larger salary.

When out of work, take the first respectable job that offers, heeding not the disproportion between your faculties and your task. If you put your manhood into your labor, you will soon be given something better to do.

One of the saddest sights is that of a young man who, without ever having asked himself if he possessed sufficient strength of nerve to endure the strain of an intellectual career, has been graduated heavily in debt, and has sacrificed what little health and constitution he had for a college course. No one told him that, even if he should obtain his degree, he would be totally unfitted to excel in intellectual pursuits, and would be doomed to perpetual mediocrity. He thought that if he could only get through college, even if he were broken in health and in purse, he could get on somehow. He is no longer content with his former lot, his ambition is poisoned by visions of impossible goals, his vitality exhausted, his energies scattered, and so the youth who might have become a useful farmer or a skillful mechanic, staggers under his load of pecuniary obligation, ill health, and unsatisfied ambition, until death relieves him of his misery.

This question of a right aim in life has become exceedingly perplexing in our complicated age. It is not a difficult problem to solve when one is the son of a Zulu or the daughter of a Bedouin. The condition of the savage hardly admits of but one choice; but as one rises higher in the scale of civilization and creeps nearer to the great centres of activity, the difficulty of a correct decision increases with its importance. In proportion as one is hard pressed in competition is it of the sternest necessity for him to choose the right aim, so as to be able to throw the whole of his energy and enthusiasm into the struggle for success. The dissipation of strength or hope is fatal to prosperity even in the most attractive field.

Gladstone says there is a limit to the work that can be got out of a human body, or a human brain, and he is a wise man who wastes no energy on pursuits for which he is not fitted.

"Blessed is he who has found his work," says Carlyle. "Let him ask no other blessedness. He has a work — a life purpose; he has found it, and will follow it."

In choosing an occupation do not ask yourself how you can make the most money or gain the most notoriety, but choose that work which will call out all your powers and develop your manhood into the greatest strength and symmetry. Not money, not notoriety, not fame even, but power is what you want. Manhood is greater than wealth, grander than fame. Character is greater than any career. Each faculty must be educated, and any deficiency in its training will appear in whatever you do. The hand must be educated to be graceful, steady, and strong. The eye must be educated to be alert, discriminating, and microscopic. The heart must be educated to be tender, sympathetic, and true. The memory must be drilled for years in accuracy, retention, and comprehensiveness. The world does not demand that you be a lawyer, minister, doctor, farmer, scientist, or merchant. It does not dictate what you shall do, but it does require that you be a master in whatever you undertake. If you are a master in your line, the world will applaud you and all doors will fly open to you. But the world condemns all botches, abortions, and failures.

"Whoever is well educated to discharge the duty of a man," says Rousseau, "cannot be badly prepared to fill any of those offices that have relation to him. It matters little to me whether my pupils be designed for the army, the pulpit, or the bar. Nature has destined us to the offices of human life antecedent to our destination concerning society. To live is the profession I would teach him. When I have done with him, it is true he will be neither a soldier, a lawyer, nor a divine. Let him first be a man. Fortune may remove him from one rank to another as she pleases; he will be always found in his place."

In 1744, at the treaty of the government of Virginia with the Six Nations at Lancaster, Pa., the Indians were invited to send six youths to Williamsburg College to be educated free.

It is a rule of Indian courtesy not to answer important questions on the day they are asked. After deliberating they declined the invitation. They said that they had sent several young men to the colleges of the northern provinces; and, when they returned, they were poor runners, ignorant of how to get a living in the woods, could not bear cold or hunger, could not build a cabin, take a deer, or kill an enemy, and spoke their own language badly. They were not fit for hunters, warriors, or councilors; they were totally good for nothing. "If the gentlemen of Virginia will send us a dozen of their sons, we will take great care of their education, instruct them in all we know, and make men of them."

In the great race of life common sense has the right of way. Wealth, a diploma, a pedigree, talent, genius, without tact and common sense, cut but a small figure. The incapables and the impracticables, though loaded with diplomas and degrees, are left behind. Not what do you know, or who are you, but what can you do, is the interrogation of the century.

George Herbert has well said: "What we are is much more to us than what we do." An aim that carries in it the least element of doubt as to its justice or honor or right should be abandoned at once. The art of dishing up the wrong so as to make it look and taste like the right, has never been more extensively cultivated than in our day. It is a curious fact that reason will, on pressure, overcome a man's instinct of right. An eminent scientist has said that a man could soon reason himself out of the instinct of decency if he would only take pains and work hard enough. So when a doubtful but attractive future is placed before one, there is a great temptation to juggle with the wrong until it seems the right, just as Hermann or Keller apparently changes a rabbit into an omelet. Yet any aim that is immoral carries in itself the germ of certain failure, in the real sense of the word — failure that is physical and spiritual.

There is no doubt that every person has a special adaptation for his own peculiar part in life. A very few — the geniuses, we call them — have this marked in an unusual degree, and very early in life.

Madame de Staël was engrossed in political philosophy at an age when other girls are dressing dolls. Mozart, when but four years old, played the clavichord, and composed minuets and other pieces still extant. The little Chalmers would preach often from a stool in the nursery, with solemn air and earnest gestures. Goethe wrote tragedies at twelve, and Grotius published an able philosophical work before he was fifteen. Pope "lisped in numbers." Chatterton wrote good poems at eleven, and Cowley published a volume of poetry in his sixteenth year. Thomas Lawrence and Benjamin West drew likenesses almost as soon as they could walk. Liszt played in public at twelve. Canova made models in clay while a mere child. Bacon exposed the defects of Aristotle's philosophy when but sixteen. Napoleon was at the head of armies when throwing snowballs at Brienne. Kean played Shylock the first night almost as well as he ever did.

All these showed their bent while young, and followed it in active life. But precocity is not common, and, except in rare cases, we must discover the bias in our natures, and not wait for the proclivity to make itself manifest. When found, it is worth more to us than a vein of gold.

"It is a vain thought," said George Eliot, "to flee from the work that God appoints us, for the sake of finding a greater blessing to our own souls, as if we could choose for ourselves where we shall find the fullness of the Divine Presence, instead of seeking it where alone it can be found, — in loving obedience."

"I do not forbid you to preach," said a Bishop to a young clergyman, "but nature does."

"The age has no aversion to preaching as such," said Phillips Brooks, "it may not listen to your preaching." But though it may not listen to your preaching, it will wear your boots, or buy your flour, or see stars through your telescope. It has a use for every person, and it is his business to find out what that use is.

Lowell said: "It is the vain endeavor to make ourselves what we are not, that has strewn history with so many broken purposes, and lives left in the rough."

You have not found your place until all your faculties are roused, and your whole nature consents and approves of the work you are doing; not until you are so enthusiastic in it that you take it to bed with you. You may be forced to drudge at uncongenial toil for a time, but emancipate yourself as soon as possible. Carey, the "Consecrated Cobbler," before he went as a missionary said: "My business is to preach the gospel. I cobble shoes to pay expenses."

If your vocation be a humble one, elevate it with more manhood than others put into it. Put into it brains and heart and energy and economy. Broaden it by originality of methods. Extend it by enterprise and industry. Study it as you would a profession. Learn everything that is to be known about it. Concentrate your faculties upon it, for the greatest achievements are reserved for the man of single aim, in whom no rival powers divide the empire of the soul. *Better adorn your own than seek another's place.*

Go to the bottom of your business if you would climb to the top. Nothing is small which concerns your business. Master every detail. This was the secret of A. T. Stewart's and of John Jacob Astor's great success. They knew everything about their business.

As to the responsibility for our environments which has troubled great minds in all ages, and as to what we shall do, a noted clergyman says: "You are not responsible for your parentage, or grand-parentage. You are not responsible for any of the cranks that may have lived in your ancestral line, and who a hundred years before you were born may have lived a style of life that more or less affects you to-day. You are not responsible for the fact that your temperament is sanguine, or melancholic, or bilious, or lymphatic, or nervous. Neither are you responsible for the place of your nativity, whether among the granite hills of New England, or the cotton plantations of Louisiana, or on the banks of the Clyde, or the Dnieper, or the Shannon, or the Seine. Neither are you responsible for the religion taught in your father's house, or for his religion. Do not bother yourself about what you cannot help, or about circumstances that you did not decree. Take things as they are and decide the question so that you shall be able safely to say: 'To this end was I born.' How will you decide it? By direct application to the only Being in the universe who is competent to tell you — the Lord Almighty."

As love is the only excuse for marriage, and the only thing which will carry one safely through the troubles and vexations of married life, so love for an occupation is the only thing which will carry one safely and surely through the troubles which overwhelm ninety-five out of every one hundred who choose the life of a merchant, and very many in every other career.

A famous Englishman said to his nephew, "Don't choose medicine, for we have never had a murderer in our family, and the chances are that in your ignorance you may kill a patient; as to the law, no prudent man is willing to risk his life or his fortune to a young lawyer, who has not only no experience, but is generally too conceited to know the risks he incurs for his client, who alone is the loser; therefore, as the mistakes of a clergyman in doctrine or advice to his parishioners cannot be clearly determined in this world, I advise you by all means to enter the church."

"I felt that I was in the world to do something, and thought I must," said Whittier, thus giving the secret of his great power. It is the man who must enter law, literature, medicine, the ministry, or any other of the overstocked professions, who will succeed. His certain call, that is his love for it, and his fidelity to it, are the imperious factors of his career. If a man enters a profession simply because his grandfather made a great name in it, or his mother wants him to, with no love or adaptability for it, it were far better for him to be a motor-man on an electric car at one dollar and seventy-five cents a day. In the humbler work, his intelligence may make him a leader; in the other career he might do as much harm as a boulder rolled from its place upon a railroad track, a menace to the next express.

Only a few years ago marriage was the only "sphere" open to girls, and the single woman had to face the disapproval of her friends. Lessing said: "The woman who thinks is like a man who puts on rouge, ridiculous." Not many years have elapsed since the ambitious woman who ventured to study or write would keep a bit of embroidery at hand to throw over her book or manuscript when callers entered. Dr. Johnson likened a woman speaking to a dog walking on his hind legs. "It is not surprising that she does not do it well," he said; "the wonder is that she does it at all." Dr.

Gregory said to his daughters: "If you happen to have any learning, keep it a profound secret from the men, who generally look with a jealous and malignant eye on a woman of great parts and a cultivated understanding." Women who wrote books in those days would deny the charge as though a public disgrace. All this has changed, and what a change it is! As Frances Willard says, the greatest discovery of the century is the discovery of woman. We have emancipated her, and are opening countless opportunities for our girls outside of marriage. Formerly only a boy could choose a career, now his sister can do the same. This freedom is one of the greatest glories of the nineteenth century. But with freedom comes responsibility, and under these changed conditions every girl should have a definite aim.

"Girls, you cheapen yourselves by lack of purpose in life," says Rena L. Miner. "You show commendable zeal in pursuing your studies; your alertness in comprehending and ability in surmounting difficult problems have become proverbial; nine times out of every ten you outrank your brothers thus far; but when the end is attained, the goal reached, whether it be the graduating certificate from a graded school, or a college diploma, for nine out of every ten it might as well be added thereto, 'dead to further activity,' or, 'sleeping until marriage shall resurrect her.'

"Crocheting, placquing, dressing, visiting, music, and flirtations make up the sum total for the expense and labor expended for your existence. If forced to earn your support, you are content to stand behind a counter, or teach school term after term in the same grade, while the young men who graduated with you walk up the grades. as up a ladder. to professorship and good salary, from which they swing off into law, physics, or perhaps, the legislative firmament, leaving difficulties and obstacles like nebulæ in their wake. You girls, satisfied with mediocrity, have an eye mainly for the 'main chance' — marriage. If you marry wealthy, — which is marrying well according to the modern popular idea, — you dress more elegantly, cultivate more fashionable society, leave your thinking for your husband and your minister to do for you, and become in the economy of life but a sentient nonentity. If you are true to the grand passion, and accept with it poverty, you bake, brew, scrub, spank the children, and talk with your neighbor over the back fence for recreation, spending the years literally like the horse in a treadmill, all for the lack of a purpose, — a purpose sufficiently potent to convert the latent talent into a gem of living beauty, a creative force which makes all adjuncts secondary, like planets to their central sun. Choose some one course or calling, and master it in all its details, sleep by it, swear by it, work for it, and, if marriage crowns you, it can but add new glory to your labor."

Dr. Hall says that the world has urgent need of "girls who are mother's right hand; girls who can cuddle the little ones next best to mamma, and smooth out the tangles in the domestic skein when things get twisted; girls whom father takes comfort in for something better than beauty, and the big brothers are proud of for something that outranks the ability to dance or shine in society. Next, we want girls of sense, — girls who have a standard of their own regardless of conventionalities, and are independent enough to live up to it; girls who simply won't wear a trailing dress on the street to gather up microbes and all sorts of defilement; girls who don't wear a high hat to the theatre, or lacerate their feet and endanger their health with high heels and corsets; girls who will wear what is pretty and becoming and snap their fingers at the dictates of fashion when fashion is horrid and silly. And we want good girls, — girls who are sweet, right straight out from the heart to the lips; innocent and pure and simple girls, with less knowledge of sin and duplicity and evil-doing at twenty than the pert little schoolgirl of ten has all too often. And we want careful girls and prudent girls, who think enough of the generous father who toils to maintain them in comfort, and of the gentle mother who denies herself much that they may have so many pretty things, to count the cost and draw the line between the essentials and non-essentials; girls who strive to save and not to spend; girls who are unselfish and eager to be a joy and a comfort in the home rather than an expense and a useless burden. We want girls with hearts,—girls who are full of tenderness and sympathy, with tears that flow for other people's ills, and smiles that light outward their own beautiful thoughts. We have lots of clever girls, and brilliant girls, and witty girls. Give us a consignment of jolly girls, warm-hearted and impulsive girls; kind and entertaining to their own folks, and with little desire to shine in the garish world. With a few such girls scattered around, life would freshen up for all of us, as the weather does under the spell of summer showers."

> "They talk about a woman's sphere,
>   As though it had a limit;
> There's not a place in earth or heaven,
> There's not a task to mankind given,
> There's not a blessing or a woe,
> There's not a whisper, Yes or No,
> There's not a life, or death, or birth,
> That has a feather's weight of worth,
>   Without a woman in it."

"Do that which is assigned you," says Emerson, "and you cannot hope too much or dare too much. There is at this moment for you an utterance brave and grand as that of the colossal chisel of Phidias, or trowel of the Egyptians, or the pen of Moses or Dante, but different from all these."

"The best way for a young man to begin, who is without friends or influence is," said Russell Sage, "first, by getting a position; second, keeping his mouth shut; third, observing; fourth, being faithful; fifth, making his employer think he would be lost in a fog without him; and sixth, being polite."

"Close application, integrity, attention to details, discreet advertising," are given as the four steps to success by John Wanamaker, whose motto is, "Do the next thing."

"There lives not a man on earth, outside of a lunatic asylum," says Bulwer, "who has not in him the power to do good. What can writers, haranguers, or speculators do more than that? Have you ever entered a cottage, ever traveled in a coach, ever talked with a peasant in the field, or loitered with a mechanic at the loom, and not found that each of those men had a talent you had not, knew some things you knew not? The most useless creature that ever yawned at a club, or counted the vermin on his rags, under the sun of Calabria, has no excuse for want of intellect. What men want is not talent, it is purpose; in other words, not the power to achieve, but the will to labor."

Whatever you do in life, be greater than your calling. Most people look upon an occupation or calling as a mere expedient for earning a living. What a mean, narrow view to take of what was intended for the great school of life, the great man-developer, the character-builder; that which should broaden, deepen, heighten, and round out into symmetry, harmony, and beauty, all the God-given faculties within us! How we shrink from the task and evade the lessons which were intended for the unfolding of life's great possibilities into usefulness and power, as the sun unfolds into beauty and fragrance the petals of the flower.

> I am glad to think
> I am not bound to make the world go round;
> But only to discover and to do,
> With cheerful heart, the work that God appoints.
> JEAN INGELOW.

There is only one constant factor that can enter into all professions and businesses — the service of mankind. It need interfere with no honest calling, or with its success. That Christian factor is the only thing that gives the highest success, the most enduring life — a worthy immortality. We do not choose our parts in life and have nothing to do with those parts. Our simple duty is confined to playing them well. — EPICTETUS.

"'What shall I do to be forever known?'
   Thy duty ever!
'This did full many who yet sleep all unknown,' —
   Oh, never, never!
Think'st thou, perchance, that they remain unknown
   Whom thou know'st not?
By angel trumps in heaven their praise is blown,
   Divine their lot."

CHAPTER VII.

CONCENTRATED ENERGY.

This one thing I do. — St. Paul.

The one prudence in life is concentration; the one evil is dissipation; and it makes no difference whether our dissipations are coarse or fine. . . . Everything is good which takes away one plaything and delusion more, and sends us home to add one stroke of faithful work. — Emerson.

Let thine eyes look right on, and let thine eyelids look straight before thee. Turn not to the right hand nor to the left. — Proverbs.

> The man who seeks one thing in life, and but one,
> May hope to achieve it before life be done;
> But he who seeks all things, wherever he goes,
> Only reaps from the hopes which around him he sows,
> A harvest of barren regrets.
> — Owen Meredith.

The longer I live, the more deeply am I convinced that that which makes the difference between one man and another — between the weak and powerful, the great and insignificant, is energy — invincible determination — a purpose once formed, and then death or victory. — Fowell Buxton.

> One science only will one genius fit.
> — Pope.

He did it with all his heart and prospered.
— 2 Chronicles.

"There was not room enough for us all in Frankfort," said Nathan Mayer Rothschild, speaking of himself and his four brothers. "I dealt in English goods. One great trader came there, who had the market to himself; he was quite the great man, and did us a favor if he sold us goods. Somehow I offended him, and he refused to show me his patterns. This was on a Tuesday. I said to my father, 'I will go to England.' On Thursday I started. The nearer I got to England, the cheaper goods were. As soon as I got to Manchester, I laid out all my money, things were so cheap, and I made a good profit."

FRANCIS PARKMAN

"He who would do some great thing in this short life must apply himself to the work with such a concentration of his forces, as, to idle spectators, who live only to amuse themselves, looks like insanity."

"I hope," said a listener, "that your children are not too fond of money and business, to the exclusion of more important things. I am sure you would not wish that."

"I am sure I would wish that," said Rothschild; "I wish them to give mind, and soul, and heart, and body, and everything to business; that is the way to be happy." "Stick to one business, young man," he added, addressing a young brewer; "stick to your brewery, and you may be the great brewer of London. But be a brewer, and a banker, and a merchant, and a manufacturer, and you will soon be in the Gazette."

Not many things indifferently, but one thing supremely, is the demand of the hour. He who scatters his efforts in this intense, concentrated age, cannot hope to succeed.

"Goods removed, messages taken, carpets beaten, and poetry composed on any subject," was the sign of a man in London who was not very successful at any of these lines of work, and reminds one of Monsieur Kenard, of Paris, "a public scribe, who digests accounts, explains the language of flowers, and sells fried potatoes."

The great difference between those who succeed and those who fail does not consist in the amount of work done by each, but in the amount of intelligent work. Many of those who fail most ignominiously, do enough to achieve grand success; but they labor at haphazard, building up with one hand only to tear down with the other. They do not grasp circumstances and change them into opportunities. They have no faculty of turning honest defeats into telling victories. With ability enough, and time in abundance, — the warp and woof of success, — they are forever throwing back and forth an empty shuttle, and the real web of life is never woven.

If you ask one of them to state his aim and purpose in life, he will say: "I hardly know yet for what I am best adapted, but I am a thorough believer in genuine hard work, and I am determined to dig early and late all my life, and I know I shall come across something — either gold, silver, or at least iron." I say most emphatically, no. Would an intelligent man dig up a whole continent to find its veins of silver and gold? The man who is forever looking about to see what he can find, never finds anything. We find what we seek with all our heart, and if we look for nothing in particular, we find just that and no more. The bee is not the only insect that visits the flower, but it is the only one that carries honey away. It matters not how rich the materials we have gleaned from the years of our study and toil in youth, if we go out into life with no well-defined idea of our future work, there is no happy conjunction of circumstances that will arrange them into an imposing structure, and give it magnificent proportions.

"What an immense power over the life," says Elizabeth Stuart Phelps, " is the power of possessing distinct aims. The voice, the dress, the look, the very motions of a person, define and alter when he or she begins to live for a reason. I fancy that I can select, in a crowded street, the busy, blessed women who support themselves. They carry themselves with an air of conscious self-respect and self-content, which a shabby alpaca cannot hide, nor a bonnet of silk enhance, nor even sickness nor exhaustion quite drag out."

The wind never blows fair for that sailor who knows not to what port he is bound.

"The weakest living creature," says Carlyle, "by concentrating his powers on a single object, can accomplish something; whereas the strongest, by dispersing his over many, may fail to accomplish anything. The drop, by continually falling, bores its passage through the hardest rock. The hasty torrent rushes over it with hideous uproar and leaves no trace behind."

"When I was young I used to think it was thunder

that killed men," said a shrewd preacher; "but as I grew older, I found it was lightning. So I resolved to thunder less, and lighten more."

This is the age of concentration or specialization of energy. The problem of the day is to get ten horse-power out of an engine that shall occupy the space of a one horse-power engine and no more. The solution of that problem will solve in its turn the lesser problem of flying. Just so society demands a ten man-power out of one individual. It crowns the man who knows one thing supremely, and can do it better than anybody else, even if it only be the art of raising turnips. If he raises the best turnips by reason of concentrating all his energy to that end, he is a benefactor to the race, and is recognized as such.

"Lord, help me to take fewer things into my hands, and to do them well," is a prayer recommended by Paxton Hood to an overworked man.

If a salamander be cut in two, the front part will run forward and the other backward. Such is the progress of him who divides his purpose. Success is jealous of scattered energies.

No one can pursue a worthy object steadily and persistently with all the powers of his mind, and yet make his life a failure. You can't throw a tallow candle through the side of a tent, but you can shoot it through an oak board. Melt a charge of shot into a bullet, and it can be fired through the bodies of four men. Focus the rays of the sun in winter, and you can kindle a fire with ease.

The giants of the race have been men of concentration, who have struck sledge-hammer blows in one place until they have accomplished their purpose. The successful men of to-day are men of one overmastering idea, one unwavering aim, men of single and intense purpose. "Scatteration" is the curse of American business life. Too many are like Douglas Jerrold's friend, who could converse in twenty-four languages, but had no ideas to express in any one of them.

One of the hardest tasks for a boy or a girl is to concentrate the whole attention upon the lesson of the morrow; for the student in college to prepare for the next recitation without running to the ball-field, or allowing his gaze to wander around the room, or doing anything else in order to cheat himself out of what he ought to do. In study, as in business, we must not only strike the iron while it is hot, but strike it until it is made hot.

William A. Mowry tells a story of one of the foremost of American scholars, who found himself spending two hours a day in preparing his Latin lesson. He determined to get that lesson in an hour and fifty minutes, and succeeded. When he afterwards sat down to learn his Latin, he bent every energy to accomplish it in the shortest possible time. He found by daily trials, that he could learn it in an hour and forty-five minutes, and that the time required was diminishing. Concentrating all his powers upon the task, day by day, he soon found himself studying only an hour and a half upon it, then five, ten, fifteen, and even thirty minutes less. Encouraged, he redoubled his efforts, and within a few months the lesson could be learned in less than half an hour, a thing absolutely impossible with his habits of study when he entered the school. But he had done something more than to learn a Latin lesson in a shorter time. He had learned something of the value of concentration. The acquisition of such power is of more value than the acquisition of knowledge.

Mr. Mowry gives another good illustration of this power in his "Talks with My Boys." A boy of fifteen once agreed to commit seven long stanzas of poetry in twenty minutes, with his companions allowed to use every possible effort to disturb him, provided they would not touch him. Amid such a pandemonium as only boys can make, the task was accomplished. This boy, George S. Boutwell, was afterwards governor of Massachusetts, United States Senator, and Secretary of the United States Treasury.

"The only valuable kind of study," said Sydney Smith, "is to read so heartily that dinner-time comes two hours before you expected it; to sit with your Livy before you and hear the geese cackling that saved the Capitol, and to see with your own eyes the Carthaginian sutlers gathering up the rings of the Roman knights after the battle of Cannæ, and heaping them into bushels, and to be so intimately present at the actions you are reading of, that when anybody knocks at the door it will take you two or three seconds to determine whether you are in your own study or on the plains of Lombardy, looking at Hannibal's weather-beaten face and admiring the splendor of his single eye."

Don't dally with your purpose.

"The one serviceable, safe, certain, remunerative, attainable quality in every study and pursuit is the quality of attention," said Charles Dickens. "My own invention, or imagination, such as it is, I can most truthfully assure you would never have served me as it has, but for the habit of commonplace, humble, patient, daily, toiling, drudging attention." When asked on another occasion the secret of his success, he said: "I never put one hand to anything on which I could throw my whole self." "Be a whole man at everything," wrote Joseph Gurney to his son, "a whole man at study, in work, in play."

"I go at what I am about," said Charles Kingsley, "as if there was nothing else in the world for the time being. That's the secret of all hard-working men; but most of them can't carry it into their amusements."

Many a man fails to become a great man by splitting into several small ones, choosing to be a tolerable Jack-

of-all-trades rather than to be an unrivaled specialist.
Such people produce admiration but not conviction.

"Many persons seeing me so much engaged in active
life," said Edward Bulwer Lytton, "and as much about
the world as if I had never been a student, have said to
me, 'When do you get time to write all your books?
How on earth do you contrive to do so much work?'
I shall surprise you by the answer I made. The answer
is this — 'I contrive to do so much by never doing too
much at a time. A man to get through work well must
not overwork himself; or, if he do too much to-day, the
reaction of fatigue will come, and he will be obliged to
do too little to-morrow. Now, since I began really and
earnestly to study, which was not till I had left college,
and was actually in the world, I may perhaps say that
I have gone through as large a course of general reading
as most men of my time. I have traveled much and I
have seen much; I have mixed much in politics, and
in the various business of life; and in addition to all
this, I have published somewhere about sixty volumes,
some upon subjects requiring much special research.
And what time do you think, as a general rule, I have
devoted to study, to reading and writing? Not more
than three hours a day; and, when Parliament is sitting, not always that. But then, during these three
hours, I have given my whole attention to what I was
about."

S. T. Coleridge possessed marvelous powers of mind,
but he had no definite purpose; he lived in an atmosphere of mental dissipation which consumed his energy,
exhausted his stamina, and his life was in many respects
a miserable failure. He lived in dreams and died in
reverie. He was continually forming plans and resolutions. but to the day of his death they remained
resolutions and plans. He was always just going to do
something, but never did it. "Coleridge is dead,"
wrote Charles Lamb to a friend, "and is said to have

left behind him above forty thousand treatises on metaphysics and divinity — not one of them complete!"

Every great man has become great, every successful man has succeeded, in proportion as he has confined his powers to one particular channel.

Hogarth would rivet his attention upon a face and study it until it was photographed upon his memory, when he could reproduce it at will. He studied and examined each object as eagerly as though he would never have a chance to see it again, and this habit of close observation enabled him to develop his work with marvelous detail. The very modes of thought of the time in which he lived were reflected from his works. He was not a man of great education or culture except in his power of observation.

Great men who have written books in prison know the value of concentrated observation. The slightest circumstance, as the appearance of a visitor, the passing of an officer or prisoner by the door of the cell, would be seized and utilized as though it were the last thing to be seen for a year.

With an immense procession passing up Broadway, the streets lined with people, and bands playing lustily, Horace Greeley would sit upon the steps of the Astor House, use the top of his hat for a desk, and write an editorial for the "New York Tribune" which would be quoted far and wide.

Offended by a pungent article, a gentleman called at the "Tribune" office and inquired for the editor. He was shown into a little seven-by-nine sanctum, where Greeley sat, with his head close down to his paper, scribbling away at a two-forty rate. The angry man began by asking if this was Mr. Greeley. "Yes, sir; what do you want?" said the editor quickly, without once looking up from his paper. The irate visitor then began using his tongue, with no reference to the rules of propriety, good breeding, or reason. Meantime Mr. Greeley continued to write. Page after page was dashed off in the most impetuous style, with no change of features, and without paying the slightest attention to the visitor. Finally, after about twenty minutes of the most impassioned scolding ever poured out in an editor's office, the angry man became disgusted, and abruptly turned to walk out of the room. Then, for the first time, Mr. Greeley quickly looked up, rose from his chair, and slapping the gentleman familiarly on his shoulder, in a pleasant tone of voice said: "Don't go, friend; sit down, sit down, and free your mind; it will do you good,—you will feel better for it. Besides, it helps me to think what I am to write about. Don't go."

One unwavering aim has ever characterized successful men.

"I resolved, when I began to read law," said Edward Sugden, afterwards Lord St. Leonard, "to make everything I acquired perfectly my own, and never go on to a second reading till I had entirely accomplished the first. Many of the competitors read as much in a day as I did in a week; but at the end of twelve months my knowledge was as fresh as on the day it was acquired, while theirs had glided away from their recollection."

"See a great lawyer like Rufus Choate," says Dr. Storrs, "in a case where his convictions are strong and his feelings are enlisted. He saw long ago, as he glanced over the box, that five of those in it were sympathetic with him; as he went on he became equally certain of seven; the number now has risen to ten; but two are still left whom he feels that he has not persuaded or mastered. Upon them he now concentrates his power, summing up the facts, setting forth anew and more forcibly the principles, urging upon them his view of the case with a more and more intense action of his mind upon theirs, until one only is left. Like the blow of a hammer, continually repeated until the iron bar crumbles beneath it, his whole force comes with ceaseless percussion on that one mind till it has yielded, and accepts the conviction on which the pleader's purpose is fixed. Men say afterward, 'He surpassed himself.' It was only because the singleness of his aim gave unity, intensity, and overpowering energy to the mind."

"Daniel Webster," said Sydney Smith, "struck me much like a steam-engine in trousers."

As Adams suggests, Lord Brougham, like Canning, had too many talents; and, though as a lawyer he gained the most splendid prize of his profession, the Lord Chancellorship of England, and merited the applause of scientific men for his investigations in science, yet his life on the whole was a failure. He was "everything by turns and nothing long." With all his magnificent abilities he left no permanent mark on history or literature, and actually outlived his own fame.

Miss Martineau says, "Lord Brougham was at his château at Cannes when the daguerreotype process first came into vogue. An artist undertook to take a view of the château with a group of guests on the balcony. He asked His Lordship to keep perfectly still for five seconds, and he promised that he would not stir, but alas,— he moved. The consequence was that where Lord Brougham should have been there was only a blur. So stands the view to this hour.

"There is something," remarks Miss Martineau, "very typical in this. In the picture of our century, as taken from the life by history, this very man should have been the central figure. But, owing to his want of steadfastness, there will be forever a blur where Lord Brougham should have been. How many lives are blurs for want of concentration and steadfastness of purpose."

What a contrast is afforded by the unwavering aim of William Pitt, who lived, ay, and died for the sake of political supremacy. Everything yielded to his lofty aim. He neglected everything else, was careless of his friends and expenditures, so that even with an income of £10,000 a year, and no family, he died hopelessly in debt. He tore by the roots from his heart a love most deep and tender, because it ran counter to his ambition. He was totally indifferent to posthumous fame, so that he did not take pains to transmit to posterity a single one of his speeches. He bent all his energies to the acquisition of power, and wielded the sceptre of England for a quarter of a century. There was no turning to the right or left. He went straight to his goal. There was "no dreaming away time or building air-castles; but one look and purpose, forward, onward, and upward, straight to success."

Fowell Buxton attributed his success to ordinary means and extraordinary application, and being a whole man to one thing at a time. It is ever the unwavering pursuit of a single aim that wins. "*Non multa, sed multum*"—not many things, but much, was Coke's motto.

It is the almost invisible point of a needle, the keen, slender edge of a razor or an axe, that opens the way for the huge bulk that follows. Without point or edge the bulk would be useless. It is the man of one line of work, the sharp-edged man, who cuts his way through obstacles, and achieves brilliant success. While we should shun that narrow devotion to one idea which prevents the harmonious development of our powers, we should avoid on the other hand the extreme versatility of one of whom W. M. Praed says:—

> "His talk is like a stream which runs
> With rapid change from rocks to roses,
> It slips from politics to puns,
> It glides from Mahomet to Moses;
> Beginning with the laws that keep
> The planets in their radiant courses,
> And ending with some precept deep
> For skinning eels or shoeing horses."

If you can get a child learning to walk to fix his eyes on any object, he will generally navigate to that point without capsizing, but distract his attention and down goes the baby.

He who vacillates in his course, "yawing," as sailors say, first this way, then that, is pretty sure to be cast away before he has half finished the voyage of life. Weathercock men are nature's failures. No one can succeed who has not a fixed and resolute purpose in his mind, and an unwavering faith that he can accomplish his purpose. One little hair's-breadth above or below a direct aim, and a man has begun his downward course. "When I have once taken a resolution," said Cardinal Richelieu, "I go straight to my aim; I overthrow all, I cut down all."

The young man seeking a position to-day is not asked what college he came from or who his ancestors were, but "*What can you do?*" is the great question. It is special training that is wanted. Most of the men at the head of great firms and great enterprises have been promoted step by step from the bottom.

"Beware of making a purchase there," said an eminent Frenchman to one who wished to buy land and settle in a certain district; "I know the men of that department; the pupils who come from it to our veterinary school at Paris do not strike hard upon the anvil; they want energy, and you will not get a satisfactory return on any capital you may invest there."

By exercising this art of concentration in a higher degree than did his brother generals, Grant was able to bring the Civil War to a speedy termination. This trait was strongly marked in the character of Washington. One way of acquiring the power of concentration is by close, accurate observation. This was the main factor in Darwin's wonderful success.

"I know that he can toil terribly," said Cecil of Walter Raleigh, in explanation of the latter's success.

As a rule, what the heart longs for the head and the hands may attain. The currents of knowledge, of wealth, of success, are as certain and fixed as the tides of the sea. In all great successes we can trace the power of concentration, riveting every faculty upon one unwavering aim; perseverance in the pursuit of an undertaking in spite of every difficulty; and courage which enables one to bear up under all trials, disappointments, and temptations.

Chemists tell us that there is power enough in a single acre of grass to drive all the mills and steam-cars in the world, could we but concentrate it upon the piston-rod of the steam-engine. But it is at rest, this acre of grass, and so, in the light of science, it is comparatively valueless.

What a great discrepancy there is between men and the results they achieve! It is due to the difference in their power of calling together all the rays of their ability, and concentrating them upon one point. Such a power will find a way, or make one. A versatile man is usually a smatterer.

Dr. Mathews says that the man who scatters himself upon many objects soon loses his energy, and with his energy his enthusiasm, adding, "and how is success possible without enthusiasm?" Dr. J. W. Alexander thus exhorted young ministers: "Live for your sermon — live in your sermon. Get some starling to cry Sermon, sermon, sermon." Rufus Choate advised young lawyers to "carry the jury at all hazards; move heaven and earth to carry the jury, and then fight it out with the judges on the law questions as best you can." Commodore Macdonough on Lake Champlain concentrated the fire of all his vessels upon the "big ship" of Downie, regardless of the fact that the other British ships were all hurling cannon-balls at his little fleet. The guns of the big ship were silenced, and then the others were taken care of easily. William Wirt wrote of a former

Chief Justice of the United States: "There is John Marshall, whose mind seems to be little less than a mountain of barren and stupendous rocks,—an inexhaustible quarry from which he draws his materials and builds his fabrics, rude and Gothic, but of such strength that neither time nor force can beat them down; a fellow who would not turn off a single step from the right line of his argument though a paradise should rise to tempt him."

"Never study on speculation," says Waters; "all such study is vain. Form a plan; have an object; then work for it; learn all you can about it, and you will be sure to succeed. What I mean by studying on speculation is that aimless learning of things because they may be useful some day; which is like the conduct of the woman who bought at auction a brass door-plate with the name of Thompson on it, thinking it might be useful some day!"

Definiteness of aim is characteristic of all true art. He is not the greatest painter who crowds the greatest number of ideas upon a single canvas, giving all the figures equal prominence. He is the genuine artist who makes the greatest variety express the greatest unity, who develops the leading idea in the central figure, and makes all the subordinate figures, lights, and shades point to that centre and find expression there. So in every well-balanced life, no matter how versatile in endowments, or how broad in culture, there is one grand central purpose, in which all the subordinate powers of the soul are brought to a focus, and where they will find fit expression. In nature we see no waste of energy, nothing left to chance. Since the shuttle of creation shot for the first time through chaos, design has marked the course of every golden thread. Every leaf, every flower, every crystal, every atom, even, has a purpose stamped upon it which unmistakably points to the crowning summit of all creation — man.

Young men are often told to aim high, but we must aim at what we would hit. He who cannot see an angel in the rough marble can never call it out with mallet and chisel. No, a general purpose is not enough. The arrow shot from the bow does not wander around to see what it can hit on its way, but flies straight to the mark. The magnetic needle does not point to all the lights in the heavens to see which it likes best. They all attract it. The sun dazzles, the meteor beckons, the stars twinkle to it, and try to win its affections; but the needle, true to its instinct, and with a finger that never errs in sunshine or in storm, points steadily to the North Star; for, while all the other stars must course with untiring tread around their great centres through all the ages, the North Star, alone, distant beyond human comprehension, moves with stately sweep on its circuit of more than 25,000 years, for all practical purposes of man, stationary, not only for a day but for a century. So all along the path of life other luminaries will beckon to lead us from our cherished aim — from the course of truth and duty; but let no moons which shine with borrowed light, no meteors which dazzle but never guide, turn the needle of our purpose from the North Star of its hope

CHAPTER VIII.

"ON TIME," OR THE TRIUMPH OF PROMPTNESS.

"On the great clock of time there is but one word — NOW."
Note the sublime precision that leads the earth over a circuit of five hundred millions of miles back to the solstice at the appointed moment without the loss of one second, — no, not the millionth part of a second, — for ages and ages of which it traveled that imperiled road. — EDWARD EVERETT.

"Who cannot but see oftentimes how strange the threads of our destiny run? Oft it is only for a moment the favorable instant is presented. We miss it, and months and years are lost."

By the street of by and by one arrives at the house of never. — CERVANTES.

Whilst we are considering when we are to begin, it is often too late to act. — QUINTILIAN.

When a fool has made up his mind the market has gone by. — SPANISH PROVERB.

It is no use running; to set out betimes is the main point. — LA FONTAINE.

"Lose this day by loitering — 't will be the same story to-morrow, and the next more dilatory."

Let's take the instant by the forward top. — SHAKESPEARE.

"HASTE, post, haste! Haste for thy life!" was frequently written upon messages in the days of Henry VIII. of England, with a picture of a courier swinging from a gibbet. Post-offices were unknown, and letters were carried by government messengers subject to hanging if they delayed upon the road.

Even in the old, slow days of stage-coaches, when it took a month of dangerous traveling to accomplish the distance we can now span in a few hours, unnecessary delay was a crime. One of the greatest gains civilization has made is in measuring and utilizing time. We can do as much in an hour to-day as they could in twenty hours a hundred years ago; and if it was a hanging affair then to lose a few minutes, what should the penalty be now for a like offense?

Cæsar's delay to read a message cost him his life when he reached the senate house. "Delays have dangerous ends." Colonel Rahl, the Hessian commander at Trenton, was playing cards when a messenger brought a letter stating that Washington was crossing the Delaware. He put the letter in his pocket without reading it until the game was finished, when he rallied his men only to die just before his troops were taken prisoners. Only a few minutes' delay, but he lost honor, liberty, life!

Success is the child of two very plain parents — punctuality and accuracy. There are critical moments in every successful life when if the mind hesitate or a nerve flinch all will be lost.

General Putnam was ploughing with his son Daniel in eastern Connecticut when the news of the battle of Lexington reached him. "He loitered not," said Daniel, "but left me, the driver of his team, to unyoke it in the furrow, and not many days after, to follow him to camp." Alarming the militia and ordering them to join him, he rode all night and reached Cambridge the next morning at sunrise, still wearing the checkered shirt which he had on when ploughing.

"Immediately on receiving your proclamation," wrote Governor Andrew of Massachusetts to President Lincoln on May 3, 1861, "we took up the war, and have carried on our part of it, in the spirit in which we believe the Administration and the American people intend to act, namely, as if there were not an inch of red tape in the world." He had received a telegram for troops from Washington on Monday, April 15; at nine o'clock the next Sunday he said: "All the regiments demanded from Massachusetts are already either in Washington, or in Fortress Monroe, or on their way to the defense of the Capitol."

JOHN QUINCY ADAMS

Promptness takes the drudgery out of an occupation.

"The mill can never grind with the water that is passed."

"The only question which I can entertain," he said, "is what to do; and when that question is answered, the other is, what next to do."

"The whole period of youth," said Ruskin, "is one essentially of formation, edification, instruction. There is not an hour of it but is trembling with destinies — not a moment of which, once passed, the appointed work can ever be done again, or the neglected blow struck on the cold iron."

Napoleon laid great stress upon that "supreme moment," that "nick of time" which occurs in every battle, to take advantage of which means victory, and to lose in hesitation means disaster. He said that he beat the Austrians because they did not know the value of five minutes; and it has been said that among the trifles that conspired to defeat him at Waterloo, the loss of a few moments by himself and Grouchy on the fatal morning were the most significant. Blücher was on time, and Grouchy was late. It was enough to send Napoleon to St. Helena. It is a well-known truism that has almost been elevated to the dignity of a maxim, that what may be done at any time will be done at no time.

"The fact is," says the Rev. Sydney Smith, "that, in order to do anything in this world worth doing, we must not stand shivering on the bank, and thinking of the cold and the danger, but jump in and scramble through as well as we can. It will not do to be perpetually calculating risks and adjusting nice chances. It did all very well before the flood, when a man could consult his friends upon an intended publication for one hundred and fifty years, and then live to see its success for six or seven centuries afterwards; but at present a man waits, and doubts, and hesitates, and consults his brother, and his uncle, and his cousin, and his particular friends, till, one fine day, he finds that he is sixty-five years of age, — that he has lost so much time in consulting his cousins and particular friends that he has no more time left to follow their advice."

The African Association of London wanted to send Ledyard the traveler to Africa, and asked when he would be ready to go. "To-morrow morning," was the reply. John Jervis, afterwards Earl St. Vincent, was asked when he could join his ship, and replied, "Directly." Colin Campbell, appointed commander of the army in India, and asked when he could set out, replied without hesitation, "To-morrow." "Every moment lost," said Napoleon, "gives an opportunity for misfortune."

The energy wasted in postponing until to-morrow a duty of to-day, would often do the work. How much harder and more disagreeable, too, it is to do work which has been put off. What would have been done at the time with pleasure or even enthusiasm becomes drudgery after it has been delayed for days and weeks. Letters can never be answered so easily as when first received. Many large firms make it a rule never to allow a letter to lie unanswered overnight. Promptness takes the drudgery out of an occupation. Putting off usually means leaving off, and going to do becomes going undone. Doing a deed is like sowing a seed; if not done at just the right time it will be forever out of season. The summer of eternity will not be long enough to bring to maturity the fruit of a delayed action. If a star or planet were delayed one second, it might throw the whole universe out of harmony.

"There is no moment like the present," said Maria Edgeworth; "not only so, there is no moment at all, no instant force and energy, but in the present. The man who will not execute his resolutions when they are fresh upon him, can have no hopes from them afterward. They will be dissipated, lost in the hurry and skurry of the world, or sunk in the slough of indolence." Cobbett said he owed his success to being "always ready"[1] more than to all his natural abilities combined.

"You cannot bathe twice in the same river," said Heraclitus.

"How," asked a man of Sir Walter Raleigh, "do you accomplish so much, and in so short a time?" "When I have anything to do, I go and do it," was the reply. The man who always acts promptly, even if he makes occasional mistakes, will succeed when a procrastinator will fail — even if he have the better judgment.

When asked how he managed to accomplish so much work, and at the same time attend to his social duties, a French statesman replied, "I do it simply by never postponing till to-morrow what should be done to-day." It was said of an unsuccessful public man that he used to reverse this process, his favorite maxim being "never to do to-day what might be postponed till to-morrow." How many men have dawdled away their success and allowed companions and relatives to steal it away five minutes at a time. Amos Lawrence's motto was, "Business before friends."

"To-morrow, didst thou say?" asked Cotton. "Go to — I will not hear of it. To-morrow! 'tis a sharper who stakes his penury against thy plenty — who takes thy ready cash and pays thee naught but wishes, hopes, and promises, the currency of idiots. *To-morrow!* it is a period nowhere to be found in all the hoary registers of time, unless perchance in the fool's calendar. Wisdom disclaims the word, nor holds society with those that own it. 'Tis fancy's child, and folly is its father; wrought of such stuffs as dreams are; and baseless as the fantastic visions of the evening." Oh, how many a wreck on the road to success could say: "I have spent

---

[1] "To this quality I owed my extraordinary promotion in the army," said Cobbett. "If I had to mount guard at ten, I was ready at nine; never did any man or anything wait one minute for me."

all my life in pursuit of to-morrow, being assured that to-morrow has some vast benefit or other in store for me."

"But his resolutions remained unshaken," Charles Reade continues in his story of Noah Skinner, the defaulting clerk, who had been overcome by a sleepy languor after deciding to make restitution; "by and by, waking up from a sort of heavy doze, he took, as it were, a last look at the receipts, and murmured, 'My head, how heavy it feels!' But presently he roused himself, full of his penitent resolutions, and murmured again, brokenly, 'I'll take it to — Pembroke — Street to—morrow; to—morrow.' The morrow found him, and so did the detectives, dead."

"To-morrow?" It is the devil's motto. All history is strewn with its brilliant victims, the wrecks of half-finished plans and unexecuted resolutions. It is the favorite refuge of sloth and incompetency.

"Strike while the iron is hot," and "Make hay while the sun shines," are golden maxims. Most of us need a spur to make us begin and to hold us to our task.

Very few people recognize the hour when laziness begins to set in. Some people it attacks after dinner; some after lunch; and some after seven o'clock in the evening. There is in every person's life a crucial hour in the day, which must be employed instead of wasted if the day is to be saved. With most people the early morning hour becomes the test of the day's success. Daniel Webster used often to answer twenty to thirty letters before breakfast.

A person was once extolling the skill and courage of Mayenne in Henry's presence. "You are right," said Henry, "he is a great captain, but I have always five hours' start of him." Henry rose at four in the morning, and Mayenne at about ten. This made all the difference between them. Indecision becomes a disease and procrastination is its forerunner. There is only one known remedy for the victims of indecision, and that is prompt decision. Otherwise the disease is fatal to all success or achievement. He who hesitates is lost.

A noted writer says that a bed is a bundle of paradoxes. We go to it with reluctance, yet we quit it with regret. We make up our minds every night to leave it early, but we make up our bodies every morning to keep it late. Yet most of those who have become eminent have been early risers. Peter the Great always rose before daylight. "I am," said he, "for making my life as long as possible, and therefore sleep as little as possible." Alfred the Great rose before daylight. In the hours of early morning Columbus planned his voyage to America, and Napoleon his greatest campaigns. Copernicus was an early riser, as were most of the famous astronomers of ancient and modern times. Bryant rose at five, Bancroft at dawn, and nearly all our leading authors, in the early morning. Washington, Jefferson, Webster, Clay, and Calhoun were all early risers. Henry VIII. breakfasted at seven and dined at ten.

John Jacob Astor and Cornelius Vanderbilt were accustomed to rise at set times each morning, and to retire at definite hours, even though they had company.

Walter Scott was a very punctual man. This was the secret of his enormous achievements. He made it a rule to answer all letters the day they were received. He rose at five. By breakfast-time he had broken the neck of the day's work, as he used to say. Writing to a youth who had obtained a situation and asked him for advice, he gave this counsel: "Beware of stumbling over a propensity which easily besets you from not having your time fully employed — I mean what the women call dawdling. Do instantly whatever is to be done, and take the hours of recreation after business, never before it."

Not too much can be said about the value of the

habit of rising early. Late rising is one of the first signs of family degeneracy. Eight hours is enough sleep for any man. Very frequently seven hours is plenty. After the eighth hour in bed, if a man is able, it is his business to get up, dress quickly, and go to work.

"A singular mischance has happened to some of our friends," said Hamilton. "At the instant when He ushered them into existence, God gave them a work to do, and He also gave them a competency of time; so much that if they began at the right moment, and wrought with sufficient vigor, their time and their work would end together. But a good many years ago a strange misfortune befell them. A fragment of their allotted time was lost. They cannot tell what became of it, but sure enough, it has dropped out of existence; for just like two measuring-lines laid alongside, the one an inch shorter than the other, their work and their time run parallel, but the work is always ten minutes in advance of the time. They are not irregular. They are never too soon. Their letters are posted the very minute after the mail is closed. They arrive at the wharf just in time to see the steamboat off, they come in sight of the terminus precisely as the station gates are closing. They do not break any engagement nor neglect any duty; but they systematically go about it too late, and usually too late by about the same fatal interval."

Some one has said that "promptness is a contagious inspiration." Whether it be an inspiration, or an acquirement, it is one of the practical virtues of civilization.

There is one thing that is almost as sacred as the marriage relation,— that is, an appointment. A man who fails to meet his appointment, unless he has a good reason, is practically a liar, and the world treats him as such.

"I give it as my deliberate and solemn conviction." said Dr. Fitch, "that the individual who is tardy in meeting an appointment will never be respected or successful in life." "If a man has no regard for the time of other men," said Horace Greeley, "why should he have for their money? What is the difference between taking a man's hour and taking his five dollars? There are many men to whom each hour of the business day is worth more than five dollars."

"It is not necessary for me to live," said Pompey, "but it is necessary that I be at a certain point at a certain hour."

When President Washington dined at four, new members of Congress invited to dine at the White House would sometimes arrive late, and be mortified to find the President eating. "My cook," Washington would say, "never asks if the visitors have arrived, but if the hour has arrived."

When his secretary excused the lateness of his attendance by saying that his watch was too slow, Washington replied, "Then you must get a new watch, or I another secretary."

Franklin said to a servant who was always late, but always ready with an excuse, "I have generally found that the man who is good at an excuse is good for nothing else."

On the eve of Nelson's departure on a famous cruise, his coachman said that the carriage would be at the door punctually at six o'clock. "A quarter before," said the admiral; "I have always been a quarter of an hour before my time, and it has made a man of me."

Napoleon once invited his marshals to dine with him, but, as they did not arrive at the moment appointed, he began to eat without them. They came in just as he was rising from the table. "Gentlemen," said he, "it is now past dinner, and we will immediately proceed to business."

Blücher was one of the promptest men that ever lived. He was called "Marshal Forward." John Q. Adams was never known to be behind time. The Speaker of the House of Representatives knew when to call the House to order by seeing Mr. Adams coming to his seat. Once a member said that it was time to begin. "No," said another, "Mr. Adams is not in his seat." It was found that the clock was three minutes fast, and prompt to the minute, Mr. Adams arrived.

Lord Brougham, who, in addition to other arduous duties, presided in the House of Lords, the Court of Chancery, and at the meetings of nearly a dozen literary associations, was uniformly in his chair at the appointed minute. He was as punctual as the clock.

Webster was never late at a recitation in school or college. In court, in congress, in society, he was equally punctual. Amid the cares and distractions of a singularly busy life, Horace Greeley managed to be on time for every appointment. Many a trenchant paragraph for the "Tribune," was written while the editor was waiting for men of leisure, tardy at some meeting.

The comet which visits our atmosphere but once in a thousand years is never a single second behind time.

Punctuality is the soul of business, as brevity of wit.

Every business man knows that there are moments on which hang the destiny of years. If you arrive a few moments late at the bank, your paper may be protested and your credit ruined. During the first seven years of his mercantile career, Amos Lawrence did not permit a bill to remain unsettled over Sunday. Punctuality is said to be the politeness of kings. Some men are always running to catch up with their business; they are always in a hurry, and give you the impression that they are late for a train. They lack method, and seldom accomplish much.

One of the best things about school and college life is that the bell which strikes the hour for rising, for recitations, or for lectures, teaches habits of promptness. Every young man should have a watch which is a good timekeeper; one that is *nearly* right encourages bad habits, and is an expensive investment at any price. Wear threadbare clothes if you must, but never carry an inaccurate watch.

"Oh, how I do appreciate a boy who is always on time!" says H. C. Brown. "How quickly you learn to depend on him, and how soon you find yourself intrusting him with weightier matters! The boy who has acquired a reputation for punctuality has made the first contribution to the capital that in after years makes his success a certainty!"

Promptness is the mother of confidence and gives credit. It is the best possible proof that our own affairs are well ordered and well conducted, and gives others confidence in our ability. The man who keeps his time (i. e., is punctual), as a rule, will keep his word.

Keep your business as her Majesty keeps her ships, always in trim in every detail, ready for immediate action.

"Better late than never" is not half so good a maxim as "Better never late."

A conductor's watch is behind time, and a frightful railway collision occurs. A leading firm with enormous assets becomes bankrupt, because an agent is tardy in transmitting available funds, as ordered. An innocent man is hanged because the messenger bearing a reprieve should have arrived five minutes earlier. A man is stopped five minutes to hear a trivial story and misses a train or steamer by one minute.

Grant decided to enlist the moment that he learned of the fall of Sumter. When Buckner sent him a flag of truce at Fort Donelson, asking for the appointment of commissioners to consider terms of capitulation, he promptly replied: "No terms except an unconditional and immediate surrender can be accepted. I propose to move immediately upon your works." Buckner replied that circumstances compelled him "to accept the ungenerous and unchivalrous terms which you propose."

The man who, like Napoleon, can on the instant seize the most important thing and sacrifice the others, is sure to succeed. Men often fail because they want to think the whole matter over before making any sacrifice; but the choice of the one and the sacrifice of the others come together.

"We are all so indolent by nature and by habit," said John Todd, "that we feel it a luxury to find a man of real, undeviating punctuality. We love to lean upon such a man, and we are willing to purchase such a staff at almost any price. It shows, at least, that he has conquered himself."

Many a wasted life dates its ruin from a lost five minutes. "Too late" can be read between the lines on the tombstone of many a man who has failed. A few minutes often makes all the difference between victory and defeat, success and failure.

CHAPTER IX.

CHEERFULNESS AND LONGEVITY.

I have gout, asthma, and seven other maladies, but am otherwise very well.— SYDNEY SMITH.

I feel and grieve, but, by the grace of God, I fret at nothing.— JOHN WESLEY.

> This one sits shivering in Fortune's smile,
> Taking his joy with bated, doubtful breath;
> This other, gnawed by hunger, all the while
> Laughs in the teeth of death.
>   T. B. ALDRICH.

Anxiety never yet successfully bridged over any chasm. — RUFFINI.

> " For every evil under the sun,
> There is a remedy, or there is none;
> If there be one, try and find it:
> If there be none, never mind it."

> On morning wings how active springs the mind
> That leaves the load of yesterday behind.
>   POPE.

> Blessed are the joy-makers.
>   WILLIS.

> 'T is always morning somewhere, and above
> The awakening continents, from shore to shore,
> Somewhere the birds are singing evermore.
>   LONGFELLOW.

The cheerful live longest in years, and afterward in our regards.— BOVEE.

Wondrous is the strength of cheerfulness, altogether past calculation its powers of endurance. Efforts to be permanently useful must be uniformly joyous, — a spirit all sunshine, graceful from very gladness, beautiful because bright. — CARLYLE.

> There 's a good time coming, boys, a good time coming:
> Let us aid it all we can, every woman, every man.
>   MACKAY.

GOLDSMITH says that one of the happiest persons he ever saw was a slave in the fortifications at Flanders, — a man with but one leg, deformed, and chained. He was condemned to slavery for life, and had to work from dawn till dark, yet he seemed to see only the bright side of everything. He laughed and sang, and appeared the happiest man in the garrison.

"It is from these enthusiastic fellows," says an admirer, "that you hear — what they fully believe, bless them! — that all countries are beautiful, all dinners grand, all pictures superb, all mountains high, all women beautiful. When such a one has come back from his country trip, after a hard year's work, he has always found the cosiest of nooks, the cheapest houses, the best of landladies, the finest views, and the best dinners. But with the other the case is indeed altered. He has always been robbed; he has positively seen nothing; his landlady was a harpy, his bedroom was unhealthy, and the mutton was so tough that he could not get his teeth through it."

A gentleman in Minneapolis owned a business block which was completely gutted by fire. The misfortune produced a melancholy that boded ill for his mind. In vain his friends tried to cheer him. Nothing could dispel the impenetrable gloom. He was almost on the point of suicide. He was away from home when the disaster occurred, and received the following letter from his little seven-year-old daughter: —

"Dear Papa, — I went down to see your store that was burned, and it looks very pretty all covered with ice. Love and kisses from   Lilian."

The father smiled as he read; and the man who had contemplated jumping from the train laughed aloud. The spell that had overshadowed him was at last broken by this ray of sunshine.

A cheerful man is preëminently a useful man. He does not cramp his mind, nor take half-views of men and things. He knows that there is much misery, but that misery need not be the rule of life. He sees that

OLIVER WENDELL HOLMES

"Blessed are the joy-makers."

"Mirth is God's medicine; everybody ought to bathe in it."

in every state people may be cheerful; the lambs skip, birds sing and fly joyously, puppies play, kittens are full of joyance, the whole air full of careering and rejoicing insects; that everywhere the good outbalances the bad, and that every evil has its compensating balm.

"You are on the shady side of seventy, I expect?" was asked of an old man. "No," was the reply, "I am on the sunny side; for I am on the side nearest to glory."

Travelers are told by the Icelanders, who live amid the cold and desolation of almost perpetual winter, that "Iceland is the best land the sun shines upon."

When Pandora out of curiosity removed the lid from the great box in which Hesiod says the gods had inclosed all human miseries, they flew abroad through the earth, but Hope remained at the bottom, the antidote for all.

Doctor Marshall Hall frequently prescribed "cheerfulness" for his patients, saying that it was better than anything they could get at the apothecary's. "A merry heart doeth good like a medicine." Health is the condition of wisdom, and the sign is cheerfulness. Half the people we meet think they have something about them which will ultimately kill them, and live in chronic dread of death. What is even worse, they seem anxious that other people should share with them the "enjoyment of bad health," and are ready to tell them at the slightest provocation.

You must take joy with you, or you will not find it, even in heaven. He who hoards his joys to make them more is like the man who said: "I will keep my grain from mice and birds, and neither the ground nor the mill shall have it. What fools are they who throw away upon the earth whole handfuls."

"Nothing will supply the want of sunshine to peaches," said Emerson, "and to make knowledge valuable, you must have the cheerfulness of wisdom." In answer to the question, "How shall we overcome temptation," a noted writer said, "Cheerfulness is the first thing, cheerfulness is the second, and cheerfulness is the third." A habit of cheerfulness, enabling one to transmute apparent misfortunes into real blessings, is a fortune to a young man or young woman just crossing the threshold of active life. He who has formed a habit of looking at the bright, happy side of things, who sees the glory in the grass, the sunshine in the flowers, sermons in stones, and good in everything, has a great advantage over the chronic dyspeptic, who sees no good in anything. His habitual thought sculptures his face into beauty and touches his manner with grace.

"Of all virtues," says S. C. Goodrich, "cheerfulness is the most profitable. While other virtues defer the day of recompense, cheerfulness pays down. It is a cosmetic which makes homeliness graceful and winning. It promotes health and gives clearness and vigor to the mind; it is the bright weather of the heart in contrast with the clouds and gloom of melancholy."

"The spirit that could conjure up a Hamlet or a Lear would have broken had it not possessed, as well, the humor which could produce a Falstaff, and the 'Merry Wives of Windsor.'" The London "Lancet," the most eminent medical journal in the world, gives the following scientific testimony of the value of good spirits:—

"This power of 'good spirits' is a matter of high moment to the sick and weakly. To the former it may mean the ability to survive; to the latter, the possibility of outliving, or living in spite of, a disease. It is, therefore, of the greatest importance to cultivate the highest and most buoyant frame of mind which the conditions will admit. The same energy which takes the form of mental activity is vital to the work of the organism. Mental influences affect the system, and a joyous spirit not only relieves pain, but increases the momentum of life in the body."

"I find nonsense singularly refreshing," said Talleyrand. There is good philosophy in the saying, "Laugh and grow fat." If everybody knew the power of laughter as a health tonic and life prolonger, the tinge of sadness which now clouds the American face would largely disappear, and thousands of physicians would find their occupation gone. The power of laughter was given us to serve a wise purpose in our economy. It is Nature's device for exercising the internal organs and giving us pleasure at the same time. Laughter begins in the lungs and diaphragm, setting the liver, stomach, and other internal organs into a quick, jelly-like vibration, which gives a pleasant sensation and exercise, almost equal to horseback riding. The heart beats faster, sends the blood bounding through the body, increases the respiration, and gives warmth and glow to the whole system. Laughter brightens the eye, increases the perspiration, expands the chest, forces the poisoned air from the least-used lung cells, and tends to restore that exquisite poise or balance which we call health, and which results from the harmonious action of all the functions of the body. This delicate poise, which may be destroyed by a sleepless night, a piece of bad news, by grief or anxiety, is often wholly restored by a good hearty laugh. A jolly physician is often better than all his pills.

It is not the troubles of to-day, but those of to-morrow and next week and next year, that whiten our heads and wrinkle our faces.

"Cries little Miss Fret,
In a very great pet:
'I hate this warm weather; it's horrid to tan.
It scorches my nose,
And it blisters my toes,
And wherever I go I must carry a fan.'

"Chirps little Miss Laugh:
'Why, I could n't tell half
The fun I am having this bright summer day.
I sing through the hours,
I cull pretty flowers,
And ride like a queen on the sweet-smelling hay.'"

"Men are not made to hang down either heads or lips," says a modern writer. "It is the duty of every one to extract all the happiness and enjoyment he can without and within him, and, above all, he should look on the bright side of things. As well might fog, and cloud, and vapor hope to cling to the sun-illumined landscape, as the blues and moroseness to remain in any countenance when the cheerful one comes with a hearty 'good-morning.' Don't forget to say it, with a smile, to all you meet. A busy life cannot well be otherwise than cheerful. Frogs do not croak in running water."

"I have told you," says Southey, "of the Spaniard who always put on spectacles when about to eat cherries, in order that the fruit might look larger and more tempting. In like manner I make the most of my enjoyments; and though I do not cast my eyes away from my troubles, I pack them in as small a compass as I can for myself, and never let them annoy others." We all know the power of good cheer to magnify everything.

When Garrison was locked up in the Boston city jail, he said he had two delightful companions, — a good conscience and a cheerful mind. It was Lincoln's cheerfulness that enabled him to stand up under the terrible load of the Civil War. His jests and quaint stories lightened the gloom of the darkest hours of the nation's peril.

About two things we should never fret, that which we cannot help, and that which we can help. Better find one of your own faults than ten of your neighbor's.

Henry Ward Beecher was the greatest joker in college, and shocked many church people because he was so full of fun. His sister, Harriet Beecher Stowe. said he was like "a converted bobolink who should be brought to judgment for short quirks and undignified twitters and tweedles among the daisy-heads, instead of flying in dignified paternal sweeps like a good swallow of the sanctuary, or sitting in solemnized meditation in the depths of the pine-trees like the owl." Solemnity was regarded then as evidence of Christian character; but this cheerful preacher has done much to show that religion is the most beautiful thing in the world.

Helen Hunt says there is one sin which seems to be everywhere, and by everybody is underestimated and quite too much overlooked in valuations of character. It is the sin of fretting. It is as common as air, as speech; so common that unless it rises above its usual monotone we do not even observe it. Watch any ordinary coming together of people, and we see how many minutes it will be before somebody frets — that is, makes more or less complaint of something or other, which probably every one in the room, or car, or on the street corner knew before, and which most probably nobody can help. Why say anything about it? It is cold, it is hot, it is wet, it is dry, somebody has broken an appointment, ill-cooked a meal; stupidity or bad faith somewhere has resulted in discomfort. There are plenty of things to fret about. It is simply astonishing, how much annoyance and discomfort may be found in the course of every-day living, even of the simplest, if one only keeps a sharp eye out on that side of things. Some people seem to be always hunting for deformities, discords, and shadows, instead of beauty, harmony, and light. We are born to trouble, as sparks fly upward. But even to the sparks flying upward, in the blackest of smoke, there is a blue sky above, and the less time they waste on the road, the sooner they will reach it. Fretting is all time wasted on the road.

Wordsworth, elsewhere sombre enough, in the most splendid ode ever written by mortal pen, saw wonder in the grass and glory in the flower; and that "land and sea gave themselves up to jollity;" and this was to his, one of the most reflective minds we have ever had, enough to inspire perpetual benedictions.

How true it is that if we are cheerful and contented,

all nature smiles with us; the air seems more balmy, the sky more clear, the earth has a brighter green, the trees have a richer foliage, the flowers are more fragrant, the birds sing more sweetly, and the sun, moon, and stars all appear more beautiful.

"If a word or two will render a man happy," said a Frenchman, "he must be a wretch indeed, who will not give it. It is like lighting another man's candle with your own, which loses none of its brilliancy by what the other gains."

Sir Walter Scott, who wrote, "Give me an honest laugher," was one of the happiest men in the world. He had a kind word and a pleasant smile for every one, and everybody loved him. He once threw a stone at a dog, and broke his leg. The poor creature crawled up to him, dragging the broken leg, and licked his foot. It almost broke his heart. He said it caused him the deepest remorse of his life.

"I dare no more fret than I dare curse and swear," said John Wesley.

Habitual fretters see more trouble than others. They are never so well as their neighbors. The weather never suits them. The climate is trying. The winds are too high or too low; it is too hot or too cold, too damp or too dry. The roads are either muddy or dusty.

"Mirth is God's medicine," says a wise writer; "everybody ought to bathe in it. Grim care, moroseness, anxiety — all the rust of life, ought to be scoured off by the oil of mirth." It is better than emery. Every man ought to rub himself with it. A man without mirth is like a wagon without springs, in which one is caused disagreeably to jolt by every pebble over which it runs. A man with mirth is like a chariot with springs, in which one can ride over the roughest roads and scarcely feel anything but a pleasant rocking motion.

Undoubtedly we could trace much of the moroseness in our bones past dyspepsia, back to our Puritan ancestors who groaned as they worshiped, and who for the glory of God pulled faces as long as a yardstick. They were the people who, like Jacques, sucked "melancholy out of a song, as a weasel sucks eggs."

But we have arrived at a new and better understanding of the religion of Christ. God is glorified, not by our groans, but by our thanksgivings; and all good thought and good action claim a natural alliance with good cheer.

Christ said, "to-day," not next year, not at Judgment day, but "to-day shalt thou be with me," not in purgatory, but "in paradise." How long will humanity persist in harboring thoughts of wickedness and woe, and insisting that we live in a hopeless, cheerless world where sin and death shall forever perpetuate themselves? Can we not see that sin and death are self-destructive, and must ultimately work their own annihilation? that discord will finally be swallowed up in harmony, darkness in light, error in truth, disease in health, sorrow in joy? Why not enter the protest of our belief and example against the habit of forever dwelling upon deformity, disease, and discord?

Anxiety and care may be read on nearly every American face, telling the story of our too serious civilization. Bent forms, premature gray hair, heavy steps, and feverish haste are indicative of American life. Restlessness and discontent have become chronic, and are characteristic of our age and nation. Thousands of our people die annually from depressed spirits, disappointed hopes, thwarted ambitions, and premature exhaustion. We have not yet learned to cultivate that high-minded cheerfulness which is found in great souls, self-centred and confident in their own heaven-aided powers — that lofty cheerfulness which is the great preventive of humanity's ills. We have not yet learned, as a people, that grief, anxiety, and fear, are the great enemies of human life, and should be resisted as we resist the plague. Without cheerfulness there can be no healthy action, physical, mental, or moral, for it is the normal atmosphere of our being.

But oh, for the glorious spectacles worn by the good-natured man!—oh, for those wondrous glasses, finer than the Claude Lorraine glass, which throw a sunlit view over everything, and make the heart glad with little things, and thankful for small mercies! Such glasses had honest Izaak Walton, who, coming in from a fishing expedition on the river Lea, bursts out into such grateful little talks as this: "Let us, as we walk home under the cool shade of this honeysuckle hedge, mention some of the thoughts and joys that have possessed my soul since we two met. And that our present happiness may appear the greater, and we more thankful for it, I beg you to consider with me, how many do at this very time lie under the torment of the gout or the toothache, and this we have been free from; and let me tell you, that every misery I miss is a new blessing."

Worry is a disease. It sometimes becomes a crime. In some States the unsuccessful suicide is arrested on the charge of homicide. Some people ought to be incarcerated for disturbing the family peace, and for troubling the public welfare, on the charge of intolerable fretfulness and touchiness. And it is this incessant care, this mordant anxiety that is to blame for our second national vice—hurry. Of course every one will recognize the fact that worry is the vice for which as a nation we are remarkable. "Touchiness" is a modern disease.

"Every man we meet looks as if he'd gone out to borrow trouble, with plenty of it on hand," said a French lady driving in New York.

How quickly we Americans exhaust life! With what panting haste we pursue everything! Every man you meet seems to be late for an appointment. Hurry is stamped in the wrinkles of the American face. We are men of action; we die without it; nay, we go faster and faster as the years go by, speed our machinery to the utmost, stretch the silver cord of life until it snaps. We have not even leisure to die a natural death; we go at high pressure until the boiler bursts. We have actually changed the type of our diseases, to suit our changed constitution. Instead of the lingering maladies of our fathers, we drop down and die of heart disease or apoplexy. Even death has adopted our terrible gait.

"It is not work that kills men," says Beecher; "it is worry. Work is healthy; you can hardly put more on a man than he can bear. But worry is rust upon the blade. It is not movement that destroys the machinery, but friction."

The busy bee stops not to complain that there are so many poisonous flowers and thorny boughs in his path, nor that disgusting bugs and flies are but soiling the flower from which he would gather sweets, but buzzes on, sucking up honey wherever he can find it, and passing quietly by the places where it is not.

"It is not the cares of to-day," says George Macdonald, "but the cares of to-morrow that weigh a man down. For the needs of to-day we have corresponding strength given."

"How much have cost us the evils that never happened!" exclaims Jefferson.

"Do not anticipate trouble," says Franklin, "or worry about what may never happen. Keep in the sunlight."

Charles Lamb tells of a chronic grumbler who always complained at whist, because he had so few trumps. By some artifice his companions managed to deal him the whole thirteen, hoping to extort some expression of satisfaction, but he only looked more wretched than ever as he examined his hand. "Well, Tom," said Lamb. "have n't you trumps enough this time?" "Yes," grunted Tom, "but I've no other cards."

The Puritans went through life tormented with the

fear of sin and terror of the Judgment Day, and their melancholy taints their descendants. We are a nation of dyspeptics. We can earn our bread, but cannot digest it. We believe "there is not a string tuned to mirth, but has its chord of melancholy," that evil always stands behind good, and that the devil always has the whisk of his tail in everything. It seems impossible for some people to rid themselves of an inherent gloom which colors their whole life. They cannot enjoy a beautiful day. To them it is only one of those infernal "weather-breeders." Their lives are set to a minor key, and they hear only plaintive sounds. Our religious creeds, philosophy, and hymns are tinged with the spleen of jaundice of unfortunate authors who sometimes mistook bile for inspiration.

Many writers have honestly believed they were giving the world valuable religious doctrines, when in reality they were writing an account of their own jaundice and dyspepsia.

Calvin, though unquestionably honest, was a dyspeptic and could eat but once a day. Who can say that his writings were not tinged by his malady? How can men shut out from the pure air and sunlight in convents and studies, away from the great throbbing, pulsing heart of Nature and humanity, write healthy, vigorous, religious doctrines for a hardy, healthy, robust, and practical world?

We should fight against every influence which tends to depress the mind, as we would against a temptation to crime. A depressed mind prevents the free action of the diaphragm and the expansion of the chest. It stops the secretions of the body, interferes with the circulation of the blood in the brain, and deranges the entire functions of the body. Scrofula and consumption often follow protracted depression of mind. That "fatal murmur" which is heard in the upper lobes of the lungs in the first stages of consumption, often follows depressed spirits after some great misfortune or sorrow. Victims of suicide are almost always in a depressed state from exhausted vitality, loss of nervous energy, dyspepsia, worry, anxiety, trouble, or grief.

Christ the great Teacher did not shut himself up with monks, away from temptation of the great world outside. He taught no long-faced, gloomy theology. He taught the gospel of gladness and good cheer. His doctrines are touched with the sunlight, and flavored with the flowers of the fields. The birds of the air, the beasts of the field, and happy, romping children are in them. True piety is cheerful as the day.

> Joy is the mainspring in the whole
> Of endless Nature's calm rotation.
> Joy moves the dazzling wheels that roll
> In the great timepiece of Creation.
>
> SCHILLER.

CHAPTER X.

A FORTUNE IN GOOD MANNERS.

Give a boy address and accomplishments, and you give him the mastery of palaces and fortunes wherever he goes; he has not the trouble of earning or owning them; they solicit him to enter and possess. — EMERSON.

With hat in hand, one gets on in the world. — GERMAN PROVERB.

> What thou wilt,
> Thou must rather enforce it with thy smile,
> Than hew to it with thy sword.
> SHAKESPEARE.

Politeness has been compared to an air cushion, which, although there is apparently nothing in it, eases our jolts wonderfully. — GEORGE L. CAREY.

Birth's gude, but breedin's better. — SCOTCH PROVERB.

You had better return a dropped fan genteelly than give a thousand pounds awkwardly; and you had better refuse a favor than grant it clumsily. Manner is all in everything: it is by manner only that you can please, and consequently rise. All your Greek will never advance you from secretary to envoy, or from envoy to ambassador; but your address, your air, your manner, if good, may. — CHESTERFIELD.

Conduct is three fourths of life. — MATTHEW ARNOLD.

I learnt that nothing can constitute good breeding that has not good nature for its foundation. — BULWER.

The commonest man, who has his ounce of sense and feeling, is conscious of the difference between a lovely, delicate woman and a coarse one. Even a dog feels a difference in her presence. — GEORGE ELIOT.

"Why the doose do 'e 'old 'is 'ead down like that?" asked a cockney sergeant-major angrily, when a worthy fellow soldier wished to be reinstated in a position from which he had been dismissed. "Has 'e's been han hofficer 'e hought to know 'ow to be'ave 'isself better. What huse 'ud 'e be has ha non-commissioned hofficer hif 'e did n't dare look 'is men hin the face? Hif ha man wants to be ha soldier, hi say, let 'im cock 'is chin hup, switch 'is stick habout ha bit, han give ha crack hover the 'ead to hanybody who comes foolin' round 'im, helse 'e might just has well be ha Methodist parson."

MADAME DE STAËL

"When she had passed it seemed
Like the ceasing of exquisite music."

This English is somewhat rude, but it expresses pretty forcibly the fact that a good bearing is indispensable to success as a soldier. Mien and manner have much to do with our influence and reputation in any walk of life.

"Don't you wish you had my power?" asked the East Wind of the Zephyr. "Why, when I start they hail me by storm signals all along the coast. I can twist off a ship's mast as easily as you can waft thistledown. With one sweep of my wing I strew the coast from Labrador to Cape Horn with shattered ship-timber. I can lift and have often lifted the Atlantic. I am the terror of all invalids, and to keep me from piercing to the very marrow of their bones, men cut down forests for their fires and explore the mines of continents for coal to feed their furnaces. Under my breath the nations crouch in sepulchres. Don't you wish you had my power?"

Zephyr made no reply, but floated from out the bowers of the sky, and all the rivers and lakes and seas, all the forests and fields, all the beasts and birds and men smiled at its coming. Gardens bloomed, orchards ripened, silver wheat-fields turned to gold, fleecy clouds went sailing in the lofty heaven, the pinions of birds and the sails of vessels were gently wafted onward, and health and happiness were everywhere. The foliage and flowers and fruits and harvests, the warmth and sparkle and gladness and beauty and life were the only answer Zephyr gave to the insolent question of the proud but pitiless East Wind.

The story goes that Queen Victoria once expressed herself to her husband in rather a despotic tone, and Prince Albert, whose manly self-respect was smarting at her words, sought the seclusion of his own apartment, closing and locking the door. In about five minutes some one knocked.

"Who is it?" inquired the Prince.

"It is I. Open to the Queen of England!" haughtily responded her Majesty. There was no reply. After a long interval there came a gentle tapping and the low spoken words: "It is I, Victoria, your wife." Is it necessary to add that the door was opened, or that the disagreement was at an end? It is said that civility is to a man what beauty is to a woman: it creates an instantaneous impression in his behalf.

The monk Basle, according to a quaint old legend, died while under the ban of excommunication by the pope, and was sent in charge of an angel to find his proper place in the nether world. But his genial disposition and his great conversational powers won friends wherever he went. The fallen angels adopted his manner, and even the good angels went a long way to see him and live with him. He was removed to the lowest depths of Hades, but with the same result. His inborn politeness and kindness of heart were irresistible, and he seemed to change the hell into a heaven. At length the angel returned with the monk, saying that no place could be found in which to punish him. He still remained the same Basle. So his sentence was revoked, and he was sent to Heaven and canonized as a saint.

"Bishop Fénelon is a delicious man." said Lord Peterborough; "I had to run away from him to prevent his making me a Christian."

The Duke of Marlborough "wrote English badly and spelled it worse," yet he swayed the destinies of empires. The charm of his manner was irresistible and influenced all Europe. His fascinating smile and winning speech disarmed the fiercest hatred and made friends of the bitterest enemies.

A gentleman took his daughter of sixteen to Richmond, to witness the trial of his bitter personal enemy, Aaron Burr, whom he regarded as an arch traitor. But she was so fascinated by Burr's charming manner that she sat with his friends. Her father took her from the courtroom, and locked her up, but she was so overcome by the fine manner of the accused that she believed in his innocence and prayed for his acquittal. "To this day," said she fifty years afterwards, "I feel the magic of his wonderful deportment."

Madame Récamier was so charming that when she passed around the box at the Church St. Roche in Paris, twenty thousand francs were put into it. At the great reception to Napoleon on his return from Italy, the crowd caught sight of this fascinating woman and almost forgot to look at the great hero.

"Please, Madame," whispered a servant to Madame de Maintenon at dinner, "one anecdote more, for there is no roast to-day." She was so fascinating in manner and speech that her guests appeared to overlook all the little discomforts of life.

According to St. Beuve, the privileged circle at Coppet, after making an excursion, returned from Chambéry in two coaches. Those arriving in the first coach had a rueful experience to relate — a terrific thunder-storm, shocking roads, and danger and gloom to the whole company. The party in the second coach heard their story with surprise; of thunder-storm, of steeps, of mud, of danger, they knew nothing; no, they had forgotten earth, and breathed a purer air; such a conversation between Madame de Staël and Madame Récamier and Benjamin Constant and Schlegel! they were all in a state of delight. The intoxication of the conversation had made them insensible to all notice of weather or rough roads. "If I were Queen," said Madame Tesse, "I should command Madame de Staël to talk to me every day."

"When she had passed," as Longfellow wrote of Evangeline, "it seemed like the ceasing of exquisite music."

> Our homes are cheerier for her sake,
> Our door-yards brighter blooming,
> And all about the social air
> Is sweeter for her coming. — WHITTIER.

"A woman must be truly refined to incite chivalry in the heart of man," said Madame Neckar.

"The art of pleasing," says Hazlitt, "consists in being pleased. To be amiable is to be satisfied with one's self and others."

A guest for two weeks at the house of Arthur M. Cavanaugh, M. P., who was without arms or legs, was very desirous of knowing how he fed himself; but the conversation and manner of the host were so charming that the visitor forgot to satisfy his curiosity.

"When Dickens entered a room," said one who knew him well, "it was like the sudden kindling of a big fire, by which every one was warmed."

It is said that when Goethe entered a restaurant people would lay down their knives and forks to admire him.

Philip of Macedon, after hearing the report of Demosthenes' famous oration, said: "Had I been there he would have persuaded me to take up arms against myself."

The masses could not break away from the rhythmical cadences of Wendell Phillips; they would listen spellbound for hours, even when they hated him and his cause. His inimitable manner, a kind of indefinable mesmerism, riveted their attention, and his brilliant, dazzling oratory was absolutely irresistible.

Henry Clay was so graceful and impressive in his manner that a Pennsylvania tavern-keeper tried to induce him to get out of the stage-coach in which they were riding, and make a speech to himself and his wife.

"I don't think much of Choate's spread-eagle talk," said a simple-minded member of a jury that had given five successive verdicts to the great advocate; "but I call him a very lucky lawyer, for there was not one of those five cases that came before us where he was n't on the right side." His manner as well as his logic was irresistible.

When Edward Everett took a professor's chair at Harvard after five years of study in Europe, he was almost worshiped by the students. His manner seemed touched by that exquisite grace seldom found except in women of rare culture. His great popularity lay in a magical atmosphere which every one felt, but no one could describe, and which never left him.

After Stephen A. Douglas had been abused in the Senate he rose and said: "What no gentleman should say no gentleman need answer."

A New York lady had just taken her seat in a car on a train bound for Philadelphia, when a somewhat stout man sitting just ahead of her lighted a cigar. She coughed and moved uneasily; but the hints had no effect, so she said tartly: "You probably are a foreigner, and do not know that there is a smoking-car attached to the train. Smoking is not permitted here." The man made no reply, but threw his cigar from the window. What was her astonishment when the conductor told her, a moment later, that she had entered the private car of General Grant. She withdrew in confusion, but the same fine courtesy which led him to give up his cigar was shown again as he spared her the mortification of even a questioning glance, still less of a look of amusement, although she watched his dumb, immovable figure with apprehension until she reached the door.

Julian Ralph, after telegraphing an account of President Arthur's fishing-trip to the Thousand Islands, returned to his hotel at two o'clock in the morning, to find all the doors locked. With two friends who had accompanied him, he battered at a side door to wake the servants, but what was his chagrin when the door was opened by the President of the United States!

"Why, that's all right," said Mr. Arthur when Mr. Ralph asked his pardon. "You wouldn't have got in till morning if I had not come. No one is up in the house but me. I could have sent my colored boy, but he had fallen asleep and I hated to wake him."

The Prince of Wales, the first gentleman in Europe, invited an eminent man to dine with him. When coffee was served, what was the consternation of the others to find that the guest drank from his saucer. An open titter of amusement went round the table. The Prince lifted his eyes; and, quickly noting the cause of the untimely amusement, gravely emptied his cup into his saucer and drank after the manner of his guest. Silent and abashed the other members of the princely household took the rebuke and did the same.

Queen Victoria sent for Carlyle, who was a Scotch peasant, offering him the title of nobleman, which he declined, feeling that he had always been a nobleman in his own right. He understood so little of the manners at court that, when presented to the Queen, after speaking to her a few minutes, being tired, he said, "Let us sit down, madam;" whereat the courtiers were ready to faint. But the Queen was great enough, and gave a gesture that seated all her puppets in a moment.

The Queen's courteous suspension of the rules of etiquette, and what it may have cost her, can be better understood from what an acquaintance of Carlyle said of him when he saw him for the first time. "His presence, in some unaccountable manner, rasped the nerves. I expected to meet a rare being, and I left him feeling as if I had drunk sour wine, or had had an attack of seasickness."

Some persons wield a sceptre before which others seem to bow in glad obedience. But whence do they obtain such magic power? What is the secret of that almost hypnotic influence over people which we would give anything to possess?

Courtesy is not always found in high places. Even royal courts furnish many examples of bad manners. At an entertainment given by the Prince and Princess

A FORTUNE IN GOOD MANNERS. 153

of Wales, to which, of course, only the very cream of the cream of society was admitted, there was such pushing and struggling to see the Princess, who was then but lately married, that, as she passed through the reception rooms, a bust of the Princess Royal was thrown from its pedestal and damaged, and the pedestal upset; and the ladies, in their eagerness to see the Princess, actually stood upon it.

When Catherine of Russia gave receptions to her nobles, she published the following rules of etiquette upon cards: "Gentlemen will not get drunk before the feast is ended. Noblemen are forbidden to strike their wives in company. Ladies of the court must not wash out their mouths in the drinking-glasses, or wipe their faces on the damask, or pick their teeth with forks." But to-day the nobles of Russia have no superiors in manners.

Etiquette originally meant the ticket or tag tied to a bag to indicate its contents. If a bag had this ticket it was not examined. From this the word passed to cards upon which were printed certain rules to be observed by guests. These rules were "the ticket" or the etiquette. To be "the ticket," or, as it was sometimes expressed, to act or talk by the card, became the thing with the better classes.

It was fortunate for Napoleon that he married Josephine before he was made commander-in-chief of the armies of Italy. Her fascinating manners and her wonderful powers of persuasion, were more influential than the loyalty of any dozen men in France in attaching to him the adherents who would promote his interests. Josephine was to the drawing-room and the salon what Napoleon was to the field — a preëminent leader. The secret of her personality that made her the Empress not only of the hearts of the Frenchmen, but also of the nations her husband conquered, has been beautifully told by herself. "There is only one occasion," she said to an intimate friend, "in which I would voluntarily use the words, '*I will!*'— namely, when I would say, 'I will that all around me be happy.'"

> "It was only a glad 'good-morning,'
> As she passed along the way,
> But it spread the morning's glory
> Over the livelong day."

A fine manner more than compensates for all the defects of nature. The most fascinating person is always the one of most winning manners, not the one of greatest physical beauty. The Greeks thought beauty was a proof of the peculiar favor of the gods, and considered that beauty only worth adorning and transmitting which was unmarred by outward manifestations of hard and haughty feeling. According to their ideal, beauty must be the expression of attractive qualities within — such as cheerfulness, benignity, contentment, charity, and love.

Mirabeau was one of the homeliest men in France. It was said he had "the face of a tiger pitted by smallpox," but the charm of his manner was almost irresistible.

Madame de Staël was anything but beautiful, but she possessed that indefinable something before which mere conventional beauty cowers, commonplace and ashamed. Her hold upon the minds of men was wonderful. They were the creatures of her will, and she shaped careers as if she were omnipotent. Even the Emperor Napoleon feared her influence over his people so much that he destroyed her writings and banished her from France.

Beauty of life and character, as in art, has no sharp angles. Its lines seem continuous, so gently does curve melt into curve. It is sharp angles that keep many souls from being beautiful that are almost so. Our good is less good, when it is abrupt, rude, ill timed, or ill placed. Many a man and woman might double their influence and success by a kindly courtesy and a fine manner.

Tradition tells us that before Apelles painted his wonderful Goddess of Beauty which enchanted all Greece, he traveled for years observing fair women, that he might embody in his matchless Venus a combination of the loveliest found in all. So the good-mannered study, observe, and adopt all that is finest and most worthy of imitation in every cultured person they meet.

A single grain of musk will scent a room for years without seeming to lose any part of its intrinsic value: so do we ever radiate an influence of manner appreciable to all about us and powerful for good or evil, even though we may not be conscious of its diffusion. Yet even the brute creation seems instinctively conscious of its quality, whether we be coarse or refined.

Throw a bone to a dog, said a shrewd observer, and he will run off with it in his mouth, but with no vibration in his tail. Call the dog to you, pat him on the head, let him take the bone from your hand, and his tail will wag with gratitude. The dog recognizes the good deed and the gracious manner of doing it. Those who throw their good deeds should not expect them to be caught with a thankful smile.

"Ask a person at Rome to show you the road," said Dr. Guthrie of Edinburgh, "and he will always give you a civil and polite answer; but ask any person a question for that purpose in this country [Scotland], and he will say, 'Follow your nose and you will find it.' But the blame is with the upper classes; and the reason why, in this country, the lower classes are not polite is because the upper classes are not polite. I remember how astonished I was the first time I was in Paris. I spent the first night with a banker, who took me to a pension, or, as we call it, a boarding-house. When we got there, a servant girl came to the door, and the banker took off his hat, and bowed to the servant girl, and called her mademoiselle, as if she were a lady. Now the reason why the lower classes there are so polite is because the upper classes are polite and civil to them."

A fine courtesy is a fortune in itself. The good-mannered can do without riches, for they have passports everywhere. All doors fly open to them, and they enter without money and without price. They can enjoy nearly everything without the trouble of buying or owning. They are as welcome in every household as the sunshine; and why not? for they carry light, sunshine, and joy everywhere. They disarm jealousy and envy, for they bear good will to everybody. Bees will not sting a man smeared with honey.

"A man's own good breeding," says Chesterfield, "is the best security against other people's ill manners. It carries along with it a dignity that is respected by the most petulant. Ill breeding invites and authorizes the familiarity of the most timid. No man ever said a pert thing to the Duke of Marlborough, or a civil one to Sir Robert Walpole."

The true gentleman cannot harbor those qualities which excite the antagonism of others, as revenge, hatred, malice, envy, or jealousy, for these poison the sources of spiritual life and shrivel the soul. Generosity of heart and a genial good will towards all are absolutely essential to him who would possess fine manners. Here is a man who is cross, crabbed, moody, sullen, silent, sulky, stingy, and mean with his family and servants. He refuses his wife a little money to buy a needed dress, and accuses her of extravagance that would ruin a millionaire. Suddenly the bell rings. Some neighbors call: what a change! The bear of a moment ago is as docile as a lamb. As by magic he becomes talkative, polite, generous. After the callers have gone, his little girl begs her father to keep on his "company manners" for a little while, but the sullen mood comes back and his courtesy vanishes as quickly as it came. He is the same disagreeable, contemptible, crabbed bear as before.

What friend of the great Dr. Johnson did not feel mortified and pained to see him eat like an Esquimaux, and to hear him call men "liars" because they did not agree with him. He was called the "Ursa Major" or Great Bear. Benjamin Rush said that when Goldsmith at a banquet in London asked a question about "the American Indians," Dr. Johnson exclaimed: "There is not an Indian in North America foolish enough to ask such a question." "Sir," replied Goldsmith, "there is not a savage in America rude enough to make such a speech to a gentleman."

Emerson well said: "Life is not so short but that there is always time enough for courtesy." But the touchstone of our manners is often found in the way we treat our servants and the members of our own family. Rothschild, Lawrence, Brooks, and many other millionaires treated their servants as politely as their customers.

Aristotle thus described a real gentleman more than two thousand years ago: "The magnanimous man will behave with moderation under both good fortune and bad. He will not allow himself to be exalted; he will not allow himself to be abased. He will neither be delighted with success, nor grieved with failure. He will neither choose danger, nor seek it. He is not given to talk about himself nor others. He does not care that himself should be praised, nor that other people should be blamed."

A gentleman is just a gentle man: no more, no less; a diamond polished that was first a diamond in the rough. A gentleman is gentle, modest, courteous, slow to take offence, and never giving it. He is slow to surmise evil, as he never thinks it. He subjects his appetites, refines his tastes, subdues his feelings, controls his speech, and deems every other as good as himself.

A gentleman, like porcelain-ware, must be painted before he is glazed. There can be no change after it is burned in, and all that is put on afterwards will wash off. He who has lost all, but retains his courage, cheerfulness, hope, virtue, and self-respect, is a true gentleman, and is rich still.

When Mary Queen of Scots ascended the scaffold, the jailer offered her his arm, which she accepted, saying, "I thank you, sir; this is the last trouble I shall ever give you."

"You replace Dr. Franklin, I hear," said the French Minister, Count de Vergennes, to Mr. Jefferson, who had been sent to Paris to relieve our most popular representative. "I succeed him; no man can replace him," was the felicitous reply of the man who became highly esteemed by the most polite court in Europe.

"You should not have returned their salute," said the master of ceremonies, when Clement XIV. bowed to the ambassadors who had bowed in congratulating him upon his election. "Oh, I beg your pardon," replied Clement. "I have not been pope long enough to forget good manners."

Cowper says: —

> "A modest, sensible, and well-bred man
> Would not insult me, and no other can."

"I never listen to calumnies," said Montesquieu, "because if they are untrue I run the risk of being deceived, and if they are true, of hating people not worth thinking about."

"I think," says Emerson. "Hans Andersen's story of the cobweb cloth woven so fine that it was invisible — woven for the king's garment — must mean manners, which do really clothe a princely nature."

No one can fully estimate how great a factor in life is the possession of good manners, or timely thoughtfulness with human sympathy behind it. They are the kindly fruit of a refined nature, and are the open sesame to the best of society. They vex or soothe, exalt or debase, barbarize or refine us by a constant, steady, uniform, invincible operation like that of the air we breathe. Even power itself has not half the might of gentleness, that subtle oil which lubricates our relations with each other, and enables the machinery of society to perform its functions without friction.

Thistles, and brambles, and briars, and Rocky Mountain sage-grass, and mullein stocks, and noxious weeds, grow without culture ; but the great red rose of the conservatory, its leaves packed on leaves in graceful groups that gladden the eye, its rare perfume breathing delicious fragrance upon the air, was born of a race of cultured ancestors, and has received careful culture throughout its brief but beautiful life.

"Have you not seen in the woods, in a late autumn morning," asks Emerson, "a poor fungus, or mushroom, —a plant without any solidity, nay, that seemed nothing but a soft mush or jelly,—by its constant, total, and inconceivably gentle pushing, manage to break its way up through the frosty ground, and actually to lift a hard crust on its head ? It is the symbol of the power of kindness."

"There is no policy like politeness," says Magoon ; "since *a good manner often succeeds where the best tongue has failed.*" The art of pleasing is the art of rising in the world.

The politest people in the world, it is said, are the Jews. In all ages they have been maltreated and reviled, and despoiled of their civil privileges and their social rights ; yet are they everywhere polite, affable, insinuating, and condescending. They indulge in few or no recriminations ; are faithful to old associations ; more considerate of the prejudices of others than others are of theirs ; not more worldly minded and money-loving than people generally are ; and, everything considered, they surpass all nations in courtesy, affability, and forbearance.

It was the Frenchmen at Fontenoy who politely bade the English to fire first, even when they were face to face before the battle.

In concluding the terms of peace at the close of the Franco-Prussian War, Bismarck conceded to the French the honor of firing the last shot. The German army discharged its final salute, and there was a momentary stillness in both armies. Then came the report of a single French gun, followed by the stroke of twelve on the clock tower at Versailles, and the desperate contest was over.

"Men, like bullets," says Richter, "go farthest when they are smoothest."

Napoleon was much displeased on hearing that Josephine had permitted General Lorges, a young and handsome man, to sit beside her on the sofa. Josephine explained that, instead of its being General Lorges, it was one of the aged generals of his army, entirely unused to the customs of courts. Josephine was unwilling to wound the feelings of the honest old soldier, and so allowed him to retain his seat. Napoleon commended her highly for her courtesy.

President Jefferson was one day riding with his grandson, when they met a slave, who took off his hat and bowed. The President returned the salutation by raising his hat, but the grandson ignored the civility of the negro. "Thomas," said the grandfather, "do you permit a slave to be more of a gentleman than yourself?"

"Lincoln was the first great man I talked with freely in the United States," said Fred Douglass, "who in no single instance reminded me of the difference between himself and me, of the difference in color."

"Eat at your own table," says Confucius, "as you would eat at the table of the king." If parents were not careless about the manners of their children at home, they would seldom be shocked at their behavior abroad.

When Washington visited Milford, N. H., in 1790, he was walking about the town with several officers, when he was saluted by a colored soldier who had fought under him and lost a limb in the service. Washington shook hands with the soldier and gave him a silver dollar. An attendant objected to the President of the United States showing civilities to so humble a person, but Washington rebuked him and asked if he should permit this colored man to excel him in politeness.

Andrew Jackson was as courteous, respectful, and kind to his slaves as to his white neighbors. He was a man without fear and without secrets. He never locked a door or concealed a paper.

James Russell Lowell was as courteous to a beggar as to a lord, and was once observed holding a long conversation in Italian with an organ-grinder whom he was questioning about scenes in Italy that they were each familiar with.

In hastily turning the corner of a crooked street in London, a young lady ran with great force against a ragged beggar-boy and almost knocked him down. Stopping as soon as she could, she turned around and said very kindly: "I beg your pardon, my little fellow; I am very sorry that I ran against you." The astonished boy looked at her a moment, and then, taking off about three quarters of a cap, made a low bow and said, while a broad, pleasant smile overspread his face: "You have my parding, miss, and welcome, — and welcome; and the next time you run ag'in' me, you can knock me clean down and I won't say a word." After the lady had passed on, he said to a companion: "I say, Jim, it's the first time I ever had anybody ask my parding, and it kind o' took me off my feet."

"Respect the burden, madame, respect the burden," said Napoleon, as he courteously stepped aside at St.

Helena to make way for a laborer bending under a heavy load, while his companion seemed inclined to keep the narrow path.

A Washington politician went to visit Daniel Webster at Marshfield, Mass., and, in taking a short cut to the house, came to a stream which he could not cross. Calling to a rough-looking farmer near by, he offered a quarter to be carried to the other side. The farmer took the politician on his broad shoulders and landed him safely, but would not take the quarter. The old rustic presented himself at the house a few minutes later, and was introduced as Mr. Webster, to the great surprise and chagrin of the visitor.

President Quincy was once riding to Cambridge in a crowded omnibus, when a colored woman entered. The president of Harvard University rose and gave her his seat, although at that time negroes were considered "only property." The author heard Fred Douglass say that he was ejected from a street car in Boston on account of his color.

Garrison was as polite to the furious mob that tore his clothes from his back and dragged him through the streets as he could have been to a king. He was one of the serenest souls that ever lived. Christ was courteous, even to his persecutors, and in terrible agony on the cross he cried: "Father, forgive them, for they know not what they do." The speech of Paul before Agrippa is a model of dignified courtesy, as well as of persuasive eloquence. The finest type of the coming man will be a Christian gentleman.

Good manners often prove a fortune to a young man. Mr. Butler, a merchant in Providence, R. I., had once closed his store and was on his way home when he met a little girl who wanted a spool of thread. He went back, opened the store, and got the thread. This little incident was talked of all about the city and brought him hundreds of customers. He became very wealthy, largely because of his courtesy.

A FORTUNE IN GOOD MANNERS.

Ross Winans of Baltimore owed his great success and fortune largely to his courtesy to two foreign strangers. Although his was but a fourth-rate factory, his great politeness in explaining the minutest details to his visitors was in such marked contrast with the limited attention they had received in large establishments that it won their esteem. The strangers were Russians sent by their Czar, who soon invited Mr. Winans to establish locomotive works in Russia. He did so, and soon his profits resulting from his politeness were more than $100,000 a year. Courtesy pays.

A poor curate saw a crowd of rough boys and men laughing and making fun of two aged spinsters dressed in antiquated costume. The ladies were embarrassed and did not dare enter the church. The curate pushed through the crowd, conducted them up the central aisle, and gave them choice seats, amid the titter of the congregation. These old ladies at their death left the gentle curate a large fortune, although strangers to him. Not long since a lady met the late President Humphrey of Amherst College, and she was so much pleased with his great politeness that she gave a generous donation to the college.

"Why did our friend never succeed in business?" asked a man returning to New York after years of absence; "he had sufficient capital, a thorough knowledge of his business, and exceptional shrewdness and sagacity." "He was sour and morose," was the reply; "he always suspected his employees of cheating him, and was discourteous to his customers. Hence, no man ever put good will or energy into work done for him, and his patrons went to shops where they were sure of civility!"

Some men almost work their hands off, and deny themselves many of the common comforts of life in their earnest efforts to succeed, and yet render success impossible by their cross-grained ungentlemanliness. They repel patronage, and business goes to others who are really less deserving but more companionable.

Bad manners often neutralize even honesty, industry, and the greatest energy; while agreeable manners win in spite of other defects. Take two men, possessing equal advantages in every other respect; but let one be gentlemanly, kind, obliging, and conciliating, the other disobliging, rude, harsh, and insolent, and the one will become rich while the other will starve.

A fine illustration of the business value of good manners is found in the Bon Marché, an enormous establishment in Paris where thousands of clerks are employed, and where almost everything is kept for sale. The two distinguishing characteristics of the house are one low price to all, and extreme courtesy. Mere politeness is not enough; the employees must try in every possible way to please and to make customers feel at home. Something more must be done than is done in other stores, so that every visitor will remember the Bon Marché with pleasure. By this course the business has been developed until it is said to be the largest of the kind in the world. No other advertising is so efficacious. A. T. Stewart imitated this store in his great retail house in New York.

"Thank you, my dear; please call again," spoken to a little beggar-girl, who bought a pennyworth of snuff, proved a profitable advertisement and made Lundy Foote a millionaire.

Many persons of real refinement are thought to be stiff, proud, reserved, and haughty who are not, but who are merely diffident and shy.

It is a curious fact that diffidence often betrays us into discourtesies which our hearts abhor, and which cause us intense mortification and embarrassment. Excessive shyness must be overcome as an obstacle to perfect manners. It is peculiar to the Anglo-Saxon and the Teutonic races, and has frequently been a barrier to the highest culture. It is a disease of the finest organizations and the highest types of humanity. It never attacks the coarse and vulgar. Sir Isaac Newton was the shyest man of his age. He did not acknowledge his great discovery for years for fear of attracting attention to himself. He would not allow his name to be used in connection with his theory of the moon's motion, for fear it would increase the acquaintances he would have to meet. George Washington was awkward and shy and had the air of a countryman. Archbishop Whately was so shy that he would escape notice whenever it was possible. At last he determined to give up trying to cure his shyness; "for why," he asked, "should I endure this torture all my life?" when, to his surprise, it almost entirely disappeared. Elihu Burritt was so shy that he would hide in the cellar when his parents had company.

Practice on the stage or lecture platform does not always eradicate shyness. David Garrick, the great actor, was once summoned to testify in court; and, though he had acted for thirty years with marked self-possession, he was so confused and embarrassed that the judge dismissed him. John B. Gough said that he could not rid himself of his early diffidence and shrinking from public notice. He said that he never went on the platform without fear and trembling, and would often be covered with cold perspiration.

There are many worthy people who are brave on the street, who would walk up to a cannon's mouth in battle, but who are cowards in the drawing-room, and dare not express an opinion in the social circle.

They feel conscious of a subtle tyranny in society's code, which locks their lips and ties their tongues. Addison was one of the purest writers of English and a perfect master of the pen, but he could scarcely utter a dozen words in conversation without embarrassment. Shakespeare was very shy. He retired from London at forty, and did not try to publish or preserve one of his plays. He took second or third rate parts on account of his diffidence. Byron would sometimes jump out of a window when he saw visitors coming, to avoid meeting them. Hawthorne wrote in his note-book: "When in England I was called upon at a public dinner to make a speech. I rapped on my head and it returned only a hollow sound." He was tortured through life by his shyness, and would often take a boat on the Concord River to escape visitors. He would sometimes turn his back to avoid recognition. "God may forgive sins," said he, "but awkwardness has no forgiveness in heaven or earth!"

Generally shyness comes from a person thinking too much about himself — which in itself is a breach of good breeding — and wondering what other people think about him.

"I was once very shy," said Sydney Smith, "but it was not long before I made two very useful discoveries: first, that all mankind were not solely employed in observing me; and next, that shamming was of no use; that the world was very clear-sighted, and soon estimated a man at his true value. This cured me."

What a misfortune it is to go through life apparently encased in ice, yet all the while full of kindly, cordial feeling for one's fellow men? It is a disease; for it is caused by fear, and fear is a disease. Shy people are always distrustful of their powers and look upon their lack of confidence as a weakness or lack of ability, when it may indicate quite the reverse. By teaching children early the arts of social life, such as boxing, horseback riding, dancing, elocution, and similar accomplishments, we may do much to overcome the sense of shyness. Shy people should dress well. Good clothes give ease of manner, and unlock the tongue. The consciousness of being well dressed gives a grace and ease of manner that even religion will not bestow, while inferiority of garb often induces restraint. As peculiarities in apparel are sure to attract attention, it is well to avoid bright colors and fashionable extremes, and wear plain, well-fitted garments of as good material as the purse will afford.

Beauty in dress is a good thing, rail at it who may. But it is a lower beauty, for which a higher beauty should not be sacrificed. They love dress too much who give it their first thought, their best time, or all their money; who for it neglect the culture of the mind or heart, or the claims of others on their service; who care more for dress than for their character; who are troubled more by an unfashionable garment than by a neglected duty.

When Ezekiel Whitman, a prominent lawyer and graduate of Harvard, was elected to the Massachusetts legislature, he came to Boston from his farm in countryman's dress, and went to an hotel in Boston. He went into the parlor and sat down, when he overheard a remark between some ladies and gentlemen. "Ah, here comes a real homespun countryman. Here's fun." They asked him all sorts of queer questions, tending to throw ridicule upon him, when he arose and said, "Ladies and gentlemen, permit me to wish you health and happiness, and may you grow better and wiser in advancing years, bearing in mind that outward appearances are deceitful. You mistook me, from my dress, for a country booby; while I, from the same superficial cause, thought you were ladies and gentlemen. The mistake has been mutual." Just then Governor Caleb Strong entered and called to Mr. Whitman, who, turning to the dumfounded company, said: "I wish you a very good evening." Dress, like wealth, is a power, but we must not be its slave.

"An emperor in his nightcap," says Goldsmith, "would not meet with half the respect of an emperor with a crown."

"In civilized society," says Johnson, "external advantages make us more respected. A man with a good coat upon his back meets with a better reception than he who has a bad one."

One cannot but feel that God is a lover of dress. He has put robes of beauty and glory upon all his works. Every flower is dressed in richness; every field blushes beneath a mantle of beauty; every star is veiled in brightness; every bird is clothed in the habiliments of the most exquisite taste.

Yet some fanatics will tell you that beauty is a sin, and that the loveliness and gorgeousness of nature are a consequence of the fall of man in Eden.

Some people look upon polished manners as a kind of affectation. They claim admiration for plain, solid, square, rugged characters. As well say that they like square, plain, unornamented houses made from square blocks of stone. St. Peter's is none the less strong and solid because of its elegant columns and the magnificent sweep of its arches, its carved and fretted marbles of matchless hues. Why do not such people wear their diamonds in the rough? Why not take them as made by nature? They have the same intrinsic value, but we know that all men want their diamonds polished.

Our manners like our characters are always under inspection. Every time we go into society we must step on the scales of each person's opinion, and the loss or gain from our last weight is carefully noted. Each asks, "Is this person going up or down? Through how many grades has he passed?" For example, young Brown enters a drawing-room. All present weigh him in their judgment and silently say, "This young man is gaining; he is more careful, thoughtful, polite, considerate, straightforward, truthful, industrious." Beside him stands young Jones. It is evident that he is losing ground rapidly. He is careless, indifferent, rough, profane, obscene, does not look you in the eye, is mean, small, stingy, snaps at the servants, yet is over-polite to strangers. And so we go through life, tagged with these invisible labels by all who know us. I sometimes think it would be a great advantage if one could read these ratings of his associates. We cannot long deceive the world, for that other self, who ever stands in the shadow of ourselves holding the scales of justice, that telltale in the soul, rushes to the eye or into the manner and betrays us.

But manners, while they are the garb of the gentleman, do not constitute or finally determine his character. Mere politeness can never be a substitute for moral excellence, any more than the bark can take the place of the heart of the oak. It may well indicate the kind of wood below, but not always whether it be sound or decayed. Etiquette is but a substitute for good manners and is often but their mere counterfeit.

Sincerity is the highest quality of good manners.

The following recipe is recommended to those who wish to acquire genuine good manners : —

Of Unselfishness, three drachms ;
Of the tincture of Good Cheer, one ounce ;
Of Essence of Heart's-Ease, three drachms ;
Of the Extract of the Rose of Sharon, four ounces ;
Of the Oil of Charity, three drachms, and no scruples ;
Of the Infusion of Common Sense and Tact, one ounce ;
Of the Spirit of Love, two ounces.

The Mixture to be taken whenever there is the slightest symptom of selfishness, exclusiveness, meanness, or I-am-better-than-you-ness.

Pattern after Him who gave the Golden Rule, and who was the first true gentleman that ever breathed.

CHAPTER XI.

THE TRIUMPHS OF ENTHUSIASM.

The labor we delight in physics pain. — SHAKESPEARE.

The only conclusive evidence of a man's sincerity is that he gives himself for a principle. Words, money, all things else are comparatively easy to give away; but when a man makes a gift of his daily life and practice, it is plain that the truth, whatever it may be, has taken possession of him. — LOWELL.

Let us beware of losing our enthusiasm. Let us ever glory in something, and strive to retain our admiration for all that would ennoble, and our interest in all that would enrich and beautify our life.
PHILLIPS BROOKS.

> "It can so inform
> The mind that is within them, so impress
> With quietness and beauty, and so feed
> With lofty thoughts, that neither evil tongues,
> Rash judgments, nor the sneers of selfish men,
> Nor greetings where no kindness is, nor all
> The dreary intercourse of daily life,
> Can e'er prevail against them, or destroy
> Their cheerful faith that all which they behold
> Is full of blessings."

A region of spiritual ideas and spiritual persons where youth is perpetual, where ecstasy is no transient mood, but a permanent condition, and where dwell the awful forces which radiate immortal life into the will. — E. P. WHIPPLE.

WHAT a power there is in an enthusiastic adherence to an ideal! What are hardships, contumely, slander, ridicule, persecution, toil, sickness, the feebleness of age, to a soul throbbing with an overmastering purpose?

In the Galerie des Beaux Arts in Paris is a beautiful statue conceived by a sculptor who was so poor that he lived and worked in a small garret. When his clay model was nearly done, a heavy frost fell upon the city. He knew that if the water in the interstices of the clay should freeze, the beautiful lines would be distorted. So

HUMPHRY DAVY

"Every great and commanding movement in the annals of the world is the triumph of enthusiasm. Nothing great was ever achieved without it."

he wrapped his bedclothes around the clay image. In the morning he was found dead, but his idea was saved, and other hands gave it enduring form in marble.

"I do not know how it is with others when speaking on an important question," said Henry Clay; "but on such occasions I seem to be unconscious of the external world. Wholly engrossed by the subject before me, I lose all sense of personal identity, of time, or of surrounding objects."

"A bank never becomes very successful," says a noted financier, "until it gets a president who takes it to bed with him." "Men are nothing," exclaimed Montaigne, "until they are excited." Like the new and added power of the young lover to paint in hues of paradise the ugliest object, enthusiasm gives the otherwise dry and uninteresting subject or occupation a new meaning. As the young lover has finer sense and more acute vision and sees in the object of his affections a hundred virtues and charms invisible to all other eyes, so a man permeated with enthusiasm has his power of perception heightened and his vision magnified until he sees beauty and charms others cannot discern which compensate for drudgery, privations, hardships, and even persecution. Dickens says he was haunted, possessed, spirit-driven by the plots and characters in his stories which would not let him sleep or rest until he had committed them to paper. On one sketch he shut himself up for a month, and when he came out he looked haggard as a murderer. His characters haunted him day and night.

John Jacob Astor would hang a fine fur in his counting-room as other men hang pictures; he would stroke it with enthusiasm, extol its beauty, and add that it was worth five hundred dollars in Canton.

"Herr Capellmeister, I should like to compose something; how shall I begin?" asked a youth of twelve, who had played with great skill on the piano. "Pooh, pooh," replied Mozart, "you must wait." "But you began when you were younger than I am," said the boy. "Yes, so I did," said the great composer, "but I never asked anything about it. When one has the spirit of a composer, he writes because he can't help it."

Gladstone says that what is really wanted is to light up the spirit that is within a boy. In some sense and in some degree, in some effectual degree, there is in every boy the material of good work in the world; in every boy, not only in those who are brilliant, not only in those who are quick, but in those who are stolid, and even in those who are dull, or who seem to be dull. If they have only the good will, the dullness will day by day clear away, under the influence of the good will.

Gerster, an unknown Hungarian, made fame and fortune sure the first night she appeared in opera. Her enthusiasm almost hypnotized her auditors. In less than a week she had become popular and independent. Her soul was smitten with a passion for growth, and all the powers of heart and mind were devoted to self-improvement.

The artist who played Meg Merrilies in "Guy Mannering" in the usual formal way was ill, and the "utility" woman, Charlotte Cushman, was asked to take the part. The chance for a hit flashed through her mind; she rushed upon the stage, and, to the astonishment of audience and actors alike, assumed the rôle since so famous.

"I have been so busy for twenty years trying to save the souls of other people," said Livingstone. "that I had forgotten that I have one of my own until a savage auditor asked me if I felt the influence of the religion I was advocating."

All great works of art have been produced when the artist was intoxicated with the passion for beauty and form which would not let him rest until his thought was expressed in marble or on canvas.

"Well, I've worked hard enough for it," said Malibran when a critic expressed his admiration of her D in alt, reached by running up three octaves from low D; "I've been chasing it for a month. I pursued it everywhere. — when I was dressing, when I was doing my hair; and at last I found it on the toe of a shoe that I was putting on."

"Capital composition," said Joshua Reynolds, examining a picture he wished to praise; "correct drawing, color, tone, lights, and shadows excellent; but it wants — that!" added the great artist, snapping his fingers.

"Why," says Bulwer, "nothing is so contagious as enthusiasm. It is the real allegory of the fable of Orpheus; it moves stones and charms brutes. It is the genius of sincerity, and truth accomplishes no victories without it."

"Every great and commanding moment in the annals of the world," says Emerson, "is the triumph of some enthusiasm. The victories of the Arabs after Mahomet, who, in a few years, from a small and mean beginning, established a larger empire than that of Rome, is an example. They did they knew not what. The naked Derar, horsed on an idea, was found an overmatch for a troop of cavalry. The women fought like men and conquered the Roman men. They were miserably equipped, miserably fed. They were temperance troops. There was neither brandy nor flesh needed to feed them. They conquered Asia and Africa and Spain on barley. The Caliph Omar's walking-stick struck more terror into those who saw it than another man's sword."

It was enthusiasm that enabled Napoleon to make a campaign in two weeks that would have taken another a year to accomplish. "These Frenchmen are not men, they fly," said the Austrians in consternation. In fifteen days Napoleon, in his first Italian campaign, had gained six victories, taken twenty-one standards, fifty-five pieces of cannon, had captured fifteen thousand prisoners, and had conquered Piedmont. After this avalanche a discomfited Austrian general said: "This young commander knows nothing whatever about the art of war. He is a perfect ignoramus. There is no doing anything with him." But his soldiers followed their "Little Corporal" with an enthusiasm which knew no defeat or disaster.

"There are important cases," says A. H. K. Boyd, "in which the difference between half a heart and a whole heart makes just the difference between signal defeat and a splendid victory."

"Should I die this minute," said Nelson at an important crisis, "want of frigates would be found written on my heart."

The simple, innocent Maid of Orleans with her sacred sword, her consecrated banner, and her belief in her great mission, sent a thrill of enthusiasm through the whole French army such as neither king nor statesmen could produce. Her zeal carried everything before it. Oh! what a great work each one could perform in this world if he only knew his power! But, like a bitted horse, man does not realize his strength until he has once run away with himself.

Disraeli considered enthusiasm an incomparable faculty, a divine gift, which enables a statesman to command the world.

"Underneath is laid the builder of this church and city, Christopher Wren, who lived more than ninety years, not for himself, but for the public good. Reader, if you seek his monument, look around!" Turn where you will in London, you find noble monuments of the genius of a man who never received instruction from an architect. He built fifty-five churches in the city and thirty-six halls. "I would give my skin for the architect's design of the Louvre," said he, when in Paris to get ideas for the restoration of St. Paul's Cathedral in London. His rare skill is shown in the palaces of Hampton Court and Kensington, in Temple Bar, Drury Lane

Theatre, the Royal Exchange, and the great Monument. He changed Greenwich palace into a sailor's retreat, and built churches and colleges at Oxford. He also planned for the rebuilding of London, after the Great Fire, but those in authority would not adopt his splendid plan. He worked thirty-five years upon his masterpiece, St. Paul's Cathedral. Although he lived so long, and was so healthy in later life, he was so delicate as a child that he was a constant source of anxiety to his parents. His great enthusiasm seemed to give strength to his body.

"Oh, no!" exclaimed General Marion, when a visiting British officer announced his intention to return; "it is now about our time of dining, and I hope, sir, you will give us the pleasure of your company at dinner." The stranger looked about him in astonishment, for he could see no sign of pot or pan or any other cooking utensil; but this was not the first surprise he had experienced that forenoon. He had been led into camp blindfolded, bearing a flag of truce, and expecting to see a general of commanding presence, and an army of giant men, for the band of the famous "Swamp-Fox" was then a terror to every red-coat in the Carolinas. When the bandage was removed, he was introduced to a swarthy, smoke-dried little man, scantily clad in threadbare homespun; and, in place of tall ranks of gayly dressed soldiers, he beheld a handful of sunburned, yellow-legged militiamen.

"Well, Tom," said Marion to one of his men, after the visitor had accepted his invitation, "give us our dinner;" and with a stick the soldier rolled out a heap of sweet potatoes that had been snugly roasting under the embers. "I fear, sir," continued the general, "our dinner will not prove so palatable to you as I could wish, but it is the best we have."

The officer began to eat one of the potatoes, out of politeness, but soon he laughed heartily at the strange meal. "I beg pardon, general," said he, "but one cannot always command himself, you know." "I suppose it is not equal to your style of living," suggested Marion. "No, indeed," quoth the other, "and I imagine this is one of your accidental Lent dinners. In general, no doubt, you live a great deal better." "Rather worse," answered the general, "for often we don't get even enough of this." "Heavens!" rejoined the officer, "but probably, stinted in provisions, you draw noble pay?" "Not a cent, sir," said Marion, "not a cent." "Heavens and earth!" exclaimed the Briton, "then you must be in a bad box. I don't see, general, how you can stand it." "Why, sir," returned Marion, "these things depend upon feeling. The heart is all, and when that is much interested, a man can do anything. Many a youth would think it hard to make himself a slave for fourteen years. But let him be head and ears over in love, and with such a beauteous sweetheart as Rachel, and he will think no more of fourteen years' servitude than young Jacob did. This is exactly my case. I am in love, and my sweetheart is Liberty, and I am happy indeed. I would rather fight for such blessings for my country and feed on roots, than keep aloof, though wallowing in all the luxuries of Solomon. For now, sir, I walk the soil that gave me birth, and exult in the thought that I am not unworthy of it. I look upon these venerable trees around me and feel that I do not dishonor them. The children of future generations may never hear my name, but it gladdens my heart to think that I am now contending for their freedom and all its countless blessings."

When the British officer returned, his colonel asked: "Why do you look so serious?" "I have cause, sir," said he, "to look serious." "What, has General Marion refused to treat?" "No, sir," said the officer. "Well, then, has old Washington defeated Sir Henry Clinton, and broken up our army?" "No, sir, not that, but worse." "Ah! what can be worse?" asked the colonel. "Why, sir," replied the officer, "I have seen an American general and his officers without pay, and almost without clothes, living on roots and drinking water, and all for liberty! What chance have we against such men?" And at the first opportunity the young officer threw up his commission and retired from the service, for he believed that the enthusiasm which can conquer such hardships is invincible.

Indifference never leads armies that conquer, never models statues that live, nor breathes sublime music, nor harnesses the forces of nature, nor rears impressive architecture, nor moves the soul with poetry, nor the world with heroic philanthropies. Enthusiasm, as Charles Bell says of the hand, wrought the statue of Memnon and hung the brazen gates of Thebes. It fixed the mariner's trembling needle upon its axis, and first heaved the tremendous bar of the printing-press. It opened the tubes for Galileo, until world after world swept before his vision, and it reefed the high topsail that rustled over Columbus in the morning breezes of the Bahamas. It has held the sword with which freedom has fought her battles, and poised the axe of the dauntless woodman as he opened the paths of civilization, and turned the mystic leaves upon which Milton and Shakespeare inscribed their burning thoughts.

Horace Greeley said that the best product of labor is the highminded workman with an enthusiasm for his work.

"The best method is obtained by earnestness," said Salvini. "If you can impress people with the conviction that you feel what you say, they will pardon many shortcomings. And above all, study, study, study! All the genius in the world will not help you along with any art, unless you become a hard student. It has taken me years to master a single part."

There is a "go," a zeal, a furore, almost a fanaticism for one's ideals or calling, that is peculiar to our American temperament and life. You do not find this in tropical countries. It did not exist fifty years ago. It could not be found then even on the London Exchange. But the influence of the United States and of Australia, where, if a person is to succeed, he must be on the jump with all the ardor of his being, has finally extended until what used to be the peculiar strength of a few great minds has now become characteristic of the leading nations. Enthusiasm is the being awake; it is the tingling of every fibre of one's being to do the work that one's heart desires. Enthusiasm made Victor Hugo lock up his clothes while writing "Notre Dame," that he might not leave the work until it was finished. The great actor Garrick well illustrated it when asked by an unsuccessful preacher the secret of his power over audiences: "You speak of eternal verities and what you know to be true, as if you hardly believed what you were saying yourself, whereas I utter what I know to be unreal and untrue, as if I did believe it in my very soul."

Gladstone's intense earnestness and enthusiasm have been a perpetual inspiration to his associates.

"When he comes into a room, every man feels as if he had taken a tonic and had a new lease of life," said a man when asked the reason for his selection, after he, with two companions, had written upon a slip of paper the name of the most agreeable companion he had ever met. "He is an eager, vivid fellow, full of joy, bubbling over with spirits. His sympathies are quick as an electric flash."

"He throws himself into the occasion, whatever it may be, with his whole heart," said the second, in praise of the man of his choice.

"He makes the best of everything," said the third, speaking of his own most cherished acquaintance.

The three were traveling correspondents of great English journals, who had visited every quarter of the world and talked with all kinds of men. The papers were examined, and all were found to contain the name of a prominent lawyer in Melbourne, Australia.

"If it were not for respect for human opinions," said Madame de Staël to M. Mole, "I would not open my window to see the Bay of Naples for the first time, while I would go five hundred leagues to talk with a man of genius whom I had not seen."

Enthusiasm is that secret and harmonious spirit which hovers over the production of genius, throwing the reader of a book, or the spectator of a statue, into the very ideal presence whence these works have originated. A great work always leaves us in a state of lofty contemplation if we are in sympathy with it.

"One moonlight evening in winter," writes the biographer of Beethoven, "we were walking through a narrow street of Bonn. 'Hush!' exclaimed the great composer, suddenly pausing before a little, mean dwelling, 'what sound is that? It is from my Sonata in F. Hark! how well it is played!'

"In the midst of the finale there was a break, and a sobbing voice cried: 'I cannot play any more. It is so beautiful; it is utterly beyond my power to do it justice. Oh, what would I not give to go to the concert at Cologne!' 'Ah! my sister,' said a second voice; 'why create regrets when there is no remedy? We can scarcely pay our rent.' 'You are right,' said the first speaker, 'and yet I wish for once in my life to hear some really good music. But it is of no use.'

"'Let us go in,' said Beethoven. 'Go in!' I remonstrated; 'what should we go in for?' 'I will play to her,' replied my companion in an excited tone; 'here is feeling, — genius, — understanding! I will play to her, and she will understand it. Pardon me,' he continued, as he opened the door and saw a young man sitting by a table, mending shoes, and a young girl leaning sorrowfully upon an old-fashioned piano; 'I heard music and was tempted to enter. I am a musician. I — I also overheard something of what you said. You wish to hear — that is, you would like — that is — shall I play for you?'

"'Thank you,' said the shoemaker, 'but our piano is so wretched, and we have no music.'

"'No music!' exclaimed the composer; 'how, then, does the young lady — I — I entreat your pardon,' he added, stammering as he saw that the girl was blind; 'I had not perceived before. Then you play by ear? But where do you hear the music, since you frequent no concerts?'

"'We lived at Bruhl for two years; and, while there, I used to hear a lady practicing near us. During the summer evenings her windows were generally open, and I walked to and fro outside to listen to her.'

"Beethoven seated himself at the piano. Never, during all the years I knew him, did I hear him play better than to that blind girl and her brother. Even the old instrument seemed inspired. The young man and woman sat as if entranced by the magical, sweet sounds that flowed out upon the air in rhythmical swell and cadence, until, suddenly, the flame of the single candle wavered, sank, flickered, and went out. The shutters were thrown open, admitting a flood of brilliant moonlight, but the player paused, as if lost in thought.

"'Wonderful man!' said the shoemaker in a low tone; 'who and what are you?'

"'Listen!' replied the master, and he played the opening bars of the Sonata in F. 'Then you are Beethoven!' burst from the young people in delighted recognition. 'Oh, play to us once more,' they added, as he rose to go, — 'only once more!'

"'I will improvise a sonata to the moonlight,' said he, gazing thoughtfully upon the liquid stars shining so softly out of the depths of a cloudless winter sky. Then he played a sad and infinitely lovely movement, which crept gently over the instrument, like the calm flow of moonlight over the earth. This was followed by a wild, elfin passage in triple time — a sort of grotesque interlude, like the dance of fairies upon the lawn. Then came a swift agitated ending — a breathless, hurrying, trembling movement, descriptive of flight, and uncertainty, and vague impulsive terror, which carried us away on its rustling wings, and left us all in emotion and wonder. 'Farewell to you,' he said, as he rose and turned toward the door. 'You will come again?' asked host and hostess in a breath. 'Yes, yes,' said Beethoven hurriedly, 'I will come again, and give the young lady some lessons. Farewell!' Then to me he added: 'Let us make haste back, that I may write out that sonata while I can yet remember it.' We did return in haste, and not until long past the dawn of day did he rise from his table with the full score of the Moonlight Sonata in his hand."

So absorbed was Archimedes in a problem which he had traced upon the sand that he did not know the Roman army had captured Syracuse. To the Roman soldier who rushed towards him with drawn sword, not knowing him, he said, glancing at his figures on the sand: "Hold your hand a little. Only spare my life until I have solved this problem." But the legionary cut down the greatest man of the age without a moment's warning.

Michael Angelo studied anatomy twelve years, nearly ruining his health, but this course determined his style, his practice, and his glory. He made every tool he used in sculpture, such as files, chisels, and pincers. In painting he prepared all his own colors, and would not let servants or students even mix them.

Raphael's enthusiasm inspired every artist in Italy, and his modest, charming manners disarmed envy and jealousy. He has been called the only distinguished man who lived and died without an enemy or detractor.

Again and again poor Bunyan might have had his liberty; but not the separation from his poor blind daughter Mary, which he said was like pulling the flesh from his bones; not the need of a poor family dependent upon him; not the love of liberty nor the spur of ambition could induce him to forego his plain preaching in public places. He had so forgotten his early education that his wife had to teach him again to read and write. It was the enthusiasm of conviction which enabled this poor, ignorant, despised Bedford tinker to write his immortal allegory with such fascination that a whole world has read it.

Only thoughts that breathe in words that burn can kindle the spark slumbering in the heart of another.

Rare consecration to a great enterprise is found in the work of the late Francis Parkman. While a student at Harvard, he determined to write the history of the French and English in North America. With a steadiness and devotion seldom equaled he gave his life, his fortune, his all to this one great object. Although he had ruined his health while among the Dakota Indians, collecting material for his history, and could not use his eyes more than five minutes at a time for fifty years, he did not swerve a hair's breadth from the high purpose formed in his youth, until he gave to the world the best history upon this subject ever written.

After Lincoln had walked six miles to borrow a grammar, he returned home and burned one shaving after another while he studied the precious prize.

Gilbert Becket, an English Crusader, was taken prisoner, and became a slave in the palace of a Saracen prince, where he not only gained the confidence of his master, but also the love of his master's fair daughter. By and by he escaped and returned to England, but the devoted girl determined to follow him. She knew but two words of the English language — *London* and *Gilbert*; but by repeating the first she obtained passage in a vessel to the great metropolis, and then she went from street to street pronouncing the other — "Gilbert." At last she came to the street on which Gilbert lived in prosperity. The unusual crowd drew the family to the window, when Gilbert himself saw and recognized her, and took to his arms and home his far-come princess with her solitary fond word.

The most irresistible charm of youth is its bubbling enthusiasm. Youth sees no darkness ahead, — no defile that has no outlet, — it forgets that there is such a thing as failure in the world, and believes that mankind has been waiting all these centuries for him to come and be the liberator of truth and energy and beauty.

Of what use was it to forbid the boy Händel to touch a musical instrument, or to forbid him going to school, lest he learn the gamut? He stole midnight interviews with a dumb spinet in a secret attic. The boy Bach copied whole books of studies by moonlight, for want of a candle churlishly denied. Nor was he disheartened when these copies were taken from him. The boy painter West begins in a garret, and plunders the family cat for bristles to make his brushes.

It is the enthusiasm of youth which cuts the Gordian knot age cannot untie. "People smile at the enthusiasm of youth," says Charles Kingsley; "that enthusiasm which they themselves secretly look back to with a sigh, perhaps unconscious that it is partly their own fault that they ever lost it."

How much the world owes to the enthusiasm of Dante!

Elizabeth Barrett Browning wrote prose and verse at ten and published a volume of poems at seventeen.

Tennyson wrote his first volume at eighteen, and at nineteen gained a medal at Cambridge.

"The most beautiful works of all art were done in youth," says Ruskin. "Almost everything that is great has been done by youth," wrote Disraeli. "The world's interests are, under God, in the hands of the young," says Dr. Trumbull.

It was the youth Hercules that performed the Twelve Labors. Enthusiastic youth faces the sun, its shadows all behind it. The heart rules youth; the head, manhood. Alexander was a mere youth when he rolled back the Asiatic hordes that threatened to overwhelm European civilization almost at its birth. Napoleon had conquered Italy at twenty-five. Henry Kirke White died at twenty-one, but what a record for a youth he left. Byron and Raphael died at thirty-seven, an age which has been fatal to many a genius, and Poe lived but a few months longer. Romulus founded Rome at twenty. Pitt and Bolingbroke were ministers almost before they were men. Gladstone was in Parliament in early manhood. Newton made some of his greatest discoveries before he was twenty-five. Keats died at twenty-five, Shelley at twenty-nine. Luther was a triumphant reformer at twenty-five. Ignatius Loyola made his pilgrimage at thirty. It is said that no English poet ever equaled Chatterton at twenty-one. Melancthon gained the Greek chair at Wittemburg at twenty-one. Whitefield and Wesley began their great revival as students at Oxford, and the former had made his influence felt throughout England before he was twenty-four. Victor Hugo wrote a tragedy at fifteen, and had taken three prizes at the Academy and gained the title of Master before he was twenty.

Many of the world's greatest geniuses never saw forty years. Never before has the young man, who is driven by his enthusiasm, had such an opportunity as he has to-day. It is the age of young men and young women. Their ardor is their crown, before which the languid and the passive bow.

But if enthusiasm is irresistible in youth, how much more so is it when carried into old age! Gladstone at eighty had ten times the weight and power that any man of twenty-five would have with the same ideals. The glory of age is only the glory of its enthusiasm, and the respect paid to white hairs is reverence to a heart fervent, in spite of the torpid influence of an enfeebled body. The "Odyssey" was the creation of a blind old man, but that old man was Homer. "I argue not against Heaven's hand or will," said Milton, when old, blind, and poor; "nor bate a jot of heart or hope; but still bear up and steer right onward." He was chilled with the frosts of time when he depicted the love of the first pair in Eden.

The contagious zeal of an old man, Peter the Hermit, rolled the chivalry of Europe upon the ranks of Islam.

Dandolo, the Doge of Venice, won battles at ninety-four, and refused a crown at ninety-six. Wellington planned and superintended fortifications at eighty. Bacon and Humboldt were enthusiastic students to the last gasp. Wise old Montaigne was shrewd in his gray-beard wisdom and loving life, even in the midst of his fits of gout and colic.

Dr. Johnson's best work, "The Lives of the Poets," was written when he was seventy-eight. Defoe was fifty-eight when he published "Robinson Crusoe." Newton wrote new briefs to his "Principia" at eighty-three. Plato died writing, at eighty-one. Tom Scott began the study of Hebrew at eighty-six. Galileo was nearly seventy when he wrote on the laws of motion. James Watt learned German at eighty-five. Mrs. Somerville finished her "Molecular and Microscopic Science" at eighty-nine. Humboldt completed his "Cosmos" at ninety, a month before his death. Burke was thirty-five before he obtained a seat in Parliament, yet he made the world feel his character. Unknown at forty, at forty-two Grant was one of the most famous generals in history. Eli Whitney was twenty-three when he decided to prepare for college, and was thirty when he graduated from Yale; yet his cotton-gin opened a great industrial future for the Southern States. What a power was Bismarck at eighty! Lord Palmerston was an "Old Boy" to the last. He became Prime Minister of England the second time at seventy-five, and died Prime Minister at eighty-one. Galileo at seventy-seven, blind and feeble, was working every day, adapting the principle of the pendulum to clocks. "There was nothing remarkable about Goldsmith when he was young," said Johnson; "he was a plant that flowered late in life." George Stephenson did not learn to read or write until he had reached manhood. Richard Baxter did not know a single letter at eighteen. Some of Longfellow's, Whittier's, and Tennyson's best work was done after they were seventy.

At sixty-three Dryden began the translation of the "Æneid." John Colby, brother-in-law of Daniel Webster, learned to read after he was eighty-four, that he might read the Bible. Robert Hall learned Italian when past sixty, that he might read Dante in the original. Noah Webster studied seventeen languages after he was fifty. Ludovico, at one hundred and fifteen, wrote the memoirs of his times. Cicero said well that men are like wine: age sours the bad, and improves the good.

With enthusiasm we may retain the youth of the spirit until the hair is silvered, even as the Gulf Stream softens the rigors of northern Europe.

"How ages thine heart, — towards youth? If not, doubt thy fitness for thy work."

CHAPTER XII.

TACT OR COMMON SENSE.

"Who is stronger than thou?" asked Brahma; and Force replied, "Address." — VICTOR HUGO.

Address makes opportunities; the want of it gives them. — BOVEE.

> He'll suit his bearing to the hour,
> Laugh, listen, learn, or teach.   ELIZA COOK.

A man who knows the world will not only make the most of everything he does know, but of many things he does not know; and will gain more credit by his adroit mode of hiding his ignorance, than the pedant by his awkward attempt to exhibit his erudition. — COLTON.

The art of using moderate abilities to advantage wins praise, and often acquires more reputation than actual brilliancy. — ROCHEFOUCAULD.

> Tact clinches the bargain,
> Sails out of the bay,
> Gets the vote in the Senate,
> Spite of Webster or Clay.   HOLMES.

"A loaf baked is better than a harvest contemplated. An acre in Cook County is better than a whole principality in Utopia."

"I NEVER will surrender to a nigger," said a Confederate officer, when a colored soldier chased and caught him. "Berry sorry, massa," said the negro, leveling his rifle; "must kill you den; hain't time to go back and git a white man." The officer surrendered.

"When God endowed human beings with brains," says Montesquieu, "he did not intend to guarantee them."

"Mr. President," said an old boatswain, speaking for a number of sailors who desired promotion without increase of pay; "I can put this 'ere matter so's you can see it plain. Now here I be a parent — in fact, a father. My son is a midshipman. He outranks me, don't you observe? That ain't right, don't you see?"

"Indeed," said President Grant; "who appointed

him?" "The Secretary here," replied the boatswain. "It ain't right, don't you see, that I should be beneath him. Why, if I was to go onto his ship the boy I brought up to obedience would boss his own father. Jest think o' that! An' he has better quarters 'n me, an' better grub, nice furniture 'n' all that, sleeps in a nice soft bed, an' all that. See?"

"Yes," said the President, "the world is full of inequalities. I know of a case quite similar to yours. I know of an old fellow who is a postmaster in a little town of Kentucky. He lives in a plain way in a small house. He is a nice old man, but he isn't much in rank. His son outranks him more than your son does you. His son lives in Washington, in the biggest house there, and he is surrounded by the nicest of furniture, and eats and drinks everything he takes a notion to. He could remove his father from office in a minute if he wanted to. And the old man — that's Jesse Grant, you know — does n't seem to care about the inequality in rank. I suppose he is glad to see his boy get along in the world."

The other sailors laughed, slapped the old boatswain on the back, and filed out.

When Abraham Lincoln was running for the legislature, the first time, on the platform of the improvement of the Sangamon River, he went to secure the votes of thirty men who were cradling a wheat-field. They asked no questions about internal improvements, but only seemed curious to know whether he had muscle enough to represent them in the legislature. Lincoln took up a cradle and led the gang around the field. The whole thirty voted for him.

"I do not know how it is," said Napoleon in surprise to his cook, "but at whatever hour I call for my breakfast my chicken is always ready and always in good condition." This seemed to him the more strange because sometimes he would breakfast at eight and at

HORACE GREELEY

" Common sense is the genius of our age."
" Fine sense and exalted sense are not half so useful as common sense."

other times as late as eleven. "Sire," said the cook, "the reason is, that every quarter of an hour I put a fresh chicken down to roast, so that your Majesty is sure always to have it at perfection."

Talent in this age is no match for tact. We see its failure everywhere. Tact will manipulate one talent so as to get more out of it in a lifetime than ten talents will accomplish without tact. "Talent lies abed till noon; tact is up at six." Talent is power, tact is skill. Talent knows what to do, tact knows how to do it. Talent theorizes, tact performs. Philosophers discuss, practical men act.

The world is full of theoretical, one-sided, impractical men, who have turned all the energies of their lives into one faculty until they have developed, not a full-orbed, symmetrical man, but a monstrosity, while all their other faculties have atrophied and died. We often call these one-sided men geniuses, and the world excuses their impractical and almost idiotic conduct in most matters, because they can perform one kind of work that no one else can do as well. A merchant is excused if he is a giant in merchandise, though he may be an imbecile in the drawing-room. Adam Smith could teach the world economy in his "Wealth of Nations," but he could not manage the finances of his own household. Many great men are very impractical even in the ordinary affairs of life. Isaac Newton could read the secret of creation; but, tired of rising from his chair to open the door for a cat and her kitten, he had two holes cut through the panels for them to pass at will, a large hole for the cat, and a small one for the kitten. Beethoven was a great musician, but he sent three hundred florins to pay for six shirts and half a dozen handkerchiefs. He paid his tailor as large a sum in advance, and yet he was so poor at times that he had only a biscuit and a glass of water for dinner. He did not know enough of business to cut the coupon from a bond when he wanted money, but sold the whole instrument. It was said of Dr. Johnson that he "uplifts the club of Hercules to crush a butterfly or brain a gnat." Dean Swift nearly starved in a country parish where his more practical classmate Stafford became rich. One of Napoleon's marshals understood military tactics as well as his chief, but he did not know men so well, and lacked the other's skill and tact. Napoleon might fall; but, like a cat, he would fall upon his feet. For his argument in the Florida Case, a fee of one thousand dollars in crisp new bills of large denomination was handed to Daniel Webster as he sat reading in his library. The next day he wished to use some of the money, but could not find any of the bills. Years afterward, as he turned the page of a book, he found a bank-bill without a crease in it. On turning the next leaf he found another, and so on until he took the whole amount lost from the places where he had deposited them thoughtlessly, as he read. Learning of a new issue of gold pieces at the Treasury, he directed his Secretary, Charles Lanman, to obtain several hundred dollars' worth. A day or two after he put his hand in his pocket for one, but they were all gone. Webster was at first puzzled, but on reflection remembered that he had given them away, one by one, to friends who seemed to appreciate their beauty. A professor in mathematics in a New England college, a "book-worm," was asked by his wife to bring home some coffee. "How much will you have?" asked the merchant. "Well, I declare, my wife did not say, but I guess a bushel will do."

Many a great man has been so absent-minded at times as to seem devoid of common sense.

"The professor is not at home," said his servant who looked out of a window in the dark and failed to recognize Lessing when the latter knocked at his own door in a fit of absent-mindedness. "Oh, very well," replied Lessing; "no matter, I'll call at another time."

A sailor who narrowly escaped death from a fever contracted in the West Indies sent a barrel of cranberries to his faithful nurse. A letter of grateful acknowledgment was soon received, with a postscript adding that, unfortunately, although the fruit looked pretty, it had turned sour on the passage, and had to be thrown away. "That," said the sailor, "is what I call missin' the sweetness of things 'cause you don't know how to get at it."

Louis Philippe said he was the only sovereign in Europe fit to govern, for he could black his own boots. The world is full of men and women apparently splendidly endowed and highly educated, yet who can scarcely get a living.

Not long ago three college graduates were found working on a sheep farm in Australia, one from Oxford, one from Cambridge, and the other from a German University,—college men tending brutes! Trained to lead men, they drove sheep. The owner of the farm was an ignorant, coarse sheep-raiser. He knew nothing of books or theories, but he knew sheep. His three hired graduates could speak foreign languages and discuss theories of political economy and philosophy, but he could make money. He could talk about nothing but sheep and farm; but he had made a fortune, while the college men could scarcely get a living. Even the University could not supply common sense. It was "culture against ignorance; the college against the ranch; and the ranch beat every time."

Do not expect too much from books. Bacon said that studies "teach not their own use, but that there is a practical wisdom without them, won by observation." The use of books must be found outside their own lids. It was said of a great French scholar: "He was drowned in his talents." Over-culture, without practical experience, weakens a man, and unfits him for real life. Book education alone tends to make a man too critical, too self-conscious, timid, distrustful of his abilities, too fine for the mechanical drudgery of practical life, too highly polished, and too finely cultured for every-day use.

The culture of books and colleges refines, yet it is often but an ethical culture, and is gained at the cost of vigor and rugged strength. Book culture alone tends to paralyze the practical faculties. The bookworm loses his individuality; his head is filled with theories and saturated with other men's thoughts. The stamina of the vigorous mind he brought from the farm has evaporated in college; and when he graduates, he is astonished to find that he has lost the power to grapple with men and things, and is therefore outstripped in the race of life by the boy who has had no chance, but who, in the fierce struggle for existence, has developed hard common sense and practical wisdom. The college graduate often mistakes his crutches for strength. He inhabits an ideal realm where common sense rarely dwells. The world cares little for his theories or his encyclopædic knowledge. The cry of the age is for practical men. The nineteenth century does not ask you what you know or where you came from, but what can you do?

"Men have ruled well who could not, perhaps, define a commonwealth," says Sir Thomas Browne; "and they who understand not the globe of the earth command a greater part of it."

"We have been among you several weeks," said Columbus to the Indian chiefs; "and, although at first you treated us like friends, you are now jealous of us and are trying to drive us away. You brought us food in plenty every morning, but now you bring very little and the amount is less with each succeeding day. The Great Spirit is angry with you for not doing as you agreed in bringing us provisions. To show his anger he will cause the sun to be in darkness." He knew that there was to be an eclipse of the sun, and told the day and hour it would occur, but the Indians did not believe him, and continued to reduce the supply of food.

On the appointed day the sun rose without a cloud, and the Indians shook their heads, beginning to show signs of open hostility as the hours passed without a shadow on the face of the sun. But at length a dark spot was seen on one margin; and, as it grew larger, the natives grew frantic and fell prostrate before Columbus to entreat for help. He retired to his tent, promising to save them, if possible. About the time for the eclipse to pass away, he came out and said that the Great Spirit had pardoned them, and would soon drive away the monster from the sun; but they must never offend him again. They readily promised, and when the sun had passed out of the shadow they leaped, and danced, and sang for joy. Thereafter the Spaniards had all the provisions they needed.

"Common sense," said Wendell Phillips, "bows to the inevitable and makes use of it."

The foundations of English liberty were laid by men who could not write their names. "Talent is something, but tact is everything. It is not a sixth sense, but it is like the life of all the five. It is the open eye, the quick ear, the judging taste, the keen smell, and lively touch; it is the interpreter of all riddles, the surmounter of all difficulties, the remover of all obstacles."

When Cæsar stumbled in landing on the beach of Britain, he instantly grasped a handful of sand and held it aloft as a signal of triumph, hiding forever from his followers the ill omen of his threatened fall.

Goethe, speaking of some comparisons that had been instituted between himself and Shakespeare, said: "Shakespeare always hits the right nail on the head at once; but I have to stop and think which is the right nail, before I hit."

It has been said that a few pebbles from a brook, in the sling of a David, who knows how to send them to the mark, are more effective than a Goliath's spear and a Goliath's strength with a Goliath's clumsiness.

"Get ready for the redskins!" shouted an excited man as he galloped up to the log-cabin of the Moore family in Ohio many years ago; "and give me a fresh horse as soon as you can. They killed a family down the river last night, and nobody knows where they'll turn up next!"

"What shall we do?" asked Mrs. Moore, with a pale face. "My husband went away yesterday to buy our winter supplies, and will not be back until morning."

"Husband away? Whew! that's bad! Well, shut up as tight as you can. Cover up your fire, and don't strike a light to-night." Then springing upon the horse the boys had brought, he galloped away to warn other settlers.

Mrs. Moore carried the younger children to the loft of the cabin, and left Obed and Joe to watch, reluctantly yielding the post of danger to them at their urgent request. "They're coming, Joe!" whispered Obed early in the evening, as he saw several shadows moving across the fields. "Stand by that window with the axe, while I get the rifle pointed at this one." Opening the bullet-pouch, he took out a ball, but nearly fainted as he found it was too large for the rifle. His father had taken the wrong pouch. Obed felt around to see if there were any smaller balls in the cupboard, and almost stumbled over a very large pumpkin, one of the two which he and Joe had been using to make Jack-o'-lanterns when the messenger alarmed them. Pulling off his coat, he flung it over the vegetable lantern, made to imitate a gigantic grinning face, with open eyes, nose, and mouth, and with a live coal from the ashes he lighted the candle inside. "They'll sound the war-whoop in a minute, if I give them time," he whispered, as he raised the covered lantern to the window. "Now for it!" he added, pulling the coat away. An unearthly yell greeted the appearance of the grinning monster, and the Indians fled wildly to the woods. "Quick, Joe! Light up the other one! Don't you see that's what scar't 'em so?" demanded Obed; and at the appearance of the second fiery face the savages gave a final yell and vanished in the forest. Mr. Moore and daylight came together, but the Indians did not return.

Thurlow Weed earned his first shilling by carrying a trunk on his back from a sloop in New York harbor to a Broad Street hotel. He had very few chances such as are now open to the humblest boy, but he had nameless tact and intuition. He could read men as an open book, and mould them to his will. He was unselfish. By three presidents whom his tact and shrewdness had helped to elect, he was offered the English mission, and scores of other important positions, but he invariably declined.

Lincoln selected Weed to attempt the reconciliation of the New York "Herald," which had a large circulation in Europe, and was creating a dangerous public sentiment abroad and at home by its articles in sympathy with the Confederacy. Though Weed and Bennett had not spoken to each other before for thirty years, the very next day after their interview the "Herald" became a strong Union paper. Weed was then sent to Europe to counteract the pernicious influence of secession agents. The emperor of France favored the South. He was very indignant because Charleston harbor had been blockaded, thus shutting off French manufacturers from large supplies of cotton. But the rare tact of Weed modified the emperor's views, and induced him to change to friendliness the tone of a hostile speech prepared for delivery to the National Assembly. England was working night and day preparing for war when Weed arrived upon the scene, and soon changed largely the current of public sentiment. On his return to America the city of New York extended public thanks to him for his inestimable services. He was equally successful in business, and acquired a fortune of a million dollars.

"Tell me the breadth of this stream," said Napoleon to his chief engineer, as they came to a bridgeless river which the army must cross. "Sire, I cannot. My scientific instruments are with the army, and we are ten miles ahead of it."

"Measure the width of this stream instantly."— "Sire, be reasonable!"—"Ascertain at once the width of this river, or you shall be deposed."

The engineer drew the cap-piece of his helmet down until the edge seemed just in line between his eye and the opposite bank; then, holding himself carefully erect, he turned on his heel and noticed where the edge seemed to touch the bank on which he stood, which was on the same level as the other. He paced the distance to the point last noted, and said: "This is the approximate width of the stream." He was promoted.

"Mr. Webster," said the mayor of a Western city, when it was learned that the great statesman, although weary with travel, would be delayed for an hour by a failure to make close connections, "allow me to introduce you to Mr. James, one of our most distinguished citizens." "How do you do, Mr. James?" asked Webster mechanically, as he glanced at a thousand people waiting to take his hand. "The truth is, Mr. Webster," replied Mr. James in a most lugubrious tone, "I am not very well." "I hope nothing serious is the matter," thundered the godlike Daniel, in a tone of anxious concern. "Well, I don't know that, Mr. Webster. I think it's rheumatiz, but my wife"— "Mr. Webster, this is Mr. Smith," broke in the mayor, leaving poor Mr. James to enjoy his bad health in the pitiless solitude of a crowd. His total want of tact had made him ridiculous.

"Address yourself to the jury, sir," said a judge to a witness who insisted upon imparting his testimony in a confidential tone to the court direct. The man did not understand and continued as before. "Speak to the jury, sir, the men sitting behind you on the raised benches." Turning, the witness bowed low in awkward suavity, and said, "Good-morning, gentlemen."

"If I send a man to examine a horse for me, I expect him to give me his points, not how many hairs he has in his tail," said Lincoln, when a pile of papers was handed him containing the report of a Congressional committee appointed to examine a new gun. "I should want a new lease of life," said he, "to read all this."

"What are these?" asked Napoleon, pointing to twelve silver statues in a cathedral. "The twelve Apostles," was the reply. "Take them down," said Napoleon, "melt them, coin them into money, and let them go about doing good, as their Master did."

"I don't think the Proverbs of Solomon show very great wisdom," said a student at Brown University; "I could make as good ones myself." "Very well," replied President Wayland, "bring in two to-morrow morning." He did not bring them.

"Jim Lowell writes books, and has been in England a spell," said an Adirondack guide, "but he's an ign'rant feller, for when we were making first-rate time down stream in the current, he didn't know any better than to want me to steer the canoe to the other side of the stream, just to get in the shade of the bank where we didn't get ahead at all. Now I call a man that don't know enough to keep in the current a blamed ignoramus."

"Will you lecture for us for fame?" was the telegram young Henry Ward Beecher received from a Young Men's Christian Association in the West. "Yes, F. A. M. E. Fifty and my expenses," was the answer the shrewd young preacher sent back.

Montaigne tells of a monarch who, on the sudden death of an only child, showed his resentment against Providence by abolishing the Christian religion throughout his dominions for a fortnight.

The triumphs of tact, or common sense, over talent and genius, are seen everywhere. Walpole was an ignorant man, but he held the sceptre over England for a quarter of a century. Charlemagne could hardly write his name so that it could be deciphered; but these giants knew men and things, and possessed that practical wisdom and tact which have ever moved the world.

Tact, like Alexander, cuts the knots it cannot untie, and leads its forces to glorious victory. A practical man not only sees, but seizes the opportunity. There is a certain getting-on quality difficult to describe, but which is the great winner of the prizes of life. Napoleon could do anything in the art of war with his own hands, even to the making of gunpowder. Paul was all things to all men, that he might save some. The palm is among the hardest and least yielding of all woods, yet rather than be deprived of the rays of the life-giving sun in the dense forests of South America, it is said to turn into a creeper, and climb the nearest trunk to the light.

He who would push to the front in this competitive age must be in touch with the great bustling, busy world. He must keep his mind parallel with the nature of things. He must not be one of those who explore the illimitable and grasp the infinite, but never pay cash.

In the patent-office at Washington may be seen many thousands of ingenious mechanical devices, not one in a hundred of which has ever been put to any practical use, and never will be seen outside the rooms where they are stored for exhibition. Most of these are the results of days, months, and even years of labor on the part of men whose inventive faculties ought to have enabled them to render valuable service to their fellow men; but which unfortunately, not being balanced by the necessary qualities to render them of practical value, have been squandered in the invention and construction of machines for doing what nobody ever cares to have done, or what can be accomplished by much simpler and better means.

There are many engineers who know vastly more than George Stephenson did, but he knew how to apply his knowledge.

A farmer who could not get a living sold one half of his farm to a young man who made enough money on the half to pay for it and buy the rest. "You have not tact," was his reply, when the old man asked how one could succeed so well where the other had failed.

According to an old custom a Cape Cod minister was called upon in April to make a prayer over a piece of land. "No," said he, when shown the land, "this does not need a prayer; it needs manure."

To see a man as he is you must turn him round and round until you get him at the right angle. Place him in a good light as you would a picture. The excellences and defects will appear if you get the right angle and a favorable light. How our old schoolmates have changed places in the ranking of actual life! The boy who led his class and was the envy of all has been distanced by the poor dunce who was called slow and stupid, but who had a sort of dull energy in him which enabled him to get on in the world. The class leader had only a theoretical knowledge, and could not cope with the stern realities of the age. Even genius, however rapid its flight, must not omit a single essential detail, and must be willing to work like a horse.

Shakespeare had marvelous tact; he worked everything into his plays. He ground up the king and his vassal, the fool and the fop, the prince and the peasant, the black and the white, the pure and the impure, the simple and the profound, passions and characters, honor and dishonor,—everything within the sweep of his vision he ground up into paint and spread it upon his mighty canvas.

Some people show want of tact in resenting every slight or petty insult, however unworthy their notice. Others make Don Quixote's mistake of fighting a windmill by engaging in controversies with public speakers and editors, who are sure to have the advantage of the final word. One of the greatest elements of strength in the character of Washington was found in his forbearance when unjustly attacked or ridiculed.

Artemus Ward touches this bubble with a pretty sharp-pointed pen.

"It was in a surtin town in Virginny, the Muther of Presidents and things, that I was shaimfully aboozed by a editer in human form. He set my Show up steep, and kalled me the urbane and gentlemunly manager, but when I, fur the purpuss of showin fair play all round, went to anuther offiss to get my handbills printed, what duz this pussillanermus editer do but change his toon and abooze me like a injun. He sed my wax-wurks was a humbug, and called me a horey-heded itinerent vagabone. I thort at fust Ide pollish him orf ar-lar Beneki Boy, but on reflectin that he cood pollish me much wuss in his paper, I giv it up; and I wood here take occashun to advise people when they run agin, as they sumtimes will, these miserble papers, to not pay no attenshun to um. Abuv all, don't assault a editer of this kind. It only gives him a notorosity, which is jist what he wants, and don't do you no more good than it would to jump into enny other mud-puddle. Editers are generally fine men, but there must be black sheep in every flock."

John Jacob Astor had practical talent in a remarkable degree. During a storm at sea, on his voyage to America, the other passengers ran about the deck in despair, expecting every minute to go down; but young

Astor went below and coolly put on his best suit of clothes, saying that if the ship should founder and he should happen to be rescued, he would at least save his best suit of clothes.

"Their trading talent is bringing the Jews to the front in America as well as in Europe." said a traveler to one of that race; "and it has gained for them an ascendancy, at least in certain branches of trade, from which nothing will ever displace them."

"Dey are coming to de vront, most zairtainly," replied his companion; "but vy do you shpeak of deir drading dalent all de time?"

"But don't you regard it as a talent?"

"A dalent? No! It is chenius. I vill dell you what is de difference, in drade, between dalent and chenius. Ven one goes into a man's shtore and manaches to sell him vot he vonts, dat is dalent; but ven annoder man goes into dat man's shtore and sells him vot he don't vont, dat is chenius; and dat is de chenius vot my race has got."

Tact is a national trait. The Chinese understood the art of printing, and possessed the magnetic needle and gunpowder, centuries in advance of other nations, but they did not have the practical talent to use them to any great advantage. But the English and other European nations changed the face of the civilized world with them.

Tact is a child of necessity. It is not found in people who live under a tropical sun, where there is little need of clothing, and where food is found ready prepared in the date, cocoanut, and banana. It has its highest development where man has to struggle hardest for existence.

CHAPTER XIII.

SELF-RESPECT AND SELF-CONFIDENCE.

Be a friend to yersel, and ithers will. — SCOTCH PROVERB.
A nod from a lord is a breakfast for a fool. — FRANKLIN.
The king is the man who can. — CARLYLE.
The reverence of man's self is, next to religion, the chiefest bridle of all vices. — BACON.
Self-approbation, when founded in truth and a good conscience, is a source of some of the purest joys known to man. — C. SIMMONS.
Self-reverence, self-knowledge, self-control, these three alone lead life to sovereign power. — TENNYSON.
Self-respect, — that corner-stone of all virtue. — JOHN HERSCHEL.
Above all things, reverence yourself. — PYTHAGORAS.
No one can disgrace us but ourselves. — J. G. HOLLAND.
Nothing can work me damage, except myself; the harm that I sustain I carry about with me, and never am a real sufferer but by my own faults. — ST. BERNARD.
Self-distrust is the cause of most of our failures. In the assurance of strength there is strength, and they are the weakest, however strong, who have no faith in themselves or their powers. — BOVEE.
The pious and just honoring of ourselves may be thought the fountainhead from whence every laudable and worthy enterprise issues forth. — MILTON.

A POOR Scotch weaver used to pray daily that he might have a good opinion of himself. Why not? Can I ask another to think well of me when I do not set the example? The Chinese say it never pays to respect a man who does not respect himself. If the world sees that I do not honor myself, it has a right to reject me as an impostor, because I claim to be worthy of the good opinion of others when I have not my own. Self-respect is based upon the same principles as respect for others. The scales of justice hang in every heart, and even the murderer respects the judge who condemns him; for the still small voice within says, "That is right." Justice never looks to see who is in the scales

GEORGE PEABODY

"To thine own self be true; and it must follow, as the night the day, thou canst not then be false to any man."

SELF-RESPECT AND SELF-CONFIDENCE. 203

before she strikes the balance. King or beggar, it is all the same.

"You may deceive all the people some of the time," said Lincoln, "some of the people all the time, but not all the people all the time." We cannot deceive ourselves any of the time, and the only way to enjoy our own respect is to deserve it. What would you think of a man who would neglect himself, and treat his shadow with the greatest respect?

The world has a right to look to me for my own rating. We stamp our own value upon ourselves and cannot expect to pass for more. When you are introduced into society, people look into your face and eye to see what estimate you place upon yourself. If they see a low mark, why should they trouble themselves to investigate to see if you have not rated yourself too low? They know you have lived with yourself a good while and ought to know your own value better than they.

"Good God, that I should have intrusted the fate of the country and of the administration to such hands!" exclaimed Pitt to Lord Temple, after listening in disgust to the egotistical boasting of General Wolfe, the day before his embarkation for Canada. The young soldier had drawn his sword, rapped upon the table with it, flourished it around the room, and told of the great deeds he should perform.

Little did the Prime Minister dream that this egotistical young man would rise from his bed when sick with a fever, and lead his troops to glorious victory upon the Heights of Abraham. This apparent egotism was but a prophecy of his ability to achieve.

> "One self-approving hour whole years outweighs
> Of stupid starers and of loud huzzas;
> And more true joy Marcellus exiled feels
> Than Cæsar with a senate at his heels."

"Where is now your fortress?" asked his captors

derisively of Stephen of Colonna. "Here," was the bold reply, as he placed his hand upon his heart.

"Ah! John Hunter, still hard at work!" exclaimed a physician on finding the old anatomist at the dissecting-table. "Yes, doctor, and you'll find it difficult to meet with another John Hunter when I am gone."

"Heaven takes a hundred years to form a great genius for the regeneration of an empire, and afterwards rests a hundred years," said Kaunitz, who had administered the affairs of his country with great success for half a century. "This makes me tremble for the Austrian monarchy after my death!"

"My Lord," said William Pitt in 1757 to the Duke of Devonshire, "I am sure that I can save this country, and that nobody else can." He did save it.

"Isn't it beautiful that I can sing so?" asked Jenny Lind, naïvely, of a friend.

Louis the Fourteenth said to his clergyman, "Ah! it's all very true; I am a sinner, no doubt, since you say so; but *le bon Dieu* will think twice before he casts out such a great prince as I."

"Well-matured and well-disciplined talent is always sure of a market," said Washington Irving; "but it must not cower at home and expect to be sought for. There is a good deal of cant, too, about the success of forward and impudent men, while men of retiring worth are passed over with neglect. But it usually happens that those forward men have that valuable quality of promptness and activity, without which worth is a mere inoperative property. A barking dog is often more useful than a sleeping lion."

John C. Fremont closed in almost forgotten obscurity his career as a man whose scientific attainment gave him the seat left vacant by the death of Humboldt in European academies, whose wonderful enterprise gave California to the Union, and whose position was once among the foremost in the political world. "He has been ignored," said an opponent, "simply because he is utterly lacking in self-assertion. He has a positive talent for effacing himself."

"Why, sir," said John C. Calhoun in Yale College when a fellow student ridiculed his intense application to study; "I am forced to make the most of my time, that I may acquit myself creditably when in Congress." A laugh greeted this speech, when he exclaimed, "Do you doubt it? I assure you if I were not convinced of my ability to reach the national capital as a representative within the next three years, I would leave college this very day!"

"What does Grattan say of himself?" said Curran, repeating the question of the egotistical Lord Erskine; "nothing. Grattan speak of himself! Why, sir, Grattan is a great man! Torture, sir, could not wring a syllable of self-praise from Grattan; a team of six horses could not drag an opinion of himself out of him! Like all great men, he knows the strength of his reputation, and will never condescend to proclaim its march like the trumpeter of a puppet show. Sir, he stands on a national altar, and it is the business of us inferior men to keep up the fire and incense. You will never see Grattan stooping to do either the one or the other."

What seems to us disagreeable egotism in others is often but a strong expression of confidence in their ability to attain. Great men have usually had great confidence in themselves. Wordsworth felt sure of his place in history, and never hesitated to say so. Dante predicted his own fame. Kepler said it did not matter whether his contemporaries read his books or not. "I may well wait a century for a reader since God has waited 6000 years for an observer like myself." "Fear not," said Julius Cæsar to his pilot frightened in a storm; "thou bearest Cæsar and his good fortunes."

Egotism, so common in men of rank, may be a necessity. Nature gives man large hope lest he falter before reaching the high mark she sets for him. So she has overloaded his egotism, often beyond the pleasing point, to make sure that he will persist in pushing his way upward. Self-confidence indicates reserve power. It may show that one feels equal to the occasion.

Morally considered, it is usually safe to trust those who can trust themselves, but when a man suspects his own integrity, it is time he was suspected by others. Moral degradation always begins at home.

Did not Napoleon I., when he was a poor sub-lieutenant, believe that within him lay capacities enough to shake a world?

In this busy world, men have no time to hunt about in obscure corners for retiring merit. They prefer to take a man at his own estimate until he proves himself unworthy. The world admires courage and manliness, and despises a young man who goes about "with an air of perpetual apology for the unpardonable sin of being in the world."

"If a man possesses the consciousness of what he is," said Schelling, "he will soon also learn what he ought to be; let him have a theoretical respect for himself, and a practical will soon follow." A person under the firm persuasion that he can command resources virtually has them. "Humility is the part of wisdom, and is most becoming in men," said Kossuth; "but let no one discourage self-reliance; it is, of all the rest, the greatest quality of true manliness." Froude wrote: "A tree must be rooted in the soil before it can bear flowers or fruit. A man must learn to stand upright upon his own feet, to respect himself, to be independent of charity or accident. It is on this basis only that any superstructure of intellectual cultivation worth having can possibly be built."

A youth should have that self-respect which lifts him above meanness, and makes him independent of slights and snubs.

Never chase a lie. Let it alone, and it will run itself to death. "I can work out a good character much faster than any one can lie me out of it," said Lyman Beecher.

"There is a kind of elevation which does not depend on fortune," says La Rochefoucauld. "It is a certain air which distinguishes us, and seems to destine us for great things; it is a price which we imperceptibly set on ourselves. By this quality we usurp the deference of other men, and it puts us, in general, more above them than birth, dignity, or even merit itself."

"It is only shallow-minded pretenders," said Webster, "who make either distinguished origin a matter of personal merit, or obscure origin a matter of personal reproach. A man who is not ashamed of himself need not be ashamed of his early condition. It did happen to me to be born in a log-cabin, raised amid the snow-drifts of New Hampshire, at a period so early that, when the smoke first rose from its rude chimney and curled over the frozen hills, there was no similar evidence of white man's habitation between it and the settlements on the rivers of Canada.

"Its remains still exist; I make it an annual visit. I carry my children to it, and teach them the hardships endured by the generations before them. I love to dwell on the tender recollections, the kindred ties, the early affections, and the narrations and incidents which mingle with all I know of this primitive family abode. I weep to think that none who then inhabited it are now among the living; and if ever I fail in affectionate veneration for him who raised it, and defended it against savage violence and destruction, cherished all domestic comforts beneath its roof, and through the fire and blood of seven years' revolutionary war shrunk from no toil, no sacrifice to serve his country, and to raise his children to a condition better than his own, may my name and the name of my posterity be blotted from the memory of mankind."

"I have studied all my law books," said Curran, pleading, "and cannot find a single case where the principle contended for by the opposing counsel is established."

"I suspect, sir," interrupted Judge Robinson, who owed his position to his authorship of several poorly written, but sycophantic and scurrilous pamphlets, "I suspect that your law library is rather contracted."

"It is true, my lord, that I am poor," said the young lawyer calmly, looking the judge steadily in the face; "and the circumstance has rather curtailed my library. My books are not numerous, but they are select, and I hope have been perused with proper dispositions. I have prepared myself for this high profession rather by the study of a few good books, than by the composition of a great many bad ones. I am not ashamed of my poverty, but I should be of my wealth, could I stoop to acquire it by servility and corruption. If I rise not to rank, I shall at least be honest. And should I ever cease to be so, many an example shows me that an ill-acquired elevation, by making me the more conspicuous, would only make me the more universally and the more notoriously contemptible." Judge Robinson never again sneered at the young barrister.

"Self-reliance is a grand element of character," says Michael Reynolds. "It has won Olympic crowns and Isthmian laurels; it confers kinship with men who have vindicated their divine right to be held in the world's memory."

Self-confidence and self-respect give a sense of power which nothing else can bestow.

The weak, the leaning, the dependent, the vacillating, the undecided, —

> "Know not, nor ever can, the generous pride
> That glows in him who on himself relies.

. . . .

His joy is not that he has got the crown
But that the power to win the crown is his."

This above all, — to thine own self be true;
And it must follow, as the night the day,
Thou canst not then be false to any man.
                                      SHAKESPEARE.

CHAPTER XIV.

GREATER THAN WEALTH.

> They call thee rich, I call thee poor,
> Since, if thou darest not use thy store,
> But savest it only for thine heirs,
> The treasure is not thine but theirs.
>
> COWPER.

When life is ruined for the sake of money's preciousness, the ruined life cares naught for the money. — JAPANESE PROVERB.

"Better a cheap coffin and a plain funeral after a useful, unselfish life, than a grand mausoleum after a loveless, selfish life."

Can wealth give happiness? Look round and see what gay distress, what splendid misery. — YOUNG.

Can anything be so elegant as to have few wants and serve them one's self? — EMERSON.

The fewer our wants the nearer we resemble the gods. — SOCRATES.

> Be noble! and the nobleness that lies
> In other men, sleeping, but never dead,
> Will rise in majesty to meet thine own.
>
> LOWELL.

"AND who is king to-day?" Greuze, the painter, would ask his daughter each morning during the first great revolution in France. Then he would add: "Homer and Raphael will live longer than these temporary kings."

"You are a plebeian," said a patrician to Cicero. "I am a plebeian," replied the great Roman orator; "the nobility of my family begins with me, that of yours will end with you." No man deserves to be crowned with honor whose life is a failure, and he who lives only to eat and drink and accumulate money is surely not successful. The world is no better for his living in it. He never wiped a tear from a sad face, never kindled a fire upon a frozen hearth. There is no flesh in his heart; he worships no god but gold.

WILLIAM LLOYD GARRISON

"My country is the world; my countrymen are all mankind."
"A crown is his that seldom kings enjoy"

If Adam were alive to-day, supposing him to have lived four thousand years ago, and had deposited fifty dollars in the bank every day of his life, without interest, he would have less money than Jay Gould had at the time of his death. Yet Gould's life was not a success, nor should his career be quoted to young men.

"What is the best thing to possess?" asked an ancient philosopher of his pupils. One answered, "Nothing is better than a good eye,"— a figurative expression for a liberal and contented disposition. Another said, "A good companion is the best thing in the world;" a third chose a good neighbor; and a fourth, a wise friend. But Eleazar said: "A good heart is better than them all." "True," said the master; "thou hast comprehended in two words all that the rest have said, for he that hath a good heart will be contented, a good companion, a good neighbor, and will easily see what is fit to be done by him."

Queen Caroline Matilda of Denmark wrote on the window of her prison, with her diamond ring: "Oh, keep me innocent; make others great."

"Oh, if I could only go!" thought Pierre, the French boy, as he saw a man putting up a great bill with yellow letters, announcing that Madame Malibran would sing that night. But there was no bread in the house and he had not tasted food all day. How nice a sweet orange would seem to his poor sick mother, but he had not a penny in the world. From a little box he took some old, stained paper, glanced at his sleeping mother, and ran out into the streets of London.

"Who did you say is waiting for me?" asked Malibran of her servant; "I am already worn out with company." "He is only a very pretty little boy with yellow curls, who said if he can just see you he is sure you will not be sorry, and he will not keep you a moment." "Oh, well, let him come," smiled the great singer; "I can never refuse children."

"I came to see you because my mother is very sick," began Pierre, "and we are too poor to get food and medicine. I thought, perhaps, that if you would sing my little song at some of your grand concerts, maybe some publisher would buy it for a small sum, and so I could get food and medicine for my mother." "Did you compose it?" asked Malibran, after humming the air, "you, a child!" looking at the boy attentively. "And the words, too? Would you like to come to my concert?" "Oh, yes! but I couldn't leave my mother." "I will send somebody to take care of your mother for the evening, and here is a crown with which you may go and get food and medicine. Here is also one of my tickets. Come to-night; that will admit you to a seat near me."

Pierre bought some oranges and other delicacies for his mother, and went to the Concert Hall that night. The band struck up a plaintive little melody and Madame Malibran poured forth the touching words. Pierre clasped his hands for joy, but many a bright eye in that vast audience grew dim with tears. The next day the door of his humble home opened, and Madame Malibran laid her hand on his yellow curls, as she said to his mother: "Your little boy, madame, has brought you a fortune. I was offered this morning, by the best publisher in London, three hundred pounds for his little song, and after he has realized a certain amount from the sale, little Pierre here is to share the profits. Madame, thank God that your son has a gift from heaven."

The boy fell upon his knees and asked God to bless the kind heart that had felt for the poor; and when, a few years later, Malibran sank to an early death, it was Pierre, the rich composer, who smoothed her pillow and cheered her last hours.

"What property has he left behind him?" people ask when a man dies; but the angel who receives him asks, "What good deeds hast thou sent before thee?"

"Please, sir, buy some matches!" said a little boy, with a poor thin blue face, his feet bare and red, and his clothes only a bundle of rags, although it was very cold in Edinburgh that day. "No, I don't want any," said the gentleman. "But they're only a penny a box," the little fellow pleaded. "Yes, but you see I don't want a box." "Then I'll gie ye two boxes for a penny," the boy said at last.

"And so, to get rid of him," says the gentleman who tells the story in an English paper, "I bought a box, but then I found I had no change, so I said, 'I'll buy a box to-morrow.'

"'Oh, do buy them to-nicht,' the boy pleaded again; 'I'll rin and get ye the change; for I'm very hungry.' So I gave him the shilling, and he started away. I waited for the boy, but no boy came. Then I thought I had lost my shilling; but still there was that in the boy's face I trusted, and I did not like to think badly of him.

"Late in the evening a servant came and said a little boy wanted to see me. When the child was brought in, I found it was a smaller brother of the boy who got the shilling, but, if possible, still more ragged and thin and poor. He stood a moment diving into his rags, as if he were seeking something, and then said, 'Are you the gentleman that bought matches frae Sandie?' 'Yes!' 'Weel, then, here's fourpence oot o' yer shillin'. Sandie canna coom. He's no weel. A cart ran over him and knocked him doon; and he lost his bonnet, and his matches, and your elevenpence; and both his legs are broken, and he's no weel at a', and the doctor says he'll dee. And that's a' he can gie ye the noo,' putting fourpence down on the table; and then the child broke down into great sobs. So I fed the little man; and then I went with him to see Sandie.

"I found that the two little things lived with a wretched drunken stepmother; their own father and mother were both dead. I found poor Sandie lying on a bundle of shavings; he knew me as soon as I came in, and said, 'I got the change, sir, and was coming back; and then the horse knocked me down, and both my legs are broken. And Reuby, little Reuby! I am sure I am deein'! And who will take care o' ye, Reuby, when I am gane? What will ye do, Reuby?'

"Then I took the poor little sufferer's hand and told him I would always take care of Reuby. He understood me, and had just strength to look at me as if he would thank me; then the expression went out of his blue eyes; and in a moment —

> "'He lay within the light of God,
> Like a babe upon the breast,
> Where the wicked cease from troubling,
> And the weary are at rest.'"

Heaven meant principle to that little match-boy, bruised and dying. He knew little where he was to go, but he knew better than most of those who would have spurned him from their carriages, the value of honesty, truth, nobility, sincerity, genuineness, — the qualities that go to make heaven.

"I will give a hundred French louis to any one who will venture to deliver these unfortunate people," said Count Spolverini when the swollen Adige swept away the bridge of Verona, with the exception of the centre arch. On this section stood a house whose inmates cried for help from the windows, as they saw the foundations slowly giving way. A young peasant seized a boat and pushed into the flood. He gained the pier, took the whole family into the little boat, and carried them safely to land. "Here is your money, my brave young fellow," said the count. "No," said the youth, "I do not sell my life; give the money to this poor family, who have need of it."

Robert, Duke of Normandy, eldest son of William

the Conqueror, had been struck by a poisoned arrow, and his physicians said he must die unless the venom were sucked from the wound by some one, whose life would be forfeited. Robert disdained to receive such aid, but Sibilla sucked the wound while the duke lay asleep, and died to save her husband.

During an epidemic of yellow fever in Savannah, the whole force in a leading drug-store fled except one young clerk who refused to leave the post of duty, in spite of the protestations of his friends, and remained until the proprietor ordered him to close the doors. He went at once to another store, where he worked day and night, without even removing his clothes for sleep, and allowing himself but scanty time for meals. The owner of this shop was stricken with fever, and the boy nursed him until the man died. The cook was next prostrated and he watched with her, saving her life. A bosom friend was taken ill at this time; and the clerk, without neglecting his duties, nursed him to convalescence; when he, too, was prostrated by the relentless plague.

Then the young man who had been nursed to recovery showed his gratitude, watching with the clerk day and night, although the task was too great for his strength. "I will stick to him to the last," and "I shall not sleep to-night," were his last messages sent to friends who had not dared to come near. Both died that night.

In a similar epidemic at Memphis, the members of the Relief Committee were at their wits' end, to obtain watchers, when a man with coarse features, close-cropped hair, and shuffling gait, went directly to one of the attending physicians and said: "I want to nurse."

The doctor looked at him critically, concluded he was not fitted for the work in any way, and replied: "You are not needed."

"I wish to nurse," persisted the stranger. "Try me for a week. If you don't like me, then dismiss me; if you do, pay me my wages."

"Very well," said the doctor, "I'll take you, although to be candid, I hesitate to do so." Then he added mentally, "I'll keep my eye on him."

But the man soon proved that he needed nobody's eye upon him. In a few weeks he had become one of the most valuable nurses on that heroic force. He was tireless and self-denying. Wherever the pestilence raged most fiercely he worked hardest. The suffering and the sinking adored him. To the neglected and the forgotten his rough face was as the face of an angel.

He acted so strangely on pay-days, however, that he was followed through back streets to an obscure place, where he was seen to put his whole week's earnings into a relief-box for the benefit of the yellow-fever sufferers. Not long afterwards he sickened and died of the plague; and when his body was prepared for its unnamed grave, for he had never told who he was, a livid mark was found which showed that John, the nurse, had been branded as a convicted felon.

From London in 1676 the Great Plague had spread to Eyam in Derbyshire, a beautiful village nestling among the hills. The people in terror prepared to flee, when their rector, the Rev. William Mompesson, announced his intention to remain, and advised all to follow his example. "The plague is already among us," said he, "and it is not likely that any one could avoid carrying infection with him, wherever he might go. It would be selfish cruelty to other places to try to escape amongst their people, and thus spread the danger." Of their own free will all adopted his advice, and for seven months they calmly faced death in its most terrible form, four out of every five falling victims. Mr. Mompesson labored with all his might in all the offices of a nurse and a clergyman, and escaped scathless, although his faithful wife, who ably seconded his efforts, was among those whose funeral services he was compelled to pronounce. Supplies were brought from a distance through the agency of the Earl of Derbyshire, and left on the hills above Eyam, the people leaving silver in payment at the same place. As a result of their self-sacrificing devotion there was not a case of plague in any of the surrounding villages.

That is but a low standard of greatness which measures a man by his employment or what he can buy rather than by what he is. A hod-carrier may be infinitely superior to the millionaire under whose bricks he staggers. The real world in which the laborer lives, as shown by his lofty conversation and noble living, may be as far above that of his employer as heaven is high above hell. The greatest monetary success on earth may mean the dreariest failure in the world to come.

What a shock was given to the would-be aristocratic world when President Lincoln took off his hat and bowed in silence to a colored ex-slave in Richmond, after that city had fallen. "God bless you, Massa Linkum," was the fervid exclamation of many an ignorant negro, after the Emancipation Proclamation had been delivered.

It is an interesting fact in this money-getting era that a poor author, or a seedy artist, or a college president with frayed coat-sleeves, has more standing in society and has more paragraphs written about him in the papers than many a millionaire. This is due, perhaps, to the malign influence of money-getting and to the benign effect of purely intellectual pursuits. As a rule every great success in the money world means the failure and misery of hundreds of antagonists. Every success in the world of intellect and character is an aid and profit to society. Character is a mark cut upon something, and this indelible mark determines the only true value of all people and all their work.

Dr. Hunter said: "No man was ever a great man who wanted to be one." Artists cannot help putting themselves and their own characters into their works. The vulgar artist cannot paint a virtuous picture. The gross, the bizarre, the sensitive, the delicate, all come out on the canvas and tell the story of his life.

Byron once wrote of a passion, which was one that he did not possess: —

> "A thirst for gold,
> The beggar's vice, which can but overwhelm
> The meanest hearts."

He might have written "the noblest hearts," with truth. It is absurd to suppose that any one sees any inherent sin in riches any more than he does in tennis or dancing. But Christ, who said to his disciples, "Verily I say unto you, that a rich man shall hardly enter into the Kingdom of Heaven," well understood the moral degeneracy that almost inevitably attends the struggle for great wealth. Somehow, in spite of many examples to the contrary, the race for thousands, and then millions, often strangles nobility of character and tarnishes the soul of honor.

Money-getting has well been called unhealthy when it impoverishes the mind, or dries up the sources of the spiritual life; when it extinguishes the sense of beauty, and makes one indifferent to the wonders of nature and art; when it blunts the moral sense, and confuses the distinction between right and wrong, virtue and vice; when it stifles religious impulse, and blots all thoughts of God from the soul.

Money-getting is unhealthy, when it engrosses all one's thought, leads a man to live meanly and coarsely, to do without books, pictures, music, travel, for the sake of greater gains, and causes him to find his deepest and most soul-satisfying joy, not in the culture of his heart or mind, not in doing good to himself or others, but in the adding of eagle to eagle, in the knowledge that the money in his chest is piled up higher and higher every year, that his account at the bank is constantly growing, that he is adding bonds to bonds, mortgages to mortgages, stocks to stocks.

An Arab who fortunately escaped death after losing his way in the desert, without provisions, tells of his feelings when he found a bag full of pearls, just as he was about to abandon all hope. "I shall never forget," said he, "the relish and delight that I felt on supposing it to be fried wheat, nor the bitterness and despair I suffered on discovering that the bag contained pearls."

A miser, robbed of a store of buried gold, over which he had long gloated in secret, was advised by a wise friend to bury some oyster-shells in the place where the gold had been, and visit them and chuckle over their possession daily.

In a fable an old miser is said to have kept a tame jackdaw that would steal pieces of money and hide them in a hole. The cat reproved him, as the coins would be of no use to him. The jackdaw replied: "Why, my master has a whole chestful and makes no more use of them than I."

King Midas, in the ancient myth, asked that everything he touched might be turned to gold, for then, he thought, he would be perfectly happy. His request was granted, but when his clothes, his food, his drink, the flowers he plucked, and even his little daughter, whom he kissed, were all changed into yellow metal, he begged that the Golden Touch might be taken from him. He had learned that many other things are intrinsically far more valuable than all the gold that was ever dug from the earth.

Socrates did not teach for money, but to propagate wisdom. He declared that the highest reward he could enjoy was to see mankind benefited by his labors.

Agassiz would not lecture at five hundred dollars a

night, because he had no time to make money. Charles Sumner, when a senator, declined to lecture at any price, saying that his time belonged to Massachusetts and the nation. Spurgeon would not speak for fifty nights in America at one thousand dollars a night, because he said he could do better: he could stay in London and try to save fifty souls. All honor to the comparative few in every walk of life who, amid the strong materialistic tendencies of our age, still speak and act earnestly, inspired by the hope of rewards other than gold or popular favor. These are our truly great men and women. They labor in their ordinary vocations with no less zeal because they give time and thought to higher things.

After he had conquered Mysore, Wellington was offered $500,000 by the East India Company, but he refused to touch the money.

Charles Napier was offered $100,000 by an Indian prince, as a bribe, but he refused the proffered gift of the barbarian.

Weirtz, of Brussels, said to a man who wanted to buy one of his pictures, "Keep your money. Gold is a death-blow to art." It has been said that "man's intellect receives its highest polish where gold and silver lose theirs." A little integrity is better than a great career of questionable method.

Luther's will stated that he left "no money, no treasures of any kind or description," yet the king did not sit upon his throne so securely as did Luther upon the throne of honor.

"There is a burden of care in getting riches," says Matthew Henry, "fear in keeping them, temptation in using them, guilt in abusing them. sorrow in losing them, and a burden of account at last to be given up concerning them."

"These are my jewels," said Cornelia to the Campanian lady who asked to see her gems; and she pointed with pride to her boys returning from school. The reply was worthy the daughter of Scipio Africanus and wife of Tiberius Gracchus. The most valuable production of any country is its crop of men.

He is the richest man who enriches his country most; in whom the people feel richest and proudest; who gives himself with his money; who opens the doors of opportunity widest to those about him; who is ears to the deaf, eyes to the blind, and feet to the lame. Such a man makes every acre of land in his community worth more, and makes richer every man who lives near him. On the other hand, many a millionaire has impoverished the town in which he lived, and lessened the value of every foot of land.

"I know of no great man," said Voltaire, "except those who have rendered great services to the human race." Men are measured by what they do, not by what they possess.

"Is there a physician," asks Bulwer, "who has not felt at times how that ceremonious fee throws him back from the garden-land of humanity into the market-place of money — seems to put him out of the pale of equal friendship, and say: 'True, you have given health and life. Adieu! there, you are paid for it'?"

When a letter from Washington was read in Congress, suggesting the propriety of bombarding Boston, a solemn silence ensued, for all the members knew that their presiding officer, John Hancock, was a large owner of real estate in that town. To give him an opportunity to speak, the body resolved itself into a committee of the whole, when Mr. Hancock said: "It is true, sir, nearly all my property in the world is in houses and other real estate in the town of Boston; but if the expulsion of the British army from it, and the liberties of our country, require their being burnt to ashes, issue the order for that purpose immediately."

Barrows of Cambridge resigned his professorship to make a place for his pupil, Isaac Newton.

If we work upon gold it will perish; if upon brass, time will efface it; if we rear temples, they will crumble into dust. But if we work upon immortal minds — if we imbue them with high principles, with the just fear of God, with manhood and the respect of it — we engrave on these tables something which no time can efface, but which will grow brighter through all eternity.

" Education — a debt due from present to future generations," was the sentiment found in a sealed envelope opened during the centennial celebration at Danvers, Mass. In the same envelope was a check for twenty thousand dollars for a town library and institute. The sender was George Peabody, one of the most remarkable men of this century, once a poor boy, but then a millionaire banker. At another banquet given in his honor at Danvers, years afterwards, he gave two hundred and fifty thousand dollars to the same institute. " Steadfast and undeviating truth," said he, " fearless and straightforward integrity, and an honor ever unsullied by an unworthy word or action, make their possessor greater than worldly success or prosperity. These qualities constitute greatness."

Neither a man's means, nor his worth, are measurable by his money. If he has a fat purse and a lean heart, a broad estate and a narrow understanding, what will his " means " do for him — what will his " worth " gain him? What sadder sight is there than an old man who has spent his whole life getting instead of growing? He has piled up books, statuary, and paintings, with his wealth, but he is a stranger amongst them. His soul has shriveled to that of a miser, and all his nobler instincts are dead.

The honesty and integrity of A. T. Stewart won for him a great reputation, and the young schoolmaster who began life in New York on less than a dollar a day, amassed nearly forty million dollars, and there was not a smirched dollar in all those millions.

Do you call him successful who wears a bull-dog expression that but too plainly tells the story of how he gained his fortune, taking but never giving? Can you not read in that brow-beating face the sad experience of widows and orphans? Do you call him a self-made man who has unmade others to make himself,— who tears others down to build himself up? Can a man be really rich who makes others poorer? Can he be happy in whose every lineament chronic avarice is seen as plainly as hunger in the countenance of a wolf? How seldom sweet, serene, beautiful faces are seen on men who have been very successful as the world rates success! Nature expresses in the face and manner the sentiment which rules the heart.

When petitioned to license the opium traffic, the pagan emperor of China said: "Nothing will induce me to derive a revenue from the vice and misery of my people." But Christian England has been only too glad to derive an immense income from this very traffic, and Christian America still obtains large sums from the sale of licenses to dealers in alcoholic drinks. No wonder the state, which should be a father instead of a murderer, nourishes a degraded race of men, bereft of the old-fashioned virtues of pity, and benevolence, and generosity, who, wherever there is a glitter of gold, claw one another to obtain the vulgar metal.

In the days of the Abolitionists, a great "Union Saving Committee" of their opponents met at Castle Garden, New York, and decided that merchants who would not oppose the "fanatics" should be put on a "Black List" and crushed financially. Messrs. Bowen & McNamee, however, stated in their advertisements that they hoped to sell their silks, but would not sell their principles. Their independent stand created a great sensation throughout the country. People wanted to buy of men who would not sell themselves.

When Scipio Africanus was accused of peculation, he refused to disgrace himself by waiting for justification, though he had the scroll of his accounts in his hands. He immediately tore the paper to pieces before the tribunes.

When the corner-stone of the Washington monument was laid, July 4, 1848, Mr. Winthrop said: "Build it to the skies — you cannot outreach the loftiness of his principles; found it upon the massive and eternal rock — you cannot make it more enduring than his fame; construct it of the purest Parian marble — you cannot make it purer than his life."

Webster said: "America has furnished to the world the character of Washington; if our American institutions had done nothing else, that alone would have entitled them to the respect of mankind."

Where, asked Byron, —

"Where may the wearied eye repose
  When gazing on the great,
Where neither guilty glory glows,
  Nor despicable state!

"Yes, one — the first, the last, the best,
  The Cincinnatus of the West,
    Whom envy dared not hate —
Bequeathed the name of Washington,
To make men blush there was but one!"

Lord Erskine wrote to Washington: "You are the only being for whom I have an awful reverence."

Charles James Fox, in the House of Commons, spoke of that "illustrious man, before whom all borrowed greatness sinks into insignificance."

Lord Brougham said: "Until time shall be no more, will a test of the progress which our race has made in wisdom and virtue be derived from the veneration paid to the immortal name of Washington!"

Gladstone called Washington "the purest figure in history," and added: "If, among all the pedestals supplied by history for public characters of extraordinary nobility and purity, I saw one higher than all the rest, and if I were required at a moment's notice to name the fittest occupant for it, I think my choice, at any time within the last forty-five years, would have lighted, and it would now light, upon Washington!"

Fisher Ames wrote: "He changed mankind's ideas of political greatness."

Lafayette, speaking of his friend, said: "Never did I behold so superb a man."

"We look with amazement," wrote an eminent thinker, "on such eccentric characters as Alexander, Cæsar, Cromwell, Frederick, and Napoleon, but when Washington's face rises before us, instinctively mankind exclaims, 'This is the man for nations to trust and reverence, and for rulers to follow.'"

Washington practiced the profound diplomacy of truthful speech, — the consummate tact of direct attention.

Lincoln always yearned for a rounded wholeness of character; and his fellow lawyers called him "perversely honest." Nothing could induce him to take the wrong side of a case, or to continue on that side after learning that it was unjust or hopeless. After giving considerable time to a case in which he had received from a lady a retainer of two hundred dollars, he returned the money, saying: "Madam, you have not a peg to hang your case on." "But you have earned that money," said the lady. "No, no," replied Lincoln, "that would not be right. I can't take pay for doing my duty."

"The greatest works," says Waters, "have brought the least benefit to their authors. They were beyond the reach of appreciation before appreciation came. The benefactors of mankind have never stooped to the quest of lucre. Who can conceive of Socrates or St. Paul, Martin Luther or John Wesley, John Hampden or George Washington, scheming to make money?"

There should be something in a man's life greater than his occupation or his achievements; grander than acquisition or wealth; higher than genius; more enduring than fame. Men and nations put their trust in education, culture, and the refining influences of civilized life, but these alone can never elevate or save a people. Art, luxury, and degradation have been boon companions all down the centuries.

Phidias was adding the last touch of grace to Grecian art in the Parthenon when the glory of Athens departed. Rome fell when art was in its golden age, while Mars, Bacchus, and Venus sat upon the throne of the Cæsars. Wealth is demoralizing when obtained at the sacrifice of character. The more money a man or nation has, the more moral strength is needed to protect from its demoralizing influence.

A man may make millions and be a failure still. Money-making is not the highest success. The life of a well-known millionaire was not truly successful. He had but one ambition. He coined his very soul into dollars. The almighty dollar was his sun, and was mirrored in his heart. He strangled all other emotions and hushed and stifled all nobler aspirations. He grasped his riches tightly, till stricken by the scythe of death; when, in the twinkling of an eye, he was transformed from one of the richest men who ever lived in this world to one of the poorest souls that ever went out of it.

"The truest test of civilization," says Emerson, "is not the census, nor the size of cities, nor the crops; no, but the kind of man the country turns out."

Character is success, and there is no other.

The passion for wealth often stifles every noble aspiration. Rothschild was called "one of the most devout worshipers that ever laid a withered soul upon the altar of Mammon." Is it any wonder that our young men start out with a false idea of the great object of life, when they see everybody else bowing and scraping and running after the men with crowns of gold upon their heads, but with corruption in their hearts?

When a lady is married, people ask, "Did she marry well?" That is, did she marry money; not, did she marry an honest, clean, upright man? Can anything be more pitiable than a fat purse and a lean soul, a large house and a small character?

"When I asked you for anecdotes upon the age of this king," said Voltaire, while preparing his "History of Louis XIV.," "I referred less to the king himself than to the art which flourished in his reign. I should prefer details relating to Racine and Boileau, to Sully, Molière, Lebrun, Bossuet, Poussin, Descartes, and others, than to the battle of Steinkirk. Nothing but a name remains of those who commanded battalions and fleets, nothing results to the human race from a hundred battles gained; but the great men of whom I have spoken prepared pure and durable delights for generations unborn. A canal that connects the seas, a picture by Poussin, a beautiful tragedy, a discovered truth, are things a thousand times more precious than all the annals of the court, than all the narratives of war. You know that with me great men rank first, heroes last. I call great men those who have excelled in the useful or the agreeable. The ravagers of provinces are mere heroes."

"Not a child did I injure," says the epitaph of an Egyptian ruler who lived in a pagan age more than forty centuries ago. "Not a widow did I oppress. Not a herdsman did I ill treat. There were no beggars in my day, no one starved in my time. And when the years of famine came, I ploughed all the lands of the province to its northern and southern boundaries, feeding its inhabitants and providing their food. There was no starving person in it, and I made the widow to be as though she possessed a husband." What ruler can say as much in our enlightened age?

"When real history shall be written by the truthful and the wise," says Ingersoll, "the kneelers at the shrines of chance and fraud, the brazen idols once worshiped as gods, shall be the very food of scorn, while those who have borne the burden of defeat, who have earned and kept their self-respect, who have never bowed to men or power, will wear upon their brows the laurel mingled with the oak."

Emerson well said that the advantage of riches remains with him who procured them, not with the heir. "When I go into my garden with a spade," he says, "and dig a bed, I feel such an exhilaration and health, that I discover I have been defrauding myself all this time in letting others do for me what I should have done with my own hands. But not only health, but education, is in the work. Is it possible that I who get indefinite quantities of sugar, hominy, cotton, buckets, crockery-ware, and letter-paper, by simply signing my name once in three months to a check in favor of John Smith & Co., traders, get the fair share of exercise to my faculties by that act, which nature intended for me in making all these far-fetched matters important to my comfort?"

"My kingdom for a horse," said Richard III. of England amid the press of Bosworth Field. "My kingdom for a moment," said Queen Elizabeth on her death-bed. And millions of others, when they have felt earth, its riches and power slipping from their grasp, have shown plainly that deep down in their hearts they value such things at naught when really compared with the blessed light of life, the stars and flowers, the companionship of friends, and far above all else, the opportunity of growth and development here and of preparation for future life.

History shows that the time always comes when anguish and hunger rise greater than wealth and crush it. That was the story of the French Revolution. What anarchist is so base as to have threatened George W. Childs, of Philadelphia, because he was a rich man? He might blow up others, but not Mr. Childs. Is it not because the famous editor exhibited something in his character greater than wealth, that irresistibly softened hatred, drew the hungry to him for bread, the ignorant for education, the homeless for a home?

He was here to supply those needs, and the love of humanity, and the sympathy for all kinds of want and suffering,—these were the greatest things in the world to him. Doing good to others, he said, was the greatest pleasure of his life. History demonstrates what the Bible teaches, that love is the greatest thing in the world. A beautiful illustration comes to us from the life of Mr. Charles N. Crittendon, who has strikingly lived up to the Golden Rule. When he became as rich as he thought he ought to be, he took into partnership five of the heads of departments in his great wholesale house in New York. The voluntary transfer by a man of large means, of a large interest in his business to his employees without the payment of a penny, is unique in this money-grasping age.

Mr. Crittendon devotes his entire time to evangelistic work, and his fortune to founding Florence Crittendon missions for the rescue of erring girls. The story of their founding melts all hearts to tenderness and all eyes to tears. A few years ago, his little four-year-old Florence, on her dying bed, pleaded: "Papa, sing 'The Sweet By and By.'" With choking voice and breaking heart her father sang the beautiful words, and her beloved spirit floated heavenward on the wings of song.

Mr. Crittendon went down into the slums and helped

to uplift the fallen, and one night when he was pleading with a poor erring girl to leave her life of shame, he said in the words of Christ: "Neither do I condemn thee; go and sin no more." Through her tears she said, "Where can I go?"

Quick as a flash came the thought, "Where can she go? Scarce a door save a door of sin is open to her;" and then and there he determined, as a memorial to his own little Florence, to found a home where other fathers' little girls, lost in the whirlpool of shame, might be rescued and restored to a life of virtue. So on Bleecker Street, New York, a few years ago, was opened the first Florence Crittendon Mission, a large double four-story house, where food and shelter and clothing and a home are freely given, and under the influence of Mother Prindle, the W. C. T. U. matron, hundreds become Christian women. Over five hundred girls annually find a home here, and three fourths of them are redeemed.

Mr. Crittendon has also established Florence Crittendon missions in New Brunswick, N. J., San José, Sacramento, Los Angeles, and San Francisco, California.

It is the dream of his life to found a Florence Crittendon mission in every large city in America and Europe, and plans to that end are made with the Woman's Christian Temperance Union, under the leadership of Miss Frances E. Willard and Lady Henry Somerset.

Thank God! there are some things beyond the reach of "influence" and better than the madness for a brown-stone front. Gold cannot vie with virtue, and social position does not create manhood. Trusts and monopolies only control the lower things of life.

There are men who choose honesty as a soul companion. They live in it, with it, by it. They embody it in their actions and lives. Their words speak it. Their faces beam it. Their actions proclaim it. Their hands are true to it. Their feet tread its path. They are full of it. They love it. It is to them like a God. Not gold, or crowns, or fame, could bribe them to leave it. It makes them beautiful men, noble, great, brave, righteous men.

"No man has come to true greatness," said Phillips Brooks, "who has not felt in some degree that his life belongs to his race, and that what God gives him, He gives him for mankind."

> "The rank is but the guinea's stamp
> The man's the gowd for a' that."

> "The noblest men that live on earth
> Are men whose hands are brown with toil,
> Who, backed by no ancestral graves,
> Hew down the woods and till the soil,
> And win thereby a prouder name
> Than follows king's or warrior's fame."

CHAPTER XV.

THE PRICE OF SUCCESS.

The gods sell anything and to everybody at a fair price. — EMERSON.
To color well requires your life. It cannot be done cheaper. — RUSKIN.
There is no fate! Between the thought and the success, God is the only agent. — BULWER.

> "We have but what we make, and every good
> Is locked by nature in a granite hand,
> Sheer labor must unclench."

> "By hammer and hand all arts do stand."

To be thrown upon one's own resources is to be cast into the very lap of fortune. — FRANKLIN.
Heaven never helps the man who will not act. — SOPHOCLES.
The talent of success is nothing more than doing what you can do well, and doing well whatever you do, without a thought of fame. — LONGFELLOW.
There is no road to success but through a clear, strong purpose. A purpose underlies character, culture, position, attainment of whatever sort. — T. T. MUNGER.
Mankind worships success, but thinks too little of the means by which it is attained, — what days and nights of watching and weariness, how year after year has dragged on, and seen the end still far off: all that counts for little, if the long struggle do not close in victory. — H. M. FIELD.

"WHAT a heavenly mournful expression!" exclaims Miss Sybil in Bulwer's "Kenelm Chillingly," as she gazes at the baby; "it seems so grieved to have left the angels!"

"That is prettily said, cousin Sybil," replied the clergyman, "but the infant must pluck up courage and fight its way among mortals with a good heart, if it wants to get back to the angels again."

The same principle obtains in the performance of even trivial tasks.

An ancient Greek thought to save his bees a laborious

SAMUEL F. B. MORSE

"What hath God wrought." (*First telegraphic message.*)

"A constant struggle, a ceaseless battle to bring success from inhospitable surroundings, is the price of all great achievements."

flight to Hymettus. He cut their wings and gathered flowers for them to work upon at home, but they made no honey.

"Oh, if I could thus put a dream on canvas!" exclaimed an enthusiastic young artist, pointing to a most beautiful painting. "Dream on canvas!" growled the master, "it is the ten thousand touches with the brush you must learn to put on canvas that make your dream."

"Not so very long to do the work itself," said a great artist, when asked the time required to paint a cottage scene with an old woman trying to thread a needle near the open door, "but it took me twenty years to get that pose of the figure, and to correctly represent that sunlight coming in at the door."

"You charge me fifty sequins," said a Venetian nobleman to a sculptor, "for a bust that cost you only ten days' labor." "You forget," said the artist, "that I have been thirty years learning to make that bust in ten days."

"If only Milton's imagination could have conceived his visions," says Waters, "his consummate industry alone could have carved the immortal lines which enshrine them. If only Newton's mind could reach out to the secrets of nature, even his genius could only do it by the homeliest toil. The works of Bacon are not midsummer's-night dreams, but, like coral islands, they have risen from the depths of truth, and formed their broad surfaces above the ocean by the minutest accretions of persevering labor. The conceptions of Michael Angelo would have perished like a night's phantasy, had not his industry given them permanence."

"There is but one method of attaining excellence," said Sydney Smith, "and that is hard labor."

The mottoes of great men often give us glimpses of the secret of their characters and success. "Work! work! work!" was the motto of Sir Joshua Reynolds,

David Wilkie, and scores of other men who have left their mark upon the world. Voltaire's motto was "Toujours au travail" (always at work). Scott's maxim was "Never be doing nothing." Michael Angelo was a wonderful worker. He even slept in his clothes ready to spring to his work as soon as he awoke. He kept a block of marble in his bedroom that he might get up in the night and work when he could not sleep. His favorite device was an old man in a go-cart, with an hour-glass upon it, bearing this inscription: "Ancora imparo" (still I'm learning). Even after he was blind he would ask to be wheeled into the Belvidere, to examine the statues with his hands. Cobden used to say, "I'm working like a horse without a moment to spare." It was said that Händel, the musician, did the work of a dozen men. Nothing ever daunted him. He feared neither ridicule nor defeat. Lord Palmerston worked like a slave, even in his old age. Being asked when he considered a man in his prime, he replied, "Seventy-nine," that being his own age. Humboldt was one of the world's great workers. In summer he arose at four in the morning for thirty years. He used to say work was as much of a necessity as eating or sleeping. Sir Walter Scott was a phenomenal worker. He wrote the "Waverley Novels" at the rate of twelve volumes a year. He averaged a volume every two months during his whole working life. What an example is this to the young men of to-day, of the possibilities of an earnest life! Edmund Burke was one of the most prodigious workers that ever lived.

Daniel Webster said, "I have worked for more than twelve hours a day for fifty years." Charles James Fox became a great orator, yet few people outside of his personal friends had any idea of how he struggled to perfect himself in "the art of all arts." He never let an opportunity for speaking or self-culture pass unimproved. Henry Clay could have been found almost daily for years in some old Virginia barn, declaiming to the cattle for an audience. He said, "Never let a day go by without exercising your power of speech." Cæsar controlled men by exciting their fear; Cicero by captivating their affections and swaying their passions. The influence of one perished with its author; that of the other continues to this day. Beecher used to practice speaking for years in the woods and pastures.

"Work or starve," is nature's motto, — and it is written on the stars and the sod alike, — starve mentally, starve morally, starve physically. It is an inexorable law of nature that whatever is not used, dies. "Nothing for nothing," is her maxim. If we are idle and shiftless by choice, we shall be nerveless and powerless by necessity.

We are the sum of our endeavors. "Our reward is in the race we run, not in the prize."

"I acquired all the talent I have," said John Sebastian Bach, "by working hard: and all who like to work as hard will succeed just as I have done."

"What is the secret of success in business?" asked a friend of Cornelius Vanderbilt. "Secret! there is no secret about it." replied the commodore; "all you have to do is to attend to your business and go ahead." If you would adopt Vanderbilt's method, know your business, attend to it, and keep down expenses until your fortune is safe from business perils.

A Southern student at Andover bought some wood, and went to Professor Stuart to learn whom he could get to saw it. "I am out of a job of that kind," said Mr. Stuart; "I will saw it myself."

Do not choose your life-work solely for the money that you can make by it. It is a contemptible estimate of an occupation to regard it as a mere means of making a living. The Creator might have given us our bread ready-made. He might have kept us in luxurious Eden forever; but He had a grander and nobler end in view when He created man, than the mere satisfaction of his animal appetites and passions. There was a divinity within man, which the luxuries of Eden could never develop. There was an inestimable blessing in that curse which drove him from the garden, and compelled him forever to earn his bread by the sweat of his brow. It was not without significance that the Creator concealed our highest happiness and greatest good beneath the sternest difficulties, and made their attainment conditional upon a struggle for existence. "Our motive power is always found in what we lack." Never feel above your business. All legitimate occupations are respectable. "The ploughman may be a Cincinnatus, or a Washington, or he may be brother to the clod he turns." During the Revolutionary War the soldiers were trying to raise a heavy timber which they could scarcely lift from the ground. A young corporal stood by, urging the men to lift hard, and shouting, "Now, boys, right up." when a superior officer rode up, dismounted, and lifted with the men. When the timber was in place the officer asked the corporal why he did not help. "I am a corporal," he replied. "I am George Washington," responded the officer. "You will meet me at your commander's headquarters."

Depend upon it, there is always something wrong about the young man or woman who looks upon manual labor as degrading. Manual labor was never considered degrading until slavery came into existence.

"Laboremus" (we must work) was the last word of the dying Emperor Severus, as his soldiers gathered around him. "Labor," "achievement," was the great Roman motto, and the secret of her conquest of the world. The greatest generals returned from their triumphs to the plough. Agriculture was held in great esteem, and it was considered the highest compliment to call a Roman a great agriculturist. Many of their family names were derived from agricultural terms, as

Cicero from "cicer," a chick-pea, and Fabius from "faba," a bean, etc. The rural tribes held the foremost rank in the early days of the Empire. City people were regarded as an indolent, nerveless race.

Rome was a mighty nation while industry led her people, but when her great conquest of wealth and slaves placed her citizens above the necessity of labor, that moment her glory began to fade; vice and corruption, induced by idleness, doomed the proud city to an ignominious history. Cicero, Rome's great orator and statesman, said: "All artisans are engaged in a disgraceful occupation;" and Aristotle, a stranger to Christian philosophy, said: "The best regulated cities will not permit a mechanic to be a citizen, for it is impossible for one who leads the life of a mechanic, or hired servant, to practice a life of virtue. Some were born to be slaves." But fortunately, there came One mightier than Rome, Cicero, or Aristotle, whose magnificent life and example forever lifted the ban from labor, and redeemed it from disgrace. He gives significance to labor and dignity to the most menial service. Christ did not say, "Come unto me, all ye pleasure-hunters, ye indolent, and ye lazy;" but, "Come all ye that labor and are heavy laden." A noble manhood or womanhood will lift any legitimate calling into respectability.

It is manhood nature is after, not money or fame. Oh, what price will she not pay for a man! Ages and æons were nothing for her to spend in preparing for his coming, or in making his existence possible. She has rifled the centuries for his development, and placed the universe at his disposal. The world is but his kindergarten, and every created thing but an object-lesson from the unseen universe. Nature resorts to a thousand expedients to develop a perfect type of her grandest creation. To do this she must induce him to fight his way up to his own loaf. She never allows him once to lose sight of the fact that it is the struggle to attain that develops the man. The moment we put our hand upon that which looks attractive at a distance, and which we struggle so hard to reach, nature robs it of its charm by holding up before us another prize still more attractive. The toy which the child could not be induced to give up, he forsakes willingly when he sees the orange. So we relinquish one prize to pursue another, but with the added strength, developed in the struggle to attain the last.

Nature has left man in this unstable equilibrium, lest the satisfaction from the possession of that which he struggled so hard to get rob him of his ambition for new conquests. The struggle to obtain is the great gymnasium of the race. Nature puts pleasure in the acquisition of that which the heart covets, but the moment we place our hand upon the prize, the charm vanishes ; its usefulness is gone ; it can develop no more character, no more stamina, no more manhood. What if —

> "That which shone afar so grand
> Turns to ashes in the hand?
> On again : the virtue lies
> In the struggle, not in the prize."

Labor is the great schoolmaster of the race. It is the grand drill in life's army, without which we are only confused and powerless when called into action. What a teacher industry is! It calls us away from conventional instructors, books, and theories, and brings us into the world's great school — into actual contact with men and things. The perpetual attrition of mind upon mind rasps off the rough edges of unpractical life and gives polish to character. It teaches patience, perseverance, forbearance, and application. It teaches method and system, by compelling us to crowd the most possible into every day and hour. Industry is a perpetual call upon the judgment. the power of quick decision ; it makes ready men, practical men.

"To have any chance of success, I must be more steady than other men," Lord Campbell wrote to his father as an excuse for not visiting home; "I must be in chambers when they are at the theatre; I must study when they are asleep; I must, above all, remain in town when they are in the country."

Why does a bit of canvas with the "Angelus" on it bring one hundred and twenty-five thousand dollars, while that of another artist brings but a dollar? Because Millet put one hundred and twenty-five thousand dollars' worth of brains and labor into his canvas, while the other man put only a dollar's worth into his. Work is worthless unless mixed with brains.

A blacksmith makes five dollars' worth of iron into horseshoes, and gets ten dollars for them. The cutler makes the same iron into knives, and gets two hundred dollars. The machinist makes the same iron into needles, and gets sixty-eight hundred dollars. The watchmaker takes it and makes it into mainsprings, and gets two hundred thousand dollars; or into hair-springs, and gets two million dollars, sixty times the value of the same weight of gold.

So it is with our life material which is given us at birth. Do something with it we must. We cannot throw it away, for even idleness leaves its curse upon it. One young man works his up into objects of beauty and utility. He mixes brains with it. Another botches and spoils his without purpose or aim until, perhaps late in life, he comes to his senses and tries to patch up the broken and wasted pieces; but it is a sorry apology to leave, in payment for a life of magnificent possibilities.

"Why, my lord," said a flippant English clergyman to the Bishop of Litchfield, "it is the easiest thing in the world to preach. Why, very often, I choose my text after I go into the pulpit, and then go on and preach a sermon, and think nothing of it." "Ah, yes," said the bishop, "that agrees exactly with what I hear your people say, for they hear the sermon, and they, too, think nothing of it."

The world is full of just-a-going-to-bes,— subjunctive heroes who might, could, would, or should be this or that but for certain obstacles or discouragements,— prospectuses which never become published works. They all long for success, but they want it at a discount. The "one price" for all is too high. They covet the golden round in the ladder, but they do not like to climb the difficult steps by which alone it can be reached. They long for victory, but shrink from the fight. They are forever looking for soft places and smooth surfaces where there will be the least resistance, forgetting that the very friction which retards the train upon the track, and counteracts a fourth of all the engine's power, is essential to its locomotion. Grease the track, and, though the engine puffs and the wheels revolve, the train will not move an inch.

Work is difficult in proportion as the end to be attained is high and noble. God has put the highest price upon the greatest worth. If a man would reach the highest success he must pay the price himself. No titled pedigree, no money inherited from ancestors with long bank accounts, can be given in exchange for this commodity. He must be self-made or never made.

The Romans arranged the seats in their two temples to Virtue and Honor, so that no one could enter the second without passing through the first. Such is the order of advance,— Virtue, Toil, Honor.

All would like to succeed, but this is not enough. Who would be satisfied with the success which may be had for the wishing? You can have what you desire, if you will pay the price. But how much do you want to succeed? Will you pay the price? How eager are you to strive for success? How much can you endure? How long can you wait?

Do you long for an education? Would you, if necessary, wear threadbare clothes in college, and board yourself? Would you, like Thurlow Weed, study nights by the light of a camp-fire in a sugar-orchard? Would you walk through the snow two miles, with pieces of rag carpet tied about your feet for shoes, that you might, like him, borrow a coveted book? Have you the stamina to go on with your studies when too poor to buy bread, and when you can appease the pangs of hunger only by tying tighter and tighter about your body a girdle, as did Samuel Drew or Kitto? Would you, like John Scott, rise at four and study until ten or eleven at night, tying a wet towel around your head to keep awake; would you, when too poor to buy books, borrow and copy three folio volumes of precedents, and the whole of Coke on Littleton, with the boy who became Lord Eldon? Would you be disheartened by Wilberforce's suggestion to a student of law: "You must make up your mind to live like a hermit and work like a horse"? Can you eat sawdust without butter, as the great lawyer, Chitty, asked the young man who came to him for advice about studying law? Have you the determination that would hammer an education from the stone-quarry, with Hugh Miller; the patience that would spend a lifetime tracing the handwriting of the Creator down through the ages in the strata of the rocks? Would you work on a farm for twelve long years for a yoke of oxen and six sheep, with Henry Wilson? Do you love learning well enough to walk forty miles to obtain a book you could not afford to buy, with Abraham Lincoln? Not that we would recommend such extreme measures; but if you saw no way open except such as was traveled by these and many other great men, would you be equal to the stern ordeal, and learn from experience that "the royal road to learning" is a myth, and that the real road is one that tears the brow with its thorns, and exhausts the heart with its disappointments?

Would you be an orator and sway the minds of men? Would you train your voice for months on the seashore with only the wild waves for your audience, with Demosthenes? Would you, like him, cure yourself of a peculiar shrug by practicing with naked shoulders under the sharp points of suspended swords? Could you stand calm and unmoved in Faneuil Hall, amid hisses and showers of rotten eggs, with Wendell Phillips? Have you the stamina that would keep you on your feet in Parliament with a Disraeli when every sentence is hailed with derisive laughter? Could you stand your ground, as he did, until you had compelled the applause of "the first gentlemen in the world"? Have you the determination that carried Curran again and again to speak in that august Parliament from which he had been so often hissed? Would you persevere, like Savonarola, Cobden, Sheridan, and scores of others who broke down completely at their first attempts, in spite of repeated and ignominious failures? If, like Daniel Webster, you could not manage to declaim throughout your whole school course, could you still find courage to become a public speaker? Would you black boots for the students at Oxford with George Whitefield? Would you, like Beecher, begin preaching in a church of nineteen members in an obscure town in Indiana, and act as sexton, janitor, and minister? Would you, like Anna Dickinson, face the jeers and hisses, and even the pistol-bullets of the Molly Maguires? Would you preach Christ and Him crucified amid the scorn of skeptics, the pangs of martyrdom?

Do you yearn to be an artist, and transfer to canvas or set free from marble the beauty which haunts your soul? Would you join Michael Angelo in carrying mortar for the frescoers up long ladders, to catch some suggestions from their words or work?

Would you, at sixty-five, while the pope yet sleeps, don your overalls and dig your own ochre in the rear of the Vatican, and devote your whole day to your art? Could you work patiently for seven long years decorating the Sistine Chapel with the "Story of the Creation" and the immortal "Last Judgment"? Would you refuse remuneration for this work, lest you be swerved from the ideal dominating your soul? Would you rise at dead of night, seize hammer and chisel, and call from the rough marble the angel which haunts your dreams and will not let you sleep?

Would you excel in literature? Would not the dread of rejected manuscript, returned with thanks, dishearten you after you had given it years of your ripest thought and great sacrifice? Are you willing to live unrecognized and die unknown? You would have written Shakespeare's plays, but could you wait two hundred years for recognition, and die without even receiving mention from your greatest contemporary? Would you pay Goethe's price for distinction? "Each bon mot of mine," said he, "has cost a purse of gold. Half a million of my own money, the fortune I inherited, my salary, and the large income derived from my writings for fifty years back, have been expended to instruct me in what I know." Would you have laboriously created and dictated "Paradise Lost" in a world you could not see, and then sell it for fifteen pounds, in an age in which a learned London critic could say: "The blind schoolmaster has written a tedious poem on 'The Fall of Man,' and unless length has merit, it has none"? Would not the grating of the jail door and the long nights in a dungeon dampen your ardor for the authorship of even the immortal "Pilgrim's Progress"? Would you endure the agonies of a De Quincey in order to write his matchless visions and analyses? Would you live on the border-land of want and woe and temptation for many years, with Poe, even for the sake of pioneering human thought into unexplored regions of weird and mystic speculation, of exquisite, ethereal beauty? Would you endure the misery of Cowper that you might wail your anguish in song, or dally with the story of the inimitable John Gilpin? Could you, with Euripides, be content to devote three days to five lines, that those lines might live centuries after your language had ceased to be spoken? Could you have the patience and perseverance of Moore, that you might produce ten immortal lines a day? Could you have the persistence of Isaac Newton, who, after spending long years on an intricate calculation, had his papers destroyed by his dog Diamond, and then cheerfully began to replace them? Have you the courage of Carlyle, who, after he had lent the manuscript of the "French Revolution" to a friend, whose servant carelessly used it to kindle the fire, calmly went to work and rewrote it? Would you wheel supplies in a barrow through the streets of Philadelphia, with a Franklin?

Would you be a soldier? Could you, like Napoleon, wait for an appointment seven years after you had prepared yourself thoroughly, and use all your enforced leisure in further intense study? Could you, while losing nine battles out of every ten, still press on with an iron determination which would win you Blücher's title of "Marshal Forward"? Could you, while losing more battles than you won, go on with Washington and conquer by the power of your character?

Would you bless your race by inventions or discoveries? Could you cheerfully earn the means to carry on your experiments by working in Richard Arkwright's barber-shop in a basement, with this sign over your door: "Come to the Subterraneous Barber — a Clean Shave for a Halfpenny"? Could you plod on with enthusiasm after seeing a mob tear down the mill you had erected for the employment of your machinery? Is incessant labor for fifteen weary years too great a price to pay for George Stephenson's first successful locomotive? Is thirty years too long to spend with Watt

THE PRICE OF SUCCESS.

amid want and woe in perfecting the condensing-engine? Is your determination strong enough to carry you to the verge of ruin, time and again, and to enable you when your credit is exhausted, and your wife has turned against you, to burn the palings of your fence and the furniture and floor of your house, and then add the shelves of your pantry to the fire which develops an enamel like Palissy's? If cast into prison, could you experiment with the straw in your cell, with Galileo? Can you lie more than once in a debtor's prison and live on charity much of the time, for ten years, to win the triumph of Goodyear, whose friend could truthfully say: "If you see a man with an India-rubber coat on, India-rubber shoes, and India-rubber cap, and in his pocket an India-rubber purse, with not a cent in it, that is Goodyear"? Could you have the heart to perfect an invention beyond almost any other at its first introduction, only to find with Eli Whitney or Elias Howe, that those whom it was intended to bless refused to use it at first, and later tried to steal it?

Could you wait eight years for a patent on telegraphy with Samuel F. B. Morse, and then almost fight for a chance to introduce it? Could you invent a hay-tedder, and then pay a farmer for trying it on his hay, because he said it would "knock the seeds off"? Would you, after inventing McCormick's reaper, have the persistence to introduce it into England amid the ridicule of the press, the "London Times" calling it "a cross between an Astley chariot, a wheelbarrow, and a flying-machine"? Would you live in the woods for years to reproduce Audubon's drawings of North American birds, after they had been destroyed by Norway rats, or toil over Alps and Andes with Agassiz, or go with Pliny to describe the volcano, Mt. Ætna, that was to destroy your life? Would your passion for art give you nerve like that of Vernet to sketch the towering wave on the Mediterranean that threatened to engulf your vessel?

Would your patience suffice to practice on Händel's harpsichord in secret until every key was hollowed by your fingers to resemble the bowl of a spoon? If a physician, would you inoculate yourself with a yellow-fever or cholera bacillus, to test its power? Would you take three grains of opium to test the power of a new antidote you believed you had discovered, permanganate of potash?

In politics, could you persevere to be a candidate sixteen times in vain, to be elected Governor Marcus Morton of Massachusetts in 1840 by a majority of but one vote? Could you endure the most bitter persecution for years, to rank with William Lloyd Garrison as a benefactor of an unfortunate race? After acquiring fortune, could you give up your well-earned leisure, devote years of almost hopeless drudgery, and risk all your wealth, amid the scoffs of men, in a seemingly futile attempt to bind two continents together by an electric cord, with Cyrus W. Field?

Success is the child of drudgery and perseverance. Fame never comes because it is craved.

If you are built of such material as this, you will succeed; if not, in spite of all your dreams and wishes you will fail. Most people look upon poverty as bad fortune, and forget that it has ever been the priceless spur in nearly all great achievements, all down the ages.

Jean Paul Richter, who suffered greatly from poverty, said that he would not have been rich for worlds.

"How unfortunate it is for a boy to have rich parents," said James Gordon Bennett to George W. Childs. "If you and I had been born that way, we would never have done anything worth mentioning."

"I began life with a sixpence," said Girard, "and believe that a man's best capital is his industry."

How nature laughs at puny society caste, and at attempts to confine greatness behind brown-stone fronts!

She drops an idiot on Fifth Avenue or Beacon Street, where a millionaire looked for a Webster or a Sumner, and leaves a Garfield in a log-cabin in the wilderness, where humble parents expected only a pioneer. She astonishes a poor blacksmith with a Burritt, and gives a dunce to a wealthy banker. A fool may be born in a palace, and the Saviour of the world in a stable. Truly royal men and women look out of cold and miserable attic windows, from factories and poorhouses, upon people much their inferiors, though dressed in broad-cloths and satins, whose dishonesty and craft have overcome them in the battle of life.

What an army of young men enters the success-contest every year as raw recruits! Many of them are country youths flocking to the cities to buy success. Their young ambitions have been excited by some book, or fired by the story of some signal success, and they dream of becoming Astors or Girards, Stewarts or Wanamakers, Vanderbilts or Goulds, Lincolns or Garfields, until their innate energy impels them to try their own fortune in the magic metropolis. But what are you willing to pay for "success," as you call it, young man? Do you realize what that word means in a great city in the nineteenth century, where men grow gray at thirty and die of old age at forty, — where the race of life has become so intense that the runners are treading on the heels of those before them; and "woe to him who stops to tie his shoestring"? Do you know that only two or three out of every hundred will ever win permanent success, and only because they have kept everlastingly at it; and that the rest will sooner or later fail and many die in poverty because they have given up the struggle?

It is said of the young men who entered business on State Street, Boston, forty years ago, that even their names are almost forgotten. Most of them were killed in the fierce struggle of competition.

Read the diary of an old man on Long Wharf, Boston, where the battle waged less fiercely: "Of all I knew in business, only five have succeeded in forty years. All the others failed or died in want." Of a thousand depositors in the Union Bank, all but six failed or died poor. "Bankruptcy," said one of the old bank directors, "is like death and almost as certain. They fall single and alone, and are thus forgotten, but there is no escape, and he is fortunate who fails young." In Pemberton Square among the lawyers, an old friend of Rufus Choate and Daniel Webster tells us there are two thousand attorneys in Boston, and only four hundred get a living by their profession, and only now and then one becomes distinguished.

In a work on business, published in eighteen hundred and fifty-two, Edwin T. Freedley gave a select list of the first-class wholesale houses in Philadelphia. On reëxamining the list twenty-three years later, he found but two out of seventeen of the importing firms he had mentioned; two out of twenty-two dry goods houses: four out of twenty-five dry goods jobbing houses; nine of the silk firms; eight out of twenty-five drug houses; one out of seventeen boot and shoe jobbers; and a total of only twenty-five out of the one hundred and seventy-seven wholesale firms he had considered the most solid in the City of Brotherly Love. The thought of this cold reality is appalling, and we almost shrink from effort when success seems so much like a lottery with very few prizes.

But he who would succeed must pay the price. He must not look for a "soft job." Into work which he feels to be a part of his very existence he must pour his whole heart and soul. He must be fired by a determination which knows no defeat, which cares not for hunger or ridicule, which spurns hardships and laughs at want and disaster. They were not men of luck and broadcloth, nor of legacy and laziness, but men inured to hardship and deprivation, — not afraid of threadbare clothes and honest poverty, men who fought their way to their own loaf, — who have pushed the world up from chaos into the light of the highest civilization. They were men who, as they climbed, expanded and lifted others to a higher plane and opened wider the doors of narrow lives.

> If thou canst plan a noble deed,
> And never flag till it succeed,
> Though in the strife thy heart should bleed ;
> Whatever obstacles control,
> Thine hour will come, — go on, true soul,
> Thou 'lt win the prize, — thou 'lt reach the goal.
> CHARLES MACKAY.

No pain, no palm ; no thorns, no throne; no gall, no glory; no cross, no crown. — PENN.

CHAPTER XVI.

CHARACTER IS POWER.

Character is power — is influence ; it makes friends ; creates funds ; draws patronage and support ; and opens a sure and easy way to wealth, honor, and happiness. — J. HAWES.

>When all have done their utmost, surely he
>Hath given the best who gives a character
>Erect and constant.
>   LOWELL.

I'm called away by particular business, but I leave my character behind me. — SHERIDAN.

As there is nothing in the world great but man, there is nothing truly great in man but character. — W. M. EVARTS.

>The spirit of a single mind
>Makes that of multitudes take one direction,
>As roll the waters to the breathing wind.   BYRON.

Character must stand behind and back up everything — the sermon, the poem, the picture, the play. None of them is worth a straw without it. — J. G. HOLLAND.

The alleged power to charm down insanity, or ferocity in beasts, is a power behind the eye. — EMERSON.

Character is the diamond that scratches every other stone. — BARTOL.

"DAREST thou kill Caius Marius?" said the unarmed Roman to the assassin sent to his dungeon. The Cimbrian quailed before the captive's eye, dropped his weapon, and fled.

Learning that Napoleon would soon pass alone through a long dim passage, a young man hid there to slay the ruthless invader of his country. As the emperor approached, his massive head bowed in thought, the young man raised his weapon, took careful aim, and was about to press the trigger when a slight noise betrayed his presence. Napoleon looked up, and comprehended the situation at a glance. He did not speak, but gazed intently upon the youth, a smile of haughty

GEORGE WASHINGTON

"That tower of strength
Which stood four square to all the winds that blew."

challenge upon his face. The weapon fell from nerveless hands, and the hero of a hundred fields passed on in silence, his head again bowed in meditation upon affairs of state. To him it was but one incident in a crowded career, a mere personal triumph soon lost sight of amid memories of battles which shook the world with the thunder of his victorious legions. To the young man it was the experience of a lifetime, a crushing, bewildering sense of his own inferiority in comparison with the enormous, ponderous weight of character of a man who threw every fibre and faculty and power of his being into the life he was living. As well might the glowworm match himself against the lightning!

"Let a king and a beggar converse freely together." said Bulwer, "and it is the beggar's fault if he does not say something which makes the king lift his hat to him." What is that to which the king would make obeisance? Information? No. He would not lift his hat to that. Is there not something which the poorest and humblest may have in equal or greater proportion than the monarch — manliness? We admire wisdom, but we bow our heads before a man, whether he be a child of misfortune or a king.

"Be you only whole and sufficient," says Emerson, "and I shall feel you in every part of my life and fortune, and I can as easily dodge the gravitation of the globe as escape your influence." Character is power.

"No, say what you have to say in her presence, too," said King Cleomenes of Sparta, when his visitor Anistagoras asked him to send away his little daughter Gorgo, ten years old, knowing how much harder it is to persuade a man to do wrong when his child is at his side. So Gorgo sat at her father's feet, and listened while the stranger offered more and more money if Cleomenes would aid him to become king in a neighboring country. She did not understand the matter, but when she saw her father look troubled and **hesitate,** she took hold of his hand and said, "Papa, come away — come, or this strange man will make you do wrong." The king went away with the child, and saved himself and his country from dishonor. Character is power, even in a child. When grown to womanhood, Gorgo was married to the hero Leonidas. One day a messenger brought a tablet sent by a friend who was a prisoner in Persia. But the closest scrutiny failed to reveal a single word or line on the white waxen surface, and the king and all his noblemen concluded that it was sent as a jest. "Let me take it," said Queen Gorgo; and, after looking it all over, she exclaimed, "There must be some writing underneath the wax!" They scraped away the wax and found a warning to Leonidas from the Grecian prisoner, saying that Xerxes was coming with his immense host to conquer all Greece. Acting on this warning Leonidas and the other kings assembled their armies and checked the mighty host of Xerxes, which is said to have shaken the earth as it marched.

During the Revolutionary War, Richard Jackson was accused of an intention to join the British army, and admitted the truth of the charge. He was committed to the rude county jail, from which he could have escaped easily; but he considered himself held by due process of law, and his sense of duty forbade flight under such circumstances.

He asked leave of the sheriff to go out and work by day, promising to return each night. Consent was given readily, as his character for simple honesty was well known, and for eight months he went out each morning and returned at evening. At length the sheriff prepared to take him to Springfield, to be tried for high treason. Jackson said this would be needless trouble and expense, for he could go just as well alone. Again his word was taken, and he set off alone. On the way he was overtaken by Mr. Edwards of the council of Massachusetts, who asked whither he was going. "To Springfield, sir," was the reply, "to be tried for my life."

The proof was complete, and Jackson was condemned to death. When the president of the council asked if a pardon should be granted, member after member opposed, until Mr. Edwards told the story of his meeting with Jackson in the woods. By common consent a pardon was at once made out. The childlike simplicity and integrity of the man had saved his life. Character is power.

In the great monetary panic of 1857, a meeting was called of the various bank presidents of New York city. When asked what percentage of specie had been drawn during the day, some replied fifty per cent., some even as high as seventy-five per cent., but Moses Taylor of the City Bank said: "We had in the bank this morning, $400,000; this evening, $470,000." While other banks were badly " run," the confidence in the City Bank under Mr. Taylor's management was such that people had deposited in that institution what they had drawn from other banks. Character gives confidence.

"One man speaks with the accent of conviction, and his words are edicts. Nations run to obey, as if to obey was the only joy they coveted. Another speaks hesitatingly and only makes us question whether the gift of speech be, on the whole, a blessing."

We can calculate the efficiency of an engine to the last ounce of pressure. Its power can be as accurately determined as the temperature of a room. But who can rightly determine the inherent force of a man of predominant character? Who can estimate the influence of a single boy or girl upon the character of a school? Traditions, customs, manners have been changed for several school generations by one or two strong characters, who in their own small way, but none the less important, have become school heroes — as much real forces in life as if they were locomotives dragging loads of cars. Any teacher will tell you that many a school has been pulled up grade, or run down, by just such imperious characters.

When war with France seemed imminent, in 1798, President Adams wrote to George Washington, then a private citizen in retirement at Mount Vernon: "We must have your name, if you will permit us to use it; there will be more efficacy in it than in many an army." Character is power.

Wellington said that Napoleon's presence in the French army was equivalent to forty thousand additional soldiers, and Richter said of the invincible Luther, "His words were half battles."

St. Bernard had such power over men that mothers hid their sons, wives their husbands, companions their friends, lest they should be persuaded to enter the monastery.

"You could not stand with Burke under an archway while a shower of rain was passing," said Dr. Johnson, "without discovering that he was an extraordinary man."

Warren Hastings said he thought himself the basest of men while Burke was hurling at him his terrible denunciations when on trial for his alleged misrule in India.

"Hence it was," said Franklin, speaking of the influence of his known integrity of character, "that I had so much weight with my fellow citizens. I was but a bad speaker, never eloquent, subject to much hesitation in my choice of words, hardly correct in language, and yet I generally carried my point."

"The man behind the sermon," said William M. Evarts, "is the secret of John Hall's power." In fact if there is not a man with a character behind it nothing about it is of the slightest consequence.

John Brown (of Ossawatomie) said: "One good,

strong, sound man is worth one hundred, nay, one thousand men without character, in building up a state."

We all believe in the man of character. What power of magic lies in a great name! Theodore Parker used to say that Socrates was worth more to a nation than many such states as South Carolina.

Jefferson once wrote to Washington: "The confidence of the whole nation centres in you." There was not a throne in Europe that could stand against Washington's character, and in comparison with it the millions of the Rothschilds would look ridiculous. What are the works of avarice compared with the names of Lincoln, Grant, or Garfield? A few names have ever been the salt which has preserved the nations from premature decay.

"It is the nature of party in England," said John Russell, "to ask the assistance of men of genius, but to follow the guidance of men of character."

"My road must be through character to power," wrote Canning in 1801. "I will try no other course; and I am sanguine enough to believe that this course, though not perhaps the quickest, is the surest."

Power is the great goal of ambition, and it is only through a noble character that one can arrive at a personality strong enough to move men and nations.

"The thought, the feeling in the central man in a great city touches all who are in it who think and feel," said C. T. Brooks. "The very boys catch something of his power, and have something about them that would not be there if he were not in the town."

During the civil war in France, Montaigne alone kept his castle gates unbarred, and was not molested. His character was more powerful than the king's guards. Truly, as Pope says, he's armed without that's innocent within.

History and biography show many wonderful instances of the immunity accorded to men of character.

A strange talisman seemed to surround them. Read the lives of William Penn. Roger Williams. Xavier. Livingstone, and of many others who courted danger for the sake of religion or science, and why is it that they have been spared by the savage spear? Character is protection.

In the army, fleeing from Moscow amid the bewildering snows of a biting Russian winter, was a German prince whose sterling character had endeared him to all his soldiers. One bitter night, in the ruins of a shed built for cattle, all lay down to sleep, cold, tired, and hungry. At dawn the prince awoke, warm and refreshed, and listened to the wind as it howled and shrieked around the shed. He called his men, but received no reply. Looking around, he found their dead bodies covered with snow, while their cloaks were piled upon himself — their lives given to save his.

"There is a time for all things," said the Reverend Peter J. G. Muhlenburg to his congregation at Woodstock, Va., about the close of seventeen hundred and seventy-five; "a time to preach and a time to pray, but those times have passed away. There is a time to fight and that time has now come." So saying, he flung aside his ministerial robes and stood before them in the full uniform of a Virginia colonel. Nearly every man in his congregation joined him; and, with others quickly rallied from a distance, he marched to do noble service in the Revolutionary War, from which he returned an honored major-general.

"I fear, my Attilia, that, for this year, our little fields must remain unsown," said Quintius Cincinnatus to his wife, as the deputies of the Roman Senate led him away to a consulship, when the great empire was in danger. They had found him holding the plough, clad in plain attire, and apparently destitute of ambition for office. By his moderation, humanity, and justice in the midst of factional jealousy, he soon restored public tranquillity, and returned to his plough.

CHARACTER IS POWER.   257

Another exigency soon arose, when the Eternal City needed character, and the senate made him dictator, with unlimited power. He restored public confidence, reorganized the army, defeated a powerful enemy, and then, having refused any share of the rich spoil, he resigned the dictatorship which he had held but fourteen days, and resumed work upon his farm as calmly as if nothing had happened.

"O sir, we are beaten," exclaimed the general in command of Sheridan's army, retreating before the victorious Early. "No, sir," replied the indignant Sheridan; "you are beaten, but this army is not beaten." Drawing his sword, he waved it above his head, and pointed it at the pursuing host, while his clarion voice rose above the horrid din in a command to charge once more. The lines paused, turned, —

> "And with the ocean's mighty swing,
> When heaving to the tempest's wing,
> They hurled them on the foe;"

and the Confederate army was wildly routed.

How could an ancient battle be won by bringing upon the field, bound upright upon his familiar charger, the corpse of Douglas, of whose death his troops were ignorant? When Clan Alpine's best were borne backward in Scott's "Lady of the Lake," why would one blast upon his bugle-horn have been worth a thousand men, if blown by Roderick Dhu, then lying in his blood at Stirling Castle? Surely a living private were better than a dead general, and scores of mountaineers could blow as loud a blast as Roderick. The power all emanated from the character or spirit of which the clay on horseback was known as the outward embodiment, and the stirring bugle-call the voice.

One of the most dramatic illustrations of the force of manhood in action, and at the same time in restraint, comes to us from the Civil War. The following thrilling description of the charge at New Market Heights is an extract from General Butler's speech on the Civil-Rights Bill:—

"Now, sir, you will allow me to state how I got over my prejudices. I think the House got over theirs after the exhibition we had yesterday. I think no man will get up here and say he speaks only to white men again. He must, at first, show himself worthy before he can speak for some colored men in the House, after what occurred yesterday.

"I came into command in Virginia in eighteen hundred and sixty-three. I there organized twenty-five regiments, with some that were sent to me, and disciplined them. Still, all my brother officers of the regular army said my colored soldiers would not fight, and I felt it was necessary that they should fight to show that their race was capable of the duties of citizens; for one of the highest duties of citizens is to defend their own liberties and their country's flag and honor. I went myself with the colored troops to attack the enemy at New Market Heights, which was the key to the enemy's flank on the north side of James River. When the flash of dawn was breaking, I placed a column of three thousand colored troops, in close column by division, right in front, with guns at right shoulder shift.

"I said: 'That work must be taken by the weight of your column: no shot must be fired;' and to prevent their firing I had the caps taken from the nipples of their guns. Then I said: 'Your cry, when you charge, will be "Remember Fort Pillow;"' and as the sun rose up in the heavens the order was given 'Forward,' and they marched forward, steadily as if on parade—went down the hill, across the marsh, and as they got into the brook they came within range of the enemy's fire, which vigorously opened upon them. They broke a little as they forded the brook, and the column wavered. Oh, it was a moment of intensest anxiety, but they formed again as they reached the firm ground, marching steadily on with closed ranks under the enemy's fire, until the head of the column reached the first line of abatis, some one hundred and fifty yards from the enemy's works. Then axemen ran to the front to cut away the heavy obstructions of defense, while one thousand men of the enemy with their artillery concentrated, from the redoubt, poured a heavy fire upon the head of the column hardly wider than the clerk's desk. The axemen went down under the murderous fire; other strong hands grasped the axes in their stead, and the abatis was cut away. Again, at double-quick, the column goes forward to within forty yards of the fort, to meet there another line of abatis. The column halts. And there a very fire of hell is poured upon them. The abatis resists and holds, the head of the column seemed literally to melt away under the shot and shell, the flags of the leading regiments go down, but a brave black hand seizes the colors; strong hands and willing hearts seize the heavy, sharpened trees and drag them away, and the column went forward, and, with a shout which now rings in my ear, they went over that redoubt like a flash, and the enemy never stopped running for four miles.

"It became my painful duty, sir, to follow in the track of that charging column, and there, in a space not wider than the clerk's desk and three hundred yards long, lay the dead bodies of five hundred and forty-three of my colored soldiers, slain in defense of their country, and who had laid down their lives to uphold its flag and its honor as a willing sacrifice; and, as I rode along among them, guiding my horse this way and that way, lest he should profane with his foot what seemed to me the sacred dead, and I looked on their bronzed faces upturned in the shining sun to heaven, as if in mute appeal against the wrongs of that country for which they had given their lives, and whose flag had only been to them a flag of stripes, on which no star of glory had ever shone for them,— feeling that I had wronged them in the past, and believing what was the future of my country to them,— among my dead comrades there I swore to myself a solemn oath: 'May my right hand forget its cunning and my tongue cleave to the roof of my mouth, if I ever fail to defend the rights of these men who have given their blood for me and my country this day and for their grace forever;' and, God helping me, I will keep that oath."

On the 2d of September, 1792, the populace broke into the prisons of Paris, crowded almost to suffocation with aristocrats and priests. These fell like grain before the scythe of the reaper. But in the midst of that wild revel of blood, a *sans culotte* recognized the Abbé Sicard, who had spent his life teaching the deaf and dumb, and in whose house —

> "The cunning fingers finely twined
> The subtle thread that knitteth mind to mind;
> There that strange bridge of signs was built where roll
> The sunless waves that sever soul from soul,
> And by the arch, no bigger than a hand,
> Truth traveled over to the silent land."

"Behold the bosom through which you must pass to reach that of this good citizen," said Mounot, who knew the abbé only by sight and reputation; "you do not know him. He is the Abbé Sicard, one of the most benevolent of men, the most useful to his country, the father of the deaf and dumb." And the murderers around embraced him, and wished to carry him home in their arms. Even in that bloodstained throng the power of a noble character was still supreme.

The Franks had maintained a siege of the Roman walls of Paris until the starving garrison began to despair, although their fortifications were strong enough. No warrior was willing to incur the risk of going out in search of provisions. But Genevieve, a maid of the garrison, went down the Seine in a little boat, beyond the camp of the besiegers, and succeeded in persuading the different Gallic tribes to send supplies to their famished brethren.

The Franks withdrew; but, in a later attempt when Genevieve was absent, they seized the city and closed the gates in mysterious fear that she might return, the guards being specially instructed to deny her admittance. But in the homely gown and veil of a peasant she entered unsuspected, and appeared before the Frank leader Hilperik in the midst of a wild carousal. What passed in that interview is not known beyond the fact that the barbarian granted safety to his captives and mercy to all the people. She is regarded to this day the patron saint of Paris.

Character, when expressed, is only reflex action: it is the doing what we have always resolved to do when the chance came. Character is like stock in trade; the more of it a man possesses, the greater his facilities for adding to it. Just as a man prizes his character, so is he.

Sir Philip Sidney, mortally wounded at Zutphen, was tortured by thirst from his great loss of blood. Water was carried to him. A wounded soldier borne by on a litter fixed his eyes upon the bottle with such a wistful gaze that Sidney insisted on giving it to him, saying, "Thy necessity is greater than mine." Sidney died, but this deed alone would have made his name honored when that of the king he served is forgotten. Florence Nightingale tells of soldiers suffering with dysentery, who, scorning to report themselves sick lest they should force more labor on their overworked comrades, would go down to the trenches and make them their death-beds. Say what you will, there is in the man who gives his time, his strength, his life, if need be, for something not himself, — whether he call it his queen, his country, his colors, or his fellow man, — something more truly

Christian than in all the ascetic fasts, humiliations, and confessions that have ever been made.

Porsena threatened Caius Mutius with torture, when the latter coolly stretched his right hand into the campfire, and watched it burn to a crisp without a groan. The Tuscan freed his prisoner, and concluded a treaty with Rome, the country which reared such men as Mutius and Horatius.

"I have read," Emerson says, "that they who listened to Lord Chatham felt that there was something finer in the man than anything which he said." It has been complained of Carlyle that when he has told all his facts about Mirabeau they do not justify his estimate of the latter's genius. The Gracchi, Agis, Cleomenes, and others of Plutarch's heroes do not in the record of facts equal their own fame. Sir Philip Sidney and Sir Walter Raleigh are men of great figure and of few deeds. We cannot find the smallest part of the personal weight of Washington in the narrative of his exploits. The authority of the name of Schiller is too great for his books. This inequality of the reputation to the works or the ancedotes is not accounted for by saying that the reverberation is longer than the thunder-clap; but something resided in these men which begot an expectation that outran all their performance. The largest part of their power was latent. This is that which we call character, — a reserved force which acts directly by presence, and without means. What others effect by talent or eloquence. the man of character accomplishes by some magnetism. "Half his strength he puts not forth." His victories are by demonstration of superiority, and not by crossing bayonets. He conquers, because his arrival alters the face of affairs. "O Iole! how didst thou know that Hercules was a god?" "Because," answered Iole, "I was content the moment my eyes fell on him. When I beheld Theseus, I desired that I might see him offer battle, or at least drive his horses in the chariot-race; but Hercules did not wait for a contest; he conquered whether he stood, or walked, or sat, or whatever else he did."

There are men and women in every country who conquer before they speak, and who exert an influence out of all proportion to their ability, and people wonder what is the secret of their power over men. It is natural for all classes to believe in and to follow character, for character is power. Even the murderer respects the justice of the judge who pronounces his death-sentence. Something in him instinctively feels and indorses its right and justice. Never did Cæsar exert a greater influence over the Roman people than when he lay upon the marble floor of the senate, pierced by cruel daggers, — his wounds so many open mouths pleading for him.

It was said of Sheridan : "Had he possessed principle he might have ruled the world." How few young men realize that their success in life depends more upon what they are than upon what they know. It was character, not ability, that elected Washington and Lincoln to the presidency.

Webster bid high for the presidency. The price was his honor — all his former convictions. When a farmer heard that he had lost the nomination, he said : " The South never pays its slaves."

What is this principle that Napoleon and Webster lacked? Is it not a deathless loyalty to the highest ideal which the world has been able to produce up to the present date? This is what we admire and respect in strong men whose roots are deep in the ground and whose character is robust enough to keep them like oaks in their places when all around is whirling.

"Trying to run without a pilot," was the only comment of a captain, as a passenger once pointed to a wreck lying upon the rocks. This would form a pertinent inscription over Byron, Burns, and many a premature grave. Character is safety.

When promised protection in Turkey if he would embrace the Mohammedan religion, the exiled Kossuth replied: "Between death and shame, I have never been dubious. Though once the governor of a generous people, I leave no inheritance to my children. That were at least better than an insulted name. God's will be done. I am prepared to die." "These hands of mine," he said at another time, "are empty but clean."

"Mamma," exclaimed the young Princess Victoria, "I cannot see who is to come after Uncle William unless it is myself." When told that she was the heir apparent, she said: "I will be good."

More than half a century has elapsed since this princess of eighteen years was roused from slumber on the 21st of June, 1837, and summoned to appear before the Archbishop of Canterbury. Without even time to dress, she hastily threw a wrapper over her nightrobes, and, with slippers on bare feet, and hair in disorder, she went before the archbishop and was saluted "Queen." The king was dead, and business of state will not wait for ladies' toilets. With all the dignity, innocence, and good sense of a true woman, the young queen extended her hand for the customary kiss of allegiance. Character, courtesy, and sound judgment have distinguished her wonderful reign of over half a century, and not once has she ceased to be a real queen.

When Petrarch approached the tribunal to take the customary oath as a witness, he was told that such was the confidence of the court in his veracity that his word would be sufficient, and he would not be required to swear to his testimony.

Hugh Miller was offered the position of cashier in a large bank, but declined, saying that he knew little of accounts, and could not get a bondsman. "We do not require bonds of you," said Mr. Ross, president of the bank. Miller did not even know that Ross knew him.

Our characteristics are always under inspection whether we realize it or not.

"No man ever entered Mr. Pitt's closet who did not feel himself a braver man when he came out," said an eminent soldier who knew Chatham well.

When Florence Nightingale entered the hospital at the Crimea, the whole atmosphere seemed changed. From those rough soldiers, tossing on beds of anguish, there came not a word to shock the most fastidious.

Vittoria Colonna wrote her husband, when the princes of Italy urged him to desert the Spanish cause, to which he was bound by every tie of faithfulness, "Remember your honor, which raises you above kings. By that alone, and not by titles and splendor, is glory acquired — the glory which it will be your happiness and pride to transmit unspotted to your posterity."

When Thoreau lay dying, a Calvinistic friend asked anxiously, "Henry, have you made your peace with God?" "John," whispered the dying naturalist, "I didn't know God and myself had quarreled."

Lincoln, although President of a great people, was the laughing-stock of the aristocratic and fashionable circles of Europe. The illustrated papers of all Christendom caricatured the awkwardness and want of dignity of this backwoods graduate. Politicians were shocked at the simplicity of his state papers, and wished to make them more conventional; but Lincoln only replied, "The people will understand them." Even in Washington he was ridiculed as "the ape," "stupid blockhead," and "satyr." On reading these terrible denunciations and criticisms, he once said, "Well, Abraham Lincoln, are you a man or are you a dog?" After the repulse at Fredericksburg he said, "If there is a man out of hell that suffers more than I do, I pity him." But the great heart of the common people beat in unison with his. The poor operatives in European cotton-mills sometimes nearly starved for lack of cotton, but they never petitioned their government to break Lincoln's blockade. Working people, the world over, believed in and sympathized with him.

No man ever lived of whom it could have been more truly said that, —

> " The elements
> So mixed in him that nature might stand up
> And say to all the world, ' This is a man.' "

The world, it is said, is always looking for men who are not for sale; men who are honest, sound from centre to circumference, true to the heart's core; men whose consciences are as steady as the needle to the pole; men who will stand for the right if the heavens totter and the earth reels; men who can tell the truth, and look the world and the devil right in the eye; men that neither brag nor run; men that neither flag nor flinch; men who can have courage without shouting to it; men in whom the courage of everlasting life runs still, deep, and strong; men who know their message and tell it; men who know their places and fill them; men who know their own business and attend to it; men who will not lie, shirk, nor dodge; men who are not too lazy to work, not too proud to be poor; men who are willing to eat what they have earned, and wear what they have paid for; men who are not afraid to say "No" with emphasis, and who are not ashamed to say, "I can't afford it."

"How true it is that many millionaires, like the butternut, impoverish the ground upon which they grow; others are like the olive-trees which enrich the very soil upon which they feed. Others are affluent souls, which enrich by their very presence, whose smiles are full of blessing, and whose touch has a balm of healing in it like the touch of Him of Nazareth."

If there is any one power in the world that will make itself felt, it is character. There may be little culture, slender abilities, no property, no position in "society;" yet, if there be a character of sterling excellence, it will demand influence and secure respect.

"A man, Cæsar, is born," says Emerson, "and for ages after, we have a Roman empire. Napoleon changes the front of the world. Bacon turns in a new direction the thought of the human race. Newton interprets the thoughts of God. Franklin unlocks the temple of Nature."

"A right act strikes a chord that extends through the whole universe, touches all moral intelligence, visits every world, vibrates along its whole extent, and conveys its vibrations to the very bosom of God."

Do you not see a quality greater than leadership or generalship in Moses at the Red Sea, Leonidas at Thermopylæ, Horatius at the bridge, Winkelried at Lake Zurich, Napoleon at Arcola or Lodi, Ney guarding the rear of the Grand Army, Nelson at the Nile, Wolfe at Quebec, Allen at Ticonderoga, Arnold at Saratoga, Washington at Yorktown, Perry at Lake Erie, Jackson at New Orleans, Farragut on the Mississippi, Grant at Vicksburg, Sheridan at Winchester, or in scores of others who have achieved triumphs in war or in peace?

Louis XIV. asked Colbert how it was that, ruling so great and populous a country as France, he had been unable to conquer so small a country as Holland. "Because," said the minister, "the greatness of a country does not depend upon the extent of its territory, but on the character of its people."

The characters of great men are the dowry of a nation. Chateaubriand said he saw Washington but once, yet it inspired his whole life. An English tanner whose leather gained a great reputation said he should not have made it so good had he not read Carlyle. It is said that Franklin reformed the manners of a whole workshop in London. Ariosto and Titian inspired each other and heightened each other's glory. "Tell me

whom you admire, and I will tell you what you are."
A book or work of art puts us in the mood or train of
thought of him who produced it. Is Michael Angelo
dead ? Ask the hundreds of thousands who have gazed
with rapt souls upon his immortal works at Rome. In
how many thousands of lives has he lived and reigned?
Are Washington, Grant, and Lincoln dead ? Did they
ever live more truly than to-day ? What American
heart or home does not enshrine their characters ?

Picture to yourself, if you can, Egypt without a
Moses, Babylon without a Daniel, Athens without a
Demosthenes, Phidias, Socrates, or Plato. What was
Carthage two hundred years before Christ without her
Hannibal? What was Rome without her Cæsar, her
Cicero, Marcus Aurelius ? What is Paris without her
Napoleon, and Hugo, and Père Hyacinthe ? What is
England without her Newton, Shakespeare, Milton, Pitt,
Burke, Gladstone ? What is Boston without such characters as Garrison, and Phillips, and Whittier, and Emerson, and Holmes ? What is New York without such men
as Peter Cooper, or Horace Greeley ? What is California without her Stanford, or Chicago without her
Armour, Pullman, and Field ? In these cities millions
of lesser note have planned, and toiled, and worshiped,
— have lived and died, and have made the real history
which should receive our most careful attention ; but
the leaven of the thoughts, the genius, the character
of a few eminent men and women has so leavened the
whole lump of life in either city, that they are largely
typical of its history. What were the Crusades without
Peter the Hermit, Godfrey de Bouillon, and Richard
Cœur de Lion ? Take from England a score of names
like Gladstone's, and who would read her history ?

Through all the centuries of Italy's degradation
Dante's name was the watchword of the country, while
in the brain of many a slave still echoed the impassioned words of Cicero, of the Scipios, and the Gracchi.

Byron said: "The Italians talk Dante, write Dante, and think Dante at this moment to an excess which would be ridiculous but that he deserves their admiration." Even degenerate Greece is not dead to the influence of the intellectual and moral giants of her golden age. Indeed, they still hold sway throughout the earth, more potent than when living, in the realms of thought and feeling. Our minds are shaped by the combined influence of the minds of men called dead, nearly as strongly as by those with whom we associate in life; our creeds are sanctified by the devotion of martyrs in whose sufferings under persecution we share through sympathy, and are thereby ennobled; our deeds are such as we feel that our ideals would have performed under like conditions.

> "But strew his ashes to the wind
> Whose sword or voice has served mankind —
> And is he dead, whose glorious mind
> Lifts thine on high?
> To live in hearts we leave behind
> Is not to die."

Every thought which enters the mind, every word we utter, every deed we perform, makes its impression upon the inmost fibre of our being, and the resultant of these impressions is our character. The study of books, of music, or of the fine arts, is not essential to a lofty character. Those most accomplished in learning and art have often been the worst of men and women. Indeed, bookworms who become all books, and artists who become all art, are usually weak. Low, aimless lives leave their mark upon the character as truly as the Creator branded Cain with his guilt. On the other hand, there are men in whom the very dogs on the street believe. Character is power.

Turner was on the hanging-committee of the Royal Academy when the artist Bird presented a picture of merit for which no place could be found. After pleading hard for it, only to be met by the constant assertion of impracticability, Turner took down one of his own cherished pictures, and hung Bird's in its place.

Amos Lawrence gave the odd half cent and the odd quarter of a yard to his customer. It was a little thing, but it indicated his character.

We resemble insects which assume the color of the leaves and plants they feed upon, for sooner or later we become like the food of our minds, like the creatures that live in our hearts. Every act of our lives, every word, every association, is written with an iron pen into the very texture of our being. The ghosts of our murdered opportunities, squandered forces, killed time, forever rise up to rebuke us, and will not down. How hard it is to learn that like begets like; that an acorn will always become an oak, if anything; that birds of a feather will flock together; that there is a magnetic affinity between kindred things which inevitably brings them together, and that they must communicate their own properties and nothing else; that they can do no differently.

Association with the good can only produce good; with the wicked, evil. No matter how sly, how secret, no matter if our associations have been in the dark, their images will sooner or later appear in our faces and conduct. The idols of the heart look through our eyes, appear in our manners, and betray their worshipers. Our associates, our loves, hates, struggles, triumphs, defeats, dissipations, aspirations, intrigues, honesty, dishonesty, all leave their indelible autographs upon the soul's window and are published to the world. Black hearts cast black shadows upon the face which all our will power cannot drive away. What a panorama passes across the face of a dissipated life! Behold the barrooms, the dens of infamy, the dissipated wretches, the polluted companions, the disgusting scenes, the askings and denyings of passions, the struggles for victory, the broken resolutions, the sore defeats. But oh! what radiance glorifies the faces of those who have overcome temptation and disciplined their powers in striving for self-improvement!

Did you ever see a pure and noble woman enter a room where a lot of coarse, rough men were talking and telling stories? The whole character and tone of the company rises. The very atmosphere seems purer. The entire company is transformed. Sometimes we see such a woman transform a whole neighborhood. On the other hand, one bad woman may sometimes ruin a hundred young men.

We do not need an introduction to a great man to feel his greatness. If you meet a cheerful man on the street on a cold day, you seem to feel the mercury rise several degrees.

Our manners, our bearing, our presence, tell the story of our lives, though we do not speak, and the influence of every act is felt in the utmost part of the globe. Every man that ever lived contributed something towards making me what I am. The chisel of every member of society contributed a blow to the marble of my life, and influenced its destiny.

He is the greatest man, to me, at least, who emancipates me from the imprisonment of my surroundings and environments, who loosens my tongue, and unlocks the floodgates of my possibilities. He is a lens to my defective vision. I see things in a broader light, my horizon extends, my possibilities expand. My nerves thrill with the consciousness of added force. My whole being vibrates with the magnetic currents from another soul.

Anger begets anger, and hate, hate; the passions are contagious. Actors tell us that they often go upon the stage with heavy hearts and melancholy moods, when they have to play light and gay characters, without the slightest feeling of sympathy with the parts they have taken; yet so powerful is the law of association that the moment they assume the attitude of the character, the real feelings which belong to it come to them. Everything reproduces itself, and cannot do otherwise. One discordant instrument spoils the harmony of the finest orchestra, and one mischief-making man or woman ruins the peace of a town.

"Character is always known," says Emerson. "Thefts never enrich; alms never impoverish; murder will speak out of stone walls. The least mixture of a lie — for example, the taint of vanity, any attempt to make a good impression, a favorable appearance — will instantly vitiate the effect. But speak the truth and all nature and all spirits help you with unexpected furtherance."

Character is the poor man's capital.

Believe with Stevens that every man has in himself a continent of undiscovered possibilities. Happy is he who acts the Columbus to his own soul.

Luther says that the prosperity of a country depends, not on the abundance of its revenues, nor on the strength of its fortifications, nor on the beauty of its public buildings; but it consists in the number of its cultivated citizens, in its men of education, enlightenment, and character; here are to be found its true interest, its chief strength, its real power.

> "Rather the ground that's deep enough for graves,
> Rather the stream that's strong enough for waves,
>   Than the loose sandy drift
> Whose shifting surface cherishes no seed
> Either of any flower or any weed,
>   Whichever way it shift."

CHAPTER XVII.

ENAMORED OF ACCURACY.

> "Antonio Stradivari has an eye
> That winces at false work and loves the true."

Accuracy is the twin brother of honesty. — C. SIMMONS.

Genius is the infinite art of taking pains. — CARLYLE.

There is no error in this book. — KORAN.

I hate a thing done by halves. If it be right, do it boldly; if it be wrong, leave it undone. — GILPIN.

Doing well depends upon doing completely. — PERSIAN PROVERB.

> If I were a cobbler, it would be my pride
> The best of all cobblers to be;
> If I were a tinker, no tinker beside
> Should mend an old kettle like me.
>   OLD SONG.

If a man can write a better book, preach a better sermon, or make a better mouse-trap than his neighbor, though he build his house in the woods, the world will make a beaten path to his door. — EMERSON.

> Seize upon truth, where'er 't is found,
> Amongst your friends, amongst your foes,
> On Christian or on heathen ground;
> The flower 's divine where'er it grows.
>   WATTS.

"SIR, it is a watch which I have made and regulated myself," said George Graham of London to a customer who asked how far he could depend upon its keeping correct time; "take it with you wherever you please. If after seven years you come back to see me, and can tell me there has been a difference of five minutes, I will return you your money." Seven years later the gentleman returned from India. "Sir," said he, "I bring you back your watch."

"I remember our conditions," said Graham. "Let me see the watch. Well, what do you complain of?" "Why," said the man, "I have had it seven years, and there is a difference of more than five minutes."

"Indeed! In that case I return you your money." "I would not part with my watch," said the man, "for ten times the sum I paid for it." "And I would not break my word for any consideration," replied Graham; so he paid the money and took the watch, which he used as a regulator.

He learned his trade of Tampion, the most exquisite mechanic in London, if not in the world, whose name on a timepiece was considered proof positive of its excellence. Character is power. When a person once asked him to repair a watch upon which his name was fraudulently engraved, Tampion smashed it with a hammer, and handed the astonished customer one of his own masterpieces, saying, "Sir, here is a watch of my making." Graham invented the "compensating mercury pendulum," the "dead escapement," and the "orrery," none of which has been much improved since. The clock which he made for Greenwich Observatory has been running one hundred and fifty years, yet it needs regulating but once in fifteen months. Tampion and Graham lie in Westminster Abbey, because of the accuracy of their work.

To insure safety, a navigator must know how far he is from the equator, north or south, and how far east or west of some known point. as Greenwich, Paris, or Washington. He could be sure of this knowledge when the sun is shining, if he could have an absolutely accurate timekeeper; but such a thing has not yet been made. In the sixteenth century Spain offered a prize of a thousand crowns for the discovery of an approximately correct method of determining longitude. About two hundred years later the English government offered £5,000 for a chronometer by which a ship six months from home could get her longitude within sixty miles; £7,500 if within forty miles; £10,000 if within thirty miles; and in another clause £20,000 for correctness within thirty miles, a careless repetition. The watch-

GALILEO

"The better is always enemy to the best."

makers of the world contested for the prizes, but 1761 came, and they had not been awarded. In that year John Harrison asked for a test of his chronometer. In a trip of one hundred and forty-seven days from Portsmouth to Jamaica and back, it varied less than two minutes, and only four seconds on the outward voyage. In a round trip of one hundred and fifty-six days to Barbadoes, the variation was only fifteen seconds. The £20,000 was paid to the man who had worked and experimented for forty years, and whose hand was as exquisitely delicate in its movement as the mechanism of his chronometer.

"Make me as good a hammer as you know how," said a carpenter to the blacksmith in a New York village before the first railroad was built; "six of us have come to work on the new church, and I've left mine at home." "As good a one as I know how?" asked David Maydole, doubtfully, "but perhaps you don't want to pay for as good a one as I know how to make." "Yes, I do," said the carpenter, "I want a good hammer."

It was indeed a good hammer that he received, the best, probably, that had ever been made. By means of a longer hole than usual, David had wedged the handle in its place so that the head could not fly off, a wonderful improvement in the eyes of the carpenter, who boasted of his prize to his companions. They all came to the shop next day, and each ordered just such a hammer. When the contractor saw the tools, he ordered two for himself, asking that they be made a little better than those for his men. "I can't make any better ones," said Maydole; "when I make a thing, I make it as well as I can, no matter whom it is for."

The storekeeper soon ordered two dozen, a supply unheard of in his previous business career. A New York dealer in tools came to the village to sell his wares, and bought all the storekeeper had, and left a standing order for all the blacksmith could make.

David might have grown very wealthy by making goods of the standard already attained; but throughout his long and successful life he never ceased to study still further to perfect his hammers in the minutest detail. They were usually sold without any warrant of excellence, the word "Maydole" stamped on the head being universally considered a guaranty of the best article the world could produce. Character is power, and is the best advertisement in the world.

"Yes," said he one day to the late James Parton, who told this story, "I have made hammers in this little village for twenty-eight years." "Well," replied the great historian, "by this time you ought to make a pretty good hammer."

"No, I can't," was the reply, "I can't make a pretty good hammer. I make the best hammer that's made. My only care is to make a perfect hammer. I make just as many as people want and no more, and I sell them at a fair price. If folks don't want to pay me what they're worth, they're welcome to buy cheaper ones somewhere else. My wants are few, and I'm ready any time to go back to my blacksmith's shop, where I worked forty years ago, before I thought of making hammers. Then I had a boy to blow my bellows, now I have one hundred and fifteen men. Do you see them over there watching the heads cook over the charcoal furnace, as your cook, if she knows what she is about, watches the chops broiling? Each of them is hammered out of a piece of iron, and is tempered under the inspection of an experienced man. Every handle is seasoned three years, or until there is no shrink left in it. Once I thought I could use machinery in manufacturing them; now I know that a perfect tool can't be made by machinery, and every bit of the work is done by hand."

"In telling this little story," said Parton, "I have told thousands of stories. Take the word hammer out of it, and put glue in its place, and you have the history of Peter Cooper. By putting in other words, you can make the true history of every great business in the world which has lasted thirty years."

"We have no secret," said Manager Daniel J. Morrill, of the Cambria Iron Works, employing seven thousand men at Johnston, Pa. "We always try to beat our last batch of rails. That is all the secret we've got, and we don't care who knows it."

"I don't try to see how cheap a machine I can produce, but how good a machine," said the late John C. Whitin of Northbridge, Mass., to a customer who complained of the high price of some cotton machinery. Business men soon learned what this meant; and when there was occasion to advertise any machinery for sale, New England cotton manufacturers were accustomed to state the number of years it had been in use and add, as an all-sufficient guaranty of Northbridge products, "Whitin make." Put character into your work: it pays.

"My whole ambition is to establish for myself, and to deserve, the reputation of a man of science," wrote Joseph Henry, when a young man. As a natural result of following his ambition in this way, Professor Joseph Henry could say years afterward, when his name was held in high honor in every department of science: "The various offices of honor and responsibility which I hold, nine in number, have all been pressed upon me: I never occupied a position for which I have, of my own will and action, been made a candidate."

"Madam," said the sculptor H. K. Brown, as he admired a statue in alabaster made by a youth in his teens, "this boy has something in him." It was the figure of an Irishman who worked for the Ward family in Brooklyn years ago, and gave with minutest fidelity not merely the man's features and expression, but even the patches in his trousers, the rent in his coat, and the creases in his narrow-brimmed stove-pipe hat. Mr. Brown saw the statue at the house of a lady living at Newburg-on-the-Hudson. Six years later he invited her brother, J. Q. A. Ward, to become a pupil in his studio. To-day the name of Ward is that of the most prosperous of all American sculptors.

"Sculpture is the simplest thing in the world," said a rustic. "All you have to do is to take a big chunk of marble and a hammer and chisel, make up your mind what you are about to create, and then chip off all the marble you don't want."

"From whom did the artist paint that head?" asked a visitor of a "model" in a gallery. "From yours obediently, madam. I sit for the 'eads of all 'is 'oly men." "He must find you a very useful person?" "Yes, madam, I order his frames, stretch his canvas, wash his brushes, set his palette, and mix his colors. All he's got to do is to shove 'em on."

"Paint me just as I am, warts and all," said Cromwell, to the artist who had omitted a mole, thinking to please the great man.

"I can remember when you blacked my father's shoes," said one member of the House of Commons to another in the heat of debate. "True enough," was the prompt reply, "but did I not black them well?"

"It is easy to tell good indigo," said an old lady. "Just take a lump and put it into water, and if it is good, it will either sink or swim, I am not sure which; but never mind, you can try it for yourself."

John B. Gough told of a colored preacher who, wishing his congregation to fresco the recess back of the pulpit, suddenly closed his Bible and said, "There, my bredren, de Gospel will not be dispensed with any more from dis pulpit till de collection am sufficient to fricassee dis abscess."

When troubled with deafness, Wellington consulted a celebrated physician, who put strong caustic into his ear, causing an inflammation which threatened his life. The doctor apologized, expressed great regrets, and said that the blunder would ruin him. "No," said Wellington, "I will never mention it." "But you will allow me to attend you, so people will not withdraw their confidence?" "No," said the Iron Duke, "that would be lying."

"Suppose you had called to see Jenny Lind on a day when she was singing," said Mrs. Reeves; "she would probably come into the room with a bundle of music in her hand, put it on a chair and sit down upon it, talk away pleasantly enough for a few minutes, turn to a passage in one of the pieces and hum it over. Having satisfied herself of her correctness, she would replace it and sit down again as calmly as possible, and resume the conversation at the point it was broken off."

"I am reading over Macbeth," said Mrs. Siddons, when found musing over Shakespeare after she had left the stage; "and I am amazed to discover some new points in the character which I never found out in acting it."

"One language well learned," says Robert Waters, "is better than a smattering of twenty. For in the proper learning of one language you get a training of the mind, an increase of mental power, which is never gotten by smatterings."

"Father," said a boy, "I saw an immense number of dogs — five hundred, I am sure — in our street, last night." "Surely not so many," said the father. "Well, there were one hundred, I'm quite sure." "It could not be," said the father; "I don't think there are a hundred dogs in our village." "Well, sir, it could not be less than ten: this I am quite certain of." "I will not believe you saw ten even," said the father; "for you spoke as confidently of seeing five hundred as of seeing this smaller number. You have contradicted yourself twice already, and now I cannot believe you." "Well, sir," said the disconcerted boy, "I saw at least our Dash and another one."

We condemn the boy for exaggerating in order to tell a wonderful story; but how much more truthful are they who "never saw it rain so before," or who call day after day the hottest of the summer or the coldest of the winter?

There is nothing which all mankind venerate and admire so much as simple truth, exempt from artifice, duplicity, and design. It exhibits at once a strength of character and integrity of purpose in which all are willing to confide.

There are a thousand ways of lying. Ten lies are acted for every one spoken. Society is a lying organization. To say nice things merely to avoid giving offence; to keep silent rather than speak the truth; to equivocate, to evade, to dodge, to say what is expedient rather than what is truthful; to shirk the truth; to face both ways; to exaggerate; to seem to concur with another's opinions when you do not; to deceive by a glance of the eye, a nod of the head, a smile, a gesture; to lack sincerity; to assume to know or think or feel what you do not — all these are but various manifestations of hollowness and falsehood resulting from want of accuracy.

We find no lying, no inaccuracy, no slipshod business in nature. Roses blossom and crystals form with the same precision of tint and angle to-day as in Eden on the morning of creation. The rose in the queen's garden is not more beautiful, more fragrant, more exquisitely perfect, than that which blooms and blushes unheeded amid the fern-decked brush by the roadside, or in some far-off glen where no human eye ever sees it. The crystal found deep in the earth is constructed with the same fidelity as that formed above ground. Even the tiny snowflake whose destiny is to become an apparently insignificant, and a wholly unnoticed part of an enormous bank, assumes its shape of ethereal beauty as faithfully as if preparing for some grand exhibition. Planets rush with dizzy sweep through almost limitless courses, yet return to equinox or solstice at the appointed second, their very movement being "the uniform manifestation of the will of God."

The marvelous resources and growth of America have developed an unfortunate tendency to overstate, overdraw, and exaggerate. It seems strange that there should be so strong a temptation to exaggerate in a country where the truth is more wonderful than fiction. The positive is stronger than the superlative, but we ignore this fact in our speech. Indeed, it is really difficult to ascertain the exact truth in America. Read the advertisements in our papers and magazines. No one believes half of them, yet enough is believed to bring fortunes to thousands who would starve if they told the unvarnished truth about their goods, patent medicines, and wares. How many American fortunes are built on misrepresentation, needlessly, for nothing else is half so strong as truth.

"Does the devil lie?" was asked of Sir Thomas Browne. "No, for then even he could not exist." Truth is necessary to permanency.

In Siberia a traveler found men who could see the satellites of Jupiter with the naked eye. These men have made little advance in civilization, yet they are far superior to us in their accuracy of vision. It is a curious fact that not a single astronomical discovery of importance has been made through a large telescope, the men who have advanced our knowledge of that science the most, working with ordinary instruments backed by most accurately trained minds and eyes.

A double convex lens three feet in diameter is worth $60,000. Its adjustment is so delicate that the human hand is the only instrument thus far known suitable for giving the final polish, and one sweep of the hand more than is needed. Alvan Clark says, would impair the correctness of the glass. During the test of the great glass which he made for Russia, the workmen turned it a little with their hands. "Wait, boys, let it cool before making another trial," said Clark; "the poise is so delicate that the heat from your hands affects it."

Mr. Clark's love of accuracy has made his name a synonym of exactness the world over. Character is power; put it into your work.

"No, I can't do it, it is impossible," said Webster, when pressed to speak on a question soon to come up, toward the close of a Congressional session. "I am so pressed with other duties that I have n't time to prepare myself to speak upon that theme." "Ah, but, Mr. Webster, you always speak well upon any subject. You never fail." "But that's the very reason," said the orator, "because I never allow myself to speak upon any subject without first making that subject thoroughly my own. I have n't time to do that in this instance. Hence I must refuse."

When Andrew Johnson, in a great speech at Washington, said that he had begun his political career as an alderman, and had held office through all the branches of the legislature, a man in the audience shouted, "From a tailor up." "Some gentleman says I have been a tailor," said the President; "that does not disconcert me in the least, for when I was a tailor, I had the reputation of being a good one, and making close fits. I was always punctual with my customers, and always did good work."

Rufus Choate would plead before a shoemaker justice of the peace, in a petty case, with all the fervor and careful attention to detail with which he addressed the United States Supreme Court.

"Whatever is right to do," said an eminent writer, "should be done with our best care, strength, and faithfulness of purpose; we have no scales by which we can weigh our faithfulness to duties, or determine their relative importance in God's eyes. That which seems a trifle to us may be the secret spring which shall move the issues of life and death."

"There goes a man that has been in hell," the Florentines would say when Dante passed, so realistic seemed to them his description of the nether world.

"Here I stand; I cannot do otherwise, God help me!" exclaimed Luther at the Diet of Worms, facing his foes. Many a man has faced death rather than vary a hair's breadth from truth.

"There is only one real failure in life possible," said Canon Farrar; "and that is, not to be true to the best one knows."

"It is quite astonishing," Grove said of Beethoven, "to find the length of time during which some of the best known instrumental melodies remained in his thoughts till they were finally used, or the crude, vague, commonplace shape in which they were first written down. The more they are elaborated, the more fresh and spontaneous they become."

Leonardo da Vinci would walk across Milan to change a single tint or the slightest detail in his famous picture of the Last Supper. Napoleon, when sleepless, would examine the returns of his army, which he kept under his pillow. During an overture at the opera he would set himself such a problem as this: "I have ten thousand men at Strasburg, fifteen thousand at Magdeburg, twenty thousand at Würzburg. By what stages must they march so as to arrive at Ratisbon on three successive days?" "Easy writing," said Sheridan, "is commonly d—d hard reading." He wrote and rewrote most of his brilliant comedies, again and again. "Bolingbroke," said Swift, "would plod whole days and nights like the lowest clerk in his office." "Every line was then written twice over by Pope," said his publisher Dodsley, of manuscript brought to be copied.

"I gave him a clean transcript, which he sent me some time afterward for the press with every line written twice over a second time." · Gibbon wrote his memoir nine times, and the first chapters of his history eighteen times. Of one of his works Montesquieu said to a friend: "You will read it in a few hours, but I assure you it has cost me so much labor that it has whitened my hair." He had made it his study by day and his dream by night, the alpha and omega of his aims and objects. "He who does not write as well as he can on every occasion," said George Ripley, "will soon form the habit of not writing well on any occasion." Sir Isaac Newton said that whatever service he had rendered to humanity was not owing to any extraordinary sagacity he possessed, but solely to industry and patient thought. He wrote "Principia" with great care. His great love of accuracy appears in all his works. Pascal wrote one of his professional letters sixteen times. Buffon wrote his "Epoques de la Nature" eleven times before he was willing to have it published.

An accomplished entomologist thought he would perfect his knowledge by a few lessons under Professor Agassiz. The latter handed him a dead fish and told him to use his eyes. Two hours later he examined his new pupil, but soon remarked, "You have n't really looked at the fish yet. You'll have to try again." After a second examination he shook his head, saying, "You do not show that you can use your eyes." This roused the pupil to earnest effort, and he became so interested in things he had never noticed before that he did not see Agassiz when he came for the third examination. "That will do," said the great scientist. "I now see that you can use your eyes."

For many years Michael Angelo studied anatomy even more than the physicians of his day. He drew his figures in skeleton, added muscles, fat, and skin successively, and then draped them.

Reynolds said he could go on retouching a picture forever.

The captain of a Nantucket whaler told the man at the wheel to steer by the North Star, but was awakened towards morning by a request for another star to steer by, as they had "sailed by the other."

Stephen Girard was precision itself. He did not allow those in his employ to deviate in the slightest degree from his iron-clad orders. He believed that no great success is possible without the most rigid accuracy in everything. Although one of his captains had saved several thousand dollars by not buying a cargo of coffee as instructed, he discharged the man at once, saying, "You should have obeyed your orders if you had broken me."

He did not vary from a promise in the slightest degree. People knew that his word was not "pretty good," but absolutely good. He left nothing to chance. Every detail of business was calculated and planned to a nicety. He was as exact and precise even in the smallest trifles as Napoleon; yet his brother merchants attributed his superior success to good luck.

In 1805 Napoleon broke up the great camp he had formed on the shores of the English Channel, and gave orders for his mighty host to defile toward the Danube. Vast and various as were the projects fermenting in his brain, however, he did not content himself with giving the order, and leaving the elaboration of its details to his lieutenants. To details and minutiæ which inferior captains would have deemed too microscopic for their notice, he gave such exhaustive attention that, before the bugle had sounded for the march, he had planned the exact route which every regiment was to follow, the exact day and hour it was to leave that station, as well as the precise moment when it was to reach its destination. These details, so thoroughly premeditated, were carried out to the letter, and the result or fruit of that memorable march was the victory of Austerlitz, which sealed the fate of Europe for ten years.

When a noted French preacher speaks in Notre Dame, the scholars of Paris throng the cathedral to hear his fascinating, eloquent, and polished discourses. This brilliant finish is the result of most patient work, as he delivers but five or six sermons a year. Dr. Wayland gave the thought of two years to his sermon on the moral dignity of missions.

When Sir Walter Scott visited a ruined castle about which he wished to write, he wrote in a notebook the separate names of the grasses and wild flowers growing near, saying that only by such means can a writer be natural.

Macaulay never allowed a sentence to stand until it was as good as he could make it.

Besides his scrapbooks, Garfield had a large case of some fifty pigeon-holes, labeled "Anecdotes," "Electoral Laws and Commissions," "French Spoliation," "General Politics," "Geneva Award," "Parliamentary Decisions," "Public Men," "State Politics," "Tariff," "The Press," "United States History," etc.; every valuable hint he could get being preserved in the cold exactness of black and white. When he chose to make careful preparation on a subject, no other speaker could command so great an array of facts. Accurate people are methodical people, and method means character.

"I know of only three Germans in the United States who have mastered English," says Robert Waters. "I mean Mr. Carl Schurz, the late Professor Schem, and John B. Stallo of Ohio; and of only one American who has mastered German, Mr. Bayard Taylor. The rest are mere smatterers, who have learned just enough 'to get along;' and this is all they wanted to do."

"Am offered 10,000 bushels wheat on your account at $1.00. Shall I buy, or is it too high?" telegraphed a San Francisco merchant to one in Sacramento. "No price too high," came back over the wire instead of "No. Price too high," as was intended. The omission of a point cost the Sacramento dealer $1,000. How many thousands have lost their wealth or lives, and how many frightful accidents have occurred through carelessness in sending messages!

"The accurate boy is always the favored one," said President Tuttle. "Those who employ men do not wish to be on the constant lookout, as though they were rogues or fools. If a carpenter must stand at his journeyman's elbow to be sure his work is right, or if a cashier must run over his bookkeeper's columns, he might as well do the work himself as employ another to do it in that way; and it is very certain that the employer will get rid of such a blunderer as soon as he can."

Twenty things half done do not make one well done.

"If you make a good pin," said a successful manufacturer, "you will earn more than if you make a bad steam-engine."

All bad work is lying. It is thoroughly dishonest. You pay for having work done well; if it is done badly and dishonestly, you are robbed.

'T is strange, but the masterpiece, a perfect man, is the result of such an extreme delicacy, that the most unobserved flaw in the boy will neutralize the most aspiring genius, and spoil the work.

"There are women," said Fields, "whose stitches always come out, and the buttons they sew on fly off on the mildest provocation; there are other women who use the same needle and thread, and you may tug away at their work on your coat, or waistcoat, and you can't start a button in a generation."

"Carelessness," "indifference," "slouchiness." "slipshod financiering," could be truthfully written over the graves of thousands who have failed in life. How many clerks, cashiers, clergymen, editors, and professors in colleges have lost position and prestige by carelessness and inaccuracy!

"You would be the greatest man of your age, Grattan," said Curran, "if you would buy a few yards of red tape and tie up your bills and papers." Curran realized that methodical people are accurate as a rule, and successful.

Of method or system, Fuller says: "Marshal thy notions into a handsome method. One will carry twice more weight trussed and packed up in bundles, than when it lies untowardly flapping and hanging about his shoulders." Cecil says: "Method is like packing things in a box; a good packer will get in half as much again as a bad one." Said Walter Scott: "When a regiment is under march, the rear is often thrown into confusion because the front does not move steadily and without interruption. It is the same thing with business. If that which is first in hand be not instantly, steadily, and regularly dispatched, other things accumulate behind, till affairs begin to press all at once, and no human brain can stand the confusion."

Bergh tells of a man beginning business who opened and shut his shop regularly at the same hour every day for weeks, without selling two cents' worth, yet whose application attracted attention and paved the way to fortune.

"He who every morning plans the transactions of the day," says Victor Hugo, "and follows out that plan, carries a thread that will guide him through the labyrinth of the most busy life. The orderly arrangement of his time is like a ray of light which darts itself through all his occupations. But where no plan is laid, where the disposal of time is surrendered merely to the chance of incidents, all things lie huddled together in one chaos, which admits of neither distribution nor review."

A. T. Stewart was extremely systematic and precise

in all his transactions. Method ruled in every department of his store, and for every delinquency a penalty was rigidly enforced. His eye was upon his business in all its ramifications; he mastered every detail and worked hard.

From the time Jonas Chickering began to work for a piano-maker, he was noted for the pains and care with which he did everything. To him there were no trifles in the manufacturing of pianos. Neither time nor labor was of any account to him, compared with accuracy and knowledge. He soon made pianos in a factory of his own. He determined to make an instrument yielding the fullest and richest volume of melody with the least exertion to the player, withstanding atmospheric changes, and preserving its purity and truthfulness of tone. He resolved each piano should be an improvement upon the one which preceded it; perfection was his aim. To the end of his life he gave the finishing touch to each of his instruments, and would trust it to no one else. He permitted no irregularity in workmanship or sales, and was characterized by simplicity, transparency, and straightforwardness.

He distanced all competitors. Chickering's name was such a power that one piano-maker had his name changed to Chickering by the Massachusetts legislature, and put it on his pianos; but Jonas Chickering sent a petition to the legislature, and the name was changed back. Character has a commercial as well as an ethical value.

Joseph M. W. Turner was intended by his father for a barber, but he showed such a taste for drawing that a reluctant permission was given for him to follow art as a profession. He soon became skillful, but as he lacked means he took anything to do that came in his way, frequently illustrating guidebooks and almanacs. But though the pay was very small the work was never careless. His work was worth several times what he received for it, but the price was increased and work of higher grade given him simply because men seek the services of those who are known to be faithful, and employ them in as lofty work as they seem able to do. And so he toiled upward until he began to employ himself, his work sure of a market at some price, and the price increasing as other men began to get glimpses of the transcendent art revealed in his paintings, an art not fully comprehended even in our day. He surpassed the acknowledged masters in various fields of landscape work, and left matchless studies of natural scenery in lines never before attempted. What Shakespeare is in literature, Turner is in his special field, the greatest name on record.

The demand for perfection in the nature of Wendell Phillips was wonderful. Every word must exactly express the shade of his thought; every phrase must be of due length and cadence; every sentence must be perfectly balanced before it left his lips. Exact precision characterized his style. He was easily the first forensic orator America has produced. The rhythmical fullness and poise of his periods are remarkable.

Lord Brougham had such a love for excellence that no amount of labor seemed too great for him. No matter what he did, no one should do it better. To this one thing he owed his success.

Roger Williams was the best shoemaker in town, and one of the best statesmen later in life. Franklin was noted for his thoroughness even when a printer.

Alexander Dumas prepared his manuscript with the greatest care. When consulted by a friend whose article had been rejected by several publishers, he advised him to have it handsomely copied by a professional penman, and then change the title. The advice was taken, and the article eagerly accepted by one of the very publishers who had refused it before. Many able essays have been rejected because of poor penmanship.

One of the first articles which George H. Lewes sent to the "Edinburgh Review" was returned with a request to rearrange it throughout. Although greatly vexed, Lewes complied, and was so much pleased with the result that he never again sent a paper to the press until it had been rewritten from one to three times. Macaulay wrote his best essays two or three times.

We must strive after accuracy as we would after wisdom, or hidden treasure, or anything we would attain. Determine to form exact business habits. Avoid slipshod financiering as you would the plague. Careless and indifferent habits would soon ruin a millionaire. Nearly every very successful man is accurate and painstaking. Accuracy means character, and character is power.

CHAPTER XVIII.

LIFE IS WHAT WE MAKE IT.

> The tissue of the life to be
> We weave with colors all our own,
> And in the field of destiny
> We reap as we have sown.
> WHITTIER.

> Men at some times are masters of their fates;
> The fault, dear Brutus, is not in our stars,
> But in ourselves, that we are underlings.
> SHAKESPEARE.

Every one is the son of his own works. — CERVANTES.

He that would bring home the wealth of the Indies, must carry out the wealth of the Indies. — OLD ADAGE.

A vase is begun; why, as the wheel goes round, does it turn out a pitcher? — HORACE.

All looks yellow to the jaundiced eye. — POPE.

> "Let's find the sunny side of men,
>   Or be believers in it :
> A light there is in every soul
>   That takes the pains to win it.
> Oh! there's a slumbering good in all,
>   And we perchance may wake it :
> Our hands contain the magic wand :
>   This life is what we make it."

"THERE is dew in one flower and not in another," said Beecher, "because one opens its cup and takes it in, while the other closes itself and the drop runs off."

Are you dissatisfied with to-day's success? It is the harvest from yesterday's sowing. Do you dream of a golden morrow? You will reap what you are sowing to-day. We get out of life just what we put into it. The world has for us just what we have for it. It is a mirror which reflects the faces we make. If we smile and are glad, it reflects a cheerful, sunny face. If we

HENRY WARD BEECHER

"From the same materials one builds palaces and another hovels; one rears a stately edifice while his brother, vacillating and incompetent, lives forever amid ruins."

are sour, irritable, mean, and contemptible, it still shows us a true copy of ourselves. The world is a whispering-gallery which returns the echo of our own voices. What we say of others is said of us. We shall find nothing in the world which we do not first find in ourselves.

It rests with the workman whether a rude piece of marble shall be squared into a horse-block, or carved into an Apollo, a Psyche, or a Venus de Milo. It is yours, if you choose, to develop a spiritual form more beautiful than any of these, instinct with immortal life, refulgent with all the glory of character.

About the middle of the eighteenth century a lighthouse, called Dunston Pillar, was built on Lincoln Heath to guide travelers over a trackless, barren waste, a veritable desert, almost in the heart of England. But now it stands in the midst of a fertile region. No barren heath has been visible, even from its top, for more than a generation. Superphosphate of lime has effected this magic transformation. Many a barren, useless life has been made fruitful by the inspiration of a high ideal. Improvement hardly less radical is possible even in the best of lives. Apply the superphosphate of lofty purpose and your useless life will blossom like the rose.

Somehow we seem to have an innate conviction that, although we are free, yet there is a kind of fatality within us which hedges us about, limits our liberty, places bounds to our possibilities, and gives direction to our action. But freedom is also a part of fate, and what seems like inexorable destiny is but natural limitation. Knowledge, energy, push, annul fate. The broader we become, the more freedom we have. We are given all the liberty we can use. Fate recedes as knowledge advances. Only he who determines to rise superior to what is commonly meant by destiny will ever achieve great success.

"I saw a delicate flower had grown up two feet high," said Thoreau, "between the horse's path and the wheel-track. An inch more to the right or left had sealed its fate, or an inch higher; and yet it lived to flourish as much as if it had a thousand acres of untrodden space around it, and never knew the danger it incurred. It did not borrow trouble, nor invite an evil fate by apprehending it."

"I resolved that, like the sun, so long as my day lasted, I would look on the bright side of everything," said Hood.

"There is always a black spot in our sunshine," says Carlyle; "it is the shadow of ourselves." Get out of your own light.

Our minds are given us but our characters we make. The lie never told for want of courage, the licentiousness never indulged in for fear of public rebuke, the irreverence of the heart, are just as effectual in staining the character as though the world knew all about them. A good character is a precious thing, above rubies, gold, crowns, or kingdoms, and the work of making it is the noblest on earth.

"I live in a constant endeavor to fence against the infirmities of ill health and other evils by mirth," said Sterne; "I am persuaded that every time a man smiles — but much more so when he laughs — it adds something to his fragment of life."

"This pemmican is the finest flavored pemmican I have ever seen," said one of a crew in search of John Franklin, when they were reduced to starvation diet.

Take life like a man. Take it just as though it was — as it is — an earnest, vital, essential affair. Take it just as though you personally were born to the task of performing a merry part in it — as though the world had waited for your coming. Take it as though it were a grand opportunity to do and to achieve, to carry forward great and good schemes.

"A gay, serene spirit is the source of all that is noble and good," said Schiller. "Whatever is accomplished of the greatest and the noblest sort flows from such a disposition. Petty, gloomy souls that only mourn the past and dread the future are not capable of seizing on the holiest moments of life."

"What luck that it was not my arms!" exclaimed a soldier when both legs were shot away at Chancellorsville.

"Painful?" asked the young women in surprise, when asked in the fairy tale if it was not a terrible experience to pass through the magical mill at Apolda. "Oh, no! On the other hand, it is quite delightful! It is just like waking in the morning after a good night's rest, to see the sun shining in your room, and to hear the trees rustling, and the birds twittering in the branches." No wonder, then, that old women were anxious to be thrown in at the top, wrinkled and bent, without hair or teeth, if they could come out below young and pretty, with cheeks as rosy as an apple.

"I want to become young again," said an old woman one day to a servant who sat smoking near the mill. "And, pray," said the man, "what is your name?" "The children call me Mother Redcap," was the answer; "I was very happy in my youth, and I wish above all things to be young again." "Sit down, then, on this bench, Mother Redcap;" and the man went into the mill, and opening a thick book, returned with a long strip of paper.

"Is that the bill?" asked the old woman. "Oh, no!" replied the man, "we charge nothing here; only you must sign your name to the paper." "And why should I do that?" The servant smiled as he answered: "This paper is only a list of all the follies you have ever committed. It is complete, even to the present hour. Before you can become young again, you must pledge yourself to commit them all over again in the very same order as before. To be sure, there is quite a long list. From the time you were sixteen until you were thirty, there was at least one folly every day, and on Sunday there were two; then you improved a little until you were forty; but after that the follies have been plenty enough, I assure you!"

"I know that what you say is all true," said the old woman, sighing; "and I hardly think it will repay one to become young again at such a price." "Neither do I think so," said the man; "very few, indeed, could it ever repay. So we have an easy time of it — seven days of rest every week! The mill is always still, at least of late years."

"Now, couldn't we strike out just a few things?" pleaded the old lady, with a tap on the man's shoulder. "Suppose we leave off about a dozen things that I remember with sorrow. I wouldn't mind doing all the rest." "No, no!" said the servant, "we are not allowed to leave off anything; the rule is, all or none!" "Very well, then," said she, turning away, "I shall have nothing to do with your old mill."

"Why, Mother Redcap, you come back older than you went!" exclaimed her neighbors when she returned to her distant home. "We never thought there was any truth in the story about that mill." "What does it matter about being young again?" asked the old woman, coughing a little, dry cough; "if one will try to make it so, old age may be as beautiful as youth!"

At the gateway of life each soul finds as it were a block of purest marble (time), a chisel and mallet (ability and opportunity), placed at his disposal by an unseen messenger. What shall he do with the marble? He may chisel out an angel or a devil; he may rear a palace or a hovel. One shapes his marble into a statue which enchants the world or sculptures it into frozen music. Another chisels his into disgusting forms which shall demoralize man in all time and poison every beholder.

"In the same family and under the same circumstances one rears a stately edifice, while his brother, vacillating and incompetent, lives forever amid ruins." From the same materials he may fashion vessels of honor or dishonor. We find what we are looking for. The geologist sees design and order in the very pavement-stones. The botanist reads volumes in the flowers and grasses which most men tread thoughtlessly beneath their feet. The astronomer gazes with rapt soul into the starry depths, while his fellows seldom glance upward.

Nature takes on our moods; she laughs with those who laugh and weeps with those who weep. If we rejoice and are glad the very birds sing more sweetly, the woods and streams murmur our song. But if we are sad and sorrowful a sudden gloom falls upon Nature's face; the sun shines, but not in our hearts, the birds sing, but not to us. The music of the spheres is pitched in a minor key.

If I trust, I am trusted; if I suspect, I am suspected; if I love, I am loved; if I hate, I am despised. Every man is a magnet and attracts to himself kindred spirits and principles until he is surrounded by a world all his own, good or bad like himself; so all the bodily organs and functions are tied together in closest sympathy. If one laughs, all rejoice; if one suffers, all the others suffer with it.

The future will be just what we make it. Our purpose will give it its character. One's resolution is one's prophecy. There is no bright hope, no bright outlook for the man who has no great inspiration. A man is just what his resolution is. Tell us his purpose and there is the interpretation of him, of his manhood. There, too, is the revelation of his destiny. Leave all your discouraging pessimism behind. Do not prophesy evil, but good. Have the purpose within you to bring along better times, and better times will come. Men who hope large things are public benefactors. Men of hope to the front.

"Well, Robert, where have you been walking this afternoon?" asked Mr. Andrews of one of his pupils at the close of a holiday. "Oh, I have been to Brown Heath, and round by Camp Mount, and home through the meadows. But it was very dull. I hardly saw a single person. I would much rather have gone by the turnpike road."

"Well, where have you been?" asked the teacher of another pupil who came in while Robert was talking. "Oh, sir," replied Master William, "I never had such a pleasant walk before in my life. I found a curious plant (mistletoe) which grows right out from the bark of an oak-tree just as well as if its roots were deep in the ground. I saw a woodpecker, and a large wheat-ear, and gathered some beautiful flowers in the meadows. I followed a strange bird because I thought its wing was broken, but it led me into a bog, where I got very wet, and then it flew off with no sign of a broken wing. Perhaps it only meant to get me away from its nest. But I don't mind my wetting, because I met an old man burning charcoal near the bog, who told me all about his business, and gave me a pretty little dead snake. Then I went to the top of the high hill, and saw all the country spread out below me like a map. Next, because the hill is called Camp Mount, I looked for the ruins of the old camp, and found them; and then I went down to the river, and to twenty other places, and so on and so forth, till I have brought home curiosities enough, and thoughts enough, to last me a week."

Mr. Andrews told him all about his curiosities; and, when he learned that William who had seen so much had gone over the same ground as Robert, who saw nothing at all, he said: "So it is. One man walks through the world with his eyes open, another with his eyes shut. I have known sailors who had been in all quarters of the world, and could tell you of nothing but the signs of the tippling-houses and the price of the liquor that was sold there. While many a silly, thoughtless youth is whirled through Europe without gaining a single idea, the observing eye and inquiring mind find matter for improvement and delight in every ramble. You, then, William, continue to use your eyes. And you, Robert, learn that eyes were given to you for use."

Each of these young men had created his own little world.

"'T is in ourselves that we are thus or thus," says Iago. "Our bodies are our gardens, to the which our wills are gardeners: so that if we will plant nettles, or sow lettuce, set hyssop and weed up thyme, supply it with one gender of herbs, or distract it with many, either to have it sterile with idleness, or manured with industry, why, the power and corrigible authority of this lies in our wills."

Whipple says that each man's levity, bigotry, ignorance, vice, or littleness erects a wall of adamant between himself and whatever is profound, comprehensive, wise, good, or great.

It has been well said that from the same materials one man builds palaces, another hovels; one warehouses, another villas; bricks and mortar are mortar and bricks until the architect makes them something else. The block of granite which was an obstacle in the path of the weak becomes a stepping-stone in the pathway of the resolute. The difficulties which dishearten one man only stiffen the sinews of another, who looks on them as a sort of mental spring-board by which to vault across the gulf of failure on to the sure, solid ground of full success.

In every human ear, according to Corti, is a harp of 8,700 strings, varying in length from one five-hundredth to one two-hundredth of an inch. If a well-tuned violin be held near a piano, when the E string is struck the E string of the violin will vibrate in unison, and give forth a distinct tone of the same pitch. Other strings evoke their corresponding tones. In like manner the 8,700 strings of the human harp have such a wide compass that any appreciable sound finds its corresponding tone-string, and the sound is conveyed through the auditory nerve to the brain.

Our souls are harps strung to finer harmony, their compass varying according to the wholeness or halfness of our lives, the greater or less degree of our culture. The world is full of melody. Every atom, touched by unseen fingers, is vibrant with sweetest music, yet there is only now and then a soul sensitive enough to catch the finer strains. Rarely a poet or philosopher reads the "books in the running brooks, sermons in stones," or sees "God in everything." Only now and then an Agassiz, from a single track in the old red sandstone or a single fossil bone, can reconstruct a whole skeleton — reinvesting with flesh and reanimating with life an animal whose very species has been extinct for centuries. There is only now and then a Hugh Miller who can trace the footprints of the Creator down through the ages, and read the records of the past imprinted in the rocks. But rarer, far rarer than these, are they who can catch responsively the higher music of sentient being, with its joys and hopes; of earnest, aspiring, struggling souls, tolerant, serious, yet sunny; of the glorious diapason of the fullness of the compassion and love of God.

Some people, like the bee, seem to gather honey from every flower; while others, like the spider, carry only poison away. One person finds happiness everywhere and in every occasion, carrying his own holiday with him. Another always appears to be returning from a funeral. One sees beauty and harmony wherever he looks, his very tears affording him visions of resplendent rainbows as the sunbeams of Hope fall upon him. Another is blind to beauty; the lenses of his eyes seem to be smoked glass, draping the whole world in mourning.

Though all have eyes, all do not see, yet all eyes are constructed exactly alike. The same beautiful light impinges upon all retinas, but how different the images presented! While one man sees only gravel, fodder, and firewood upon Boston Common, another is ravished with its beauty. One sees in a matchless rose nothing but rose-water for sore eyes; another penetrates its purpose, and reads in the beauty of its blended colors and its wonderful fragrance the thoughts of God. The rose becomes a lens through which he gazes into the very heart of the Creator.

"My body must walk the earth," said an ancient poet, "but I can put wings on my soul, and plumes to my hardest thought."

If we would get the most out of life, we must learn not merely to look but to see. The sun is not partial to the rainbow and the rose; he scatters his beauty everywhere — the only defect is in our vision.

"Though our character is formed by circumstances," said John Stuart Mill, "our own desires can do much to shape those circumstances; and what is really inspiriting and ennobling in the doctrine of free will is the conviction that we have real power over the formation of our own character; our will, by influencing some of our circumstances, being able to modify our future habits or capacities of willing."

As we may look without seeing and listen without hearing, so we may work without accomplishing anything. Michael Angelo was once commanded by his prince to mould a beautiful statue of snow — an illustrious example of the fact that it is not necessary to be idle in order to throw away time. That statue, though instinct with ideal beauty stamped upon it by an immortal hand, melted, and every trace of the sculptor's greatness was washed away. Oh, what precious hours we have all wasted, writing in oblivion's book! Wasted? worse than wasted, for the knowledge that we were working uselessly tended to beget a habit of aimless and careless work. Who has not worked for annihilation, painting in colors that fade, carving in stone that crumbles? Who has not built upon the sand, and written upon the water?

What we are to be really, we are now potentially. As the future oak lies folded in the acorn, so in the present lies our future. Our success will be, can be, but a natural tree, developed from the seeds of our own sowing: the fragrance of its blossoms and the richness of its fruitage will depend upon the nourishment absorbed from our past and present.

Ruskin tells us that the earth we tread beneath our feet is composed of clay and sand and soot and water; and he tells us that, if nature has her perfect work (in these things), the clay will become porcelain, and may be painted upon and placed in the king's palace; then, again, it may become clear and hard and white, and have the power of drawing to itself the blue and the red, the green and the purple rays of the sunlight, and become an opal. The sand will become very hard and white, and have the power of drawing to itself the blue rays of the sunlight, and become a sapphire. The soot will become the hardest and whitest substance known, and be changed into a diamond. The water in the summer is a dewdrop, and in the winter crystallizes into a star. Even so the homeliest lives, by drawing to themselves the coloring of truth, sincerity, charity, and faith, may become crystals and gems "of purest ray serene."

> "Our acts our angels are, or good or ill,
> Our fatal shadows that walk by us still."

LIFE IS WHAT WE MAKE IT.

All are architects of fate,
   Working in these walls of time;
Some with massive deeds and great,
   Some with ornaments of rhyme;
For the structure that we raise,
   Time is with materials filled;
Our to-days and yesterdays
   Are the blocks with which we build.

LONGFELLOW.

CHAPTER XIX.

THE VICTORY IN DEFEAT.

'T is said best men are moulded of their faults.
SHAKESPEARE.

They never fail who die in a great cause.   BYRON.

"Failures are but the pillars of success."
Our greatest glory is not in never falling, but in rising every time we fall. — CONFUCIUS.

Adversity is the diamond-dust Heaven polishes its jewels with.
LEIGHTON.

Who falls for the love of God, shall rise a star.
BEN JONSON.

Nor deem the irrevocable Past
As wholly wasted, wholly vain,
If, rising on its wrecks, at last
To something nobler we attain.
LONGFELLOW.

What is defeat? Nothing but education; nothing but the first steps to something better — WENDELL PHILLIPS.

A great career, though balked of its end, is still a landmark of human energy. — SMILES.

Let Fortune empty her whole quiver on me,
I have a soul that, like an ample shield,
Can take in all, and verge enough for more;
Fate was not mine, nor am I Fate's:
Souls know no conquerors.   DRYDEN.

Sometimes the truest lives of all
Are lived by those who fail.
MYRON HANFORD VEON.

NEARLY a hundred thousand Romans are assembled in the Colosseum to see the hated Christians struggle for their lives with the wild beasts of the amphitheatre. The grand spectacle is preceded by a duel between two rival gladiators, trained to fight to the death to amuse the populace. When a gladiator hit his adversary in such contests he would say "hoc habet" (he has it), and look up to see whether he should kill or spare. If

ROBERT E. LEE

"The world will be blind indeed if it does not reckon among its great ones heroes without laurels and conquerors without the jubilation of triumph."

the people held their thumbs up, the victim would be left to recover; if down, he was to die. If he showed the least reluctance in presenting his throat for the death-blow, there would rise a scornful shout: "Recipe ferrum" (receive the steel). Prominent persons would sometimes go into the arena and watch the death agonies of the vanquished, or taste the warm blood of some brave hero.

The two rival gladiators, as they entered, had shouted to the emperor: "Ave, Cæsar, morituri te salutant" (Hail, Cæsar, those about to die salute thee). Then in mortal strife they fought long and desperately, their faces wet with perspiration and dark with the dust of the arena. Suddenly an aged stranger in the audience leaps over the railing, and, standing bareheaded and barefoot between the contestants, bids them stay their hands. A hissing sound comes from the vast audience, like that of steam issuing from a geyser, followed by cries of "Back, back, old man." But the gray-haired hermit stands like a statue. "Cut him down, cut him down," roar the spectators, and the gladiators strike the would-be peacemaker to earth, and fight over his dead body.

But what of it? What is the life of a poor old hermit compared with the thousands who have met their deaths in that vast arena? The unknown man died, indeed, but his death brought Rome to her senses, and no more gladiatorial contests disgraced the Colosseum, while in every province of the empire the custom was utterly abolished, to be revived no more. The vast ruin stands to-day a monument to the victory in the hermit's defeat.

No man fails who does his best, for if the critical world ignore him, his labor is weighed in the scales of Omniscient Justice. As there is no effect without cause, no loss of energy in the world, so conscientious persistence cannot fail of its ultimate reward.

One of the first lessons of life is to learn how to get victory out of defeat. It takes courage and stamina, when mortified and embarrassed by humiliating disaster, to seek in the wreck or ruins the elements of future conquest. Yet this measures the difference between those who succeed and those who fail. You cannot measure a man by his failures. You must know what use he makes of them. What did they mean to him? What did he get out of them?

I always watch with great interest a young man's first failure. It is the index of his life, the measure of his success-power. The mere fact of his failure does not interest me much; but how did he take his defeat? What did he do next? Was he discouraged? Did he slink out of sight? Did he conclude that he had made a mistake in his calling, and dabble in something else? Or did he up and at it again with a determination that knows no defeat?

"I thank God I was not made a dexterous manipulator," said Humphry Davy, "for the most important of my discoveries have been suggested to me by failures."

"God forbid that I should do this thing, and flee away from them," said Judas Maccabæus, when, with only eight hundred faithful men, he was urged to retire before the Syrian army of twenty thousand. "If our time be come, let us die manfully for our brethren, and let us not stain our honor."

"Sore was the battle," says Miss Yonge; "as sore as that waged by the three hundred at Thermopylæ, and the end was the same. Judas and his eight hundred were not driven from the field, but lay dead upon it. But their work was done. The moral effect of such a defeat goes further than many a victory. Those lives, sold so dearly, were the price of freedom for Judea. Judas's brothers, Jonathan and Simon, laid him in his father's tomb, and then ended the work that he had begun; and when Simon died, the Jews, once so trodden on, were the most prosperous race in the East. The temple was raised from its ruins, and the exploits of the Maccabees had nerved the whole people to do or die in defense of the holy faith of their fathers."

After a long and desperate but vain struggle to free his country from the iron rule of Rome, Vercingetorix surrendered himself to Cæsar on condition that his army should be allowed to return home without molestation. He was held a prisoner for six years, then dragged in chains over the cold stones of Rome to grace an imperial triumph, and killed in his dungeon the following night. Yet no one would think of naming any one else if asked who was the bravest and noblest among the Gallic leaders.

"Be of good comfort, Master Ridley, and play the man," said Latimer, as he stood with his friend at the stake; "we shall this day light such a candle by God's grace in England as I trust shall never be put out;" and every word had more influence than would the preaching of a hundred sermons against the intolerance of the age. So incensed did the people become that, besides Cranmer, burned two years later, very few others were sacrificed; and of these it is said that they were secretly tried and burned at night, surrounded by soldiers, for fear of riots by the populace enraged at such injustice and cruelty.

There is something grand and inspiring in a young man who fails squarely after doing his level best, and then enters the contest again and again with undaunted courage and redoubled energy. I have no fears for the youth who is not disheartened at failure.

"It is defeat," says Henry Ward Beecher, "that turns bone to flint, and gristle to muscle, and makes men invincible, and formed those heroic natures that are now in ascendency in the world. Do not, then, be afraid of defeat. You are never so near to victory as when defeated in a good cause."

Failure becomes the final test of persistence and of an iron will. It either crushes a life, or solidifies it. The wounded oyster mends his shell with pearl.

"Failure is, in a sense," says Keats, "the highway to success, inasmuch as every discovery of what is false leads us to seek earnestly after what is true, and every fresh experience points out some form of error which we shall afterward carefully avoid."

"We mount to heaven," says A. B. Alcott, "mostly on the ruins of our cherished schemes, finding our failures were successes."

No man is a failure who is upright and true. No cause is a failure which is in the right. There is but one failure, and that is not to be true to the best that is in us.

Of what avail would it be for a man without a kingdom, without an army, to oppose the most powerful monarch of Europe? William the Silent was a learned philosopher, an accomplished linguist, of good family and great wealth, and a lover of peace. Yet, as a mere citizen of little Holland, on what could he rely should he attempt to wage war against overwhelming odds, except the justice of his cause and the weight of his character?

Philip II. was a nephew of the emperor of Germany, husband of the queen of England, and ruler in his own right of Spain, Holland, Belgium, and most of Italy, Oran, Tunis, the Cape Verde, Canary, and Philippine Islands, the Antilles, Mexico, and Peru. While his neighbors were weakened by quarrels, his resources were unrivaled. His cause was supported by the arms, wealth, glory, genius, and religion of Europe.

Philip determined to establish the Inquisition in the Netherlands, and William resolved to consecrate himself to the defense of the liberties of his country.

The struggle was prodigious. At last William died, but Philip was not a victor. Holland, indeed, was without a leader, but the vast Spanish monarchy was tottering to its fall. From the beginning of the contest, "the figure of the king becomes smaller and smaller until it finally disappears, while that of the Prince of Orange grows and grows, until it becomes the most glorious figure of the century." Proscribed, impoverished, calumniated, surrounded by assassins, often a fugitive, and finally a lifeless lump of clay, William had maintained throughout a solidity of character against which beat in vain the waves of corrupt wealth and injustice. Character is power.

Raleigh failed, but he left a name ever to be linked with brave effort and noble character. Kossuth did not succeed, but his lofty career, his burning words, and his ideal fidelity will move men for good as long as time shall last. O'Connell did not win his cause, but he did achieve enduring fame as an orator, patriot, and apostle of liberty.

Viewed in this light, the retreat of Xenophon's Ten Thousand outshines the conquests of Alexander; and the retreat of Sir John Moore to Corunna was as great as the victories of Wellington.

"Gentlemen, apply to my young friend, Mr. Whitney, he can make anything," said the widow of General Greene, when some officers who had served under her husband in the Revolution said it was impossible to extend the culture of cotton, on account of the trouble and expense of separating the seed from the fibre. Eli Whitney had gone from his Massachusetts home, in 1792, to teach in Georgia.

Mrs. Greene, at whose house he was visiting, introduced Mr. Whitney to the officers and some planter guests, and recommended him as a young man of great integrity and ingenuity. The young teacher said that he had never seen cotton or cotton-seed, but promised to see what he could do. He found a little in Savannah, and shut himself up in a basement to experiment. He had to make his own tools, and even draw his wire, as none could then be bought in Savannah. He hammered and tinkered all winter, but at last his machine was successful.

Mr. Miller, who had recently married Mrs. Greene, offered to become an equal partner with Mr. Whitney, furnishing funds for perfecting, patenting, and making the machines. People came to see the wonderful device, but Mr. Miller refused to show it, as it was not yet patented.

Some of the visitors broke open the building by night and carried off the gin. Soon the partners found that machines that infringed upon theirs were upon the market. Mr. Whitney established a manufactory in New Haven, but was hampered greatly by a long sickness, while suits to defend the patent swallowed all the money of the partners. Again Whitney was sick, and had but just recovered when his manufactory burned with all his machines and papers, leaving him bankrupt. Just then came the news that British manufacturers rejected cotton cleaned by his machine, saying that the process was injurious. He went to England and at last overcame this prejudice, when his cotton-gin was again in demand. A suit against an infringer was decided against him by a Georgia jury, although the judge charged in his favor. The market was flooded with infringements. Not until 1807, the last year of his patent, was a suit decided in his favor, Judge Johnson saying: —

"The whole interior of the Southern States was languishing and its inhabitants emigrating for want of some object to engage their attention and employ their industry, when the invention of this machine at once opened views to them which set the whole country in active motion. From childhood to age, it has presented to us a lucrative employment. Individuals who were depressed with poverty and sunk in idleness have suddenly risen to wealth and respectability. Our debts have been paid off. Our capitals have increased, and our lands have trebled themselves in value."

Whitney was obliged to engage in another kind of business to gain a livelihood, on account of the injustice of his fellow countrymen, yet one of the world's greatest victories grew out of his apparent defeat. Instead of a pound of cleaned cotton as the result of a day's work of an able-bodied man, he had made it possible for him to clean hundreds of pounds. His invention increased the production of cotton in the South more than a thousand fold, and was worth, according to conservative men, more than a thousand millions of dollars to the United States. What an inspiration there is in this career for discouraged souls in life's great battles!

"No language," says E. P. Whipple, "can fitly express the meanness, the baseness, the brutality, with which the world has ever treated its victims of one age and boasts of them in the next. Dante is worshiped at that grave to which he was hurried by persecution. Milton in his own day was 'Mr. Milton, the blind adder, that spit his venom on the king's person;' and soon after, 'the mighty orb of song.' These absurd transitions from hatred to apotheosis, this recognition just at the moment when it becomes a mockery, sadden all intellectual history."

"Even in this world," says Mrs. Stowe, "they will have their judgment-day; and their names, which went down in the dust like a gallant banner trodden in the mire, shall rise again all glorious in the sight of nations."

What cared Garrison or Phillips for the rotten eggs, the jeers and hisses in Faneuil Hall? What did Demosthenes, Curran, or Disraeli care for the taunts and hisses that drove them from the rostrum? They felt within the power of greatness, and knew that the time would come when they would be heard. Mortified by

humiliation and roused by defeat, they were spurred
into a grander eloquence. Those apparent defeats which
would have silenced forever men of ordinary mould,
only excited in these men a determination which, like
the waters of the Hellespont, " ne'er felt retiring ebb."
Who can estimate the world's debt to weak, deformed,
and apparently defeated men, whose desperate struggles
to redeem themselves from perpetual scorn have made
them immortal ? It was Byron's club-foot and shyness
which caused him to pour forth his soul in song. It
was to Bedford jail that we owe the finest allegory in
the world. Bunyan wrote nothing of note before or
after his twelve years' imprisonment.

Death wins no victory over such men. Regulus might
be destroyed bodily by cruel torture, but his spirit
animated Rome to blot Carthage from the face of the
earth. Winkelried did indeed fall beneath the Austrian
spears, but Switzerland is free. Wallace was quartered :
Scotland never. Lincoln became the victim of an assassin, but none the less his work went forward. Never
was martyr yet whose death did not advance the cause
he advocated tenfold more than could possibly have been
accomplished by his voice or pen.

He who never failed has never half succeeded. The
defeat at Bull Run was really the greatest victory of
the Civil War, for it sent the cowards to the rear and
the politicians home. It was the lightning-flash in the
dark night of our nation's peril which gave us glimpses
of the weak places in our army. It was the mirror
which showed us the faces of the political aspirants.

"The angel of martyrdom is brother to the angel of
victory." What cared Savonarola though the pope
excommunicated him because he could not bribe him ?
What cared he for the live coals on his feet ? He would
still tell the Italian people of their terrible sins, and he
knew that though they should burn him at the stake,
his ashes would plead for him and speak louder than

his tongue had ever done. He shrank not from telling the dying Lorenzo to restore liberty to Florence and return what he had stolen from the people, before he would grant him absolution. Though the prince turned his face to the wall, rather than purchase forgiveness on such terms, Savonarola was inflexible, and the monarch died unabsolved. On the way to the scaffold, the bishop said, "I separate thee from the Church militant and triumphant." Savonarola corrected him, saying, "Not triumphant, that is not yours to do."

"Heaven is probably a place for those who have failed on earth. The world will be blind indeed if it does not reckon among its great ones such martyrs as miss the palms but not the pains of martyrdom, heroes without laurels and conquerors without the jubilations of triumph."

Uninterrupted successes at the beginning of a career are dangerous. Beware of the first great triumph. It may prove a failure. Many a man has been ruined by over-confidence born of his first victory. The mountain oak, tossed and swayed in the tempest until its proud top sweeps the earth, is all the stronger for its hundred battles with the elements if it only straighten up again. The danger is not in a fall, but in failing to rise.

All the great work of the world has been accomplished by courage, and the world's greatest victories have been born of defeat. Every blessing that we enjoy — personal security, individual liberty, and constitutional freedom — has been obtained through long apprenticeships of evil. The right of existing as a nation has only been accomplished through ages of wars and horrors. It required four centuries of martyrdom to establish Christianity, and a century of civil wars to introduce the Reformation.

"There are some whom the lightning of fortune blasts, only to render holy," says Bulwer. "Amidst all that humbles and scathes — amidst all that shatters from their life its verdure, smites to the dust the pomp and summit of their pride, and in the very heart of existence writeth a sudden and strange defeature, they stand erect, — riven, not uprooted, a monument less of pity than of awe! There are some who pass through the lazar-house of misery with a step more august than a Cæsar's in his hall. The very things which, seen alone, are despicable and vile, associated with them become almost venerable and divine; and one ray, however dim and feeble, of that intense holiness which, in the infant God, shed majesty over the manger and the straw, not denied to those who, in the depth of affliction, cherished his patient image, flings over the meanest localities of earth an emanation from the glory of Heaven!"

Even from the dreary waste and desolation of his bereavement at Fordham, the stricken soul of Edgar A. Poe blossomed in those matchless flowers of funeral song, the delicately ethereal dirges, "Ulalume" and "Annabel Lee," which alone would immortalize their author.

To know how to wring victory from defeat, and make stepping-stones of our stumbling-blocks, is the secret of success.

What matters it —

> "If what shone afar so grand
> Turned to ashes in the hand?
> On again, the virtue lies
> In the struggle, not the prize."

Raphael died at thirty-seven, in the very flush of young manhood, before he had finished his "Transfiguration." Yet he had produced the finest picture in the world, and it was carried in his funeral procession, while all Rome mourned their great loss.

Even the defeat of death found victorious voice in the unequaled requiem of Mozart.

There is something sublime in the resolute, fixed

purpose of suffering without complaining, which makes disappointment often better than success. Constant success shows us only one side of the world; for as it surrounds us with friends who tell us only of our merits, so it silences those enemies from whom only we can learn our defects.

Columbus was carried home in chains, on his third voyage, from the world he had discovered. Although the indignant people remonstrated, and his friend the queen had him set free, persecution followed him when he again crossed the Atlantic westward. At the age of seventy, after the "long wandering woe" of this fourth and final voyage, he was glad to reach Spain at last. He hoped for some reward — at least enough to keep soul and body together. But his appeals were fruitless. He lived for a few months after his return, poor, lonely, and stricken with a mortal disease. Even towards his death he was a scarcely tolerated beggar. He had to complain that his frock had been taken and sold, that he had not a roof of his own, and lacked wherewithal to pay his tavern bill. It was then that, with failing breath, he uttered the words, sublime in their touching simplicity, "I, a native of Genoa, discovered in the distant West, the continent and isles of India." He expired at Valladolid, May 20, 1506, his last words being, "Lord, I deliver my soul into thy hands." Thus Columbus died a neglected beggar, while a pickle-dealer of Seville, whose highest position was that of second mate of a vessel, gave his name to the greatest continent on the globe. But was the Genoese mariner a failure? Ask more than a hundred millions of people who inhabit the world he found a wilderness. Ask the grandest republic the sun ever shone upon if Columbus was a failure.

Joan of Arc was burned alive at Rouen, without even a remonstrance from Charles VII., who owed her his crown. Was the life of Joan of Arc a failure? Ask a nation besprinkled with her bronze and marble statues if the memory of the Maid of Orleans is not enshrined in every Frenchman's heart.

"A heroic Wallace, quartered upon the scaffold," said Carlyle, "cannot hinder that his Scotland become, one day, a part of England; but he does hinder that it become, on tyrannous, unfair terms, a part of it; commands still, as with a god's voice, from his old Valhalla and Temple of the brave, that there be a just, real union as of brother and brother, not a false and merely semblant one as of slave and master."

Leonidas and his three hundred may perish after defending a little mountain-pass against the vast Persian army for three days in hand to hand conflict; but their defeat shall prove a nation's victory, and they shall live in song and story when Xerxes and his vast horde will be remembered only because they were repulsed at Thermopylæ and vanquished at Salamis and Platæa.

When the troop-laden English ship Birkenhead was found to be foundering in stress of weather, the officer in charge of the battalion ordered his men to stand at "parade rest" while the boats rowed away with the women and children. They kept their places as the water swashed higher and higher around their feet, and, when it reached their waists, unstrapped their belts and held aloft their cartridge-boxes until with a wild lurch the wreck went down. Think you there was no victory in this apparent defeat? Character is power and triumphs over physical weakness.

"A man, true to man's grave religion," says Bulwer, "can no more despise a life wrecked in all else, while a hallowing affection stands out sublime through the rents and chinks of fortune, than he can profane with rude mockery a temple in ruins — if still left there the altar."

The exertion of all your strength of mind or body may result in nothing but failure in the eyes of a critical world, but what you have done is already weighed in the scales of Omniscient Justice, and can in no way avoid its legitimate reward. Your deed is registered —

> "In the rolls of Heaven, where it will live,
> A theme for angels when they celebrate
> The high-souled virtues which forgetful earth
> Has witnessed."

CHAPTER XX.

NERVE — GRIT, GRIP, PLUCK.

When you get into a tight place, and everything goes against you, till it seems as if you could not hold on a minute longer, never give up then, for that's just the place and time that the tide'll turn. — HARRIET BEECHER STOWE.

I find nothing so singular in life as this, that everything opposing appears to lose its substance the moment one actually grapples with it. — HAWTHORNE.

> " Never give up: for the wisest is boldest,
> Knowing that Providence mingles the cup;
> And of all maxims, the best, as the oldest,
> Is the stern watchword of 'Never give up!'"
>
> Be firm ; one constant element of luck
> Is genuine, solid, old Teutonic pluck.
> Stick to your aim; the mongrel's hold will slip,
> But only crowbars loose the bull-dog's grip;
> Small though he looks, the jaw that never yields
> Drags down the bellowing monarch of the fields !
>
> HOLMES.

"LET it split," said a professor, when told that his principles, if carried out, would split the world to pieces; "there are enough more planets."

"Soldiers, you are Frenchmen," said Napoleon, coolly walking among his disaffected generals when they threatened his life in the Egyptian campaign ; "you are too many to assassinate, and too few to intimidate me." "How brave he is!" exclaimed the ringleader, as he withdrew, completely cowed.

"General Taylor never surrenders," said old "Rough and Ready" at Buena Vista, when Santa Anna with 20,000 men offered him a chance to save his 4,000 soldiers by capitulation. The battle was long and desperate, but at length the Mexicans were glad to avoid

ULYSSES S. GRANT

"I know no such unquestionable badge and ensign of a sovereign mind as that tenacity of purpose which, through all changes of companions, or parties, or fortunes, changes never, bates no jot of heart or hope, but wearies out opposition and arrives at its port."

further defeat by flight. When Lincoln was asked how Grant impressed him as a general, he replied, "The greatest thing about him is cool persistency of purpose. He has the grip of a bulldog; when he once gets his teeth in, nothing can shake him off. It was "On to Richmond," and "I shall fight it out on this line if it takes all summer," that settled the fate of the Rebellion.

When Cæsar was captured by pirates, they offered to release him for twenty talents. "It is too little," said the Roman, "you shall have fifty. But when I am free I will crucify every one of you." He kept his word.

"Oh! if the duke has said that, of course t' other fellow must give way," said Sydney Smith, just before the battle of Waterloo, when told that Wellington had decided to keep his position at all events.

"Go it, William!" an old boxer was overheard saying to himself in the midst of a fight; "at him again! — never say 'die'!"

When Philip threatened to prohibit the enjoyment of all their privileges, the Lacedæmonians asked whether he would also prohibit their dying.

"My sword is too short," said a Spartan youth to his father. "Add a step to it, then," was the only reply.

It is said that the snapping-turtle will not release his grip, even after his head is cut off. He is resolved, if he dies, to die hard. It is just such grit that enables many a man to succeed, for what men call luck is generally the prerogative of valiant souls. It is the final effort that brings victory. It is the last pull of the oar, with clenched teeth and knit muscles, that shows what Oxford boatmen call "the beefiness of the fellow." Chauncey Depew said to a class of young men: "After choosing your profession, put up this motto over your door, 'Stick, dig, save.'"

As late as 1861 Grant wrote to a friend, telling his satisfaction at an increase of salary in the leather business at Galena, Ill., from $600 to $800 a year. He expressed a hope of reaching what then seemed his highest ambition, a partnership in the firm. In May, 1861, he communicated with the general in command at Washington, asking to be assigned to military duty not for one, three, or six months, but until the close of the war, in such capacity as might offer. No notice was ever taken of this request.

At forty he was an obscure citizen of Galena. At forty-two he was known as one of the greatest generals in history. Speaking of Shiloh he once said: "I thought I was going to fail, but I kept right on." It is this keeping right on that wins in the battle of life. After his defeat at the first battle of Shiloh, nearly every newspaper of both parties in the North, almost every member of Congress, and public sentiment everywhere demanded his removal. Friends of the President pleaded with him to give the command to some one else, for his own sake as well as for the good of the country. Lincoln listened for hours one night, speaking only at rare intervals to tell a pithy story, until the clock struck one. Then, after a long silence, he said: "I can't spare this man. He fights." It was Lincoln's marvelous insight and sagacity that saved Grant from the storm of popular passion, and gave us the greatest hero of the Civil War.

When Fort Henry was taken, Halleck advised Grant to defend his position. Instead, he at once marched against Fort Donelson, whose commander after four days of hard fighting sent a flag of truce to ascertain on what terms a capitulation could be arranged. "Unconditional and immediate surrender," was the reply; "I propose to move immediately upon your works;" but when night fell, he visited Buckner in the prisoner's tent, and said, "You must have lost everything; take my purse."

Grant never looked backward. Once, after several

days of hard fighting without definite result, he called a council of war. One general described the route by which he would retreat, another thought it better to retire by a different road, and general after general told how he would withdraw, or fall back, or seek a more favorable position in the rear. At length all eyes were turned upon Grant, who had been a silent listener for hours. He rose, took a bundle of papers from an inside pocket, handed one to each general, and said: "Gentlemen, at dawn you will execute those orders." Every paper gave definite directions for an advance, and with the morning sun the army moved forward to victory.

Astonished at a command to storm an important but strongly defended position, an officer rode back and said: "General, if I understand your order aright, it may involve the sacrifice of every man in my command." "I am glad, sir, that you understand my order aright," replied the silent general.

For thirty days he rained sledge-hammer blows upon Lee in the Wilderness, fighting by day, advancing by night. The country shuddered at such unheard-of carnage, and demanded his removal; but ever to his inquiring officers came the cool command, "By the left flank, forward," while he electrified the nation by the homeward dispatch, "I propose to fight it out on this line if it takes all summer." When, with the Confederacy at his feet, the storm of vengeance seemed about to burst, his magnanimous words, "Let us have peace," fell like a benediction upon the hearts of victors and vanquished alike.

When Cannæ was lost, and Hannibal was gathering in measures the rings of the Roman knights who had perished in the strife, the senate of Rome voted thanks to the defeated general, Consul Terentius Varro, for not having despaired of the republic.

Pellisier, the Crimean chief of zouaves, became angry

with a sub-officer of cavalry, and struck him across the face with a whip. The man drew a pistol and pulled the trigger, but it missed fire. "Fellow," said the grim chief coolly, "I order you a three days' arrest for not having your arms in better order."

Massena's army of 18,000 men in Genoa had been reduced by fighting and famine to 8,000. They had killed and captured more than 15,000 Austrians, but their provisions were completely exhausted; starvation stared them in the face; the enemy outnumbered them four to one, and they seemed at the mercy of their opponents. General Ott demanded a discretionary surrender, but Massena replied: "My soldiers must be allowed to march out with colors flying, and arms and baggage; not as prisoners of war, but free to fight when and where we please. If you do not grant this, I will sally forth from Genoa sword in hand. With eight thousand famished men I will attack your camp, and I will fight till I cut my way through it." Ott knew the temper of the great soldier, and agreed to accept the terms if he would surrender himself, or if he would depart by sea so as not to be quickly joined by reinforcements. Massena's only reply was: "Take my terms, or I will cut my way through your army." Ott at last agreed, when Massena said: "I give you notice that ere fifteen days are passed I shall be once more in Genoa," and he kept his word.

Napoleon said of this man, who was orphaned in infancy and cast upon the world to make his own way in life: "When defeated, Massena was always ready to fight a battle over again, as though he had been the conqueror."

"The battle is completely lost," said Dessaix, looking at his watch, when consulted by Napoleon at Marengo; "but it is only two o'clock, and we shall have time to gain another." He then made his famous cavalry charge, and won the field, although a few minutes before the French soldiers all along the line were momentarily expecting an order to retreat.

At the magazine of the Mare Island Navy Yard, California, sailors from the U. S. S. Boston were filling shells when suddenly the whole building went up in fire and smoke. All present were killed instantly. About a quarter of a mile distant a young girl was driving in a pony-cart, when the explosion occurred, and almost immediately afterward a doctor rushed from the naval hospital towards the scene of the disaster. Realizing the situation, she asked the doctor to jump into the cart, and galloped to the ruins. Other magazine buildings, in which shells were exploding every moment, had caught fire. Explosives were stored in those buildings in quantities sufficient to blow up Pike's Peak. Yet the doctor and the girl entered the pall of smoke amid the mangled dead. Collins, the watchman, half blinded and bewildered by a blow from a fragment of timber, was groping his way from building to building, to prevent further disaster by shutting the iron doors and shutters. The girl coolly wrapped a bandage round his injured head, and then looked for other wounded until more help arrived. For this deed of Bessie McDougal, a general order of the Secretary of the Navy was read from the quarterdeck of every vessel in our service, tendering the thanks of the nation.

About sunset, July 6, 1881, a tempest burst with terrible fury in Iowa. In an hour every creek had overflowed its banks, and the Des Moines River had risen six feet; while every stream bore buildings, lumber, logs, and other débris madly towards the Mississippi. Kate Shelley, a girl of eighteen, stood at a window listening to the wild tumult without, when she happened to glance in the direction of Honey Creek railroad bridge. Through the deep darkness she saw the bright headlight of a locomotive move steadily along for a moment, and drop suddenly. Only her mother and a little brother and sister were at home, but Kate lighted an old lantern, donned a waterproof cloak, and hastened to Honey Creek. She found a turbulent torrent against whose swollen flood she could not stand. She climbed through cruel briars and bushes up the steep bank to the track, crept out to the last tie of the broken bridge, swung her lantern, and shouted at the top of her voice. A faint answer out of the yawning pit came from the engineer, the only survivor of the crew of a wrecked freight train. He said that he was safe for the time on some broken timbers, and urged her to go to Moingona Station, a mile away, to seek help for him and warn the fast express, then nearly due. Buffeted by the gale, she struggled along to the high trestle, five hundred feet long, over the Des Moines, when a wild gust put out her light. She had no matches, so she crawled painfully over the dizzy structure, frequent lurid flashes making her shudder at the sight of the rushing waters far below. She reached the station, told her story, and fell unconscious just before the express came along. The legislature voted her a gold medal for bravery.

"Well," said Barnum to a friend in 1841, " I am going to buy the American Museum." "Buy it!" exclaimed the astonished friend, who knew that the showman had not a dollar; "what do you intend buying it with?" "Brass," was the prompt reply, "for silver and gold have I none."

Every one interested in public entertainments in New York knew Barnum, and knew the condition of his pocket; but Francis Olmstead, who owned the Museum building, consulted numerous references all telling of "a good showman, who would do as he agreed," and accepted a proposition to give security for the purchaser. Mr. Olmstead was to appoint a money-taker at the door, and credit Barnum towards the purchase with all above expenses and an allowance of fifty dollars per month to support his wife and three children. Mrs. Barnum gladly assented to the arrangement, and offered, if need be, to cut down the household expenses to a little more than a dollar a day. Some six months later Mr. Olmstead happened to enter the ticket-office at noon, and found Barnum eating for dinner a few slices of bread and some corned beef. "Is this the way you eat your dinner?" he asked.

"I have not eaten a warm dinner since I bought the Museum, except on the Sabbath; and I intend never to eat another until I get out of debt." "Ah! you are safe, and will pay for the Museum before the year is out," said Mr. Olmstead, slapping the young man approvingly on the shoulder. He was right, for in less than a year Barnum had paid every cent out of the profits of the establishment.

"We discount only our own bills, and not those of private persons," said the cashier of the Bank of England, when a large bill was offered drawn by Anselm Rothschild of Frankfort, on Nathan Rothschild of London. "Private persons!" exclaimed Nathan, when told of the cashier's remark; "I will make these gentlemen see what sort of private persons we are." Three weeks later he presented a five-pound note at the bank at the opening of the office. The teller counted out five sovereigns, looking surprised that Baron Rothschild should have troubled himself about such a trifle. The baron examined the coins one by one, weighing them in the balance, as he said "the law gave him the right to do," put them into a little canvas bag, and offered a second, then a third, fourth, fiftieth, thousandth note. When a bag was full, he handed it to a clerk in waiting, and proceeded to fill another. In seven hours he had changed £21,000, and, with nine employees of his house similarly engaged, had occupied the tellers so busily in changing $1,050,000 worth of notes that no one else could receive attention. The bankers laughed,

but the next morning Rothschild appeared with his
nine clerks and several drays to carry away the gold,
remarking, "These gentlemen refuse to pay my bills;
I have sworn not to keep theirs. They can pay at their
leisure, only I notify them that I have enough to employ them for two months." The smiles faded from
the features of the bank officials, as they thought of a
draft of $55,000,000 in gold which they did not hold.
Next morning notice was given in the newspapers that
the Bank of England would pay Rothschild's bills as
well as its own.

Three hundred thousand men had fought with sullen
fury all day, but the French had been steadily repulsed
until Macdonald was sent with 16,000 infantry to pierce
the Austrian centre. The archduke at once doubled
his lines, brought up his reserve cavalry, and wheeled
two hundred cannon in front of the threatened point.
Straight towards such overwhelming odds, for about
two miles, Macdonald led his melting ranks, before the
astonished gaze of both armies, which seemed to have
ceased fighting elsewhere to watch the march of such a
forlorn hope; then, amid the concentrated fire of 100,-
000 Austrians, he halted a moment to reform his shattered columns. His eye fell upon only 1,500 living
Frenchmen in his battalions, behind which trailed a
long black line of the dead and dying, in which lay ten
out of every eleven with whom he had set out.

Men of steel might well shrink from that fire of hell
which blazed at their breasts, but Macdonald's watchword was ever duty, and his soldiers had caught the
spirit of their chief. Only one look does he give to
that windrow of death; and then, glancing from his
falling heroes to the dense mass of foemen in front,
the single word "forward" rings like a clarion call
above the horrid din. Cheerily as at a holiday parade
drums beat and trumpets peal; with elastic bound the
remaining few leap over the smoking cannon, rush

through charging squadrons of cavalry, and plunge into the serried columns of infantry beyond, which seem fairly pulverized at the moral shock of such an onset. Into the breach thus opened sweep the cuirassiers of the Old Guard, sent by Napoleon to support the brave Macdonald. The Austrians are wildly routed, Wagram is won, and the fate of Europe is sealed for four years.

The powder of the garrison of Fort Henry was exhausted, on that summer day of 1777, and the Indians were pressing closer and closer, emboldened by the silence of the guns. Ebenezer Zane suddenly remembered that there was a keg in his house, some two hundred feet away, and so informed Colonel Shepard, in command. A volunteer was called for to attempt the forlorn task of going for it, exposed to close fire from the savages. Every man offered and contended eagerly for the honor, but Elizabeth Zane insisted upon going, saying that her life was less valuable for defense than that of a man. She was just graduated from a school in Philadelphia, and, with other young ladies, had been aiding the soldiers by casting bullets, making cartridges, and loading rifles. Consent was given reluctantly, and she passed quickly to her brother's house, the Indians watching in silent wonder. But when she was seen running back with the powder, a volley of bullets followed her, but without effect. The powder saved the fort, where now is Wheeling, West Virginia.

Amid difficulties and dangers before unknown, with hordes of savages around him, and winter at hand, La Salle, while exploring the Mississippi, brooded not "on the redoubled ruin that had befallen him — the desponding friends, the exulting foes, the wasted energies, the crushing load of debt, the stormy past, the dark and lowering future. His mind was of a different temper. He had no thought but to grapple with adversity, and out of the fabric of his ruin to rear the fabric of triumphant success."

"Hard pounding, gentlemen," said Wellington at Waterloo to his officers, "but we will see who can pound the longest."

"It is very kind of them to 'sand' our letters for us," said young Junot coolly, as an Austrian shell scattered earth over the dispatch he was writing at the dictation of his commander-in-chief. The remark attracted Napoleon's attention and led to the promotion of the scrivener.

Erskine, the great advocate, was a hero at the bar; but when he entered the House of Commons, there was something in the fixed imperiousness and scorn of Pitt which made him feel inwardly weak and fluttered. Erskine had flashes of heroism; Pitt had consistent and persistent grit.

A Swedish boy fell out of a window and was badly hurt, but with clenched lips he kept back the cry of pain. The king, Gustavus Adolphus, who saw him fall, prophesied that the boy would make a man for an emergency. And so he did, for he became the famous General Bauer.

The Spartan boy was dishonest enough to steal a fox, but proud enough to let the beast eat out his vitals rather than risk detection.

"There is room enough up higher," said Webster to a young man hesitating to study law because the profession was so crowded. This is true in every department of activity. The young man of to-day who would succeed must hold his ground and push hard. Whoever attempts to pass through the door to success will find it labeled in large letters, "Push."

After a severe two hours' lesson from her father, Taglioni, the great danseuse, would fall exhausted. Attendants would then resuscitate her by sponging and friction, when, after a few hours' rest, she would be ready for an evening performance.

"I have often had occasion," says Washington Irving, "to remark the fortitude with which women sustain the most overwhelming reverses of fortune. Those disasters which break down the spirit of a man, and prostrate him in the dust, seem to call forth all the energies of the softer sex, and give such intrepidity and elevation to their character that at times it approaches to sublimity."

The historian Aquetil refused to bend his knee to Bonaparte. He chose rather the direst poverty, and was reduced to three sous a day. "I have still," said he, "two sous a day left for the conqueror of Marengo and Austerlitz. I do not need the emperor's help to die."

For hours John B. Gough tried to speak on temperance to the students at Oxford, amid shouting, hooting, cat-calls, derisive yells, impertinent and insulting questions, and every conceivable annoyance, not excepting personal violence. But he would not give up, and finally captured the good will of the young men by appealing to their sense of fair play in the novel proposition that speaker and audience should divide the time equally between them. "You shall conduct things according to your ideas for twenty minutes while I listen, and then I will talk for twenty minutes while you listen." He soon charmed them so much with his wonderful oratory that they were eager to give him their share of time.

The perfection of grit is the power of saying "No," with emphasis that cannot be mistaken. Learn to meet hard times with a harder will, and more determined pluck. The nature which is all pine and straw is of no use in times of trial, we must have some oak and iron in us. The goddess of fame or of fortune has been won by many a poor boy who had no friends, no backing, or anything but pure grit and invincible purpose to commend him.

A sun-browned country youth called on Bishop Simpson, then president of Asbury University. His plain clothes led the bishop to ask what he had to depend upon. "My two hands, sir," replied the boy who afterward became a United States Senator.

The barriers are not yet erected which shall shut out aspiring talent. Give a boy health and the alphabet, and it rests with him what his future shall be. Those who wait for luck and legacies never amount to much. Who ever knew of a man becoming wise or good by luck? Those who have failed in life usually believe in luck, fate, or destiny. They will cite numerous examples of men who have made "lucky hits," or who have been "lucky dogs."

"The chapter of accidents is the bible of the fool."

Emerson says: "Shallow men believe in luck, believe in circumstances: it was somebody's name, or he happened to be there at the time, or it was so then, and another day it would have been otherwise. Strong men believe in cause and effect. All successful men have agreed in one thing,—they were causationists. They believed that things went not by luck but by law; that there was not a weak or a cracked link in the chain that joins the first and last of things."

Goethe says that industry is nine tenths of genius, and adds: "It never occurs to fools that merit and good fortune are closely united."

"Diligence is the mother of good luck," said Franklin.

"I may here impart the secret of what is called good and bad luck," said Addison. "There are men who, supposing Providence to have an implacable spite against them, bemoan in the poverty of old age the misfortunes of their lives. Luck forever runs against them, and for others. One with a good profession lost his luck in the river, where he idled away his time a-fishing. Another with a good trade perpetually burnt up his luck by his hot temper, which provoked all his employees to leave him. Another with a lucrative business lost his luck by amazing diligence at everything but his own business. Another who steadily followed his trade, as steadily followed the bottle. Another who was honest and constant to his work, erred by his perpetual misjudgment,—he lacked discretion. Hundreds lose their luck by indorsing, by sanguine expectations, by trusting fraudulent men, and by dishonest gains. A man never has good luck who has a bad wife. I never knew an early-rising, hard-working, prudent man, careful of his earnings and strictly honest, who complained of his bad luck. A good character, good habits, and iron industry are impregnable to the assaults of the ill luck that fools are dreaming of. But when I see a tatterdemalion creeping out of a grocery late in the forenoon with his hands stuck into his pockets, the rim of his hat turned up, and the crown knocked in, I know he has had bad luck,—for the worst of all luck is to be a sluggard, a knave, or a tippler."

There is no luck, for all practical purposes, to him who is not striving, and whose senses are not all eagerly attent. What are called accidental discoveries are almost invariably made by those who are looking for something. A man incurs about as much risk of being struck by lightning as by accidental luck. There is, perhaps, an element of luck in the amount of success which crowns the efforts of different men; but even here it will usually be found that the sagacity with which the efforts are directed and the energy with which they are prosecuted measure pretty accurately the luck contained in the results achieved. Apparent exceptions will be found to relate almost wholly to single undertakings, while in the long run the rule will hold good. Two pearl-divers, equally expert, dive together and work with equal energy. One brings up a pearl, while the other returns empty-handed. But let both persevere and at the end of five, ten, or twenty years it will be found that they succeeded almost in exact proportion to their skill and industry.

"With the aid or under the influence of pluck," says the London "Lancet," "it is possible not only to surmount what appear to be insuperable obstructions, but to defy and repel the ennuities of climate, adverse circumstances, and even disease. Many a life has been saved by the moral courage of a sufferer. It is not alone in bearing the pain of operations or the misery of confinement in a sick-room, this self-help becomes of vital moment, but in the monotonous tracking of a weary path, and the vigorous discharge of ordinary duty. How many a victim of incurable disease has lived on through years of suffering, patiently and resolutely hoping against hope, or, what is better, living down despair, until the virulence of a threatening malady has died out, and it has ceased to be destructive, although its physical characteristics remained!" Some patients absolutely refuse to die. What can a doctor do with such cases but let them live? Even his pills will not kill them.

"The ruin which overtakes so many merchants," says Whipple, "is due not so much to their lack of business talent as to their lack of business nerve. How many lovable persons we see in trade, endowed with brilliant capacities, but cursed with yielding dispositions, — who are resolute in no business habits and fixed in no business principles, — who are prone to follow the instincts of a weak good nature against the ominous hints of a clear intelligence, now obliging this friend by indorsing an unsafe note, and then pleasing that neighbor by sharing his risk in a hopeless speculation, — and who, after all the capital they have earned by their industry and sagacity has been sunk in benevolent attempts to assist blundering or plundering incapacity, are doomed, in their bankruptcy, to be the mark of bitter taunts from growling creditors and insolent pity from a gossiping public."

"A somewhat varied experience of men has led me, the longer I live," says Huxley, "to set less value on mere cleverness; to attach more and more importance to industry and physical endurance. Indeed, I am much disposed to think that endurance is the most valuable quality of all; for industry, as the desire to work hard, does not come to much if a feeble frame is unable to respond to the desire. No life is wasted unless it ends in sloth, dishonesty, or cowardice. No success is worthy of the name unless it is won by honest industry and brave breasting of the waves of fortune."

Has God abdicated? Is the universe an infinite chaos, in which order has no throne? Is law a fable? Is life a Babel? Is the world a Pandemonium? Then is there such a game of chance as men call luck. But as long as the smallest atom or the largest sun, the invisible animalcule or the most glorious archangel, the soul soaring from its tenement of clay or the sparrow falling to the earth, acknowledge equally His ruling power, Nature will play no blindman's-buff. If ten deaf, dumb, and blind men were placed in line in a ten-acre lot, and left to wander until all who lived long enough were in line once more, the thing would be accomplished only at the death of the ninth man. Has luck ever made a fool speak words of wisdom; an ignoramus utter lectures on science; a dolt write an Odyssey, an Æneid, a Paradise Lost, or a Hamlet; a loafer become a Girard or Astor, a Rothschild, Stewart, Vanderbilt, Field, Gould, or Rockefeller; a coward win at Yorktown, Wagram, Waterloo, or Richmond; a careless stonecutter carve an Apollo, a Minerva, a Venus de Medici, or a Greek Slave? Does luck raise rich crops on the land of the sluggard, weeds and brambles on that of the industrious farmer? Does luck make the drunkard sleek and attractive, and his home cheerful, while the temperate man looks haggard and suffers want and misery? Does luck starve honest labor, and pamper idleness? Does luck put common sense at a discount, folly at a premium? Does it cast intelligence into the gutter, and raise ignorance to the skies? Does it imprison virtue, and laud vice? Did luck give Watt his engine, Franklin his captive lightning, Whitney his cotton-gin, Fulton his steamboat, Morse his telegraph, Blanchard his lathe, Howe his sewing-machine, Goodyear his rubber, Bell his telephone, Edison his phonograph?

If you are told of the man who, worn out by a painful disorder, tried to commit suicide, but only opened an internal tumor, effecting a cure; of the Persian condemned to lose his tongue, on whom a bungling operation merely removed an impediment of speech; of a painter who produced an effect long desired by throwing his brush at a picture in rage and despair; of a musician who, after repeated failures in trying to imitate a storm at sea, obtained the result desired by angrily running his hands together from the extremities of the keyboard, — bear in mind that even this "luck" came to men as the result of action, not inaction.

One merchant lost his store, his only property, in the Chicago fire. A competitor just across the street occupied a store which was saved. In consequence of the great demand for business blocks after the fire and the enormous increase of business, the latter became wealthy. Here, indeed, circumstances seemed to govern the relative success and failure of these two men; but they were circumstances over which neither had control. The one might have provided for the contingency of such loss by insuring his store and goods; but even in so doing he was liable to select companies that would be ruined by the enormous demand upon them, and so made unable to pay the insurance. The good fortune of the other seemed inevitable. Such a calamity as befell the first, and such an opportunity as was afforded the second, independently of their volition in both instances, comes to not more than one man in ten thousand. As Juvenal says, "A lucky man is rarer than a white crow."

Realizing that "unlucky people" are usually shiftless and lazy, Baron Rothschild and P. T. Barnum would have no business relations with them, for philosophical reasons. A. T. Stewart had a similar aversion, but was somewhat superstitious in his belief that it did not pay him to trade with them in any way. He said that if the first person to whom he sold goods from a newly opened lot was unlucky, he would lose on the entire lot. An old woman who sold apples in front of his little downtown store as a pretense to cover her real business of begging, so impressed him with the idea that she was his guardian angel that he personally moved her things in front of his new store, so anxious was he to have her there. Grover Cleveland also believed in luck. During his first candidacy for the office of President of the United States, he said : " I am certain to be elected : it's just my luck."

"Luck is ever waiting for something to turn up," says Cobden; "labor, with keen eyes and strong will, will turn up something. Luck lies in bed, and wishes the postman would bring him the news of a legacy; labor turns out at six o'clock, and with busy pen or ringing hammer lays the foundation of a competence. Luck whines; labor whistles. Luck relies on chance; labor, on character."

Stick to the thing and carry it through. Believe you were made for the place you fill, and that no one else can fill it as well. Put forth your whole energies. Be awake, electrify yourself; go forth to the task. Only once learn to carry a thing through in all its completeness and proportion, and you will become a hero. You will think better of yourself; others will think better of you. The world in its very heart admires the stern, determined doer.

> "I like the man who faces what he must
> With step triumphant and a heart of cheer;
> Who fights the daily battle without fear;
> Sees his hopes fail, yet keeps unfaltering trust
> That God is God; that somehow, true and just,
> His plans work out for mortals; not a tear
> Is shed when fortune, which the world holds dear,
> Falls from his grasp; better, with love, a crust
> Than living in dishonor; envies not,
> Nor loses faith in man; but does his best,
> Nor even murmurs at his humbler lot;
> But with a smile and words of hope, gives zest
> To every toiler; he alone is great,
> Who by a life heroic conquers fate."

CHAPTER XXI.

THE REWARD OF PERSISTENCE.

Every noble work is at first impossible. — CARLYLE.

The falling drops at last will wear the stone. — LUCRETIUS.

Victory belongs to the most persevering. — NAPOLEON.

Success in most things depends on knowing how long it takes to succeed. — MONTESQUIEU.

Perpetual pushing and assurance put a difficulty out of countenance, and make a seeming impossibility give way. — JEREMY COLLIER.

> I hate inconstancy — I loathe, detest,
> Abhor, condemn, abjure the mortal made
> Of such quicksilver clay that in his breast
> No permanent foundation can be laid.
> BYRON.

> An enterprise, when fairly once begun,
> Should not be left till all that ought is won.
> SHAKESPEARE.

"Unstable as water, thou shalt not excel."

The nerve that never relaxes, the eye that never blenches, the thought that never wanders, — these are the masters of victory. — BURKE.

In the lexicon of youth, which fate reserves for a bright manhood, there is no such word as fail. — BULWER.

"THE pit rose at me!" exclaimed Edmund Kean in a wild tumult of emotion, as he rushed home to his trembling wife. "Mary, you shall ride in your carriage yet, and Charles shall go to Eton!" He had been so terribly in earnest with the study of his profession that he had at length made a mark on his generation. He was a little dark man with a voice naturally harsh, but he determined, when young, to play the character of Sir Giles Overreach, in Massinger's drama, as no other man had ever played it. By a persistency that nothing seemed able to daunt, he so trained himself to play the character that his success, when it did come, was overwhelming, and all London was at his feet.

"I am sorry to say that I don't think this is in your line," said Woodfall the reporter, after Sheridan had made his first speech in Parliament. "You had better have stuck to your former pursuits." With head on his hand Sheridan mused for a time, then looked up and said, "It is in me, and it shall come out of me." From the same man came that harangue against Warren Hastings which the orator Fox called the best speech ever made in the House of Commons.

"I had no other books than heaven and earth, which are open to all," said Bernard Palissy, who left his home in the south of France in 1828, at the age of eighteen. Though only a glass-painter, he had the soul of an artist, and the sight of an elegant Italian cup disturbed his whole existence; and from that moment the determination to discover the enamel with which it was glazed possessed him like a passion. For months and years he tried all kinds of experiments to learn the materials of which the enamel was compounded. He built a furnace, which was a failure, and then a second, burning so much wood, spoiling so many drugs and pots of common earthenware, and losing so much time, that poverty stared him in the face, and he was forced to try his experiments in a common furnace, from lack of ability to buy fuel. Flat failure was the result, but he decided on the spot to begin all over again, and soon had three hundred pieces baking, one of which came out covered with beautiful enamel. To perfect his invention he next built a glass-furnace, carrying the bricks on his back. At last the time came for a trial; but, though he kept the heat up six days, his enamel would not melt. His money was all gone, but he borrowed some, and bought more pots and wood, and tried to get a better flux. When next he lighted his fire, he attained no result until his fuel was gone. Tearing off the pal-

CHARLES ROBERT DARWIN

" 'T is dogged that does it."

" The very reputation of being strong-willed, plucky, and indefatigable, is of priceless value. It cows enemies, and dispels opposition to our undertakings."

ings of his garden fence, he fed them to the flames, but in vain. His furniture followed to no purpose. The shelves of his pantry were then broken up and thrown into the furnace; and the great burst of heat melted the enamel. The grand secret was learned. Persistence had triumphed again.

"For me, too," said Mendelssohn, "the hour of rest will come; do the next thing."

"If you work hard two weeks without selling a book," wrote a publisher to an agent, "you will make a success of it."

"Know thy work and do it," said Carlyle; "and work at it like a Hercules. One monster there is in the world — an idle man."

"Whoever is resolved to excel in painting, or, indeed, in any other art," said Reynolds, "must bring all his mind to bear upon that one object from the moment that he rises till he goes to bed."

"Those who are resolved to excel must go to their work, willing or unwilling, morning, noon, and night," said Reynolds; "they will find it no play, but very hard labor."

"I have no secret but hard work," said Turner the painter.

"Young gentlemen," said Francis Wayland, "remember that nothing can stand days' work."

"My sons," said a dying farmer to his three indolent boys, "a great treasure lies hid in the estate which I am about to leave to you." "Where is it hid?" asked the eager sons in chorus. "I am about to tell you," gasped the sick man; "you will have to dig for it" — but here his spirit departed. The sons turned over every sod upon the estate, without finding any buried gold; but they learned to work, and when the fields were sown, an enormous harvest repaid their thorough digging.

"The man who is perpetually hesitating which of

two things he will do first," said William Wirt, "will do neither. The man who resolves, but suffers his resolution to be changed by the first counter-suggestion of a friend — who fluctuates from opinion to opinion, from plan to plan, and veers like a weather-cock to every point of the compass, with every breath of caprice that blows, can never accomplish anything great or useful. Instead of being progressive in anything, he will be at best stationary, and, more probably, retrograde in all.

"Who first consults wisely, then resolves firmly, and then executes his purpose with inflexible perseverance, undismayed by those petty difficulties which daunt a weaker spirit — that man can advance to eminence in any line."

We are told that perseverance built the pyramids on Egypt's plains, erected the gorgeous temple at Jerusalem, inclosed in adamant the Chinese Empire, scaled the stormy, cloud-capped Alps, opened a highway through the watery wilderness of the Atlantic, leveled the forests of the new world, and reared in its stead a community of states and nations. Perseverance has wrought from the marble block the exquisite creations of genius, painted on canvas the gorgeous mimicry of nature, and engraved on a metallic surface the viewless substance of the shadow. Perseverance has put in motion millions of spindles, winged as many flying shuttles, harnessed thousands of iron steeds to as many freighted cars, and set them flying from town to town and nation to nation, tunneled mountains of granite, and annihilated space with the lightning's speed. Perseverance has whitened the waters of the world with the sails of a hundred nations, navigated every sea and explored every land. Perseverance has reduced nature in her thousand forms to as many sciences, taught her laws, prophesied her future movements, measured her untrodden spaces, counted her myriad hosts of worlds, and computed their distances, dimensions, and velocities.

Lofty mountains are wearing down by slow degrees. The ocean is gradually but slowly filling up, by deposits from its thousand rivers. The Niagara Falls have worn back seven miles through the hard limestone, over which they pour their thundering columns of water, and will by and by drain the great lake which feeds the boiling chasm. The Red Sea and whole regions of the Pacific Ocean are gradually filling up by the labors of a little insect, so small as to be almost invisible to the naked eye.

The slow penny is surer than the quick dollar. The slow trotter will out-travel the fleet racer. Genius darts, flutters, and tires; but perseverance wears and wins. The all-day horse wins the race. The afternoon-man wears off the laurels. The last blow drives home the nail.

"Are your discoveries often brilliant intuitions?" asked a reporter of Thomas A. Edison. "Do they come to you while you are lying awake nights?"

"I never did anything worth doing by accident," was the reply, "nor did any of my inventions come indirectly through accident, except the phonograph. No, when I have fully decided that a result is worth getting I go ahead on it and make trial after trial until it comes. I have always kept strictly within the lines of commercially useful inventions. I have never had any time to put on electrical wonders, valuable simply as novelties to catch the popular fancy. *I like it,*" continued the great inventor. "I don't know any other reason. You know some people like to collect stamps. Anything I have begun is always on my mind, and I am not easy while away from it until it is finished."

A man who thus gives himself wholly to his work is certain to accomplish something; and if he have ability and common sense, his success will be great.

"Acting does not, like Dogberry's reading and writing, 'come by nature,'" said the elder Kean; "with all the high qualities which go to the formation of a great exponent of the book of life (for so the stage may justly be called), it is impossible, totally impossible, to leap at once to fame. 'What wound did ever heal but by slow degrees?' says our immortal author; and what man, say I, ever became an 'actor' without a long and sedulous apprenticeship? I know that many think to step from behind a counter or jump from the high stool of an office to the boards, and take the town by storm in Richard or Othello, is as 'easy as lying.' Oh, the born idiots! they remind me of the halfpenny candles stuck in the windows on illumination-nights; they flicker and flutter their brief minute, and go out unheeded. Barn-storming, my lads, barn-storming, — that's the touchstone; by that I won my spurs; so did Garrick, Henderson, and Kemble; and so, on the other side of the water, did my almost namesake Lekain and Talma."

How Bulwer wrestled with the fates to change his apparent destiny! His first novel was a failure; his early poems were failures; and his youthful speeches provoked the ridicule of his opponents. But he fought his way to eminence through ridicule and defeat.

Gibbon worked twenty years on his "Decline and Fall of the Roman Empire." Noah Webster spent thirty-six years on his dictionary. What a sublime patience he showed in devoting a life to the collection and definition of words. George Bancroft spent twenty-six years on his "History of the United States." Newton rewrote his "Chronology of Ancient Nations" fifteen times. Titian wrote to Charles V.: "I send your majesty the Last Supper, after working on it almost daily for seven years." He worked on his Pietro Martyn eight years. George Stephenson was fifteen years perfecting his locomotive; Watt, twenty years on his condensing-engine. Harvey labored eight long years before he published his discovery of the circulation of the blood. He was then called a crack-brained impostor by his fellow physicians. Amid abuse and ridicule he waited twenty-five years before his great discovery was recognized by the profession.

Newton discovered the law of gravitation before he was twenty-one, but one slight error in a measurement of the earth's circumference interfered with a demonstration of the correctness of his theory. Twenty years later he corrected the error, and showed that the planets roll in their orbits as a result of the same law which brings an apple to the ground.

Missionaries preached ten years in Madagascar before they obtained a convert. Dr. Judson labored five years in Burmah, and Dr. Morrison seven in China, before one native became a Christian. For fifteen years in Tahiti, and seventeen in Bengal, the work seemed all in vain.

An Italian music-teacher once told a pupil who wished to know what could be hoped for with study: "If you will study a year I will teach you to sing well; if two years, you may excel. If you will practice the scale constantly for three years, I will make you the best tenor in Italy; if for four years, you may have the world at your feet."

Sothern, the great actor, said that the early part of his theatrical career was spent in getting dismissed for incompetency.

"The only merit to which I lay claim," said Hugh Miller, "is that of patient research — a merit in which whoever wills may rival or surpass me; and this humble faculty of patience when rightly developed may lead to more extraordinary development of ideas than even genius itself."

"Never depend upon your genius," said John Ruskin, in the words of Joshua Reynolds; "if you have talent, industry will improve it; if you have none, industry will supply the deficiency."

Patience is the guardian of faith, the preserver of peace, the cherisher of love, the teacher of humility. Patience governs the flesh, strengthens the spirit, sweetens the temper, stifles anger, extinguishes envy, subdues pride; she bridles the tongue, restrains the hand, tramples upon temptations, endures persecutions. Patience is the courage of virtue, enabling us to lessen pain of mind or body; it does not so much add to the number of our joys as it tends to diminish the number of our sufferings. Labor is still, and ever will be, the inevitable price set upon everything which is valuable.

Savages believe that, when they conquer an enemy, his spirit enters into them, and fights for them ever afterwards. So the spirit of our conquests enters us, and helps us to win the next victory.

Blücher may have been routed at Ligny yesterday, but to-day you hear the thunder of his guns at Waterloo hurling dismay and death among his former conquerors.

Opposing circumstances create strength. Opposition gives us greater power of resistance. To overcome one barrier gives us greater ability to overcome the next.

Who will not befriend the persevering, energetic youth, the fearless man of industry?

Be sure that your trade, your profession, your calling in life is a good one — one that God and goodness sanction; then be true as steel to it. Think for it, plan for it, work for it, live for it; throw your mind, might, strength, heart, and soul into your actions for it, and success will crown you her favored child. No matter whether your object be great or small, whether it be the planting of a nation or a batch of potatoes, the same perseverance is necessary. Everybody admires an iron determination, and comes to the aid of him who directs it for good.

Don't damp fires and cool off boilers while but two thirds across the Atlantic; keep up the heat.

C. C. Coffin says that in February, 1492, a poor, gray-haired man, his head bowed with discouragement almost to the back of his mule, rode slowly out through the beautiful gateway of the Alhambra. From boyhood he had been haunted with the idea that the earth is round. He believed that the piece of carved wood picked up four hundred miles at sea, and the bodies of two men unlike any other human beings known, found on the shores of Portugal, had drifted from unknown lands in the west. But his last hope of obtaining aid for a voyage of discovery had failed. King John of Portugal, while pretending to think of helping him, had sent out secretly an expedition of his own.

He had begged bread, drawn maps and charts to keep him from starving; he had lost his wife; his friends had called him crazy, and forsaken him. The council of wise men, called by Ferdinand and Isabella, ridiculed his theory of reaching the east by sailing west.

"But the sun and moon are round," said Columbus, "why not the earth?"

"If the earth is a ball, what holds it up?" asked the wise men.

"What holds the sun and moon up?" inquired Columbus.

"But how can men walk with their heads hanging down, and their feet up, like flies on a ceiling?" asked a learned doctor; "how can trees grow with their roots in the air?"

"The water would run out of the ponds and we should fall off," said another philosopher.

"This doctrine is contrary to the Bible, which says, 'The heavens are stretched out like a tent:'— of course it is flat; it is rank heresy to say it is round," said a priest.

He left the Alhambra in despair, intending to offer

his services to Charles VII., but he heard a voice calling his name. An old friend had told Isabella that it would add great renown to her reign at a trifling expense if what the sailor believed should prove true. "It shall be done," said Isabella, "I will pledge my jewels to raise the money. Call him back."

Columbus turned and with him turned the world. Not a sailor would go voluntarily; so the king and queen compelled them. Three days out in his vessels scarcely larger than fishing-schooners, the Pinta floated a signal of distress for a broken rudder. Terror seized the sailors, but Columbus calmed their fears with pictures of gold and precious stones from India. Two hundred miles west of the Canaries, the compass ceased to point to the North Star. The sailors are ready to mutiny, but he tells them the North Star is not exactly north. Twenty-three hundred miles from home, though he tells them it is but seventeen hundred, a bush with berries floats by, land birds fly near, and they pick up a piece of wood curiously carved. On October 12, Columbus raised the banner of Castile over the western world.

What is difficulty for but to teach us the necessity of redoubled exertion? danger but to give us fresh courage? impossibilities but to inspire us to the enforcement of victory? Longfellow has well illustrated this tenacity of purpose: —

> "The divine insanity of noble minds,
> That never falters nor abates,
> But labors, and endures, and waits
> Till all that it foresees it finds,
> Or what it cannot find, creates."

"How hard I worked at that tremendous shorthand, and all improvement appertaining to it," said Dickens. "I will only add to what I have already written of my perseverance at this time of my life, and of a patient and continuous energy which then began to be matured within me, and which I know to be the strong point of my character, if it have any strength at all, that there, on looking back, I find the source of my success."

Cyrus W. Field had retired from business with a large fortune when he became possessed with the idea that by means of a cable laid upon the bottom of the Atlantic Ocean, telegraphic communication could be established between Europe and America. He plunged into the undertaking with all the force of his being. The preliminary work included the construction of a telegraph line one thousand miles long, from New York to St. John's, Newfoundland. Through four hundred miles of almost unbroken forest they had to build a road as well as a telegraph line across Newfoundland. Another stretch of one hundred and forty miles across the island of Cape Breton involved a great deal of labor, as did the laying of a cable across the St. Lawrence.

By hard work he secured aid for his company from the British government, but in Congress he encountered such bitter opposition from a powerful lobby that his measure only had a majority of one in the Senate. The cable was loaded upon the Agamemnon, the flagship of the British fleet at Sebastopol, and upon the Niagara, a magnificent new frigate of the United States Navy; but, when five miles of cable had been paid out, it caught in the machinery and parted. On the second trial, when two hundred miles at sea, the electric current was suddenly lost, and men paced the decks nervously and sadly, as if in the presence of death. Just as Mr. Field was about to give the order to cut the cable, the current returned as quickly and mysteriously as it had disappeared. The following night, when the ship was moving but four miles an hour and the cable running out at the rate of six miles, the brakes were applied too suddenly just as the steamer gave a heavy lurch, breaking the cable.

Field was not the man to give up. Seven hundred

miles more of cable were ordered, and a man of great skill was set to work to devise a better machine for paying out the long line. American and British inventors united in making a machine. At length in mid-ocean the two halves of the cable were spliced and the steamers began to separate, the one headed for Ireland, the other for Newfoundland, each running out the precious thread, which, it was hoped, would bind two continents together. Before the vessels were three miles apart, the cable parted. Again it was spliced, but when the ships were eighty miles apart, the current was lost. A third time the cable was spliced and about two hundred miles paid out, when it parted some twenty feet from the Agamemnon, and the vessels returned to the coast of Ireland.

Directors were disheartened, the public skeptical, capitalists were shy, and but for the indomitable energy and persuasiveness of Mr. Field, who worked day and night almost without food or sleep, the whole project would have been abandoned. Finally a third attempt was made, with such success that the whole cable was laid without a break, and several messages were flashed through nearly seven hundred leagues of ocean, when suddenly the current ceased.

Faith now seemed dead except in the breast of Cyrus W. Field, and one or two friends, yet with such persistence did they work that they persuaded men to furnish capital for another trial even against what seemed their better judgment. A new and superior cable was loaded upon the Great Eastern, which steamed slowly out to sea, paying out as she advanced. Everything worked to a charm until within six hundred miles of Newfoundland, when the cable snapped and sank. After several fruitless attempts to raise it, the enterprise was abandoned for a year.

Not discouraged by all these difficulties, Mr. Field went to work with a will, organized a new company, and made a new cable far superior to anything before used, and on July 13, 1866, was begun the trial which ended with the following message sent to New York:—

"HEART'S CONTENT, *July* 27.

"We arrived here at nine o'clock this morning. All well. Thank God! the cable is laid and is in perfect working order. CYRUS W. FIELD."

The old cable was picked up, spliced, and continued to Newfoundland, and the two are still working, with good prospects for usefulness for many years.

In Revelations we read: "He that overcometh, I will give him to sit down with me on my throne."

Successful men, it is said, owe more to their perseverance than to their natural powers, their friends, or the favorable circumstances around them. Genius will falter by the side of labor, great powers will yield to great industry. Talent is desirable, but perseverance is more so.

"How long did it take you to learn to play?" asked a young man of Geradini. "Twelve hours a day for twenty years," replied the great violinist. Lyman Beecher's father, when asked how long it took him to write his celebrated sermon on the "Government of God," replied, "About forty years."

A Chinese student, discouraged by repeated failures, had thrown away his book in despair, when he saw a poor woman rubbing an iron bar on a stone to make a needle. This example of patience sent him back to his studies with a new determination, and he became one of the three greatest scholars of China.

"Generally speaking," said Sydney Smith, "the life of all truly great men has been a life of intense and incessant labor. They have commonly passed the first half of life in the gross darkness of indigent humility, — overlooked, mistaken, condemned by weaker men, — thinking while others slept, reading while others rioted, feeling something within them that told them they should not always be kept down among the dregs of the world. And then, when their time has come, and some little accident has given them their first occasion, they have burst out into the light and glory of public life, rich with the spoils of time, and mighty in all the labors and struggles of the mind."

Malibran said: "If I neglect my practice a day, I see the difference in my execution; if for two days, my friends see it; and if for a week, all the world knows my failure." Constant, persistent struggle she found to be the price of her marvelous power.

When an East India boy is learning archery, he is compelled to practice three months drawing the string to his ear before he is allowed to touch an arrow.

"If I am building a mountain," said Confucius, "and stop before the last basketful of earth is placed on the summit, I have failed."

Lady Franklin labored incessantly for twelve long years to rescue her husband from the polar seas. Nothing could daunt her or induce her to abandon the hopeless search until she had proven that he died after traversing before unknown seas seeking a northwest passage.

Benjamin Franklin had this tenacity of purpose in a wonderful degree. When he started in the printing business in Philadelphia, he carried his material through the streets on a wheelbarrow. He hired one room for his office, work-room, and sleeping-room. He found a formidable rival in the city and invited him to his room. Pointing to a piece of bread from which he had just eaten his dinner, he said: "Unless you can live cheaper than I can you cannot starve me out."

All are familiar with the misfortune of Carlyle while writing his "History of the French Revolution." After the first volume was ready for the press, he loaned the manuscript to a neighbor who left it lying on the floor,

THE REWARD OF PERSISTENCE.   351

and the servant girl took it to kindle the fire. It was a bitter disappointment, but Carlyle was not the man to give up. After many months of poring over hundreds of volumes of authorities and scores of manuscripts, he reproduced that which had burned in a few minutes.

Audubon, the naturalist, had spent two years with his gun and note-book in the forests of America, making drawings of birds. He nailed them all up securely in a box and went off on a vacation. When he returned he opened the box only to find a nest of Norwegian rats in his beautiful drawings. Every one was ruined. It was a terrible disappointment, but Audubon took his gun and note-book and started for the forest. He reproduced his drawings even better than those he had before.

Robert Ainsworth worked many years on a Latin dictionary. His wife became angry because he robbed her of his time, and burned all his manuscript. He rewrote it, but never forgave his wife.

A merchant went to a sculptor and wanted to hire him by the day to carve a statue. "Wretch," was the reply, "I have been twenty-five years learning how to make that statue in twenty-five days."

When Dickens was asked to read one of his selections in public he replied that he had not time, for he was in the habit of reading the same piece every day for six months before reading it in public. "My own invention," he says, "such as it is, I assure you, would never have served me as it has but for the habit of commonplace, humble, patient, toiling attention."

Addison amassed three volumes of manuscript before he began the "Spectator."

Every one admires a determined, persistent man. Marcus Morton ran sixteen times for governor of Massachusetts. At last his opponents voted for him from admiration of his pluck, and he was elected by one majority. Lord Eldon copied the whole of Coke upon Littleton twice over because too poor to buy books.

Gibbon wrote his memoirs over nine times. Such persistence always triumphs.

A teacher was drilling some boys on the hard verses in the third chapter of Daniel. When they read the chapter the third time an easily discouraged scholar came to the names Shadrach, Meshach, and Abednego, stopped short, and in a most discouraged voice said, "Teacher, there's them three fellers again."

We all know plenty of men who seem to get along pretty well until they come to "them three fellers again," when they stop and will go no further until the obstruction is removed.

Webster declared to the teachers at Phillips Academy that he never could declaim before the school. He said he committed piece after piece and rehearsed them in his room, but when he heard his name called in the academy and all eyes turned towards him the room became dark and everything he ever knew fled from his brain; but Webster became the great orator of America. Indeed, it is doubtful whether Demosthenes himself surpassed Webster's great reply to Hayne in the United States Senate. Webster's tenacity was illustrated by a circumstance which occurred in the academy. The principal punished him for shooting pigeons by compelling him to commit one hundred lines of Vergil. He knew the principal was to take a certain train that afternoon, so he went to his room and committed seven hundred lines. He went to recite them to the principal just before train time. After repeating the hundred lines he kept right on until he had recited two hundred. The principal kept looking at his watch and grew nervous, but Webster kept right on. The principal finally stopped him and asked him how many more he had learned. "About five hundred more," said Webster, and kept on.

"You can have the rest of the day for pigeon-shooting," said the principal.

Great writers have ever been noted for their tenacity of purpose. Their works have not been flung off from minds aglow with genius, but have been elaborated and elaborated into grace and beauty, until every trace of their efforts has been obliterated. Bishop Butler worked twenty years incessantly on his "Analogy," and even then was so dissatisfied that he wanted to burn it. Rousseau says he obtained the ease and grace of his style only by ceaseless inquietude, by endless blotches and erasures. Vergil worked eleven years on the Æneid. The note-books of great men like Hawthorne and Emerson are tell-tales of the enormous drudgery, of the years put into a book which may be read in an hour. Montesquieu was twenty-five years writing his "Esprit de Louis," yet you can read it in sixty minutes. Adam Smith spent ten years on his "Wealth of Nations." A rival playwright once laughed at Euripides for spending three days on three lines, when he had written five hundred lines. "But your five hundred lines in three days will be dead and forgotten, while my three lines will live forever," he replied.

Ariosto wrote his "Description of a Tempest" sixteen different ways. He spent ten years on his "Orlando Furioso," and only sold one hundred copies at fifteen pence each. The proof of Burke's "Letters to a Noble Lord" (one of the sublimest things in all literature) went back to the publisher so changed and blotted with corrections that the printer absolutely refused to correct it, and it was entirely reset. Adam Tucker spent eighteen years on the "Light of Nature." A great naturalist spent eight years on the "Anatomy of the Day Fly." Thoreau's New England pastoral, "A Week on the Concord and Merrimac Rivers," was an entire failure. Seven hundred of the one thousand copies printed were returned from the publishers. Thoreau wrote in his diary: "I have some nine hundred volumes in my library, seven hundred of which I wrote myself." Yet he says he took up his pen with as much determination as ever.

The rolling stone gathers no moss. The persistent tortoise outruns the swift but fickle hare. An hour a day for twelve years more than equals the time given to study in a four years' course at a high school. The reading and re-reading of a single volume has been the making of many a man. "Patience," says Bulwer, "is the courage of the conqueror; it is the virtue *par excellence*, of Man against Destiny — of the One against the World, and of the Soul against Matter. Therefore, this is the courage of the Gospel; and its importance in a social view — its importance to races and institutions — cannot be too earnestly inculcated."

Want of constancy is the cause of many a failure, making the millionaire of to-day a beggar to-morrow. Show me a really great triumph that is not the reward of persistence. One of the paintings which made Titian famous was on his easel eight years; another, seven. How came popular writers famous? By writing for years without any pay at all; by writing hundreds of pages as mere practice-work; by working like galley-slaves at literature for half a lifetime with no other compensation than — fame. "Never despair," says Burke; "but if you do, work on in despair." "He who has put forth his total strength in fit actions," says Emerson, "has the richest return of wisdom."

"There is also another class," says a moralist, "chiefly among the fair sex, who are incapable of making up their minds, even with the help of others; who change and change and repent again, and return to their first resolution, and then regret that they have done so when too late. They hesitate between a walk and a drive, between going in one direction or another, and fifty other things equally immaterial; and always end the matter by doing what they fancy, at any rate, is the least agreeable and eligible of the two. Of course this disposition, shown in these trifles, will be shown in more important matters; and a most distressing and unfortunate disposition it is, both for themselves and those around them. Now, the only remedy for such a turn of mind is resolutely to keep to the first decision, whatever it may be, without dwelling on its advantages or disadvantages, and allowing any useless regrets after the thing is done; and even if a mistake is often made at the outset, from want of the habit of ready and unwavering judgment, it will be far less mischievous than weak and wretched indecision."

Success is not measured by what a man accomplishes, but by the opposition he has encountered, and the courage with which he has maintained the struggle against overwhelming odds, as Alexander learned by defeat the art of war.

The head of the god Hercules is represented as covered with a lion's skin with claws joined under the chin, to show that when we have conquered our misfortunes, they become our helpers. Oh, the glory of an unconquerable will!

> Yet nerve thy spirit to the proof,
> And blench not at thy chosen lot;
> The timid good may stand aloof,
> The sage may frown, — yet faint thou not:
> Nor heed the shaft too surely cast,
> The foul and hissing bolt of scorn;
> For with thy side shall dwell at last,
> The victory of endurance born.
>
> BRYANT.

> The heights by great men reached and kept
>   Were not attained by sudden flight,
> But they, while their companions slept,
>   Were toiling upward in the night.
>
> We have not wings, we cannot soar;
>   But we have feet to scale and climb,
> By slow degrees, by more and more,
>   The cloudy summit of our time.
>
> LONGFELLOW.

CHAPTER XXII.

A LONG LIFE, AND HOW TO REACH IT.

> Not in the world of light alone,
>   Where God has built His blazing throne,
> Nor yet alone on earth below,
>   With belted seas that come and go,
> And endless isles of sunlit green,
>   Is all the Maker's glory seen —
> Look in upon thy wondrous frame,
>   Eternal wisdom still the same. HOLMES.

Pile luxury as high as you will, health is better. — JULIA WARD HOWE.

O blessed health ! thou art above all gold and treasure; 't is thou who enlargest the soul, and openest all its powers to receive instruction and to relish virtue. He that has thee has little more to wish for ; and he that is so wretched as to want thee, wants everything without thee. — STERNE.

> No chronic tortures racked his aged limb,
> For luxury and sloth had nourished none for him.
>   BRYANT, *The Old Man's Funeral.*

" Health and cheerfulness make beauty."

The nearer men live to each other, the shorter their lives are. — DR. PARR.

Some men dig their graves with their teeth. — SYDNEY SMITH.

> " Nor love, nor honor, wealth, nor power,
>   Can give the heart a cheerful hour
>   When health is lost."

The stomach begs and clamors, and listens to no precepts. And yet it is not an obdurate creditor ; for it is dismissed with small payment if you only give it what you owe, and not as much as you can. — SENECA.

Shut the door to the sun and you will open it to the doctor.
                                                    ITALIAN PROVERB.

> Joy, temperance, and repose,
> Slam the door on the Doctor's nose.   LONGFELLOW.

> 'T is the sublime of man,
> Our noontide majesty, — to know ourselves,
> Part and proportion of a wondrous whole.   COLERIDGE.

THE greatest artist the world has known painted a picture, the most beautiful ever seen. Day by day, for

WILLIAM EWART GLADSTONE

"Don't let your heart grow cold, and you shall carry youth with you into the teens of your second century."

years, he wrought upon this masterpiece, developing it from a mere sketch until it became a picture which all who saw delighted to look upon. But notwithstanding his wonderful power, the artist could never attain in this work the perfection sought. His colors seemed to change in the night. The rosy flush imparted to cheek and lip were lost as often as they were renewed. The flashing eyes grew dull and leaden, and seemed to sink into the canvas. The beautiful flesh lost its rose-leaf tint, and became sallow and unnatural. The painter's art was baffled, and he knew not why.

Yet his hand had not lost its cunning, his colors were not impure, his conception was not at fault. His work was well done, but it was spoiled in the night by an enemy, a rival painter whom none praised and whose work no one admired. Jealous of the fame his rival had won by joyous, glorious pictures, while his own sombre works were shunned, he crept by night to the studio of the other, and with palette spread with shadow tints, wrought ruin with the work he could not imitate. Thus the painting which should have excelled all others never attained perfection, and was ruined at last beyond all hope of restoration.

Again and again the two painters have repeated their efforts upon other canvas, with similar results, as a rule. Their names are Health and Disease, and they paint upon human canvas. The first rises and retires early, and works as much as possible in the open air, in the blessed sunlight, where keen winds blow in winter and zephyrs in spring and summer, where golden harvests wave and fruit-laden trees sway in the autumn breezes, where fountains murmur and rivulets sing, where men work and romping children play, where cattle are afield, and birds and bees on the wing. The other sleeps through the early hours, but comes forth when Nature is asleep; and under the flickering street-lights or the light of the silent stars, or in dark nooks and corners sometimes by day, his withering touch falls upon the fairest work of his rival, injuring it all and utterly ruining much of it. Only a very few paintings are kept almost wholly out of the reach of Disease, yet how wonderful are they in their comparative perfection!

A vase of exquisite beauty, found in a marble sarcophagus near Rome during the sixteenth century, was bought by the Duchess of Portland for ten thousand dollars and loaned to the British Museum. The visitor is powerfully impressed with its matchless symmetry; but, on examining it closely, he sees that the surface is seamed with cracks, and that in some places holes have been closed by a kind of cement. He is told that a madman once struck this beautiful vase with his cane, and broke it into a hundred pieces. The fragments were put together again at great cost and trouble; yet the vase is practically a wreck.

The world is full of men and women like this vase — marred, scarred, broken, patched, mere shadows of their former selves. They look fairly well, but their constitutions have been broken by dissipation, by exposure, by overwork, by ignorance, by violation in some way of the laws of nature. Many of them have patched the pieces together by drugs, physicians, climate, or travel; but, like the vase, they can withstand no strain. Mocked by an ambition for success, but with no strength to attain it, they drag out a miserable existence.

"I am certain," says Horace Mann, "I could have performed twice the labor, both better and with greater ease to myself, had I known as much of the laws of health and life at twenty-one as I do now. In college I was taught all about the motions of the planets, as carefully as though they would have been in danger of getting off the track if I had not known how to trace their orbits; but about my own organization, and the conditions indispensable to the healthful functions of my own body, I was left in profound ignorance. Nothing could be more preposterous. I ought to have begun at home, and taken the stars when it should have become their turn. The consequence was, I broke down at the beginning of my second college year, and have never had a well day since. Whatever labor I have since been able to do, I have done it all on credit instead of capital — a most ruinous way, either in regard to health or money. For the last twenty-five years, so far as it regards health, I have been put, from day to day, upon my good behavior; and during the whole of this period, as an Hibernian would say, if I had lived as other folks do for a month, I should have died in a fortnight."

The age of sawdust puddings and plank beds is past. Pascal's doctrine that disease is the natural condition of Christians, and that the body is the natural enemy of the soul, is exploded. Muscular Christianity is the demand of the hour. The body is no longer looked upon as the devil chained to the soul, to be mortified and starved to keep the passions down. Pale, emaciated, spiritual shadows are no longer in demand in the pulpit. A diet of bread and water is no longer regarded as conducive to real piety. Tallness is no longer the only sign of virtue, nor do width and weight any longer indicate a tendency to crime; nor is muscle associated with rowdyism. The hero of the ancients had the strength of ten men, and his servant could eat granite rock. The Cid had such power of resistance that he could sleep with a leper and not contract the disease. The Romans despised physical weakness and deformity. The great and wise Cato conceived the plan of banishing all the decrepit, deaf, and helpless to the island of Esculapius in the Tiber, where they perished of hunger and exposure. This was the reward of a slave for a life of menial servitude. The Greeks also banished their weak and deformed when they could no longer serve the state. A magnificent physique was the great object of their games, contests, and festivities. They deified health in the young and beautiful goddess Hygeia. Compare the pale, chestless, calfless, attenuated young men of to-day with the stalwart youths of Greece and Rome. What a magnificent physical perfection distinguishes the North American Indians. When the painter West was taken by prominent Italians to see the treasures of the Vatican, he was first shown the celebrated statue of Apollo. "Oh!" he exclaimed, "a Mohawk Indian!" They are born with good physiques, and their training all tends in the same direction; and the average Indian boy of fifteen can withstand more fatigue than athletes among the white men. Smallpox and bullets are about the only things that can kill them. Compare these with the thousands of haggard students in our American colleges, muscle-starved, book-crammed, and "sicklied o'er with the pale cast of thought." What a sad commentary it is upon the institutions whose avowed object is to help young men in making their way in a hard, practical world, that so many break down utterly and are compelled to spend the rest of their lives hunting for health. The first requisite to success is to be a first-class animal. The brain gets a great deal of credit that belongs to the stomach.

With rare exceptions, the great prizes of life fall to those of stalwart, robust physique. If you have a bodily weakness, such as lack of vigor or physical stamina, the effect will show itself in everything you do, and cripple your whole lifework. Every one who knows you reads your weakness and lack of tone in your unsteady eye and hesitating step. It appears in every letter you write, in every speech you make, in everything you do; you cannot disguise it, and you will fall as far below success as you fall below the health-line. Every faculty of the mind sympathizes with every defect and weakness of the body.

The world is full of half-done, botched work, the result of weak and sickly lives. The tendency of civilization has been to deteriorate bodily stamina. Cities are the graves of the physiques of our race. Long residence in cities lowers the type of physical manhood. If towns were not constantly recruited from the country, the constitutions and intellects of their inhabitants would rapidly decline in vigor. Most of the stalwart men of our large centres were born in the country, but each succeeding generation of their descendants becomes weaker.

How quickly we Americans exhaust life. With what panting haste we pursue everything. Every American you meet seems to be late for a train. Hurry is stamped in the wrinkles of the American face. We pride ourselves upon being practical men, men who strike sledge-hammer blows in our business, men who make business of recreation, even. We are men of action, we die without it; nay, we go faster and faster as the years go by, speed our machinery to the utmost, stretch the silver cord of life until it snaps. We have not even leisure to die a natural death, we go at high pressure until the boiler bursts. We have actually changed the type of our diseases, to suit our changed constitution. Instead of the lingering maladies of our fathers, we drop down and die of heart disease or apoplexy, now so common, formerly so rare. Even death has adopted our terrible gait.

Nature is a great economist. She makes the most of every opportunity, she works up all odds and ends. After you are wrecked and useless she leaves the wreck upon the rocks or reef on which you were stranded, and hoists her signal of danger, as a warning to others.

You lose your life, but nature wants to use you for a warning. You lose your health, but the tell-tales are left in your face to show the world how it went. If by drink, nature hangs out as her sign a red flag of distress, it may be, on your nose, in front of your eyes, where you can't escape it, and where everybody you meet reads the terrible warning. Though your life is a failure, and you have become useless, nature can still afford to keep you as an object-lesson to warn your fellows.

Nature is no sentimentalist. A bullet will not swerve a hair's breadth from its course, though a Lincoln or a Garfield stand in its way. A drop of prussic acid will kill a king as quickly as his meanest vassal. Water will drown you, even though you are saving your own child from death. Fire will burn you to a cinder, even while you are trying to snatch your dear ones from the flames. Every atom in the universe has immutable law stamped upon it. The rose blooms in your garden to-day under the same laws that unfolded the petals of the first flower in Eden. In all the sidereal ages the stars have returned from their vast journeys through trackless space, with the same unvarying accuracy as when they began to roll on the morning of creation. They have never once lost their way in their wild path through space, nor varied a second in a century. Not one whit less are we subject to the immutable laws of God.

We sometimes hear a clergyman consoling a mother, distracted over the death of her darling child, by telling her that a mysterious Providence has taken it from her for wise reasons, and that she must find comfort in her bereavement. What! has God snatched from loving parents a beautiful child just blooming into youth? Does the Creator of harmony produce discord? Does the Author of health and beauty smite his noblest work ere it is finished—a work into which He has breathed his own image, and which He has endowed with aspirations and possibilities as high as heaven itself? It is a libel upon Him who fashioned the human body, so wonderfully and fearfully wrought, that it may withstand the ravages of time for a century. Away with such sickly sentimentalism and blasphemy!

God does not murder nor torture his children. He rather tries in a thousand ways to induce them to keep the laws of health, which, if obeyed, would carry them into the teens of their second century. He has shielded us on every hand by kindly hints. He coaxes us by pleasure, and drives us by pain. He tries in every way to prolong life after we have forfeited every right to it, and have become useless drones. The faithful heart often beats the funeral march some time after death, and is the last servant to leave the body, lest some spark of life yet remain, which it might fan into a living flame. When alcohol goads on the drunkard's heart faster and faster, and robs it of a part of its nine hours of rest, which it should have every day, and which it must snatch between the beats, Nature even thickens its walls, in order to enable it to do the additional work imposed upon it, which is equivalent to raising fifteen tons one foot each day. It matters not that the poor wretch has forfeited every right to live, by violating every law of health; Nature helps him just the same.

Our nerves are sentinels placed thickest where there is the most danger. Pain has a use and purpose beyond those of happiness or pleasure. It tends to restrict the hurtful practices of life. Nature thus compels us to recognize her established order, or laws. The very sensitiveness and delicacy of our nerves, which give exquisite pleasure when used aright, give intense suffering when they are abused. A cinder might ruin the eye if the pain did not compel its prompt removal. Gazing at the sun would destroy the child's sight, were it not for the sensitiveness of the nerves, which compels the closing of the lids. Pain is the great monitor of our lives, ever reminding us of approaching danger. Few children would grow up without being disfigured and mutilated, were they not constantly warned by sensitive nerves. A paralytic was once advised by his physician to take a warm foot-bath; and, because of the loss of the sensitiveness of the nerves in that foot, he actually scalded his skin without knowing that the water was hot.

In the alleys and by-ways of our cities we often see the sign, "Dangerous Passing." The Creator has put up such signs all along the pathway of life. We read them over every street and alley that leads to vice and degradation. We read over the doors that lead to the gambling dens, the saloon, the dens of infamy, "All hope abandon, ye who enter here." Dangerous Passing! We read it in the deformed and crippled lives of those who have disregarded its warning, in the botched, half-finished work of the weak and inefficient. We read it in the ruined lives, the lost opportunities, the blighted hopes of those who heed it not; we read it in the prematurely old. All who have violated Nature's laws carry about in their bodies the unmistakable signs which the world may read as a terrible warning.

"It is continued temperance which sustains the body for the longest period of time, and which most surely preserves it free from sickness," writes Humboldt, when asked the secret of his success. No employer will keep in his office a drunkard, a gambler, or a profligate, for the very good reason that these vices not only debase the body, but also glut the mind with thoughts of which business has no part. Drink has become the curse of the world. Whole battalions of splendid young men who started in life with glowing hopes have been swept away by whiskey and rum.

The pen is not made nor the hand formed that has the power to adequately describe the horror and the

A LONG LIFE, AND HOW TO REACH IT. 365

power of this curse. The very instinct of self-preservation should keep a man from a saloon, as it does from a pesthouse. Dr. Richardson, a high authority, says that alcohol is the most insidious destroyer of health, happiness, and life.

"My recipe for self-preservation is exercise," said David Dudley Field. "I am a very temperate man, and have always been so. I have taken care of myself, and as I have a good constitution I suppose that is the reason I am so well." Exercise is indeed a great life-preserver.

When the pores of the body are kept open by regular exercise, the pores of the imagination are apt to be closed against tainted subjects. *Sana mens in sano corpore*, is a well-understood maxim. Says Frederick W. Robertson, England's most spiritual preacher: "It is wonderful how views of life depend upon exercise and right management of the physical constitution."

Healthy thoughts and healthy doctrines must come from healthy minds, and healthy minds cannot exist apart from healthy bodies.

The Sultan once consulted his physician in regard to a troublesome malady. Believing that only fresh air and exercise were needed, and knowing how little the world values plain, simple things, the doctor said: "Here is a ball which I have stuffed with rare and precious herbs. Your Highness must take this bat and beat this ball until you perspire freely; you must do this every day." The Sultan followed these directions, and was cured of his disease without realizing that he was only taking exercise.

When asked if he got any exercise, the great Frenchman La Harpe replied: "When my head gets fatigued I put it out of the window for a while." The Arabs say that Allah does not count from the allotted years of our lives the days spent in the chase. An English manufacturer stated before a committee of the House of Commons that he had removed the means of ventilation from his factory, as he noticed that the men ate a great deal more when they breathed pure air, and he could not afford it.

"Youth will never live to age," says Sidney, "unless they keep themselves in health with exercise, and in heart with joyfulness."

But work conduces to longevity in a greater degree than even cheerfulness or mere exercise.

Dr. Abernethy's advice to a lazy rich man, full of gout and idle humors, unhappy and without appetite, troubled with over-indulgence, and pampered with soft beds and rich food, was to "live upon sixpence a day, and earn it:" a golden sentence, a Spartan maxim which would save half the ill temper, the quarrels, the bickerings, and wranglings of the poor rich people, and would rub the rust off many a fine mind, which is now ugly and disfigured from want of use.

"I always find something to keep me busy," said Peter Cooper, when asked how he had preserved so well his strength of body and mind; "and to be doing something is the best medicine one can take. I run up and down stairs here almost as easily as I did years ago, when I never expected that my term would run into the nineties."

Life is a struggle at best. We scarcely begin to live ere we commence to die. Life and death strive in us for mastery, and we are but too confident of how the struggle will end. The enemies of human life are thick on every side. A thousand diseases dog our footsteps from the cradle to the grave. They lurk in the food we eat, in the water we drink, in the air we breathe. They watch at the door of every cold, exposure, neglect, or imprudence, seeking entrance to the citadel of life.

The plague has ever followed hard on the heels of famine and of financial depression. The germs of disease which have lurked in the system for years, perhaps, while the body was vigorous and strong, suddenly spring into activity the moment the system is depressed below the health-line, and its wonted power of resistance gone.

There is then no overplus of vitality to resist their development. Kernels of wheat which had been in a mummy's hand four thousand years sprang into life when planted. They only awaited moisture, heat, sunlight, and air to develop them. The cholera once spread all over Europe from the germs in a sailor's clothes, found in an old chest on shipboard, after lying there fifty years. They waited half a century for the proper conditions for development. We should take care never to let our systems run down below the health-line. Germs of a hundred diseases lurk just below this line, waiting for some indiscretion, some weakness, some opportunity to gain a foothold. So in the field of human society, corruption first attacks those who are physically feeble. How many are wicked only because they are physically weak! Many a youth becomes morally depraved simply because he has been a stranger to fresh air, cold water, and exercise.

Nature is ever merciful, and tries to bring compensation for the loss of any function. If you become deaf and dumb and blind, Nature develops an exquisite sense of touch. Laura Bridgman could even detect the presence of a good, or of a bad person in a room, by an agreeable or disagreeable sensation.

An electric eel cannot give shocks all the time. An overstrained bow will soon lose its tension. But who shall dare to enter God's temple to repair any mischief? The wisdom of the wisest is of no avail to rebreathe the departed breath into the lifeless clay. All the chemists in the universe cannot manufacture one drop of blood, nor can physician's skill rouse the tired heart which has once stood still. No doctor can lay his clumsy hand on the delicate brain and bid it think again. But the necessary ounce of prevention is at one's command. He must not live too intensely, if he would live long in years.

"No thinking person hearing Malibran sing," said Poe, "could have doubted that she would die in the spring of her days. She crowded ages into hours. She left the world at twenty-five, having existed her thousands of years."

Raphael, according to E. P. Whipple the greatest painter of moral beauty, and Titian, the greatest painter of sensuous beauty, were both almost equally young, though Raphael died at thirty-seven, while Titian was prematurely cut off by the plague when he was only a hundred.

Byron died, worn-out and old, at thirty-six; Burke was young at sixty-six.

Dr. Richardson says that the natural life of animals is six times the period required to become fully grown. According to this, man should live about one hundred and fifty years. That such longevity is attainable is shown by Russian statistics. In 1891 there were reported in that country eight hundred fifty-eight deaths of people between the ages of one hundred and one hundred and five years, one hundred thirty between one hundred fifteen and one hundred twenty, while three were reported to be one hundred fifty years of age, or more. But in Russia, as indeed in all European countries, the thing which surprises an American is the deliberateness with which everything is done. Everybody seems to have time enough. In Austria the wholesale stores and the banks close between noon and two o'clock. Europeans realize that rest should follow intense application, and that long-continued labor should be performed with deliberation.

"I would keep better hours if I were a boy again," said James T. Fields; "that is, I would go to bed earlier than most boys do." Nothing gives more mental and bodily vigor than sound rest when properly applied. Sleep is our replenisher.

"In all my political life," said Gladstone, "I have never been kept awake five minutes by any debate in Parliament."

Horace Greeley refused to sit up at night sessions of Congress, abruptly leaving when his hour for retiring arrived.

"I can do nothing," said Grant, "without nine hours' sleep."

Late hours are shadows from the grave.

For the evils resulting from late hours, improper diet, lack of exercise, and other forms of intemperance, men have been accustomed to seek relief in drugs, but they are beginning to realize that the aid a physician can render is almost wholly limited to cheering and encouraging his patients, and helping them to follow ordinary hygienic laws. Very many of our diseases exist only in the imagination and consciousness of the patient.

Molière said that physicians pour medicine about which they know little into bodies of which they know less, in order to cure disease about which they know nothing at all.

"We talk together," said Molière of his doctor; "he prescribes, I never take his physic, and consequently I get well." At another time he said that a doctor is a man whom people pay to relate trifles in the sick-room, until either nature has cured the patient, or physic has killed him.

Employ three physicians: First, Doctor Quiet; then, Doctor Merryman; and then, Doctor Diet.

Our beliefs are built upon models, and an ideal body can never be built upon a deformed and sick model. The model in the mind must be perfect, if we would obtain perfection of the body.

The very fact that we are conscious that the physical

manhood of our race should be lifted out of its bondage to a higher level, and that the Great Teacher commanded us not only to be perfect, but "perfect even as our Father in Heaven is perfect," is proof that such perfection is possible. God has not given the bird an instinct for the South in winter, without a South to match it; nor has he mocked us with ideals, longings, and aspirations which we have no power to attain. The very consciousness that we are capable of performing infinitely more than we ever do accomplish, is an indication that such perfection is possible, and that we shall have time and opportunity somewhere to develop into that perfect model. Man has an ideal in his soul, of the physical man, as well as of the moral man, and He who gave this ideal will give the opportunity for its realization.

Although we cannot defy death, it is now well known that we can greatly delay it by carefully observing the laws of health, especially in regard to diet. The chief characteristics of old age are found to be deposits of a gelatinous and fibrinous character in the human system, producing gradual ossification. Man begins life in a gelatinous condition, and ends it in an osseous or bony one — soft in infancy, hard in old age. This process is desirable in childhood; but, as we grow older, it is thought we may retard it more and more by swallowing less and less of the carbonates and phosphates of lime, the principal agents by which the transformation is effected. For this purpose the best drink is distilled water, while fruits, fish, poultry, veal, and lamb are much better than beef, bread, or salt meat of any kind. In this, as in other things, the best way to conquer Nature is to learn and obey her laws.

The body has its claims, — it is a good servant; treat it well, and it will do your work; attend to its wants and requirements, listen kindly and patiently to its hints, occasionally forestall its necessities by a little indulgence, and your consideration will be repaid with interest. But task it, and pine it, and suffocate it, make it a slave instead of a servant, it may not

complain much, but, like the weary camel in the desert, it will lie down and die.
CHARLES ELAM.

> O Father, grant Thy love divine,
> To make these mystic temples Thine.
> When wasting age and wearying strife
> Have sapped the leaning walls of life ;
> When darkness gathers over all,
> And the last tottering pillars fall,
> Take the poor dust Thy mercy warms,
> And mould it into heavenly forms.

HOLMES.

CHAPTER XXIII.

BE BRIEF.

I saw one excellency was within my reach — it was brevity, and I determined to obtain it. — JAY.

Brevity is the best recommendation of speech, whether in a senator or an orator. — CICERO.

> Words are like leaves, and where they most abound,
> Much fruit of sense beneath is rarely found.
> POPE.

The fewer the words, the better the prayer. — LUTHER.

Be comprehensive in all you say or write. — JOHN NEAL.

> Brevity is very good
> When we are, or are not, understood.
> BUTLER.

Concentration alone conquers. — CHAS. BUXTON.

BE brief, let us say with Sargent. Come to the point. Begin very near where you mean to leave off. Brevity is the soul of wisdom as well as of wit. Gems are not reckoned by gross weight. The common air we beat aside with our breath, compressed, has the force of gunpowder, and will rend the solid rock. A gentle stream of persuasiveness may flow through the mind, and leave no sediment: let it come at a blow, as a cataract, and it sweeps all before it. Mere words are cheap and plenty enough; but ideas that rouse, and set multitudes thinking, come as gold from the mine.

The leaden bullet is more fatal than when multiplied into shot. If you want to do substantial work, concentrate; and if you wish to give others the benefit of your work, condense. Rufus Choate would express in a minute's conversation what his contemporaries would require an hour to state clearly.

One of the firm of Baring Brothers once called Stephen

Girard from a hay-loft, and said: "I came to inform you that your ship, the Voltaire, has arrived safely." "I knew that she would reach port safely," replied Girard; "my ships always arrive safe. She is a good ship. Mr. Baring, you must excuse me, I am much engaged in my haying." And he returned to his work.

While Horace Greeley would devote a column of the "New York Tribune" to an article, Thurlow Weed would treat the same subject in a few words in the "Albany Evening Journal," and put the argument into such shape as to carry far more conviction.

"Be brief," Cyrus W. Field would say to callers; "time is very valuable. Punctuality, honesty, and brevity are the watchwords of life. Never write a long letter. A business man has not time to read it. If you have anything to say, be brief. There is no business so important that it can't be told on one sheet of paper. Years ago, when I was laying the Atlantic cable, I had occasion to send a very important letter to England. I knew it would have to be read by the prime minister and by the queen. I wrote out what I had to say; it covered several sheets of paper; then I went over it twenty times, eliminating words here and there, making sentences briefer, until finally I got all I had to say on one sheet of paper. Then I mailed it. In due time I received the answer. It was a satisfactory one too; but do you think I would have fared so well if my letter had covered half a dozen sheets? No, indeed. Brevity is a rare gift, and punctuality has made many a man's fortune. If you make an appointment, be sure and keep it, and be on time; no man of business can afford to lose a moment in these busy times."

"Call upon a business man in business hours. State your business in a business way; and, when done with business matters, go about your business, and leave the business man to attend to his business."

A. T. Stewart regarded his time as his capital. No

one was admitted to his private office until he had stated his business to a sentinel at an outer door, and then to another near the office. If the visitor pleaded private business, the sentinel would say, "Mr. Stewart has no private business." When admittance was gained one had to be brief. The business of Stewart's great establishment was dispatched with a system and promptitude which surprised rival merchants. There was no dawdling or dallying or fooling, but "business" was the watchword from morning until night. He refused to be drawn into friendly conversation during business hours. He had not a moment to waste.

"Genuine good taste," says Fénelon, "consists in saying much in a few words, in choosing among our thoughts, in having order and arrangement in what we say, and in speaking with composure."

"If you would be pungent," says Southey, "be brief; for it is with words as with sunbeams — the more they are condensed, the deeper they burn."

"When one has no design but to speak plain truth," says Steele, "he may say a great deal in a very narrow compass."

The fame of the Seven Wise Men of Greece rested largely upon a single sentence by each, of only two or three words.

"The wisdom of nations lies in their proverbs."

"Have something to say," says Tryon Edwards; "say it, and stop when you 've done."

CHAPTER XXIV.

ASPIRATION.

Ah, but a man's reach should exceed his grasp,
Or what is heaven for?
ROBERT BROWNING.

Too low they build who build beneath the stars. — YOUNG.

A prayer, in its simplest definition, is simply a wish turned heavenward. — PHILLIPS BROOKS.

From the lowest depth there is a path to the loftiest height. — CARLYLE.

Our only greatness is that we aspire. — JEAN INGELOW.

Did you ever hear of a man who had striven all his life faithfully and singly towards an object, and in no measure obtained it? If a man constantly aspires, is he not elevated? Did ever a man try heroism, magnanimity, truth, sincerity, and find that there was no advantage in them — that it was a vain endeavor? — THOREAU.

"The mission of genius on earth: to uplift,
Purify and redeem by its own gracious gift
The world, in spite of the world's dull endeavor
To drag down and degrade and oppose it forever.
The mission of genius: to watch and to wait,
To renew, to redeem, and to regenerate."

Whoever is satisfied with what he does, has reached his culminating point — he will progress no more. Man's destiny is to be not dissatisfied, but forever unsatisfied. — F. W. ROBERTSON.

"Endeavor to be first in thy calling, whatever it may be; neither let any one go before thee in well doing."

"HE is gone, then! The good old man is gone. We shall never see his snowy locks again, nor his placid countenance, nor his old horse and gig jogging by. Peter Cooper is dead!" Parton says that these words of a neighbor expressed the feelings of all the people of New York, City and State. Flags were placed at half-mast from the Hudson to the Great Lakes, and from the St. Lawrence to the Alleghanies. Why was such honor paid on that April day in eighteen hundred and eighty-three to a plain citizen born ninety-two years before?

His father was a hatter in New York in Peter's earliest youth, and the boy learned to make good beaver hats of skins bought of John Jacob Astor. Peter persuaded his father to let him learn a trade in New York.

"Have you any room for an apprentice?" he asked of a carriage-maker. "Do you know anything about the business?" "No, sir." "Have you been brought up to work?" "Yes, sir." "If I take you, will you stay and work out your time?" Peter promised, and for four years he worked hard for twenty-five dollars a year and his board. He made a machine for mortising hubs, which proved very profitable to his employer.

Having been denied the ordinary school privileges of children, he tried to find some evening-school in which he could obtain help in his studies while working at his trade by day. There were no such schools then, but the young man said to himself: "If ever I prosper in business so as to acquire more property than I need, I will try to found an institution in the city of New York, wherein apprentice boys and young mechanics shall have a chance to get knowledge in the evening."

The War of 1812 spoiled the carriage business just as he finished his apprenticeship, but soon there was a sharp demand for cloth and for machinery for its manufacture. Peter invented a machine for cutting the nap on cloth, and could not make enough to supply the demand. He married Sarah Bedel, who proved to him throughout life a jewel of great price.

Peace followed; foreign goods poured in, and the demand for Peter's machines ceased. He next tried cabinet-making, but was not successful. He bought a grocery-store and was prospering a year later, when an old friend said: "I have been building a glue factory for my son; but I don't think that either he or I can make it pay. But you are the very man to do it." "I'll go and see it," said Mr. Cooper.

The price was two thousand dollars. Peter Cooper

DAVID GLASGOW FARRAGUT

"The viking of our western clime who made his mast a throne."

"The youth who does not look up will look down; and the spirit that does not soar is destined perhaps to grovel."

had just that amount. He knew nothing of making glue, and only understood that the American article was almost worthless compared with that imported from Russia. But he made the business yield him thirty thousand dollars a year, acting for twenty years without clerk, bookkeeper, salesman, or agent. When his men came to work at seven, they always found the fires burning, lighted by the master's hand. He gave close personal attention to the boiling of his glue all the forenoon; at noon he started around the city to sell glue and isinglass; and in the evening he posted books and read to his wife and children.

In 1828 he bought three thousand acres of land in Baltimore for one hundred and five thousand dollars. The Baltimore and Ohio Railroad was then building; but on account of the many curves made necessary to avoid points of rocks, the expense was so greatly increased that the stockholders talked of abandoning the project, as it was not believed that a locomotive could run on so crooked a road. Mr. Cooper urged them not to give it up, and built a locomotive which was a success, thus saving the company from bankruptcy.

When sixty years old he found that he had seven hundred thousand dollars above the capital in his various enterprises. Evening-schools had by that time been established in every ward; and he was in doubt what to do until he heard of the Polytechnic School of Paris, when his plan was formed at once. Cooper Union was built as a free gift to the city, on the site of his old grocery-store, at a cost of seven hundred thousand dollars, and has since been endowed by Mr. Cooper until his total benefaction amounts to two million dollars. When the doors were opened, two thousand young people applied for admission; and since that day, many thousand have been fitted therein for lives of usefulness. Well might a State mourn the loss of such a man!

The story of Peter Cooper's life is only another illustration of the value of an ideal and of the necessity of enthusiasm to accomplish it. No aspiration is too high; the very grandeur of it is a promise of strength for its fulfillment.

"When will they come?" asked a thousand voices again and again, as the people waited outside St. Andrew's Church, to see if the spirit of the Covenanter still lived in Scotland. The government had asserted jurisdiction over the Scottish clergy, which the latter could not conscientiously yield.

"They will not come," was the confident reply of those who had no faith in the power of principle, on that 18th day of May, 1843.

Within, the house had been called to order in the presence of the royal commissioner. The prayer was followed by silence. Moderator Welsh, "his pure and glowing spirit shining through his fragile body like a lamp through a vase of alabaster," protested against the attempt at jurisdiction, laid his protest upon the table, bowed to the commissioner, and walked towards the door. Those who would follow must abandon their charges and incomes, to become poor and houseless. The aged Chalmers, with "massive frame and lion port," follows, and then another and another until all the noblest of Scotland's clergy have left the church, four hundred ministers and as many elders. Four thousand voices unite with theirs in singing:—

> "God is our refuge and our strength,
> In straits a present aid;
> Therefore, although the earth remove,
> We will not be afraid."

"Our yearnings," says Beecher, "are homesicknesses for heaven. Our sighings are sighings for God, just as children cry themselves asleep away from home, and sob in their slumber, not knowing that they sob for their parents. The soul's inarticulate moanings are the affections yearning for the Infinite, and having no one to tell them what it is that ails them."

An old legend tells of a king and a queen who had a fair son. Twelve fairies brought each a blessing, such as wisdom, beauty, strength, the last bearing the gift of discontent. The king was angry with the twelfth fairy, and drove her away. The prince grew with great promise, but manifested no disposition to develop his talents. There was no energy, no eagerness, no ambition in his work.

Tradition says that when Solomon received the gift of an emerald vase from the queen of Sheba, he filled it with an elixir which he only knew how to prepare, one drop of which would prolong life indefinitely. A dying criminal begged for a drop of the precious fluid, but Solomon refused to prolong a wicked life. When good men asked for it, they were refused, or failed to obtain it when promised, as the king would forget or prefer not to open the vase to get but a single drop. When at last the king became ill, and bade his servants bring the vase, he found that the contents had all evaporated. So it is often with our hope, our faith, our ambition, our aspiration.

"Ere yet we yearn for what is out of our reach," says Bulwer, "we are still in the cradle. When, wearied out with our yearnings, desire again falls asleep, we are on the death-bed."

Every star in heaven, it is said, is discontented and insatiable. Gravitation and chemistry cannot content them. Ever they woo and court the eye of every beholder. Every man who comes into the world they seek to fascinate and possess, to pass into his mind, for they desire to republish themselves in a more delicate world than that they occupy. It is not enough that they are Jove, Mars, Orion, and the North Star, in the gravitating firmament: they would have such poets as Newton, Herschel, and Laplace, that they may reëxist and reappear in the finer world of rational souls, and fill that realm with their fame.

Cardinal Farnese discovered the great genius Michael Angelo walking alone amid the ruins of the Colosseum. Expressing his surprise at finding him so occupied, the modest artist replied, "I go to school that I may continue to learn."

"More than once," said Peter Force to George W. Greene the historian, "did I hesitate between a barrel of flour and a rare book; but the book always got the upper hand. Whenever I found a little more money in my purse than I absolutely needed, I published a volume of historical tracts." Although not a rich man, he accumulated a library of 22,529 bound volumes and some 40,000 pamphlets, most of them of historical value; so much so that Mr. A. P. Spofford, Librarian of Congress, persuaded that body to purchase the collection for $100,000. Mr. Force also wrote the "American Archives," perhaps the greatest treasury extant of our early history.

"Certainly it is a glorious fever, that desire to know," says Bulwer. "And there are few sights in the moral world more sublime than that which many a garret might afford, if Asmodeus would bare the roofs to our survey — viz., a brave, patient, earnest human being toiling his own arduous way, athwart the iron walls of penury, into the magnificent Infinite, which is luminous with starry souls."

"If I held Truth captive in my hand," said Malebranche, "I should open my hand and let it fly, in order that I might again pursue and capture it."

"Our sense of details, our fatal habits of reasoning, paralyze us," said Heraclitus; "we need the impulse of the pure ideal."

When the barber Ambrose Paré saw a surgical operation performed with great skill, he aspired to become a surgeon, that he might relieve suffering humanity. His whole-souled study and careful practice led him to revolutionize the art. He found it the custom to sear gunshot wounds with red-hot irons to stop the bleeding, and then dress them with boiling oil. Amputation was performed with a red-hot knife, and anæsthetics were unknown. Paré discarded the boiling oil, the red-hot knife and irons; used emollient applications instead, and stopped bleeding by means of ligatures above the wounds. The learned doctors ridiculed the man who was ignorant of Latin, but the French soldiers said: "Let Paré go with us, and we will march against any enemy and endure any fatigues."

Who has not noticed the power of love in an awkward, crabbed, shiftless, lazy man? He becomes gentle, chaste in language, enthusiastic, energetic. Love brings out the poetry in him. It is only an idea, a sentiment, and yet what magic it has wrought. Nothing we can see has touched the man, yet he is entirely transformed. So a high ambition completely transforms a human being, making him despise ease and sloth, welcome toil and hardship, and shake even kingdoms to gratify his master passion. Mere ambition has impelled many a man to a life of eminence and usefulness; its higher manifestation, aspiration, has led him beyond the stars. If the aim be right, the life in its details cannot be far wrong. Your heart must inspire what your hands execute, or the work will be poorly done. The hand cannot reach higher than does the heart.

"I, too, am a painter," said Correggio when he first looked at Raphael's Saint Cecilia. Demosthenes was so fired by the eloquence of Calistratus that he then and there resolved to be an orator, although apparently he had not the slightest qualification for such a career. His voice was weak, indistinct, and squeaky, and he had a feeble constitution.

When the temperance crusade began in Ohio, in 1874, it stirred the very depths of the soul of Frances E. Willard, the first woman ever elected president of a college. She resigned her large salary and advocated the temperance cause with her whole heart and soul. She and her mother soon became reduced to the verge of absolute want. One day she received an offer of the presidency of the Normal Institution of New York city, with a yearly salary of $2500.00, and another offer of the presidency of the Chicago W. C. T. U., a position entailing poverty and hardship. She chose the latter. For ten years, she worked in the cars, averaged one lecture a day, answered yearly some 20,000 letters, and traveled nearly 2000 miles a month. During these ten years she also wrote several books, and hundreds of pamphlets, tracts, and newspaper letters. An earnest aspiration is her incentive, "shrewd system, stern concentration, peace, and good cheer," her methods.

John Ruskin has given away most of his fortune in his efforts to teach English artisans what is beautiful.

Aspiration like that of Miss Willard or Ruskin brings blessing to its possessor and those about him. The cold ambition of Louis XIII. cost France a million lives during his reign of nearly seventy-two years, while in one third of that period Napoleon's insatiate love of power caused the loss of five million lives in Europe.

Man never reaches heights above his habitual thought. It is not enough now and then to mount on wings of ecstasy into the infinite. We must habitually dwell there. The great man is he who abides easily on heights to which others rise occasionally and with difficulty. Don't let the maxims of a low prudence daily dinned into your ears lower the tone of your high ambition or check your aspiration. Hope lifts us step by step up the mysterious ladder, the top of which no eye hath ever seen. Though we do not find what hope promised, yet we are stronger for the climbing, and we get a broader outlook upon life which repays the effort. Indeed, if we do not follow where hope beckons, we gradually slide down the ladder in despair. Strive ever to be at the top of your condition. A high standard is absolutely necessary.

"Show me a contented slave," says Burke, "and I will show you a degraded man."

About 350 B. C., according to a Roman apologue, the haruspices declared that an earthquake chasm in the forum could be filled only by casting into it that which upheld the greatness of Rome. Forth from the bewildered throng rode Marcus Curtius, clad in complete armor, and said that a brave soldier was one of the most indispensable pillars of the glory of his native land.

"O Rome! O country best beloved! Thou land in which I first drew breath!
I render back the life thou gav'st, to rescue thee from death!
Then spurring on his gallant steed, a last and brief farewell he said,
And leapt within the gaping gulf, which closed above his head."

"If I had read the life of Napoleon when I was a boy," said a great man, "my own life might have been very different. It would have filled me with an ambition to make the most of myself."

A man cannot aspire if he looks down. God has not created us with aspirations and longings for heights to which we cannot climb. Live upward. The unattained still beckons us towards the summit of life's mountains, into the atmosphere where great souls live and breathe and have their being. Even hope is but a promise of the possibility of its own fulfillment. Life should be lived in earnest. It is no idle game, no farce to amuse and be forgotten. It is a stern reality, fuller of duties than the sky of stars. You cannot have too much of that yearning which we call aspiration, for, even though you do not attain your ideal, the efforts you make will bring nothing but blessing; while he who fails of attaining mere worldly goals is too often eaten up with the canker-worm of disappointed ambition. To all will come a time when the love of glory will be seen to be but a splendid delusion, riches empty, rank vain, power dependent, and all outward advantages without inward peace a mere mockery of wretchedness. The wisest men have taken care to uproot selfish ambition from their breasts. Shakespeare considered it so near a vice as to need extenuating circumstances to make it a virtue.

Avoid the content of the Asiatic on the one hand, who ploughs with a stick like that used by his ancestors thousands of years ago, and is satisfied with the crooked furrows; and on the other hand, do not be deluded with ambition beyond your power of reasonable attainment or tortured by wishes totally disproportioned to your capacity of fulfillment. You may, indeed, confidently hope to become eminent in usefulness or power, but only as you build upon a broad foundation of self-culture; while, as a rule, specialists in ambition as in science are apt to become narrow and one-sided. Darwin was very fond of music and poetry when young, but, after devoting his life to science, he was surprised to find Shakespeare tedious. He said that if he were to live his life again, he would read poetry and hear music every day, so as not to lose the power of appreciating such things.

"Every life," says Julia Ward Howe, "has its actual blanks which the ideal must fill up, or which else remain bare and profitless forever."

"A man may aspire," says Beecher, "and yet be quite content until it is time to rise; and both flying and resting are but parts of one contentment."

The ideal is the continual image that is cast upon the brain; and these images are as various as the stars, and, like them, differ one from another in magnitude. It is the quality of the aspiration that determines the true success or failure of a life. A man may aspire to be the best billiard-player, the best jockey, the best coachman, the best wardroom politician, the best gambler, or the most cunning cheat. He may rise to be eminent in his calling; but, compared with other men, his greatest height will be below the level of the failure of him who chooses an honest profession. No jugglery of thought, no gorgeousness of trappings can make the low high — the dishonest honest — the vile pure. As is a man's ideal or aspiration, so shall his life be.

Some aspire to dress better than their neighbors, and live in finer houses, and drive better teams. How many women are as frivolous as the Empress Anne of Russia, who assembled the geniuses of her empire to build a palace of snow! "But," says Disraeli, "the youth who does not look up will look down, and the spirit that does not soar is destined perhaps to grovel."

"Every man," says Theodore Parker, "has at times in his mind the ideal of what he should be, but is not. In all men that seek to improve, it is better than the actual character. No one is so satisfied with himself that he never wishes to be wiser, better, and more holy."

What a discrepancy there is between what we are, or what we appear to be, and what we long to be.

"Men are possessed of great and divine ideas and sentiments," said Dewey, "and to paint them, sculpture them, build them in architecture, sing them in music, utter them in eloquent speech, write them in books, in essays, sermons, poems, dramas, fictions, philosophies, histories, — this is an irresistible impulse of human nature."

"Ideality," says Horace Mann, "is only the *avant-courier* of the mind; and where that in a healthy and normal state goes, I hold it to be a prophecy that realization can follow."

"Every really able man, if you talk sincerely with

him," says Emerson, "considers his work, however much admired, as far short of what it should be. What is this better, this flying ideal, but the perpetual promise of his Creator?"

"Man can never come up to his ideal standard," says Margaret Fuller Ossoli. "It is the nature of the immortal spirit to raise that standard higher and higher as it goes from strength to strength, still upward and onward."

"No true man can live a half life," says Phillips Brooks, "when he has genuinely learned that it is a half life. The other half, the higher half, must haunt him."

"If I live," wrote Rufus Choate in his diary in September, 1844, "all blockheads which are shaken at certain mental peculiarities shall know and feel a reasoner, a lawyer, and a man of business."

"'T is not what a man does which exalts him," says Browning, "but what man would do."

"It seems to me we can never give up longing and wishing while we are thoroughly alive," says George Eliot. "There are certain things we feel to be beautiful and good, and we must hunger after them."

"The flame of a common fire casts a shadow in the path of a kerosene light," says Emerson, "and this in turn casts a shadow before the electric flash. The country lad is satisfied with his surroundings until he goes to the village and sees the store, the library, the high school. This satisfies him until he goes to the city. The village lamp puts out the country light, and in turn is extinguished by Boston or New York."

Our longings are the prophecies of our destinies. Life never wholly fulfills the expectations of youthful hope. The future can never pay all that the present promises. Providence holds back part of our wages, lest we quit work. The prophecy of immortality is written in our yearnings.

"If the certainty of future fame bore Milton rejoicing through his blindness, or cheered Galileo in his dungeon," writes Bulwer, "what stronger and holier support shall not be given to him who has loved mankind as his brothers, and devoted his labors to their cause?—who has not sought, but relinquished, his own renown?—who has braved the present censures of men for their future benefit, and trampled upon glory in the energy of benevolence? Will there not be for him something more powerful than fame to comfort his sufferings and to sustain his hopes?"

The ambition that comprehends another's welfare first, is the highest we can have. Such is the secret of Ruskin's success, and of the sway that Frances Willard holds in the hearts of every good woman in America and England. Yet to have one's name on the lips of men is not a worthy ambition. Some fast horses and prize-fighters are better known than those who have high and noble ideals. Every one knows the merits of the leading contestants in international yacht-races, but only a few, perhaps only one, knows the merits of him or her who surrendered hope, or perhaps life itself, to save a home, or keep a son from the poorhouse, or to reform tenement and prison methods.

Of necessity the above illustrations come from the lives of those whom the world delights to honor; but glory is rare and of secondary importance, and the lack of it implies no thought of failure in the judgment of Him who looks beneath the frame into the heart— who understands all aspiration—and who measures with honest scales the fervor which the soul expends.

> O! who shall lightly say that Fame
> Is nothing but an empty name,
> While in that sound there is a charm
> The nerves to brace, the heart to warm,

As, thinking of the mighty dead,
  The young from slothful couch shall start,
And vow, with lifted hands outspread,
  Like them to act a noble part?

JOANNA BAILLIE.

"I wonder if ever a song was sung,
  But the singer's heart sang sweeter!
I wonder if ever a hymn was rung,
  But the thought surpassed the metre!
I wonder if ever a sculptor wrought,
Till the cold stone echoed his ardent thought!
Or if ever a painter, with light and shade,
The dream of his inmost heart portrayed!"

CHAPTER XXV.

THE ARMY OF THE RESERVE.

It is the part of a wise man to keep himself to-day for to-morrow, and not to venture all his eggs in one basket. — CERVANTES.

'T is good in every case, you know,
To have two strings unto your bow.
CHURCHILL.

"In a word, learn taciturnity. Let that be your motto."
Though you had the wisdom of Newton, or the wit of Swift, garrulousness would lower you in the eyes of your fellow creatures. — BURNS.

The leaves and a shell of soft wood are all that the vegetation of this summer has made, but the solid columnar stem, which lifts that bank of foliage into the air to draw the eye and to cool us with its shade, is the gift and legacy of dead and buried years. — EMERSON.

There is no fault nor folly of my life which does not rise up against me, and take away my joy and shorten my power of possession, of sight, of understanding. And every past effort of my life, every gleam of rightness or good in it, is with me now, to help me in my grasp of this art and its vision. — RUSKIN.

Providence is always on the side of the last reserve. — NAPOLEON I.

The man of grit carries in his presence a power which spares him the necessity of resenting insult. — E. P. WHIPPLE.

O, the toils of life!
How small they seem when love's resistless tide
Sweeps brightly o'er them! Like the scattered stones
Within a mountain streamlet, they but serve
To strike the hidden music from its flow,
And make its sparkle visible.
ANNA KATHERINE GREEN.

PHŒBUS challenged the gods, saying, "Who will outshoot the far-darting Apollo?" "I will," said Zeus. Mars shook the lots, the first falling to Apollo, who stretched his bow and shot an arrow into the farthest west. With one stride Zeus cleared the whole distance covered by his rival's arrow, and asked, "Where shall I shoot? There is no room." He was awarded the prize by the acclamation of the gods, although he had not even drawn his bow.

We feel that Jove must have performed a wonderful feat of archery had he chosen to exert his power to the utmost. We have a similar feeling when we listen to a great orator, or witness the deeds of any person of great culture or sterling character. Such people excite in us an anticipation far in advance of their performances, and convince us by what they say or do that they could do or say immeasurably greater things.

Mirabeau was forty years old before he showed a sign of his vast knowledge and tact, his mighty reserve, and then suddenly became the greatest orator and statesman of his age. His public career lasted but twenty-three months, but in that time he did more work than most great men accomplish in as many years. "Had I not lived with him," said Dumont, "I should never have had any idea of what a man may do in a single day; what business may be transacted in the course of twelve hours. A day for this man was as much as a week or a month for another." "Impossible!" said he, jumping from his chair, when his secretary said that something was impossible, "never name to me again that blockhead's word."

It is the reserve corps of an army which enables the leader to strike the decisive blow when the critical moment arrives. It is the heavy balance-wheel of an engine which distributes the power equally and insures that steadiness of motion which prevents destructive shocks, overcoming resistance that would stop the piston unaided by the stored-up momentum. It is the knowledge, experience, and character, the mental and moral wealth which you have accumulated during your whole life, that measures your real power and influence to-day; as you will learn, to your satisfaction or chagrin, when you are subjected to any severe trial. You can draw from your bank of learning or manhood just what you have stored there, not an ounce more. In any crisis you must stand or fall by your reserve power.

DANIEL WEBSTER

"It is said of Hercules, the god of force, that 'Whether he stood or walked, or sat, or whatever he did, he conquered.'"

On a cold, rainy night in 1823, in the First Baptist Church of Boston, a young clergyman preached on the "Moral Dignity of the Missionary Enterprise." The sermon seemed to awaken no interest in the mind of any of the fifty people in the congregation, and the discouraged preacher considered it a complete failure. But a printer in the audience published the sermon on account of its earnestness, and it at once attracted wide attention and had a large sale, even in England. Robert Hall read it with enthusiasm and predicted a great future for the preacher, then an obscure young man. Three years later he was elected President Wayland of Brown University.

In the latest addresses of Beecher was still felt the momentum gained in his great speeches at Manchester, Liverpool, and London. A life of struggle, of mingled defeat and triumph, rolled its undercurrent of tone to tinge the meaning and effect of Gough's ripened utterances. Forty years of conquest gave weight to the words of Webster, Choate, Disraeli, Gladstone, long after gray hairs had told of the approach of a time when their eyes should be dimmed and their natural force abated. Bismarck, out of office, has such a reserve power that even an attack of rheumatism in his feet startles Europe.

"O Iole, how did you know that Hercules was a god?" "Because," said Iole, "I was content the moment my eyes fell upon him. When I beheld Theseus, I desired that I might see him offer battle, but Hercules did not wait for a contest: he conquered whether he stood, or walked, or sat, or whatever thing he did."

"One day," said a noted rope-walker, "I signed an agreement to wheel a barrow along a rope on a given day. A day or two before I was seized with lumbago. I called in my medical man, and told him I must be cured by a certain day; not only because I should lose what I hoped to earn, but also forfeit a large sum.

"I got no better, and the doctor forbade my getting up. I told him, 'What do I want with your advice? If you cannot cure me, of what good is your advice?'

"When I got to the place, there was the doctor protesting I was unfit for the exploit. I went on, though I felt like a frog with my back. I got ready my pole and my barrow, took hold of the handles and wheeled it along the rope as well as I ever did. When I got to the end I wheeled it back again, and when this was done I was a frog again. What made me that I could wheel the barrow? It was my reserve — will."

"It is marvelous, Monsieur le Président," said the Paris correspondent of the London "Times," to Thiers, "how you deliver long improvised speeches about which you have not had time to reflect." "You are not paying me a compliment," replied the President of the French republic; "it is criminal in a statesman to improvise speeches on public affairs. The speeches you call improvised — why, for fifty years I have been rising at five in the morning to prepare them!"

"The preparation for my reply to Hayne," said Webster, "was made upon the occasion of Mr. Foote's resolution to sell the public lands. Some years before that, a senator from Alabama introduced a resolution into the Senate proposing to cede the public domains to the State in which they were situated. It struck me at that time as being so unfair and improper that I immediately prepared an article to resist it. My argument embraced the whole history of the public lands and the government's action in regard to them. Then there was another question involved in the Hayne debate. It was as to the right and practice of petition. Mr. Calhoun denied the right of petition on the subject of slavery. Calhoun's doctrine seemed to be accepted, and I made preparation to answer his proposition. It so happened that the debate did not take place. I had my notes tucked away in a pigeon-hole, and when

Hayne made that attack upon me and upon New England, I was already posted, and only had to take down my notes, and refresh my memory. In other words, if he had tried to make a speech to fit my notes, he would not have hit it better. No man is inspired with the occasion. I never was."

"I should think, if you can't break that block in ten blows, you can't do it in a hundred," said Robert Waters to a brawny-armed quarryman who had struck forty blows with a sledge on a huge piece of granite, all apparently in vain. "Oh, yes," said the workman, "every blow tells;" and soon the granite fell asunder.

"We marvel at the skill which enables a great artist to take a little color that lies inert upon his palette — a little gray and brown and white — and presently to so 'transfigure it into a living presence' that our hearts throb faster only to look upon it, and there come upon the soul all those influences which one feels beneath the shadow of the Jungfrau or the Matterhorn, or amid the awful solitudes of Mont Blanc. But back of that apparent ease and skill are the years of struggle and effort and application which have conferred the envied power."

"What though the fire bursts forth at length," said Dr. Dewey, "like volcanic fires, with spontaneous, original, native force? It only shows the intenser action of the elements beneath. What though it breaks like lightning from the cloud? The electric force had been collecting in the firmament through many a silent, calm, and clear day." You cannot blaze forth in action when an occasion is presented unless the fire has long been smouldering within you.

It is with a feeling akin to awe that we gaze upon a huge iceberg towering aloft in solitary grandeur, regardless alike of storm or calms, and responsive only to the deep currents of the ocean.

How majestically it sweeps along, how gently it pushes aside the bubble in its path, yet how resistlessly it crushes the stoutest frigate, as if it were an eggshell. How it reminds us of the steady ponderous career of a great man. But remember that the iceberg is able to hold thus to its stately course only because seven eighths of its bulk is below the waves that make ineffectual tumult around it. So the weight and force of character of great men are hidden from the casual beholder.

A glass-blower will not try to teach difficult processes to any one who has not been engaged in the business from childhood. He must have the reserve which years of practice give.

"I treasure," says Robert Collyer, of New York, "a small drawing by Millais. It is the figure of a woman bound fast to a pillar far within tide-mark. The sea is curling its waves about her feet. A ship is passing in full sail, but not heeding her or her doom. Birds of prey are hovering about her; but she heeds not the birds, or the ship, or the sea. Her eyes look right on, and her feet stand firm, and you see that she is looking directly into heaven, and telling her soul how the sufferings of this present time are not worthy to be compared with the glory that shall be revealed. I treasure it because, when I look at it, it seems a type of a great host of women who watch and wait, tied fast to their fate, while the tide creeps up about them, but who rise as the waves rise, and on the crest of the last and the loftiest are borne into the quiet haven, and hear the 'Well done!'"

"It appears to me," said Rear-Admiral Hamilton of the British navy, referring to Farragut's prompt order for the fleet to move on in spite of the torpedoes that had just sunk the Tecumseh in Mobile Bay, "that a disastrous defeat was converted into victory by (in so unexpected a contingency) the quickness of eye and power of rapid decision Farragut possessed, which saw at a glance the only escape from the dilemma the fleet was placed in, and which can only be acquired by a thorough practical knowledge in the management of fleets, and for want of which no amount of theoretical knowledge, however desirable in many respects, can make up in the moment of difficulty." The knowledge and skill and character acquired in a lifetime of faithful performance of duty constituted a reserve fund upon which he drew heavily but not in vain when his opportunity came.

What star ever shone with purer light, or commanded more admiration, in the brilliant court of France, than the plain, republican, but cultivated, Benjamin Franklin? Who ever rose to higher influence in the political circles of proud England than Cromwell, Eldon, Burke, Canning, and Brougham? To what did they owe their vast influence but to great intellectual reserve power, developed by slow and toilsome cultivation?

"Where did you get that story, Mr. Webster?" asked a man who had been deeply impressed by an anecdote related by the great orator. "I have had it laid up in my head for fourteen years, and never had a chance to use it until to-day," was the reply.

When the Franco-Prussian war was declared, it is said that Von Moltke was awakened at midnight and told of the fact. He said coolly to the official who aroused him, "Go to pigeon-hole No. — in my safe, take a paper from it, and telegraph as there directed to the different troops of the empire." He then turned over and went to sleep, and awoke at his accustomed hour in the morning. Every one else in Berlin was much excited, but Von Moltke took his morning walk as usual, and a friend who met him said: "General, you seem to be taking it very easy. Are n't you afraid of the situation? I should think you would be busy." "Ah," replied Von Moltke, "all of my work for this time has been done long beforehand and everything that can be done now has been done." Moltke had been diligently storing up a vast reserve for half a century, waiting for his opportunity, which did not come until his hair was gray.

When Napoleon unrolls his map, the eye is commanded by original power. When Chatham leads the debate, men may well listen, because they must listen. A man filled with the stored-up momentum acquired from years of careful preparation, is acting; and the ephemera of the moment, as they are brushed from his path, wonder at his enormous influence.

Washington, even while undergoing the tortures of Valley Forge, was persecuted and maligned. Dr. Benjamin Rush wrote Patrick Henry that the soldiers at Valley Forge had no head. "A Gates, a Lee, or a Conway," he wrote, "would in a few weeks render them an invincible body of men. Some of the contents of this letter ought to be made public, in order to awaken, enlighten, and alarm our country." But the brave Washington bore all this abuse in dignified silence. What a mighty reserve power he possessed in his great commanding character!

Napoleon said of Massena that he was never himself until ruin stared him in the face. Then the sight of the dead and the groans of the dying nerved him to almost superhuman energy, and he marshaled his mighty army of the reserve to the front with a will that sent terror to the hearts of the enemy.

At the very time that Luther and his followers were making such headway in Europe in opposing the Church of Rome, Ignatius Loyola, a Spanish soldier, formed the order of Jesuits for the purpose of promulgating the tenets of Catholicism. No obstacle was too great to be overcome, no land too distant to be reached, no danger too appalling to be encountered. In India, China, Japan, their zealous preaching made hosts of converts; in Paraguay they proselyted 200,000 natives; and in North America they traveled from the Gulf of St. Lawrence to the Isthmus of Panama. The world was large enough for both Luther and Loyola, and the reserve of character in each enabled him to do great work in his own way.

After singing, as never before sung, the sublime music of the greatest masters to an audience of twenty thousand in Castle Garden, New York, the Swedish Nightingale thought of the hills of her fatherland. In the low tones of deepest emotion she breathed the words, —

"'Mid pleasures and palaces though we may roam,"

but as her voice thrilled to the souls of the listening thousands, she was suddenly silenced by a storm of applause, while tears fell like rain throughout the vast assembly.

"I intend to do well by Ben Lippincott," was a frequent remark of Stephen Girard, when speaking of a favorite clerk; so, when he was twenty-one, Ben expected to hear from the great banker. But Girard seemed to talk of everything else, so the clerk mustered courage, and said, "I suppose I am free, sir, and I thought I would say something to you as to my course; what do you think I would better do?" "Yes, I know you are," said the millionaire; "and my advice is that you go and learn the cooper's trade." This was like ice to Ben's budding expectation, but he said, "If you are in earnest, I will do so." "I am in earnest," was Girard's only reply. Seeking the best cooper in Spring Garden, Ben served his apprenticeship faithfully, and reported that he was ready to begin business. "Good," said Girard, "make me three of the best barrels you can turn out." When they were delivered, the banker pronounced them first-rate, and asked the price. "One dollar," said Ben, "is as low as I can live by." "Cheap enough — make out your bill." Girard settled that bill with a check for twenty thousand dollars, saying, "There, take that, and invest it in the best possible manner; and if you are unfortunate and lose it, you have a good trade to fall back upon, which will afford you a good living."

You wonder what is the use of this thing or that which your parents or teachers ask you to learn. Sometime you may need that very thing. It may be ten years, or twenty, before you find the right place for it; but it will most likely be just what you will want, sooner or later. If you don't have it, you will be like the hunter who had no ball in his rifle when a bear met him, or like a captain who suddenly remembered on a lee shore that he had left his cable and anchor at home.

"Twenty-five years ago my teacher made me study surveying," said a man who had lost his property, "and now I am glad of it. It is just in place. I can get a good situation and a high salary."

"He who rises earlier than his competitor," said David Dudley Field, "and works more hours, within the limits of healthful endurance, will carry off the prize." The reserve time thus gained, if only an hour a day, will amount to nearly three years out of the threescore and ten vouchsafed to man.

"When I was a freshman in Williams College," said James A. Garfield, "I looked out one night and saw in the window of my only competitor for first place in mathematics a light twinkling a few minutes longer than I was wont to keep mine burning. I then and there determined to invest a little more time in preparation for the next day's recitation. I did so, and passed above my rival. I smile to-day at the old rivalry, but I am thankful for the way my attention was called to the value of a little margin of time, well employed. I have since learned that it is just such a margin, whether of time or attention or earnestness or power, that wins in every battle, great or small."

Garfield always had a book at table, and would ask his boys, as they sat about him in the home at Mentor, how they pronounced certain words and what the definitions were. He asked them to quote from this and that great author, and in a sentence to serve up their opinions concerning eminent men and women.

Garfield was said to be only one of a very few who kept up their literary studies while in Washington. He never did so well but it seemed he could easily do better. As Trevelyan said of his Parliamentary hero, Garfield succeeded because all the world could not have kept him in the background, and because once in the front he played his part with an intrepidity and a commanding ease that were but the outward symptoms of the immense reserve of energy on which it was in his power to draw.

"If I hear that my opponent has worked the wrist-machine up and down three hundred and ninety-nine times," said James J. Corbett, "I try to go a few better. If he jumps the rope half an hour steadily, I try to make it an hour." This man became the pugilistic champion of the world.

A statue of Silence, with finger on its lip, has a marvelous effect upon every visitor to a library in Cincinnati. Its power is felt as soon as the eye rests upon it. "Speech is silvern, Silence is golden; Speech is human, Silence, divine." There is often a power in silence which no speech can equal.

"Is there not something sublime," asks a newspaper, "in a hydraulic crane which lifts a Titanic engine of destruction weighing a hundred tons to a considerable height with as noiseless a calm and as much absence of apparent stress or strain as if it had been a boy soldier's pop-gun? When we further read of the hydraulic monster holding up its terrible burden motionless in mid-air until it is photographed, and then lowering it gently and quietly on a sort of extemporized cradle without the least appearance of difficulty, one can readily understand that the mental impression produced on the bystanders must have been so solemn as to manifest itself in most eloquent silence." In an English machine-shop the power of the engine is so stored in the momentum of a ponderous balance-wheel that, directed by a huge cam, it drives a punch through one, two, or three inches of steel as if it were so much wax, without perceptible hesitation or tremor. Visitors look on in speechless awe.

It is said that on the single evening Emerson spent at Craigenputtoch in 1833, Carlyle handed him a pipe, lighted one himself, and then the two sat silent until midnight, when they parted, shaking hands and congratulating each other upon the pleasant evening they had passed. "The silent man is often worth listening to," says the Japanese proverb.

"That is my speech! That is my speech!" said the sculptor Story, each time touching his statue of George Peabody, at whose unveiling in London he was asked to make an address.

Every great orator feels but too conscious that he has never been able to express to his audience the rapture which fired his soul. He feels an immense loss in the translation of the divine sentiment which wrought ecstasy in his own soul. The author, too, sees visions which the pen refuses to copy or describe. In plucking the flower, the perfume is lost.

To one admiring his statue, the Flemish sculptor Duquesne said, pointing to his forehead, "Ah! if you could but see the one which is here!" Voltaire said that he never wrote anything which satisfied him, there was such a discrepancy between his ideal and what he accomplished. Vergil wished to burn the Æneid after working upon it for eleven years.

The artist cannot transfer to canvas the most delicate touches of nature upon the human face. There is an indescribable something which all feel but no poet can portray. The finest part of a landscape is never delineated. The writer cannot draw from his brain his choicest sentiments. They elude the pen and will not stay in words. They evaporate from the choicest language and will not allow themselves to be expressed. But they are suggested to us in the works of the masters, and it is in this suggestive force of their productions rather than in what they have really done or said that their remarkable power lies.

Tears cannot drain the deepest sorrow. Words cannot express the finest sentiments of the heart.

It is roughly estimated that the steam-power of Great Britain is equal to the united strength of 1,000,000,000 men. The number of persons employed in her coal mines is but 200,000, and of these fully two thirds dig coal for other uses than for engines, leaving 66,666 men to mine the coal necessary to do the work of 1,000,000,000. The engines are made by 60,000 men, so that 126,666 men furnish the means of doing the work of 1,000,000,000, the strength of each being thus multiplied nearly eight thousand times. This gives to each man, woman, and child of a population of 35,000,000, some thirty willing slaves, born fully grown, exempt from sickness, needing no clothes, eating only fire and water, and costing merely the work of one man in eight thousand. It is this reserve power of steam which makes certain the supremacy of Britain in the industrial contest with such countries as Ireland, Spain, Portugal, Turkey, Brazil, Mexico, Argentina, India, Jamaica, China, and Japan. Herein lies the real reserve which reinforces her bayonets in every war she wages. Too late, Napoleon learned this at St. Helena, saying, "Great Britain conquered me not with her swords but with her spindles; with her spindles she subsidized all Europe, and here I am." He was right, but the real power was in the steam-engines that drove those spindles, and that energy, obtained from the coal, really came from tiny sunbeams stored up ages ago in the leaves and stems of plants. Pitt, with all his lavish expenditures, could not squander the wealth of Great Britain as fast as it was created by the genius of Watt, long since dead. It is industry at home that makes legions victorious abroad. A nation with such a reservoir of capital is like a Niagara river with its chain of inland seas behind, and sweeps everything before it in the cataract of war. Only when it meets a greater reserve, like the spirit of liberty in the breasts of the American colonists, is it swept backward, even as the winds sometimes roll the waters of Lake Erie back upon themselves, and for a time lessen the power of Niagara.

He who has occupied his leisure moments in earnest, faithful study, will have large stores in reserve upon which to draw in any emergency. After his answer to Hayne, Webster is reported to have said, "I felt as if everything I had ever seen or read or heard was floating before me in one grand panorama, and I had little else to do than to reach up and cull a thunderbolt and hurl it at him." It was his custom in studying to devote all his faculties to the work before him until he felt fatigue, and then rest. In this way he acquired the power of doing in one day what would seem a hard week's work to many able lawyers.

Back of the preparation for any career should lie the habit of wholeness of mind and conscience which can alone insure the highest success in that career. Opie mixed his colors with brains. Hugh Miller said that the mason of whom he learned his trade put his whole soul into every brick that he laid. Of Francis Horner, a man of medium ability but of unequaled influence, it was said that the Ten Commandments were stamped upon his countenance. Such men of steadfast character in all trials are "like great ships upon November seas, when winds are gruff and waters in rebellion. While other men, like fishing-smacks and shallops, crank and unsteady, must watch each flaw and gust of wind lest suddenly they be caught and whelmed, these spread a bellying sail upon a moveless yard, and heedless of cross-currents drive onward to their home."

What reserve power to bless or ban lies in the affections and passions of man! Even brutes show the might of love and gratitude or their opposites. Androcles hid himself in a cave, where he saw a lion which seemed very lame. Walking up to the beast, he gently lifted his paw, and took out a splinter. The animal seemed very grateful. Later, Androcles was captured and delivered to wild beasts in the arena of the Colosseum. A lion let loose to devour him sprang forward with a hollow roar, but recognized Androcles as one who had relieved his suffering, and fawned at his feet.

"Gentlemen," said one of three ladies, rudely bantered by one hundred and fifty young men while all were waiting the tardy arrival of the lecturer at a medical clinic, "I have been for eighteen years a missionary in China. The Chinese have no medical science, and superstitious rites are chiefly relied on in the treatment of disease. All the people are in need of medical aid, but the women are the neediest. A Chinese woman would under no circumstances go to a male physician for the treatment of any disease peculiar to her sex. She would be prevented by her womanly delicacy, and by all the notions of modesty held by those around her. She would suffer lifelong agony rather than violate her sense of propriety. Her father, her brothers, and her husband would even let her die rather than allow her to be treated by a male physician. Full of sorrow for the sufferings of these women, I have been looking to Christian America to see what hope of help for them might be there. I have been glad to find that, in some of our great medical schools, earnest and self-sacrificing women are fitting themselves for a work of mercy in Asia and other lands. Unless such women learn to do such work well there is no physical salvation for those afflicted ones. And in behalf of those women, who have no medical care while they so sorely need it, I ask from you the courtesy of gentlemen toward ladies who are studying medicine in Philadelphia." A cheer from the young men followed the remarks, and one student assured the ladies that they should be annoyed no more. The native manliness of the youths was a corps in reserve which, when called upon, conquered all their coarseness and vulgarity.

There is a reserve in every man greater than anything he ever exhibits. There is a hero in the biggest coward which an emergency great and critical enough would call forth. Heroic acts are just what every man intends to perform.

The memory of misspent years should not hang like a millstone about your neck; so long as you have a desire for better things, you still have in reserve, greater or less in proportion to the earnestness of your aspiration, the very power you need in attaining what you seek. Thousands of bad boys have changed their course radically and become good and useful men. The ablest cardinal and statesman of France in his day was known as the incorrigible boy Richelieu. Mazarin, when young, was a reckless gambler. Dumas was a worthless, idle boy. St. Augustine was called a reprobate when a boy. Whitefield, the great preacher, was a thief when young, and his mother kept a public-house. President Thiers was the worst pupil in school; he would strike his teacher when angry, and no punishment awed him. All at once he changed his course, and determined to become President of France, although he was very poor. Great men are but common men more fully developed and ripened.

He who does his best will find himself aided at an unexpected moment by another self in reserve, the reflex action of the brain. Many a mathematician, falling asleep in a vain effort to solve some intricate problem, has awakened to find the solution at his tongue's end.

On the plains of Ephesus, Chersiphoron had placed the solid jambs on either side of the door to the temple of Artemis, and had exhausted every expedient trying to place thereon the ponderous lintel, when, in sleep, the goddess told him his work was done, and he awoke to find it so.

From the grave of every martyr emanates an influence greater far than he ever exerted in life. "The cause thou fightest for," says Carlyle, "so far as it is true, no further, yet precisely so far, is very sure of victory. The falsehood alone of it will be conquered, will be abolished, as it ought to be; but the truth of it is part of Nature's own laws, coöperates with the world's eternal tendencies, and cannot be conquered."

Nature works continually by utilizing reserves. Nothing is ever lost in the material or spiritual world. Our fires to-day give back in heat and light the exact amount absorbed by tree or plant from the sun ages ago. The present generation is fed by the decomposition of the preceding.

The best of every man's work is above and beyond himself, and is accomplished in the struggle to attain a lofty ideal. The artist stands aside and points through his work to a glimpse of the universal art. In his inspired moments the individuality of the orator is melted and fused into the all-pervading fire of eloquence. The gods will help us, but we must go their way. We must move along the line of absolute truth or they will leave us to our own devices.

Amid the alternating high and low barometer, gloom and gayety, enthusiasm and discouragement, freshness and fatigue of our physical and mental environment, we cannot always be at our best.

> "But tasks in hours of sunshine willed
> May be through hours of gloom fulfilled."

"How strange it seems," said W. J. Tilley, "that some of the most wonderful and most useful inventions in the world to-day were apparently lying in ambush beside the very pathway where thousands of human feet have trod, and remained, for years, all undiscovered and unknown." They waited but for an eye that could see nature's vast reserves.

Men have groped in physical darkness for ages while walking above untold barrels of petroleum, and have crossed oceans to carry messages which a slender wire would have delivered in a minute. Muscle has been hewing wood and drawing water, while coal and electricity have tried in vain to tell us that they were destined to emancipate man from the world's drudgery and allow him to develop his higher powers.

We call a man like Shakespeare a genius, not because he makes new discoveries, but because he shows us to ourselves; shows us the great reserve in us which, like the oil-fields, awaited a discoverer; because he says that which we had thought or felt, but could not express. Genius merely holds the glass up to nature. We can never see in the world what we do not first have in ourselves. The hemisphere of our vision is really the dome enshrining our minds, and is greater or less according to the sweep of our thought, even as without or within any circumference other circumferences may be drawn without change of centre. Man is the whole of which all the things he sees without are but parts.— segments of a curve which circle themselves in his own soul. We see but the shadow of which we are the substance. Emerson says that the god of a cannibal will be a cannibal, of the crusader a crusader, and of the merchant a merchant. Beneath its apparent levity there is a vital truth in Andrew Jackson Davis's saying that an honest God is the noblest work of man; for our ideals show what we are.

Not least among our forces in reserve are those which come from that "facility and inclination, acquired by repetition," which we call habit. Any occupation is easiest to him who has familiarized himself with its processes by repeated practice, and he who has become most familiar with those processes is most likely to succeed therein. As men acquire greater and greater skill in the various trades or professions, it becomes more and more difficult for one to do many kinds of work in a satisfactory manner, in competition with others. Jacks-of-all-trades are becoming scarcer as we advance in civilization. We must concentrate our energies to definite purposes in proportion as we wish to excel. "I have but one lamp by which my feet are guided," said Patrick Henry, "and that is the lamp of experience."

Even the most refined civilization would be impossible but for the reserves of rugged men of ruder manners from which to constantly recruit its ever wasting forces.

In 1806, it is said, every legitimate monarch in Europe was imbecile. The city would have died out, rotted, and exploded long ago, but that it was reinforced from the fields. It is only country that came to town day before yesterday that is city and court to-day. The country is the great reserve of civilization.

Not what men do, but what their lives promise and prophesy, gives hope to the race. To keep us from discouragement, Nature now and then sends us a Washington, a Lincoln, a Kossuth, a Gladstone, towering above his fellows, to show us she has not lost her ideal.

We enter upon life with a physical reserve called the vital force, a mental reserve known as enterprise, and, above all, a moral reserve of conscience, from *con*, "with," and *scio*, "I know;" literally, what we know with God. "Endeavor to keep alive in your breast," said Washington, "that spark of heavenly fire called conscience." This inward monitor is akin to that instinct which prompts the bird to seek the South as a refuge from the winter that would kill it; which persuades the squirrel to bury nuts and the bee to store honey to keep them alive when trees are bare and flowers are dead. Whatever our creed, we feel that no good deed can by any possibility go unrewarded, no evil deed unpunished. Every one is conscious that there are little demons in the background of his life which only wait an opportunity to come forward and disgrace him; such as fault-finding, envy, hatred, slander, irritability, sarcasm, back-biting, and revenge. These are microbes or germs which lie dormant in the character until the moral health-line is so reduced that they develop in the filth and miasma of a degraded soul. On the other hand, the consciousness of the grand reserve of a noble past gives confidence and strength to-day. The memory of the good we have done inspires and encourages us to worthy endeavor.

The whole creation thunders the Ten Commandments. The very atoms seem to have been dipped in a moral solution. There is a moral tendency in the nature of things. It looks out of the flowers, it shines from the stars. It grows in the forest, it waves in the grass, it laughs in the harvest. Each form of existence brings from the unseen its own little lesson of wisdom, goodness, power, design, and points to something higher than itself, the great Author of its magnificence. But while we see this moral tendency in the works of nature, we find this great moral reserve strongly emphasized in man, who has a sort of instinctive faith that somehow, somewhere, nature will rid herself of the last crime, and restore the lost Paradise of Eden.

> "These rules were writ in human hearts,
> By Him who built the day,
> The columns of the universe
> No firmer based than they."

Man finds himself on a limitless ocean with no knowledge of whence he came or whither he shall go. All he knows is, that a Hand he has never seen has traced the

Golden Rule upon his heart, hung a chart in his soul, and placed a compass in his hand. He is also conscious of a pilot at the helm, never seen but always there, an angel commissioned at his birth to pilot his frail bark across the uncertain waters of life, and that consciousness is his reserve power.

We may try to stifle the voice of the mysterious angel within, but it always says "Yes" to right actions, and "No" to wrong ones. No matter whether we heed it or not, no power can change its decision one iota. Through health, through disease, through prosperity and adversity, beyond the reach of bribery or influence, this faithful servant stands behind us in the shadow of ourselves, never intruding, but weighing every act we perform, every word we utter, pronouncing the verdict " right " or " wrong."

"Virtue has resources buried in itself, which we know not," says Bulwer, "till the invading hour calls them from their retreats. Surrounded by hosts without, and when Nature itself, turned traitor, is its most deadly enemy within, it assumes a new and a superhuman power which is greater than Nature itself. Whatever be its creed — whatever be its sect — from whatever segment of the globe its visions arise, Virtue is God's empire, and from this throne of thrones He will defend it. Though cast into the distant earth, and struggling on the dim arena of a human heart, all things above are spectators of its conflict, or enlisted in its cause. The angels have their charge over it — the banners of archangels are on its side, and from sphere to sphere, through the illimitable ether, and round the impenetrable darkness at the feet of God, its triumph is hymned by harps which are strung to the glories of the Creator!"

In London, June, 1801, Benedict Arnold sits dying. In response to a feeble request, the attendant aids him to don a faded Continental uniform. The shadow of death hovers above the execrated traitor, and mortal pangs rack his emaciated frame ; but no sigh or groan comes from his bloodless lips, for his glazing eyes are fixed upon those treasured garments and his mind is busy with the past. Shoulder to shoulder he stands with Allen at Ticonderoga. Through the trackless northern wilderness he leads his determined band, and his haughty voice summons astonished Quebec to surrender. The woods of Valcour Island reverberate with the thunders of his cannon, and from his strategy at Fort Schuyler the dusky hosts of St. Leger scatter like dry leaves before the hurricane. At Stillwater, in September, his spirit animates the army which Horatio Gates commands; and up Bemis Heights in October his coal-black steed leads to glorious victory over the far-famed legionaries of Burgoyne. Treason and disgrace are forgotten, neglect and injury forgiven ; honored and respected he stands once more a giant among his brother officers in the cause of liberty ; and thus, while reënacting bygone scenes, his spirit passes from earth.

Oh, the reserve power of noble thoughts — of noble deeds ! Not subsequent misery nor crime, not degradation, not death itself, can rob them of their influence upon us ; and through the long future of eternity whatever is ours of ecstasy will be augmented, whatever is ours of agony will be diminished, by their recollection and their reward.

INDEX.

Accuracy, enamored of, 273.
Acts, "our angels are," 303.
Adams, J. Q., his punctuality, 69, 130.
Addison on luck, 330.
Æsop, monument erected to, 28.
Agassiz, Louis, too great to make money, 219; power of observation, 284.
Age, how to retard it, 370; its enthusiasm, 184.
Alcohol, Dr. Richardson on, 364.
Andersen, Hans Christian, 26.
Andrew, John A., his promptness, 122.
Androcles and the lion, 403.
Angelo, Michael, 80; his industry, 234, 242, 380; his study of anatomy, 284; his statue of snow, 302.
An iron will, 55.
Anne, Empress of Russia, and her snow palace, 385.
Annihilation, working for, 303.
Anxiety, a disease, 141, 143.
Apelles, his goddess of beauty, 155.
Aquetil and Bonaparte, 329.
Ariosto and his persistence, 353.
Aristocracy, nature's, 247.
Arkwright, Richard, 79; his industry, 244.
Armour, Philip, his career, 14.
Arnold, Benedict, his dying vision, 409.
Art and corruption, 226.
Arthur, Chester A., his politeness, 151.
Aspiration, 375.
Astor, J. J., a failure, 79, 99, 200, 226.
Audubon, his persistency, 245, 351.

Bancroft, his perseverance, 342.
Bankruptcy, 248.
Barnum, P. T., 51; and the American Museum, 324.
Barrows, Isaac, 87.
Basle, the Monk, his great politeness, 148.
Bauer, General, 328.
Baxter, Richard, on saving time, 69.
Be brief, 372.
Beecher, H. W., and "the dew-drop," 292; on defeat, 307; his cheerfulness, 138; his tact, 197; determination, 242; on aspiration, 378, 384.
Beethoven, 179, 283.
Bennett, James Gordon, his struggles, 31.
Bentham, Jeremy, 71.
Berry, Captain, 5.
Birkenhead, the English ship, 316.
Bismarck, 160.
Blücher, General, 130; his determination, 244.

Boy slavery, 78.
Boys, round, in square holes, 74.
Boys with no chance, 25.
Bright, John, 42.
Brooks, Phillips, on occupation, 98; true greatness, 231; on aspiration, 386.
Brougham, Lord, 71, 130; lack of concentration, 115.
Brown, John, 48.
Bryant on patience, 355.
Budgett, Samuel, 70.
Bunyan, 182.
Burke, Edmund, his power, 254; on patience, 354.
Burr, Aaron, his politeness, 56; 148.
Burritt, Elihu, 36, 65.
Butler, Bishop, and his persistency, 353.
Butler, General, and his colored soldiers, 258.
Buxton, Fowell, on one unwavering aim, 116.
Byron, 87; on Dante, 268; on thirst for gold, 218.

Cæsar, 8, 70, 122; and the pirates, 319; self-confidence, 205; influence of, over Romans, 263.
Calhoun, John C., his self-confidence, 205.
Calling, be greater than, 104.
Calvin, John, his dyspepsia, 144.
Campbell, Lord, 239, "must work harder than others."
Canova, Antonio, 10.
Carelessness, 287.
Carlyle, Thomas, his courage, 244; on persistence, 339; on one aim, 108; his gruffness, 152.
Carlyle and Emerson, their silence, 400; on truth, 405.
Catharine of Russia, her rules of etiquette, 153.
Cato, his three regrets, 72.
Cavanaugh, A. M., M. P., his charming manner, 150.
Chapel, Sistine, 243.
Character is power, 250, 263; is success, 226, 250, 316; is protection, 256; the poor man's capital, 272; always known, 272.
Chateaubriand on Washington, 267.
Chatham, Lord, 262.
Cheerfulness and longevity, 133.
Chesterfield, Lord, 156.
Chickering, Jonas, his precision, 289.
Childs, George W., 32; his character, 229.

412   INDEX.

Chitty, 241.
Choate, Rufus, his irresistible manner, 59, 150; power of concentration, 114, 118; his carefulness, 282; his brevity, 372, 386.
Christ, his cheerful, sunny religion, 145.
Cicero, his economy of time, 70; true nobility, 210; on disagreeable occupations, 237.
Cid, the, physical power of, 359.
Cincinnatus, Quintius, 256.
Clark, Alvan, his accuracy, 281.
Clay, Henry, 45; his graceful manner, 150; his concentration, 171; his oratory, 235.
Cleveland, Grover, on luck, 335.
Clive, Robert, 87.
Cobbett, William, "always ready," 33, 124.
Cobden, Richard, 42; on luck, 335; his determination, 242.
Coffin, C. C., on Columbus, 346.
Colbert, "the greatness of a country depends on the character of its people," 267.
Coleridge, his lack of concentration and purpose, 112.
Collyer, Robert, 394.
Colonna, Vittoria, 265.
Columbus, 18; his tact with the Indians, 192; his victory, 315; in chains, 315; his death, 315.
Commandments, Ten, in nature, 408.
Common sense and books, 191.
Compensation, 369.
Confucius on persistence, 350.
Conscience, 407.
Cook, Joseph, his great industry, 65.
Cooper, Astley, 16.
Cooper, Peter, 375.
Corti's harp, 300.
Courage, 313.
Courtesy, among the upper classes, 155.
Cowper, William, his shyness, 84; 244.
Creon, the Greek slave artist, 26.
Crittendon, C. N., his missions, 229.
Cromwell, Oliver, 84.
Cunard, Samuel, 48.
Curran, his self-respect, 208; his determination, 242.
Curtius, Marcus, his leap to death, 383.
Cushman, Charlotte, 47; enthusiasm, 172.

Dalton, Dr., 72.
Dante, "the man who had been in hell," 283.
Darling Grace, 9.
Darwin, Charles, his persistence, 61, 71, 384.
Da Vinci, Leonardo, 283.
Davy, Sir Humphry, 35, 70.
Death has adopted the American gait, 361.
Decision, 8.
De Foe, Daniel, 81.
De Genlis, Madame, 66.
Demosthenes, his perseverance, 242, 381.

Depew, Chauncey, on "grit, grip, and pluck," 319.
De Quincey, his discouragements, 243.
De Staël, Madame, her precocity, 97; her fascinating manners, 154, 179.
Dessaix, at Marengo, 322.
Devil, the, "does he lie?" 281.
Dickens, Charles, on close attention, 111; great politeness, 150; his enthusiasm, 171; on perseverance, 346, 351.
Dickinson, Anna, her courage, 242.
Disraeli, Benjamin, his courage, 242.
Dissipation, 270.
Dixey, Henry, 51.
Douglas, Stephen A., his courtesy, 151.
Douglass, Fred, 50.
Dress, importance of, 167.
Drew, David, his industry, 88.
Drew, Samuel, his perseverance, 241.
Dumas, Alexander, 45.
Dunces, noted, 86, 87.
Duty, 105.

Edison, Thomas A., 38; on perseverance, 341.
Edward, Thomas, and his menagerie, 75.
Eldon, Lord, 49; his industry, 241.
Eliot, George, on what to do, 98; on aspiration, 386.
Emerson, Ralph Waldo, on what to do, 103; on gentleness, 158, 159; enthusiasm, 173; on work, 228; on luck, 330; 386; perseverance, 354; every man his own God, 406.
Energy, concentrated, 106.
Enthusiasm, triumphs of, 170.
Erskine, Lord, 82; his flashes of heroism, 328.
Etiquette, origin of, 153.
Euler, the mathematician, 58.
Evarts, W. M., 59.
Everett, Edward, his charming manner, 151.
Exaggeration, in America, 281.

Failure, the only one possible, 283; beware of the first, 306; the test of persistence, 308.
Fairies, the twelve, and discontent, 379.
Fame, 387.
Faraday, Michael, 43, 67.
Farragut, Admiral, reserve power of, 394.
Fate recedes before knowledge, 293; all are architects of, 303.
Ferguson, 24.
Field, Cyrus W., 246; on brevity, 373; his perseverance, 347.
Field, David Dudley, reserve power of, 398.
Financiering, slip-shod, 291.
Fluctuating men never succeed, 340.
Force, Peter, his poverty, 380.
Franklin, Benjamin, on promptness, 120; his integrity, 254; on diligence, 244, 330; his perseverance, 18, 69, 92, 350.

INDEX. 413

Franklin, Lady, her perseverance, 350.
Frederick the Great, 79.
Fremont, J. C., talent for effacing himself, 204.
Frost, Charles G., his industry, 68.
Fry, Elizabeth, and the prisons, 15.
Fuller, Margaret, on the ideal, 386.

GALILEO GALILEI, 17, 46, 67, 80; his perseverance, 245.
Garfield, James A., 52, 85; his reserve power, 398.
Garrison, William Lloyd, 39, 60, 138, 162.
Geradini, his persistence, 349.
Germans, three who mastered English, 286.
Genevieve, patron saint of Paris, 260.
Gerster, her enthusiasm, 172.
Gibbon, Edward, his painstaking, 284; his perseverance, 342.
Gilpin, John, 244.
Girard, Stephen, and his drayman, 11, 50, 397; his sixpence, 246; his brevity, 372; his precision, 285.
Girls, satisfied with mediocrity, 101.
Gladstone, William E., 67; on Washington, 224.
God does not murder nor torture his children, 363; surrounds us by kindly hints, 363.
Goethe, 70, 97; fascinating manner, 150; price of success, 243; industry, 330.
Gold a death-blow to art, 220.
Goldsmith on cheerfulness, 134.
Goodyear, Charles, his industry, 245.
Gough, John B., 20; at Oxford, 329; 278.
Gould, his wealth, 211.
Graham, George, the watchmaker, 273.
Grant, U. S., in business, 320; at Shiloh and Fort Donelson, 320; his courage, 321; in the Wilderness, 321; his nine hours' sleep, 369; at Chattanooga, 7; 60; his promptness, 131; tact, 188; politeness, 151.
Grattan and the red tape, 288; self-respect, 205.
Greater than wealth, 210.
Greatness, 271.
Greeley, Horace, early struggles, 30; concentration, 113; his punctuality, 130.
Grit, the perfection of in saying "No," 329.
Grote, George, the historian, 70.

HANCOCK, JOHN, his integrity, 221.
Händel and his harpsichord, 81, 246.
Harland, Marion, her great industry, 66.
Harrison, John, and his chronometer, 275.
Harvey, his persistence, 342.
Hawthorne, Nathaniel, 16, 69.
Heaven, a place for those who fail on earth, 313.
Henry, Patrick, 60.
Henry, Professor Joseph, 277.

Hercules, his reserve power, 391.
Hermit, the, and the Colosseum, 305.
Heroism in Memphis and Savannah, 215.
Herschel, 46.
Hill, David B., 39.
Hogarth, his power of observation, 113.
Horner, Francis, his character, 402.
Howe, Elias, 245.
Howe, Julia Ward, on health, 356.
Hugo, Victor, on method, 288.
Humboldt, Alexander von, his industry, 67; on his success, 364.
Humphrey, President Amherst College, his politeness, 163.
Hunt, Helen, on fretting, 139.
Hunter, John, 68; self-confidence, 204.
Hurry a disease.
Huxley on industry and endurance, 333.

IDEAL, the, 385.
Ingersoll, on greatness, 228.
Inventions, useful, 405.
Irving, Washington, self-respect, 204; on fortitude of woman, 329.
Italian teacher on persistence, 343.

JACKS-AT-ALL-TRADES, 111.
Jackson, Andrew, his politeness, 161.
Jackson, Richard, his integrity, 252.
Jefferson, Thomas, his politeness, 158, 160.
Jerrold, Douglas, his will power, 56.
Jews, their politeness, 159; their tact, 201.
Joan of Arc, 174, 315.
Johnson, Andrew, 51; "from a tailor up," 282.
Johnson, Samuel, 71; his gruffness, 157.
Josephine, her fascinating manner, 153, 160.
Judson, Dr. A., his perseverance, 343.
Junot and Napoleon, 328.
Juvenal on a lucky man, 335.

KEAN, his precocity, 97; his persistence, 337, 342.
Kepler, his self-confidence, 45.
King Cleomenes and his daughter Gorgo, 251.
Kingsley, Charles, on concentration, 111.
Kitto, Dr., 26; his perseverance, 241.
Kossuth, his character, 264.

LABOR, the curse of, 236; the schoolmaster of the race, 238.
Lafayette on Washington, 225.
Lamb, Charles, on grumbling, 143.
"Lancet," London, on pluck of the sick, 352.
Lanman, Charles, 190.
La Salle on the Mississippi, 327.
Latimer, Ridley, and Cranmer, 307.
Laughter, its power, 137.
Lawrence, Amos, his promptness, 130; and "the odd cent," 270.
Lawyers who can't get a living, 248.
Learning, real road to, 241.
Lee, Gideon, 51.

Leonidas, 252; victory in his defeat, 316.
Lessing, his absent-mindedness, 191.
Lewis, Edmonia, 50.
Lewis, Ida, 9.
Liberty, love of, 176.
Life is what we make it, 292; a long one, and how to reach it, 356; exhausted by Americans, 361; a struggle, 366.
Lighthouse on Lincoln Heath, 293.
Lincoln, Abraham, 52, 72, 225; his humor, 138; character of, 263, 265; his politeness, 160, 203; desire for learning, 241; on Grant, 319.
Lind, Jenny, 279.
Longfellow, Henry W., 16; on perseverance, 355.
Louis XIV., his self-conceit, 204.
Love, power of, 381.
Lowell, James R., his politeness, 98; 161.
Loyola, Ignatius, 396.
Lubbock, Sir John, 69.
Luck, none for him who is not striving, 331, 334.
Lundy, Benjamin, 25, 39.
Luther, Martin, 283.
Lytton, E. Bulwer, on industry, 112, 316, 354; perseverance, 342.

MACAULAY, his accuracy, 286.
McCormick and his reaper, 245.
McDonald, bravery, at Wagram, 327.
McDougal, Bessie, her courage, 323.
Maintenon, Madame, her wonderful manner, 149.
Malibran, her enthusiasm, 172; her persistence, 350; intense life of, 367.
Manhood, nature is after, 237, 251.
Mann, Horace, on health, 358.
Manners, a fortune in, 146; in high places, 152; recipe for, 169.
Manning, Daniel, 58.
Marlborough, Duke of, his politeness, 148.
Marshall, John, his infallibility, 118.
Mary, Queen of Scots, her politeness, 158.
Massena, 6; at Genoa, 322; and Napoleon, 322; reserve power, 396.
Masters of the situation, 57.
Matsys, Quentin, 59.
Maydole and his hammer, 275.
Melancholy of our ancestors, 141.
Mendelssohn, his persistency, 339.
Method, 288.
Midas, King, his golden wish, 219.
Mill, John Stuart, 66; on circumstances, 301.
Mill, the magical, for restoring youth, 205.
Miller, Hugh, 66, 80, 241; his pluck, 343; 300; character, 264.
Milton, John, 66, 69.
Miner, Rena I. on occupation for girls, 101.
Mirabeau, his wonderful manners, 154; his reserve power, 390.
Mirth, God's medicine, 140.

Molière on physicians, 369.
Moltke, Von, reserve power of, 395.
Montaigne, his character, 255.
Montesquieu, his accuracy, 284; his pluck, 353.
Moods, our, nature reflects, 297.
Moore, his perseverance, 244.
Morrison, Dr., his courage, 343.
Morse, Professor S. F. B., his struggles with the telegraph, 245.
Morton, Governor Marcus, his persistency, 246.
Mottoes of great men, 233, 234.
Mowry, William A., on concentration, 110.
Mozart, 314.

NAPOLEON I. crossing the Alps, 6; will power, 55, 60, 97; the nick of time, 123; on promptness, 129; enthusiasm, 173; perseverance, 244; his courage, 250; his power over the army, 254; his accuracy, 283, 285; and his generals, 318.
Nature a great economist, 361.
Nature's motto, "work or starve," 235.
Nelson, Lord, 5; on promptness, 129; enthusiasm, 174.
Nerve — Grit, Grip, Pluck, 318.
Nerves, our, are sentinels, 363.
Newton, Sir Isaac, 79; persistence, 244, 342, 343, 284.
Nightingale, Florence, her character, 265.
Nilsson, Christine, 37.
Nobility, true, 215.

OBSERVATION, 281; a keen, 299.
Obstacles, 58; necessary to success, 240, 241; make men, 311.
Occupation a doubtful one, 97; don't choose for money, 235; honorable, 237.
On time, or the triumphs of promptness, 121.
Opportunity, the Man and the, 5, 7, 8, 11, 12, 13; making it, 23; preparation for, 212.
Owen, Robert, 12.

PALACES or hovels, 300.
Palisy, his pluck and grit, 245, 338.
Paradise Lost, 243.
Paré, Ambrose, 380.
Parker, Theodore, on Socrates' character, 36, 255.
Parkman, Francis, his struggles, 182.
Pascal, 80.
Passions are contagious, 271.
Peabody, George, his generosity, 222.
Pellisier, the Crimean chief, 321.
Perfection of body, 369.
Perry, Commodore, 8.
Perseverance, triumphs of, 340.
Persistence, its reward, 337.
Peter the Great an early riser, 127.
Petrarch, character of, 264.
Phelps, Elizabeth Stuart, 108.

INDEX.   415

Philip and the Lacedæmonians, 319.
Philippe, Louis, 191.
Phillips, Wendell, 41; his inimitable manner, 150; tact, 193; courage, 242; his love of perfection, 290.
Pierre and Malibran, 211.
Pilgrim's Progress, 243.
Pitt, William, 61; his power of concentration, 115; his self-confidence, 204; his grit, 328.
Plague, the, follows famine, 366.
Poe, Edgar A., his poverty, 243, 314.
Possibilities in spare moments, 63.
Poverty, 246.
Principle, 223.
Punctuality the soul of business, 130; gives confidence and credit, 131.
Purpose, an invincible, 58, 104.
Putnam, General, his promptness, 122.

QUALITY greater than leadership or generalship, 267.
Quincy, President, his courtesy, 162.

RAHL, Colonel, his fatal delay, 122.
Raleigh, Sir Walter, could toil terribly, 117, 125.
Raphael, 70; his masterpiece, 314.
Récamier, Madame, her fascinating manner, 149.
Reserve, army of the, 389.
Reynolds, Sir Joshua, 80; on persistency, 339.
Richardson, Dr., on longevity, 368.
Robert, Duke of Normandy, and the poisoned arrow, 214.
Rockefeller, John D., 15.
Rome, her motto, 236.
Rothschild, Nathan M., on concentration, 106; his poverty, 226; and the Bank of England, 325.
Rousseau, Jean Jacques, 33; on manhood, 94.
Ruskin, John, his clay, sand, soot, and water, 303; on persistence, 343, 382.

SAGE, RUSSELL, 103.
St. Bernard, his personal power, 254.
Savonarola, his industry, 242; his inflexibility, 312.
"Scatteration," 109.
Schiller, his trials, 81.
Scotch boy, Sandie, and his matches, 213.
Scott, John (Lord Eldon), energy of, 241.
Scott, Walter, his will power, 56; his punctuality, 127; his kindness, 140.
Self-confidence and self-respect, 202; give power, 208.
Seneca, his will power, 56.
Shakespeare, William, 17; tact, 199; 243.
Sharples, James, his struggles, 45.
Shelley, Kate, the bravery of, 323.
Sheridan, General, at Winchester, 8; his courage, 257, 286.
Sheridan, R. B., his pluck, 242; might have ruled the world, 263; first speech, 338.
Sherman, General, 8.

Siddons, Mrs. Scott, 279.
Sidney, Sir Philip, and the cup of water, 261.
Silence, statue of, 399.
Smeaton, John, 82.
Smiles, Samuel, 85.
Smith, Sydney, on concentration, 111, 123; on labor, 349.
Solomon and his elixir of life, 379.
Sothern, his courage, 343.
Spartan, the, boy and the fox, 328.
Spectacles, the glorious, 298.
Spencer, P. R., Spencerian system, 33.
Spurgeon, no time to make money, 220.
Steam, the power of, in Great Britain, 401.
Stephenson, George, 24, 46, 70, 86; his persistency, 244, 342; Gladstone on, 368; Horace Greeley on, 369.
Stewart, A. T., 82, 99; his honesty, 222; method, 288; on lucky people, 335.
Story, the sculptor, and his statue of George Peabody, 400.
Stowe, Harriet Beecher, 66.
Success, the child of drudgery, 246; price of, 232, 247; secret of, 314; constant, 315; early, dangerous, 313.
Sugden, Edward, his thoroughness, 114.
Sultan, the, and his stuffed ball, 305.
Sumner, no time to make money, 220.

TACT, a national trait, 201; or common sense, 187.
Talent, not shut out by barriers, 330.
Taylor, General, at Buena Vista, 318.
Thackeray, W. M., on dunces, 86.
Thiers, President, reserve power of, 392; his reprobate youth, 404.
Thoreau, his pluck, 353; and the flower in the road, 294; and his quarrel with God, 265.
Thorwaldsen, 26.
Time, killing of, 73.
Titian, his perseverance, 342.
To-morrow, the fool's motto, 121.
"Touchiness," the new disease, 142.
Tucker, Adam, his industry, 353.
Turner, J. M. W., on hard work, 339; his magnanimity, 269, 289.

UNLUCKY people usually shiftless, 335.

VANDERBILT, CORNELIUS, 13, 48; sticking to business, 235.
Varro, Terentius, and Rome, 321.
Vergil and his persistence, 353.
Victoria, Queen, and Prince Albert, 147; her politeness, 152; her character, 264.
Victory, the, in defeat, 304.
Virtue, the resources of, 409.
Voltaire, on great men, 221; on greatness, 227.

WALES, Prince of, his politeness, 152.
Wallace, Carlyle on, 316.
Walton, Isaac, 140, 298.
Wanamaker, John, 50; his motto, 104.

Ward, Artemus, 89, 200.
Ward, J. Q. A., sculptor, 278.
Washington, George, always prompt, 129; his politeness, 161; his character, 224; and the corporal, 236; his character, 244, 254, 255, 263; maligned at Valley Forge, 396.
Watt, James, 71; his persistence, 244, 342.
Wayland, Francis, on work, 339; missionary sermon, 286, 391.
Wealth, real, 222; greater than, 226, 210.
Webster, Daniel, 190; his pluck, 242, 328, 352; reply to Hayne, 392, 402; a "steam engine in trousers," 115; promptness, 130; politeness, 162; self-respect, 207; on Washington, 224; a great worker, 234; character and the presidency, 263.
Webster, Noah, his perseverance, 342.
Weed, Thurlow, 35, 38; great tact, 195; perseverance, 241; brevity, 373.
Wellington, Duke of, 8, 69, 220; Sydney Smith on, 319; at Waterloo, 328; and his physician, 279.
Wesley, John, 88.
West, Benjamin, 81.
What career, 89.
Whipple on business nerve, 332.
Whitefield, George, his energy, 242.
White, Henry Kirke, 71.
Whiting, J. C., his accuracy, 277.

Whitman, Ezekiel, 167.
Whitney, Eli, his struggles with the cotton-gin, 309.
Whittier, John G., 39, 100.
Wilberforce, advice of, 241.
Willard, Frances, on "woman the greatest discovery of the century," 101; her aspiration, 381.
William the Silent, his character and struggles, 308.
Will power, 58.
Wilson, Professor George, his will power, 56.
Wilson, Henry, 29; his perseverance, 241.
Winans, Ross, his courtesy, 163.
Winthrop, Robert C., on Washington, 224.
Wirt, William, on hesitating, 339.
Wolfe, General, 56; his self-confidence, 203.
Woman, her influence, 271.
Woman's sphere, 100, 101, 102, 103.
Wordsworth, 139.
Work, mix brains with, 239; healthy, 366.
Wren, Christopher, enthusiasm of, 174.

YOUTH, enthusiasm of, 183.

ZANE, ELIZABETH, at Fort Henry, 327.

www.ingramcontent.com/pod-product-compliance
Lightning Source LLC
Chambersburg PA
CBHW022107300426
44117CB00007B/618